boilerplate: D0565122

2018 release

Adobe® Dreamweaver® CC
The Professional Portfolio

AGAINST THE CLOCK
mastering graphic technology

Managing Editor: Ellenn Behoriam
Cover & Interior Design: Erika Kendra

10 9 8 7 6 5

Print ISBN: 978-1-946396-09-9
Ebook ISBN: 978-1-946396-10-5

4710 28th Street North, Saint Petersburg, FL 33714
800-256-4ATC • www.againsttheclock.com

Acknowledgements

ABOUT AGAINST THE CLOCK

Against The Clock, long recognized as one of the nation's leaders in courseware development, has been publishing high-quality educational materials for the graphic and computer arts industries since 1990. The company has developed a solid and widely-respected approach to teaching people how to effectively use graphics applications, while maintaining a disciplined approach to real-world problems.

Having developed the *Against The Clock* and the *Essentials for Design* series with Prentice Hall/Pearson Education, ATC drew from years of professional experience and instructor feedback to develop *The Professional Portfolio Series*, focusing on the Adobe Creative Suite. These books feature step-by-step explanations, detailed foundational information, and advice and tips from professionals that offer practical solutions to technical issues.

ABOUT THE AUTHOR

Erika Kendra holds a BA in History and a BA in English Literature from the University of Pittsburgh. She began her career in the graphic communications industry as an editor at Graphic Arts Technical Foundation before moving to Los Angeles in 2000.

Erika is the author or co-author of more than thirty books about Adobe graphic design software. She has also written several books about graphic design concepts such as color reproduction and preflighting, and dozens of articles for industry online and print journals. Working with Against The Clock for more than fifteen years, Erika was a key partner in developing *The Professional Portfolio Series* of software training books.

CONTRIBUTING EDITORS AND ARTISTS

A big thank you to the people whose comments and expertise contributed to the success of these books:

- **Tony Cowdrey,** Against The Clock, Inc., technical editor
- **Dan Cristensen,** Against The Clock, Inc., technical editor
- **Roger Morrissey,** Against The Clock, Inc., technical editor
- **Susan Chiellini**, copy editor

Images used in the projects throughout this book are in the public domain unless otherwise noted. Individual artists' credit follow:

Project 1:
Images copyright Erika Kendra.

Project 2:
Background image by Marcus dePaula on Unsplash.com.

Project 3:
adults.jpg by Alex Jones on Unsplash.com.
chalk.jpg photo by Tina Floersch on Unsplash.com.
pencils background image by Stefan Schweihofer on Pixabay.com.

Project 4:
All images used in this project are courtesy of the Getty's Open Content Program: getty.edu/about/whatwedo/opencontentfaq.html

Project 5:
back-faqs.jpg by Jordan Connor on Unsplash.com.
back-food.jpg by Aaron Paul on Unsplash.com.
back-home.jpg by Yvette de Wit on Unsplash.com.
back-mailing.jpg on Unsplash.com.
back-schedule.jpg on Unsplash.com.
burger.jpg by Niklas Rhöse on Unsplash.com.
deli.jpg by Eaters Collective on Unsplash.com.
japanese.jpg by Erik Lundqvist on Unsplash.com.
pizza.jpg by Alexandra Gorn on Unsplash.com.
southern.jpg by Eaters Collective on Unsplash.com.
taco.jpg by Christine Siracusa on Unsplash.com.

Project 7:
julia.jpg by Nicholas Ladino Silva on Unsplash.com.
dog1.jpg by Jairo Alzate on Unsplash.com.
dog2.jpg by Alexandru Rotariu on Unsplash.com.
dog3.jpg by Matthew Henry on Unsplash.com.
dog4.jpg by Josef Reckziegel on Unsplash.com.
portrait1.jpg by Thanh Tran on Unsplash.com.
portrait2.jpg by Hybrid on Unsplash.com.
portrait3.jpg by Daniel Apodaca on Unsplash.com.
portrait4.jpg by Anton Darius Sollers on Unsplash.com.

Project 8:
Images copyright Erika Kendra.

Walk-Through

Project Goals

Each project begins with a clear description of the overall concepts that are explained in the project; these goals closely match the different "stages" of the project workflow.

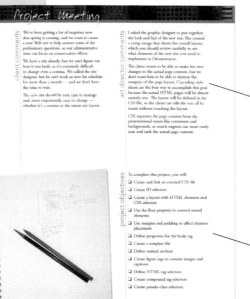

The Project Meeting

Each project includes the client's initial comments, which provide valuable information about the job. The Project Art Director, a vital part of any design workflow, also provides fundamental advice and production requirements.

Project Objectives

Each Project Meeting includes a summary of the specific skills required to complete the project.

Real-World Workflow

Projects are broken into logical lessons or "stages" of the workflow. Brief introductions at the beginning of each stage provide vital foundational material required to complete the task.

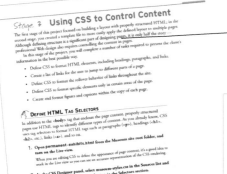

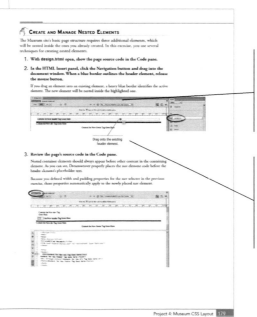

Step-By-Step Exercises

Every stage of the workflow is broken into multiple hands-on, step-by-step exercises.

Visual Explanations

Wherever possible, screen shots are annotated so that you can quickly identify important information.

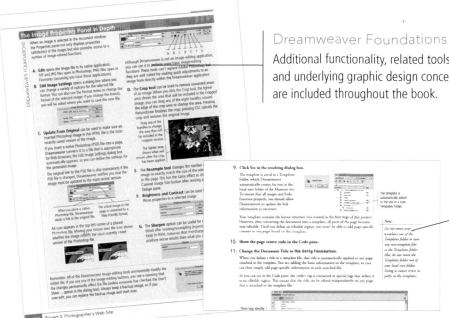

Dreamweaver Foundations

Additional functionality, related tools, and underlying graphic design concepts are included throughout the book.

Advice and Warnings

Where appropriate, sidebars provide shortcuts, warnings, or tips about the topic at hand.

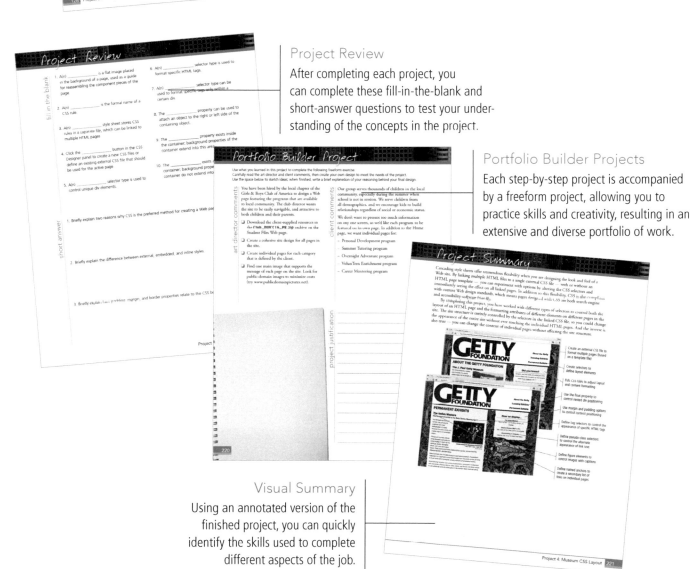

Project Review

After completing each project, you can complete these fill-in-the-blank and short-answer questions to test your understanding of the concepts in the project.

Portfolio Builder Projects

Each step-by-step project is accompanied by a freeform project, allowing you to practice skills and creativity, resulting in an extensive and diverse portfolio of work.

Visual Summary

Using an annotated version of the finished project, you can quickly identify the skills used to complete different aspects of the job.

Against The Clock's *The Professional Portfolio Series* teaches graphic design software tools and techniques entirely within the framework of real-world projects; we introduce and explain skills where they would naturally fall into a real project workflow.

The project-based approach in *The Professional Portfolio Series* allows you to get in-depth with the software beginning in Project 1 — you don't have to read several chapters of introductory material before you can start creating finished artwork.

Our approach also prevents "topic tedium" — in other words, we don't require you to read pages and pages of information about marking up text (for example); instead, we explain text-related mark-up as part of a larger project (in this case, as part of a digital book chapter).

Clear, easy-to-read, step-by-step instructions walk you through every phase of each job, from creating a new file to saving the finished piece. Wherever logical, we also offer practical advice and tips about underlying concepts and graphic design practices that will benefit you as you enter the job market.

The projects in this book reflect a range of different types of Dreamweaver jobs, from organizing a client's site and links to developing a functional site template to building a dynamic site. When you finish the eight projects in this book (and the accompanying Portfolio Builder exercises), you will have a substantial body of work that should impress any potential employer.

The eight Dreamweaver projects are described briefly here; more detail is provided in the full table of contents (beginning on Page viii).

project 1
Bistro Site Organization

❑ Exploring Site Structure

❑ Organizing the Site Navigation

❑ Naming and Titling Documents

project 2
Digital Book Chapter

❑ Preparing the Workspace

❑ Working with Semantic Markup

❑ Working with Special Characters

❑ Creating Lists

❑ Attaching an External CSS File

project 3
Arts Council Website

❑ Placing Static Foreground Images

❑ Extracting Photoshop Assets

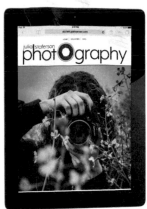

Our goal in this book is to familiarize you with the Dreamweaver tool set, so you can be more productive and more marketable in your career as a graphic designer.

It is important to keep in mind that Dreamweaver is an extremely versatile and powerful application. The sheer volume of available panels, options, and features can seem intimidating when you first look at the software interface. Most of these tools, however, are fairly simple to use with a bit of background information and a little practice.

Wherever necessary, we explain the underlying concepts and terms that are required for understanding the software. We're confident that these projects provide the practice you need to be able to create sophisticated artwork by the end of the very first project.

Contents

Contents

Getting Started

PREREQUISITES

The Professional Portfolio Series is based on the assumption that you have a basic understanding of how to use your computer. You should know how to use your mouse to point and click, as well as how to drag items around the screen. You should be able to resize and arrange windows on your desktop to maximize your available space. You should know how to access drop-down menus, and understand how check boxes and radio buttons work. It also doesn't hurt to have a good understanding of how your operating system organizes files and folders, and how to navigate your way around them. If you're familiar with these fundamental skills, then you know all that's necessary to use the Portfolio Series.

RESOURCE FILES

All of the files you need to complete the projects in this book — except, of course, the Dreamweaver application files — are on the Student Files Web page at againsttheclock.com. See the inside back cover of this book for access information.

Each archive (ZIP) file is named according to the related project (e.g., **Museum_DW18_RF.zip**). At the beginning of each project, you must download the archive file for that project and expand that archive to access the resource files that you need to complete the exercises. Detailed instructions for this process are included in the Interface chapter.

Files required for the related Portfolio Builder exercises at the end of each project are also available on the Student Files page; these archives are also named by project (e.g., **Flowers_DW18_PB.zip**).

SOFTWARE VERSIONS

This book was written and tested using the initial 2018 release of Adobe Dreamweaver CC software (version 18.0). You can find the version and build number in the Splash Screen that appears while your application is launching, or by choosing About Dreamweaver in the Dreamweaver CC/Help menu.

Because Adobe has announced periodic upgrades rather than releasing new full versions, some features and functionality might have changed since publication. Please check the Errata section of the Against The Clock Web site for any significant issues that might have arisen from these periodic upgrades.

SYSTEM REQUIREMENTS

The Professional Portfolio Series was designed to work on both Macintosh or Windows computers; where differences exist from one platform to another, we include specific instructions relative to each platform. One issue that remains different from Macintosh to Windows is the use of different modifier keys (Control, Shift, etc.) to accomplish a task. When we present key commands, we always follow the same Macintosh/Windows format — Macintosh keys are listed first, then a slash, followed by the Windows keys.

The Dreamweaver CC User Interface

Typical Dreamweaver work ranges from static HTML pages with hyperlinks to complex, dynamic, database-driven sites, where pages are generated on-the-fly based on individual user requests. Mastering the tools and techniques of the application can significantly improve your potential career options. Our goal in this book is to teach you how to use the available tools to create different types of work that you might encounter in your professional career.

The basic exercises in this introduction are designed to let you explore the Dreamweaver user interface. Whether you are new to the application or upgrading from a previous version, we recommend you follow these steps to click around and become familiar with the basic workspace.

EXPLORE THE DREAMWEAVER USER INTERFACE

The first time you launch Dreamweaver, you will see the default user interface (UI) settings as defined by Adobe. When you relaunch after you or another user has quit, the workspace defaults to the last-used settings — including open panels and the position of those panels on your screen. We designed the following exercises so you can explore different ways of controlling panels in the Dreamweaver user interface.

1. **Launch Dreamweaver.**

2. **If you see a message about syncing settings, click the Advanced button.**

   As part of your individual-user Adobe Creative Cloud (CC) membership, you can use the Sync Settings options to share certain custom assets and settings between different computers. This means you can access

   those same settings and assets on any computer where you are logged in to your CC account. (You must be logged into your CC account and connected to the internet for the sync process to work. You can open the Help menu to verify that you are signed in to your account.)

   Clicking the Advanced button in the warning dialog box opens Sync Settings pane of the Preferences dialog box, where you can customize which settings are synced.

   If you check Enable Automatic Sync, changes to the settings in your desktop application automatically upload to your CC account, and those changes automatically apply whenever and wherever you use the application.

   If you do not enable automatic syncing, you can click the Sync Settings button in the top-right corner of the user interface to initiate the sync process at any time.

3. **Click Close to dismiss the Preferences dialog box.**

4. Macintosh users: Open the Window menu and make sure the Application Frame option is toggled on.

Many menu commands and options in Dreamweaver are **toggles**, which means they are either on or off; when an option is already checked, that option is toggled on (visible or active). You can toggle an active option off by choosing the checked menu command, or toggle an inactive option on by choosing the unchecked command.

This option should be checked.

On the Windows operating system (OS), every application is contained within its own frame; all elements of the application — including the Menu bar, panels, tools, and open documents — are contained within the Application frame. On Windows, the Application Frame menu command is not available; you can't turn off the Application Frame on the Windows operating system.

Adobe also offers the Application frame to Macintosh users as an option for controlling the workspace. When the Application frame is active, the entire workspace exists in a self-contained area that can be moved around the screen; all elements of the workspace (excluding the Menu bar) move when you move the Application frame. You can toggle it on or off by choosing Window>Application Frame.

5. Macintosh users: Choose Dreamweaver>Preferences.
Windows users: Choose Edit>Preferences>.

Remember that on Macintosh systems, the Preferences dialog box is accessed in the Dreamweaver menu; Windows users access the Preferences dialog box in the Edit menu.

6. Click Interface in the list of options on the left side of the dialog box.

Preferences customize the way many of the program's tools and options function.

7. In the App Theme section, choose any option that you prefer.

The color theme defines the basic appearance of your overall workspace, including the darkness or lightness of various panels and panes throughout the application. The screen captures throughout this book use the lightest option because they reproduce better on a printed page. Feel free to use whichever theme you prefer.

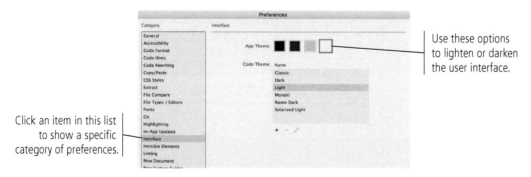

Click an item in this list to show a specific category of preferences.

Use these options to lighten or darken the user interface.

8. Click Close to close the Preferences dialog box.

9. Choose Window>Workspace Layout>Standard.

The software includes a number of built-in saved workspaces, which provide one-click access to a defined group of panels, that are designed to meet common workflows.

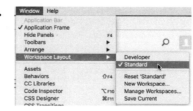

10. Choose Window>Workspace Layout>Reset Standard.

This step might or might not do anything, depending on what was done in Dreamweaver before you started this project. If you or someone else changed anything and then quit the application, those changes are remembered when Dreamweaver is relaunched. You are resetting the user interface in this step so that what you see will match our screen shots in the next exercises.

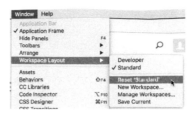

11. Review the various elements of the workspace.

When no file is open, you see a stored "Start" workspace that provides one-click access to a list of recently opened files (if any); buttons to create a new file or open an existing one; and links to additional functionality provided by the CC suite.

The (default) Standard workspace includes the Common Toolbar on the left and a set of docked, expanded panels on the right side of the workspace.

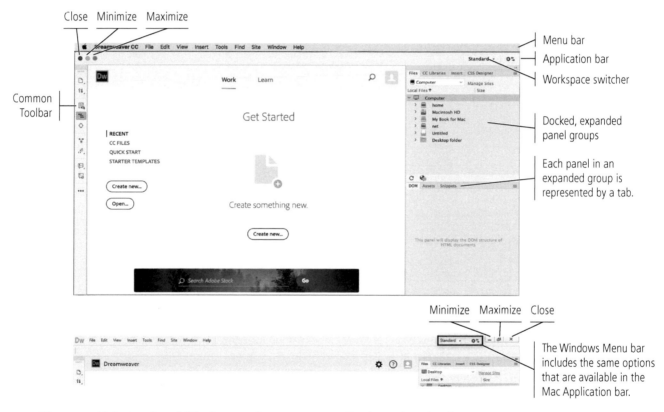

The general Macintosh and Windows workspaces are virtually identical, with a few primary exceptions:

- On Macintosh, the application's title bar appears below the Menu bar; the Close, Minimize, and Restore buttons appear on the left side of the Application bar, and the Menu bar is not part of the Application frame.

    On Windows, the Close, Minimize, and Restore buttons appear at the right end of the Menu bar, which is part of the overall Application frame.

- Macintosh users have two extra menus (consistent with the Macintosh OS structure). The Apple menu provides access to system-specific commands. The Dreamweaver menu follows the Macintosh system-standard format for all applications; this menu controls basic application operations such as About, Hide, Preferences, and Quit.

12. Continue to the next exercise.

EXPLORE WORKSPACE MANAGEMENT

As you gain experience and familiarity with the software, you will develop personal working styles and preferences. You will also find that different types of jobs often require different but specific sets of tools. In recognition of this wide range of needs, Dreamweaver includes many options for customizing the arrangement of the application's many panels. We designed the following exercise so you can explore various ways of controlling Dreamweaver's panels.

1. **On the right side of the workspace, click the Files tab in the top docked panel group and drag left, away from the dock.**

   The area where the default panels are stored is called the **panel dock**. You can move any docked panel (or panel group) away from the dock, so it appears as a separate panel (called a **floating panel**).

Note:

When we provide an instruction to "click and drag" you should hold down the mouse button while you drag.

Click the panel tab and drag to move a specific panel.

Drag from this area (called the panel **drop zone**) to move an entire panel group.

Macintosh   **Windows**

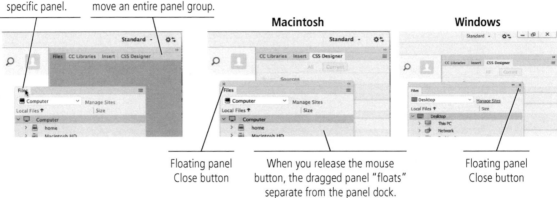

Floating panel Close button

When you release the mouse button, the dragged panel "floats" separate from the panel dock.

Floating panel Close button

2. **Click the Files panel tab again and drag back to the dock until a blue line appears to the right of the existing dock column.**

   You can move panels by dragging their tabs to another position in the dock. To move an entire panel group (including all panels in the group), you can click and drag the panel group's drop zone.

   The blue line indicates where the panel or group will appear if you release the mouse button. To add a panel to an existing panel group, drag until the target group's drop zone turns blue.

Note:

You don't need to move a panel out of the dock before placing it in a different position within the dock. We included Step 3 to show you how to float panels and panel groups.

Drag the Files panel tab until you see a blue line to the right of the existing dock column.

When you release the mouse button, the dragged panel appears to the right of the existing dock column.

3. Double-click the dock title bar above the left dock column panel.

Panels, whether docked or floating, can be collapsed to icons (called **iconic** or **iconized panels**) to save space in the document window. By default, iconized panels appear with the panel name to the right of the icon.

Double-click the title bar over a dock column to toggle between expanded and iconized modes.

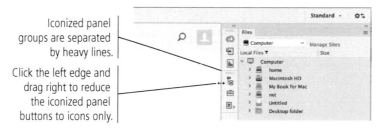

4. Click the left edge of the iconized panels and drag right.

When panels are iconized, you can reduce the panel buttons to the icons only. This can be particularly useful once you are more familiar with the application and the icons used to symbolize the various panels.

Iconized panel groups are separated by heavy lines.

Click the left edge and drag right to reduce the iconized panel buttons to icons only.

If docked panels are not iconized, you can drag the left edge of the dock column to make it wider or narrower. All panel groups in that column are affected.

You can also drag the line between two panel groups in the same dock column to make panels shorter or higher. When you drag the bottom edge of a docked group, other panels in the same column expand or contract to fit the available space. Some panels, such as the CSS Designer panel, have a smallest-possible size; depending on your monitor size, you might not be able to fully expand another panel in the same dock column if another panel would be smaller than its required minimum height.

5. Control/right-click the title bar above the iconized dock column. If the Auto-Collapse Iconic Panels option is not checked, choose that item to toggle on that option.

As we explained in the Getting Started section, when commands are different for Macintosh and Windows, we include the different commands in the Macintosh/Windows format. In this case, Macintosh users who do not have right-click mouse capability can press the Control key and click to access the contextual menu. You do not have to press Control *and* right-click to access the menus.

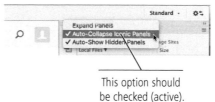

This option should be checked (active).

(If you're using a Macintosh and don't have a mouse with right-click capability, we highly recommend that you purchase one. They're inexpensive, they're available at almost any retail store, and they save significant amounts of time accessing contextual options.)

Control/right-clicking a dock title bar opens the dock contextual menu, where you can change the default panel behavior. When the Auto-Collapse Iconic Panels option is toggled on, panels collapse as soon as you click away from them. If you uncheck this option, panels will remain open until you intentionally collapse them.

6. In the left column of docked panels, click the third button in the bottom panel group (Snippets).

When panels are grouped, the button you click is the active panel in the expanded group.

Clicking a docked panel button opens the panel to the left of the panel dock.

Click here to manually collapse an expanded panel group.

Click here to open the panel Options menu.

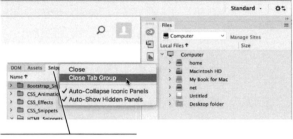

Hovering your mouse over an iconized panel button shows the name of the panel.

7. Control/right-click the Snippets panel tab and choose Close Tab Group in the contextual menu.

Choosing Close in the menu closes only the active panel. Close Tab Group closes all panels that are docked together. When panels are docked, the contextual menu options are the only way to close a panel or panel group.

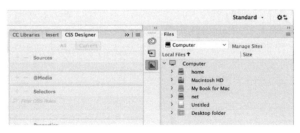

Control/right-click a panel tab to open the contextual menu.

Note:

You can also close individual panels by dragging them away from the dock or group, and then clicking the Close button on the floating panel (group).

8. Choose Window>CSS Designer.

All panels can be accessed in the Window menu.

Note:

Closing one panel from a panel group does not affect the other panels in the same group.

- If you choose a panel that's open but iconized, the panel expands to the left of its icon.

- If you choose a panel that's part of an expanded group, that panel comes to the front of the group.

- If you choose a panel in a minimized group, the panel group expands and the selected panel comes to the front of the group.

- If you choose a panel that isn't open, it appears in the same position as when it was last closed.

9. **Click the CSS Designer panel tab and drag until a blue line appears below the Files panel.**

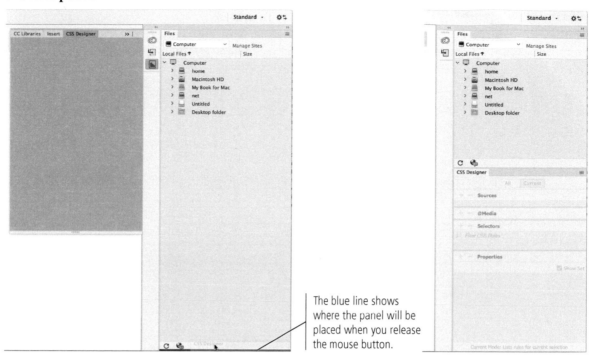

The blue line shows where the panel will be placed when you release the mouse button.

10. **In the right column of the panel dock, click the line between the two panel groups and drag up until the CSS Designer panel occupies about two-thirds of the vertical space.**

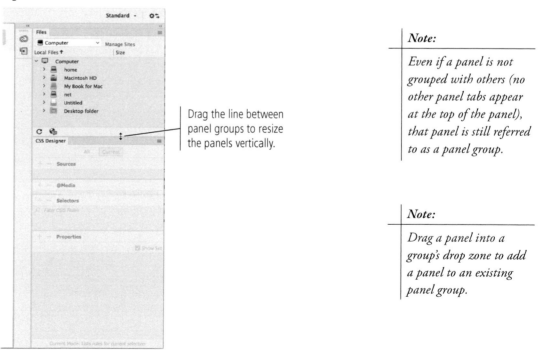

Drag the line between panel groups to resize the panels vertically.

Note:

Even if a panel is not grouped with others (no other panel tabs appear at the top of the panel), that panel is still referred to as a panel group.

Note:

Drag a panel into a group's drop zone to add a panel to an existing panel group.

11. **Double-click the CSS Designer panel tab to minimize that panel group.**

You can minimize an expanded panel group by double-clicking the active panel tab. When minimized, only the group's panel tabs are visible.

Double-click a panel tab to minimize that group in the dock.

If a docked panel is already minimized, clicking a panel tab once expands that group.

12. **Click the Insert panel button to expand that panel group. Click the Insert panel tab and then drag up and left until a blue line appears immediately below the Application/Menu bar.**

The Insert panel contains buttons for adding a number of common elements to a web page. Various commands are categorized into groups, which can be accessed using the menu at the top of the panel when it is docked in the default position.

The Insert panel can be displayed as a tabbed row at the top or bottom of the workspace, which can be especially useful if you have a small monitor. When the Insert panel appears in the tabbed format, you can click the tabs in the top row to access the different categories of options.

Note:

Because workspace preferences are largely a matter of personal taste, the projects in this book direct you to use specific panels, but you can choose where to place those elements within the interface.

Dock the Insert panel at the top of the
workspace to display it as a series of tabs.

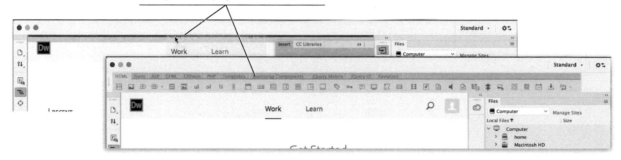

Understanding the Common Toolbar

DREAMWEAVER FOUNDATIONS

The Common Toolbar, which you can toggle on or off in the View>Toolbars submenu, appears by default on the left side of the UI when you use the Standard workspace. It provides easy access to a number of useful options. (These options will make more sense as you complete the projects in this book, in which these are explained more clearly in context.)

The Open Documents menu (⌂) lists all open files. Choosing a file in this list makes that file active in the document window.

The File Management menu (⇅) includes options for managing files that are uploaded on a remote server. You can Get files from or put files onto the server; and check files in or out to view or make changes to files that are being managed in a team setting.

The Live View Options menu (⊠) includes a number of options for managing what you see in the document window when the Live view is active.

The Toggle Visual Media Queries Bar button (≂) can be used to show or hide that element, which appears by default at the top of the document window whenever the Live view is active.

The Inspect button (◇) activates Live view and Inspect mode in the document window.

The Expand All button (⊻) can be used to expand any code blocks that have been collapsed in the Code pane.

The Format Source Code menu (⋰) includes a number of options for formatting code in the Code pane.

The Apply Comment menu (⊡) includes several options for adding comments to code in the Code pane.

The Remove Comment button (⊠) removes commenting identifiers from the selected code in the Code view.

The Customize Toolbar button (•••) opens a dialog box that you can use add or remove various options from the toolbar. If you make changes, you can always reopen the dialog box and click the Restore Defaults button to reset the toolbar to its original state.

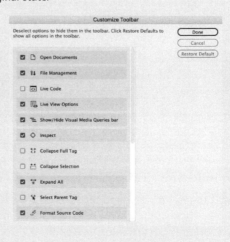

13. **Choose Window>Properties to open the Properties panel. Drag the Properties panel until you see a blue line at the bottom of the workspace, then release the mouse button to dock the Properties panel.**

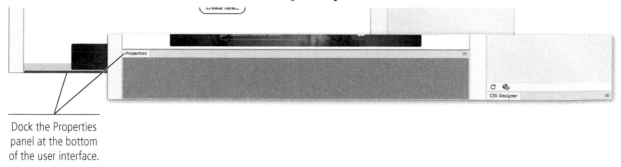

Dock the Properties panel at the bottom of the user interface.

14. **Continue to the next exercise.**

 ## CREATE A SAVED WORKSPACE

Over time you will develop personal preferences — the Files panel always appears at the top, etc. — based on your work habits and project needs. Rather than re-establishing every workspace element each time you return to Dreamweaver, you can save your custom workspace settings so they can be recalled with a single click.

1. **Click the Workspace switcher in the Application/Menu bar and choose New Workspace.**

   Again, keep in mind that we list differing commands in the Macintosh/Windows format. On Macintosh, the Workspace switcher is in the Application bar; on Windows, it's in the Menu bar.

   Saved **workspaces** (accessed in the Window>Workspace Layout menu, or in the Workspace switcher) provide one-click access to a defined group of panels.

Note:

User-defined workspaces are listed at the top of the menu.

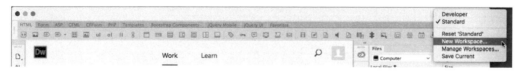

2. **In the Save Workspace dialog box, type Portfolio and click OK.**

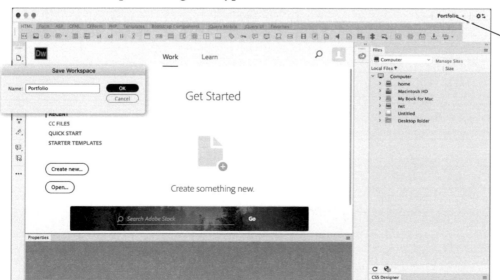

The Workspace switcher shows the name of the active workspace.

3. **Control/right-click the Files panel tab and choose Close in the menu.**

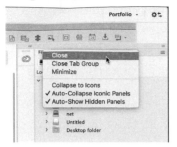

Note:

The Manage Workspaces option in the Workspace switcher opens a dialog box where you can choose a specific user-defined workspace to rename or delete.

4. **Open the Workspace switcher and choose Developer.**

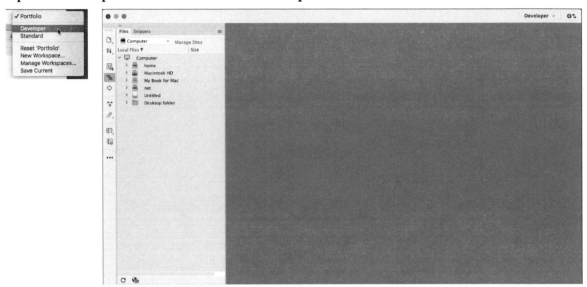

5. **Open the Workspace switcher again and choose Portfolio to restore your custom workspace.**

   Calling a saved workspace restores the last-used state of the workspace. Because you closed the Files panel after saving the workspace, Dreamweaver reverts to the last-used version of the custom workspace — without the Files panel.

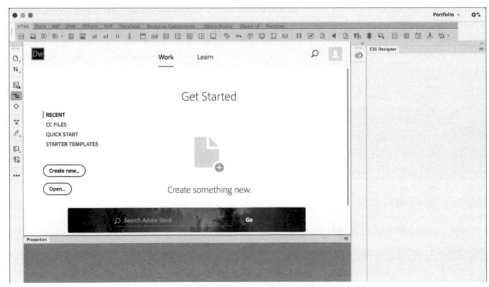

6. In the Workspace switcher menu, choose Reset 'Portfolio'.

The Reset command reverts the workspace back to the original saved state.

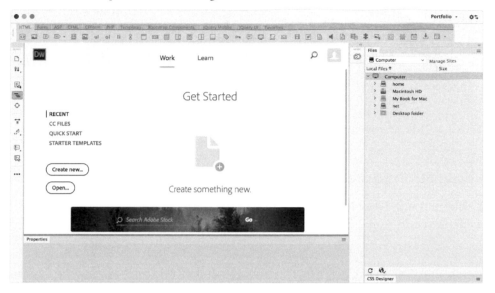

7. Continue to the next exercise.

Customizing Keyboard Shortcuts

In addition to customizing the position and appearance of panels in the workspace, you can also customize the various keyboard shortcuts used to access Dreamweaver commands (Dreamweaver>Keyboard Shortcuts on Macintosh or Edit>Keyboard Shortcuts on Windows).

The **Commands** window lists all options (in the selected product area) for which you can assign a keyboard shortcut.

Current Shortcuts for the selected command are listed immediately below the commands. You can use the **Press Key** field to assign an alternative shortcut.

Once you define custom shortcuts, you can save your choices as a set so you can access the same custom choices again without having to redo the work.

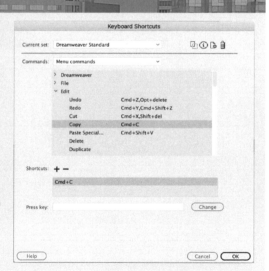

EXPLORE THE DREAMWEAVER DOCUMENT WINDOW

There is far more to using Dreamweaver than arranging panels in the workspace. What you do with those panels — and even which panels you need — depends on the type of work you are doing in a particular file. In this exercise, you import an existing site into Dreamweaver and explore some of the options for looking at files.

1. Create a new empty folder named **WIP** (**W**ork **I**n **P**rogress) on any writable disk (where you plan to save your work).

2. Download the **Interface_DW18_RF.zip** archive from the Student Files web page.

3. Macintosh users: Place the ZIP archive in your WIP folder, then double-click the file icon to expand it.

   Windows users: Double-click the ZIP archive file to open it. Click the folder inside the archive and drag it into your primary WIP folder.

   The resulting **InterfaceDW** folder contains all the files you need to complete this introduction.

Macintosh

Windows

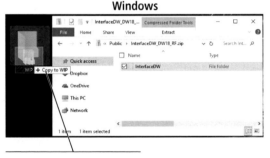

Double-click the archive file icon to expand it.

Drag the Interface folder from the archive to your WIP folder.

4. In Dreamweaver, click the Manage Sites link in the Files panel. If you don't see the Manage Sites link, open the Directory menu and choose Manage Sites from the bottom of the list.

If no sites are currently open in Dreamweaver, click the hot-text link to open the Manage Sites dialog box.

If the Manage Sites link is not available, open the Directory menu and choose the Manage Sites option.

Although Dreamweaver can be used to build individual HTML pages with no links to external files, the application is more commonly used to build entire sites. The Manage Sites dialog box is used to create new sites or import existing ones into Dreamweaver.

Note:

You can also open the Manage Sites dialog box by choosing Site>Manage Sites.

5. **Click the Import Site button in the Manage Sites dialog box. Navigate to your WIP>InterfaceDW folder, select sf-arts.ste in the list of available files, and click Open.**

The ".ste" extension identifies a Dreamweaver site file, which stores information about the site such as URL, FTP login information, etc. By importing this file into Dreamweaver, you can work with an existing site.

Note:

Depending on your system settings, the extension might not appear in your file list.

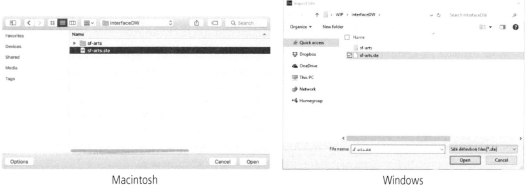

Macintosh   Windows

6. **When asked to select the local root folder of the site, navigate to and open the sf-arts folder (in your WIP>InterfaceDW folder), then click Open/Select.**

The **root folder** is simply the base folder that contains the files of your site. This is referred to as the "local" root folder because it is the folder on your computer system. When you upload site files to a web server, you place the files in the remote root folder.

Macintosh   Windows

7. **When asked to select the local images folder for the imported site, navigate to and open the sf-arts>images folder, then click Open/Select.**

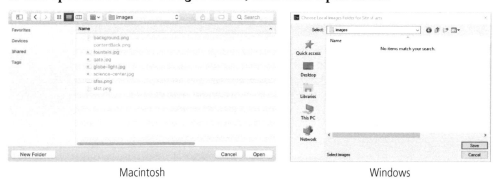

Macintosh   Windows

After you identify the local images folder, files in the site are processed and then the site is listed in the Manage Sites dialog box. The name of the site (in this case, "sf-arts") is used for internal purposes only; it has no relation to the file names in the live HTML files.

8. **Click Done to close the Manage Sites dialog box.**

   A Dreamweaver site typically includes links — from HTML pages to images, from one HTML page to another, and so on — which are the heart of interactive websites. When you import a site into Dreamweaver, the application processes the files in the site to identify links and other information required to maintain the integrity of the overall site.

   Depending on the number of files in a site, you might see a progress bar indicating that Dreamweaver is processing the files and creating a site cache, which helps the application manage the links between various files in the site.

9. **In the Files panel, click the arrow to expand the site folder.**

   The Files panel provides access to all the elements that make up a website, including page files (whether HTML, PHP, or some other format), images, downloadable PDFs, and anything else required for the site to display properly.

Click and drag the line between columns to make a column wider or narrower in the panel.

Click any column heading in the panel to sort the files by that category.

Click these arrows to expand or collapse a folder.

On Macintosh, folders are listed in alphabetical order along with other files.

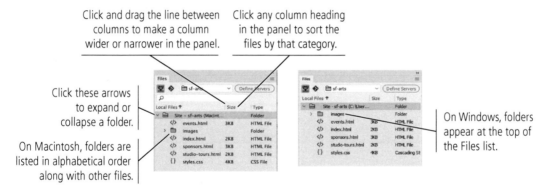

On Windows, folders appear at the top of the Files list.

10. **In the Files panel, double-click the index.html file.**

    Double-clicking a file in the Files panel opens that file in the document window.

    For Dreamweaver to effectively monitor and manage the various links to required supporting files (images, scripts, etc.), you should only open and change site files from within the Files panel. If you open and change a file outside the context of the Files panel, Dreamweaver can't keep track of those changes, which can result in broken links.

11. Open the Window>Toolbars submenu and make sure the Document option is checked.

Many menu commands are toggles, which means they are either on or off. The checkmark indicates that an option is active/visible.

Keyboard shortcuts (if available) are listed on the right side of the menu.

This option should be checked.

On Macintosh, the Document toolbar options appear in the Application bar. (Important note for Macintosh users: If you close the Application frame, the Document toolbar options do not appear even when the Window>Toolbars>Document option is checked; this appears to be a bug in the software at the time of this writing.)

On Windows, the Document toolbar appears immediately below the Menu bar.

12. Review the open file in the document window.

All open files are represented by document tabs.

Document toolbar options

The Files panel provides access to all files in the site.

Related Files bar

On Windows, the Document toolbar appears below the menu bar.

13. In the Document toolbar, click the Arrow button to the right of the Live button. Choose Design from the resulting menu.

Design view is useful for visually-oriented site design, providing a fairly accurate visual preview of the file similar to the way it will appear in a browser window. Live view (the default) will be explained in the next exercise.

The button shows whether Design or Live view is active.

Use this menu to switch between the Design and Live [Design] views.

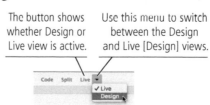

14. **Click the Design button to show only the Design view in the document window.**

Click these buttons to change which panes are visible in the document window.

Note:

The design for this site is based on the "Barren Savannah" template by Bryant Smith. The original template was found at www.free-templates.me, one of many online sources for web design templates that are free to use and modify to meet your specific needs.

15. **If necessary, scroll down to show the bottom of the page. Click the "Art & Architecture" logo to select it, then review the Properties panel.**

At this point, it isn't necessary to understand what the various properties do; you learn about all these options in later projects. For now, you should simply understand that the Properties panel is context sensitive, which means the available options depend on what is currently selected.

The selected object is an image.

The Properties panel shows options and information specific to the active selection.

Understanding New Feature Guides

As you begin to work in Dreamweaver, you will see pop-up messages with tips and/or links to videos explaining various features in the application. Each message appears only once, so you will not see a specific message twice after you close it. To show all of these messages again, open the New Feature Guides pane of the Preferences dialog box and click the Reset button. The messages will appear again after you restart the application.

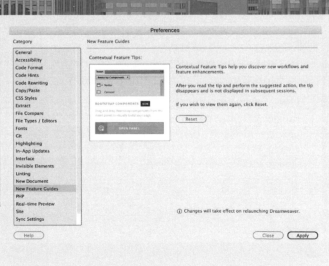

16. Double-click the word "Francisco" (in the first line of text below the logo) to select the entire word, and then review the Properties panel.

Unlike many design applications, in Dreamweaver you don't have to choose a specific tool to select objects in a document.

The selected word is editable text.

The Properties panel shows options and information related to the selected text.

17. Click the Split button in the Document toolbar.

Split view shows both the Code and Design view windows. When working in Split view, selecting an object in the Design view highlights the related code in the Code view.

Note:

Macintosh users: Code related to the selected element might not appear highlighted in the Code view. This is a bug at the time of this writing.

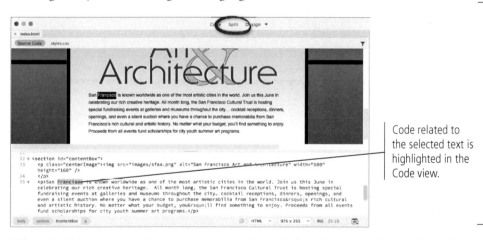

Code related to the selected text is highlighted in the Code view.

When the Split view is active, you can use the View>Split submenu to change where the various panes appear in the document window. When the window is split vertically (as it is by default), you can toggle the Design View on Top option to switch the positions of the Design and Code panes. If you choose the Split Horizontally option, you can toggle the Design View on Left option to swap the two panes.

Note:

You can also choose View>Split>Code-Code to shows the page code in two panes at the same time. This view can be useful if you need to write code in one area that specifically relates or refers to code at another point in the page.

18. **Click the Code button in the Document toolbar.**

   The Code view is useful for people who are familiar with writing code; this mode allows you to (temporarily) ignore the visual design and work solely on the code. Dreamweaver includes a umber of helpful features for working directly in the page code; you will learn about those as you complete the exercises in this book.

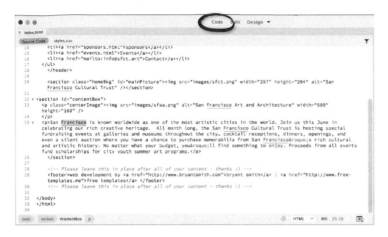

19. **Click the Design button in the Document toolbar to return to only the Design view.**

20. **Continue to the next exercise.**

 ## PREVIEW FILES IN DREAMWEAVER LIVE VIEW

Dreamweaver's Design view does a reasonably good job of allowing you to design web pages visually, but some common design elements, such as rollovers and multimedia files, are not enabled in the Design view. The Live view provides an internal method for checking many of these elements without leaving the Dreamweaver environment.

   You can't edit pages directly in Live view. However, if you are working in Split view, you can make changes to the code and then refresh the Live view to see the effect of those changes.

1. **With the sf-arts site open in the Files panel, make sure index.html is open.**

2. **In the Files panel, double-click studio-tours.html to open that page.**

   Each open file is represented by a tab at the top of the document window. You can click any tab to make the associated file active in the document window.

Each open file is represented by a document tab.

Various lines indicate the boundaries of specific objects, such as each link in the menu.

3. **Choose View>Design View Options>Visual Aids>Hide All.**

   Visual aids make it easier to identify the various elements (such as page divisions) used to create structure but which do not necessarily have a tangible physical appearance. While certainly useful, these visual aids interfere with the physical layout of the site so what you see in the document window is *not* what you get in the browser window.

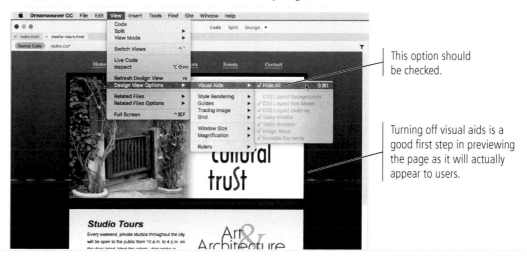

This option should be checked.

Turning off visual aids is a good first step in previewing the page as it will actually appear to users.

4. **In the Document toolbar, click the arrow button to the right of the Design button. Choose Live from the resulting menu.**

5. **Move your mouse cursor over the Events link at the top of the page.**

   Rollover elements do not function properly in Dreamweaver's Design view. The Live view provides a way to test interactive elements (such as rollovers) within the Dreamweaver environment.

In Live view, the rollover button displays as it would in a browser.

6. **Press Command/Control and click the Events link.**

One final reminder: Throughout this book, we list differing commands in the Macintosh/Windows format. On Macintosh, you need to press the Command key; on Windows, press the Control key. (We will not repeat this explanation every time different commands are required for the different operating systems.)

In Live view, pressing the Command/Control key lets you preview linked files in the local site folder directly in the Dreamweaver document window. If you click a link to an external file, you will see a "File Not Found" error message.

The active file does not change even though you navigated to a link in the Live view.

Different images and text show that the Events page is visible.

7. **In the Document toolbar, open the menu to the right of the Live button and choose Design to return to the regular Design view.**

Navigating in the Live view does not technically open the linked pages. When you return to the regular Design view, the previously active page — in this case, studio-tours.html — is still the active one.

8. **Click the Close button on the studio-tours.html tab to close that file.**

Each document has its own Close button.

9. **Click the Close button on the index.html document tab to close that file.**

On Macintosh systems, clicking the Close button on the document window closes all open files, but does not quit the application.

On Windows systems, clicking the Close (X) button on the Application frame closes all open files and quits the application.

10. **Continue to the next exercise.**

PREVIEW A FILE IN A BROWSER

As you saw in the previous exercise, the Live view can be used to verify the appearance of many common web design objects. Of course, site users will not be using Dreamweaver to view your pages, so it is always a good idea to test pages using the same method that will actually be used to display your pages — namely, the various browsers that are in common use.

Although there are some standards that govern the way browsers display web page code, the various browsers do have some different capabilities. Different operating systems also introduce display variables, so what you see in Google Chrome on a Macintosh might appear different than what you see in Chrome on Windows. As a general rule, you should test your pages on as many browsers as possible — on both Macintosh and Windows.

1. **Macintosh: Choose Dreamweaver>Preferences.**
   Windows: Choose Edit>Preferences.

   On the left side of the Preferences dialog box, click Real-Time Preview to display the related options.

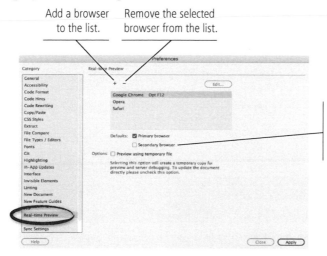

Add a browser to the list.

Remove the selected browser from the list.

Select a browser in the list and use these boxes to designate the primary and secondary browsers.

2. **Review the list of browsers that are identified by Dreamweaver.**

   When installed, Dreamweaver scans your computer for available browser applications. You likely have at least one browser in this list, and probably even more than one.

3. **If a browser is available on your system but not in Dreamweaver, click the "+" button above the list of browsers.**

4. **In the resulting Add Browser dialog box, click the Browse button and identify the location of the browser you want to add.**

5. **Click OK to return to the Preferences dialog box.**

   The list of browsers shows the defined primary and secondary browsers, which you can invoke using the associated keyboard shortcuts. To change the defaults, you can simply select a browser in the list and check the related Defaults options.

Note:

Press Option-F12/F12 to preview a page in your primary browser. Press Command/Control-F12 to preview the page in your secondary browser.

If you are using a Macintosh laptop, you also have to press the Function (FN) key to use the F key shortcuts.

6. Repeat Steps 3–5 as necessary to add all available browsers to Dreamweaver,

7. Click Apply in the Preferences dialog box to finalize your changes, then click Close to close the dialog box.

8. In the Files panel, double-click the **index.html** file to open it.

9. Click the Real-Time Preview button in the bottom-right corner of the document window and choose one of the listed browsers.

Real-Time Preview button

Note:

You can also scan the QR code with a smartphone or tablet, or type the listed http address, to preview the file directly on that device. (In this case you will be asked to sign in to your Adobe Creative Cloud account before you can preview the file.)

10. **In the resulting browser window, click the links at the top of the page to test them.**

   The Contact link on the right side of the menu opens a new, preaddressed mail message in your default email application.

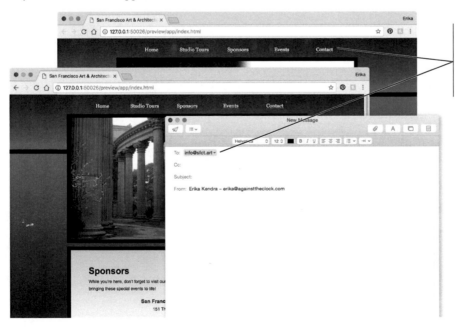

Clicking the link in a browser window correctly opens a new email message in your default email application.

Note:

A mailto: link opens a new mail message in the user's default email application. If a user does not have an email client, or has not specified one as the default option, clicking a mailto: link might open a message asking which application to use to send the email.

11. **Close the mail message without sending.**

12. **Close the browser window and return to Dreamweaver.**

13. **Close index.html, then continue to the next exercise.**

REMOVE A SITE FROM DREAMWEAVER

As you gain experience designing and developing websites, your site definition list will continue to grow. To keep your list under control, you can export site definitions and remove certain sites from the list. When you remove a site from Dreamweaver, you are not deleting the actual files and folders from your computer; you are simply removing them from Dreamweaver's view.

1. **In the Files panel, open the Directory menu and choose Manage Sites at the bottom of the list.**

2. **In the resulting Manage Sites dialog box, select the sf-arts site in the list and click the "–" button below the list of available sites.**

   In this case, you made no changes to the site definitions or files. Because you already have an STE file with the correct information, it is not necessary to re-export the site definition.

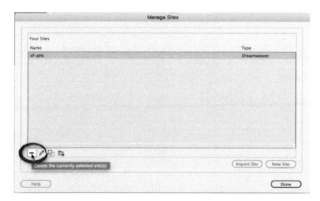

3. **Click Yes in the Warning dialog box, and then click Done to close the Manage Sites dialog box.**

   After removing the site, it no longer appears in the list of sites.

Bistro Site Organization

Your client has opened a new restaurant in a fast-growing community in Southern California. He has already designed the pages for his site, but has hired you to make sure everything works properly and then make the site available to the browsing public.

This project incorporates the following skills:

❏ Creating, exporting, and removing site definitions in Dreamweaver

❏ Moving files around in a site root folder

❏ Creating relative links between pages in a site

❏ Defining absolute links to external sites and email addresses

❏ Improving search engine optimization (SEO) with file names and titles

❏ Cloaking site files from a web server

❏ Uploading files to a web server

client comments

I already created the pages for our site, but I don't know what links to use, and I'm not sure how to create them. I've also heard that there are certain things you should do to improve a site's search engine rating — which is obviously important for a small business like mine.

art director comments

The more pages you add to a site, the more complex it becomes, until it's almost impossible to make sense of what you have and where it is located. Websites — even those with only a few pages — should be designed with a good organizational plan, making it easier to modify pages later.

Once you have a handle on the organization, make sure the pages link to each other properly. Visitors get frustrated very quickly when they're forced to return to the home page every time they want to jump to a different set of pages.

The last thing you should do is add page titles and change file names to give a better indication of what's on each page. Doing so will make the site more accessible to people with screen-reader software, and it will also improve the site's ratings on search engines.

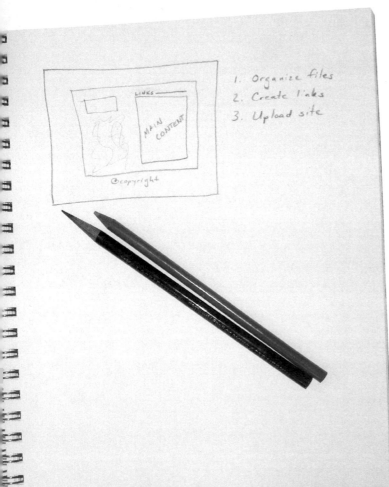

project objectives

To complete this project, you will:

- ❏ Create a Dreamweaver site definition
- ❏ Create new folders within the site root folder
- ❏ Use various methods to move files from one place to another within the site
- ❏ Create links between pages using several techniques available in Dreamweaver
- ❏ Differentiate between relative and absolute links
- ❏ Copy and paste links from one page to another
- ❏ Improve searchability and usability using page names and titles
- ❏ Cloak site files to hide them from the web server
- ❏ Upload the site files to a server so they can be viewed online

Stage 1 Exploring Site Structure

When you start a new project that involves updating an existing site, your first task is to assess the file and folder structure. Doing so gives you a good idea of what the site contains.

A small site with only a few pages requires very little organization; in fact, you *can* place all of the files — web pages and image files — in one folder (although even a small site benefits from a dedicated folder for images). Larger sites, however, require careful organization of file names, pages, and image files. A good site design with excellent organization speeds development now, and makes it much easier to update the site later.

 CREATE A NEW SITE DEFINITION

Websites are designed so all of the web pages, image files, style sheets, and other resources are stored on your local drive in a base folder called the **root folder**. Other folders can be placed inside (below) the root folder to make it easier to manage and organize files.

1. **Download Kinetic_DW18_RF.zip from the Student Files web page.**

2. **Expand the ZIP archive in your WIP folder (Macintosh) or copy the archive contents into your WIP folder (Windows).**

   This results in a folder named **Kinetic**, which contains all the files you need to complete this project.

   If necessary, refer to Page 13 of the Interface chapter for specific instructions on expanding or accessing the required resource files.

3. **In Dreamweaver, set up your workspace so the Files, Insert, and Properties panels are visible.**

   It doesn't matter which saved workspace you start with. The primary tools you need for this project are the Files, Insert, and Properties panels. We have closed all other panels to maximize the available space in our screen shots.

4. **In the Files panel, click the Manage Sites link or open the Directory menu and choose Manage Sites from the bottom of the list.**

   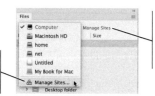

   This option performs the same function as clicking the blue Manage Sites link.

   If available, clicking Manage Sites opens the Manage Sites dialog box.

   Note:

   When a site is defined in Dreamweaver, the Manage Sites link at the top of the Files panel is replaced by a menu that defaults to Local view.

5. **Click the New Site button in the Manage Sites dialog box.**

   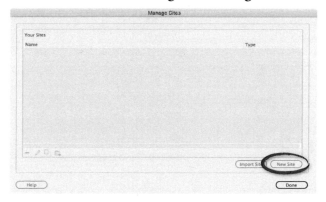

   Note:

   Ellipses in a menu or button name indicate that clicking will open a dialog box. We do not include the ellipses in our instructions.

6. **In the Site Setup dialog box, make sure Site is selected in the category list.**

7. **Type Kinetic in the Site Name field.**

   The site name can be anything that will allow you to easily recognize the project; it is only for identification within Dreamweaver. For example, you could use "Eve's site" as the site name within Dreamweaver to describe the website (www.evelynsmith.biz) that you are creating for your friend.

8. **Click the Browse for Folder button to the right of the Local Site Folder field. Navigate to the WIP>Kinetic folder and click Choose/Select Folder to return to the Site Setup dialog box.**

   Part of the process of defining a site within Dreamweaver is to specify a particular folder as the site root folder of the website. Clicking the Local Site Folder button opens a navigation dialog box where you can find the folder you want to use.

Note:

You will learn about other options in the Site Setup dialog box later in this book.

Browse for Folder button

9. **Click Save to close the Site Setup dialog box.**

10. **In the Manage Sites dialog box, make sure the Kinetic site appears in the list of sites, and then click Done.**

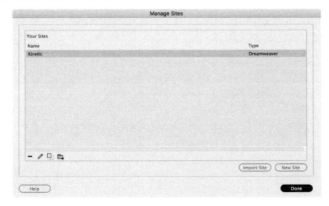

11. **Continue to the next exercise.**

EXAMINE THE SITE FILES

There are many files in the Kinetic site folder. The first step in organizing the files is to examine the web page files and understand what they contain.

1. **With Kinetic showing in the Directory menu of the Files panel, expand the site folder (if necessary) and examine the files in the site.**

Directory menu

Click this button to expand the folder.

Click here and drag left to make the panel wider.

Refresh button

This is the root folder of the current site.

Note:

If more than one site is defined, you can switch between sites using the Directory menu of the Files panel.

2. **Double-click index.html in the Files panel to open the file in Dreamweaver.**

   Using the options in the Document toolbar, close the Code pane (if necessary) and make the regular Design view active; the Live view should be turned off.

   All of the pages in this site use the same basic design. The links at the top of each page need to navigate between the pages. The copyright information at the bottom (in the footer area) needs to navigate to the copyright owner's website, which is external to your client's site.

Click this button to show only the Design view.

Choose Design in this menu to show the regular Design view.

These words will be links, which will appear on every page in the site.

This should be a link to the copyright holder's website.

3. Close index.html, then open contact.html.

As you can see, this page uses the same basic design as the index page. The specific page content also includes an email link, which you need to define so that users can click the link to send your client an email message.

These links should be the same on every page in the site.

This should be an email link to your client's email address.

Note:

The layout for this site is based on the free "Creation" template from www.templatemo.com. Photos are by Charlie Essers.

4. Close contact.html, then open menu1.html.

Again, the page uses the same basic layout as the other pages in the site. The top area of this page's primary content indicates that there are actually two menus — Dinner and Lunch. As you can see in the Files panel, two separate menu files exist. You will use the two headings at the top of the page to create links to each menu.

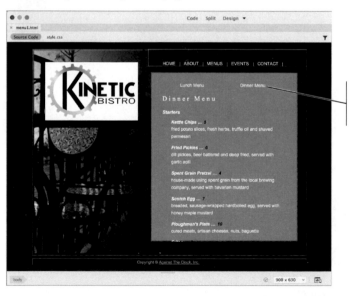

These words should link to the relevant menu page.

5. Close menu1.html, then continue to the next exercise.

PLAN FOLDER ORGANIZATION

When all files are dumped into the main site folder, it can be challenging to manage your work. A well-organized site is an easy-to-manage site. Ideally, organization occurs before the site is constructed, but Dreamweaver makes it easy to reorganize files and folders at any point in the process.

There are no absolute rules to follow for organizing files and folders — other than the general principle of keeping related components together, so you know where to find certain files when you need them.

1. **With the Kinetic site open in the Files panel, scroll to the top of the Files panel (if necessary). Control/right-click the site name and choose New Folder from the contextual menu.**

   The basic pages (home, about, contact, etc.) form the root of the site, and they should therefore appear within the root folder of the site. Other pages are better kept in folders that are named based on what they contain.

2. **Type resources and press Return/Enter to apply the new folder name.**

   If the folder name remains untitled after pressing Return/Enter, Control/right-click the untitled folder, choose Edit>Rename in the contextual menu (or press the F2 key), and retype the new folder name.

3. **Click the Refresh button in the Files panel.**

   When the Files panel is sorted by name, folders on Macintosh are alphabetized along with all other files and folders after refreshing the file list; on Windows, folders are moved to and alphabetized at the top of the list, above individual files.

   Note:

   Press F5 to refresh the file list in the Files panel.

   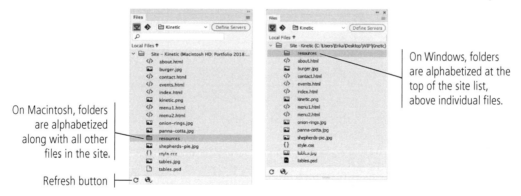

   On Macintosh, folders are alphabetized along with all other files in the site.

   Refresh button

   On Windows, folders are alphabetized at the top of the site list, above individual files.

4. **Control/right-click the main site folder again and choose New Folder from the contextual menu.**

   You want another folder at the same level as the resources folder — in the main level of the site root — so you first have to use the contextual menu for the site root folder.

5. **Type images and press Return/Enter to apply the new folder name.**

   Web design convention dictates image files be placed in a folder named "images" for easier organization. If you have many photos in various categories, you might want to create additional nested folders inside the main images folder.

6. **Repeat Steps 4–5 to create another new folder named menus in the site root folder.**

7. **Refresh the list in the Files panel.**

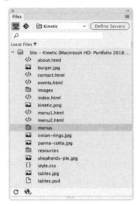

Note:

You can create a new folder inside an existing folder (called nesting) by Control/right-clicking the existing folder — instead of the root folder — and choosing New Folder from the contextual menu.

8. **Continue to the next exercise.**

Sort and Move Image Files

When you define a site in Dreamweaver, the application reads all of the pages in the site (a process that can take a few minutes in a large site), notes the links between pages, and identifies which images are used in which pages. These associations between files are stored in a cache that Dreamweaver creates when a new site is defined.

When files are moved or renamed within the site, Dreamweaver recognizes that other files are related to the moved or renamed files and prompts you to update the links in all of the affected files.

1. **With the Kinetic site open in the Files panel, Control/right-click the Local Files heading and choose Type in the contextual menu.**

   In addition to the file names and icons, you can show a variety of options in Files panel, including any notes about the files, the file size, type (format), modification date, and whether the file has been checked out by another user.

Click and drag the header edge to make a column wider or narrower.

2. **In the Files panel, click and drag burger.jpg into the images folder.**

   Make sure you drag the file directly over the name of the folder or folder icon; if you drag the file too far to the left or right, Dreamweaver will not move the file.

3. **When prompted, click Update to update the affected pages with the new location for the burger.jpg image file.**

When a browser downloads a web page, it reads the page code, requests the image files from the defined locations, and displays the images within the page. You should understand that images in web pages are not embedded into web pages; they are merged into the page by the browser.

Files being updated do not need to be open for Dreamweaver to change the required link information. If pages *are* open, links in those pages are updated, but the changes are not automatically saved; you have to manually save each open file to make the updates permanent.

If you choose Don't Update in the Update Links dialog box, the image will not appear in the page that calls for that file. If you had moved the image file using Windows Explorer or the Macintosh Finder, Dreamweaver would not have been aware of the movement, and you would not have had the opportunity to adjust the path to the image file in pages that link to that image.

The burger.jpg file is now stored in the main images folder. When you move files into a folder, that folder automatically expands in the Files panel.

Note:

To avoid potential problems if you accidentally close a file without saving, you might want to close open files before moving or renaming files in the Files panel.

4. **In the Files panel, click the Type column heading to sort the site files by type.**

By default, site files are sorted by name. You can sort by another criteria by clicking the column headings in the Files panel. Sorting by type allows you to easily find all of the images that are used in this site.

5. **Click the first JPG file in the list (onion-rings.jpg) to select that file. Press Shift and click kinetic.png to select all consecutive files between the first and the last ones you selected.**

Press Shift to select multiple consecutive files in the panel. Press Command/Control and click to select multiple, nonconsecutive files.

You can also Command/Control-click to deselect a selected file. For example, if you select a file by accident, you can deselect it by Command/Control-clicking the file name.

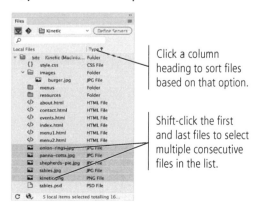

Click a column heading to sort files based on that option.

Shift-click the first and last files to select multiple consecutive files in the list.

Note:

Images in websites typically have a GIF, JPG, or PNG extension.

5. **Click the icon of any of the selected files and drag the selected files into the images folder. When asked, click Update to update all links to all of the moved files.**

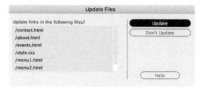 

6. **Click the down-facing arrow to the left of the images folder name to collapse the folder.**

7. **Click the Local Files column header to re-sort the files by name.**

8. **Select menu1.html and menu2.html, and move them into the menus folder. Update the links when asked.**

   This is a relatively small site, so nesting files into subfolders isn't strictly necessary. However, when you work with larger files, clearly organized subfolders can be extremely helpful in maintaining a site that is easy to update as often as necessary.

Note:

You can also copy and paste files into a folder using the Edit options in the contextual menus, or using the standard keyboard shortcuts:

*Cut:
Command/Control-X*

*Copy:
Command/Control-C*

*Paste:
Command/Control-V*

9. **Collapse the menus folder.**

10. **Select and move the file tables.psd into the resources folder.**

    In this case, you are not asked to update links. This is a layered Photoshop file that was used to create the background image behind the page content. It is not part of the actual website, but it's a good idea to keep this type of file in the site folder in case you need to make changes later. Later in this project, you will learn how to prevent this file from being uploaded as part of the site.

11. **Collapse the resources folder.**

    From the folder structure alone, the website appears to be better organized. You now know what to expect when you open each folder.

12. **Continue to the next stage of the project.**

Changing the Update Preferences

As you have seen, Dreamweaver automatically asks you to update links when you move a file in the Files panel. You can change this behavior in the General pane of the Preferences dialog box.

If you choose Always in the Update Links... menu, the affected links are automatically updated without user intervention. In other words, you do not see the Update Files dialog box during the process.

If you choose Never, links are not automatically updated when you move files in the Files panel. If you do not manually correct links, they will result in an error when clicked by a user.

Stage 2 Organizing the Site Navigation

Hyperlinks (the official term for links) can be created to link pages on a site to other pages within the same site, or to pages on other sites. A well-designed site includes links that make it easy to get to any part of a site from any other part of a site. You should carefully plan the flow of links and connections between pages — always keeping the reader's usability in mind.

Organizing links is a simple application of a science called **information architecture**, which is the organization of a website to support both usability and "findability." As you organize site links, remember that your goal is to enable visitors to see a pattern in your links, which will assist them in navigating through your site. Keep the following points in mind when you plan a site's link structure:

- You can't know how visitors will enter your site. The primary site pages (home, about us, etc.) should be accessible from every page on the site.

- When linking secondary pages such as different menus for different mealtimes, don't make users constantly click the browser's Back button. Links should allow users to navigate all sibling pages (at the same level) as easily as navigating the primary structure. For example, users should be able to access the dinner menu or lunch menu in the restaurant's site without first going back to a main "Menu" page.

Using the terms "parent," "child," and "sibling" is simply a way of describing relationships between pages. A large website cannot provide links to all of the pages from its home page. By grouping pages, grouping groups of pages, and so on, you create relationships of equality between pages that are grouped together, as well as between groups that are grouped together.

When you plan a new site, you should create this type of flowchart to make sure you create all the necessary links that make the site as user-friendly as possible. A flowchart of the required Kinetic site link structure is shown to the right.

In this stage of the project, you will learn various techniques to create the necessary links on the Kinetic site pages.

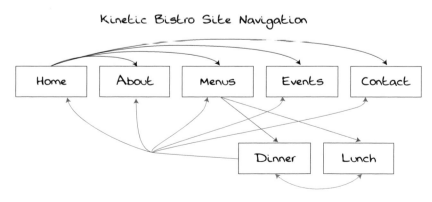

Kinetic Bistro Site Navigation

CREATE HYPERLINKS WITHIN THE SITE

Dreamweaver offers a number of options for creating the necessary links for any website structure.

- **Hyperlink Button in the HTML Insert Panel.** Clicking the Hyperlink button in the HTML Insert panel opens the Hyperlink dialog box, where you define the specific parameters of the link.

- **Insert>Hyperlink menu.** This menu command opens the same dialog box that you see when you click the Hyperlink button in the Insert panel.

- **Properties Panel Fields.** You can also simply define the specifics of a hyperlink in the Properties panel. This method offers the same options as those in the Hyperlink dialog box but does not require the dialog box interface.

- **Point to File button in the Properties panel.** To create a link using this method, simply click the Point to File button, hold down the mouse button, and drag to a file in the Files panel; Dreamweaver automatically creates a link.

- **Browse for File button in the Properties panel.** The Browse for File button opens a navigation dialog box where you can select the file that will open when a user clicks on the link.

- **Shift-Drag Method.** You can create a link directly from the document window by pressing Shift and then clicking and dragging from the link source to the destination page in the Files panel. (This method only works for text; you can't Shift-drag to create a link for an image.)

- **Quick Property Inspector in Live View.** When the Live view is active, you can use the Link button in the Quick Property Inspector, which appears attached to the selected item in the document window, to create a hyperlink.

Note:

Dreamweaver often includes several different ways to achieve the same result. You should use the method that is most efficient at the time.

1. With the **Kinetic** site open in the Files panel, open **index.html**. Make sure the Live view is not active.

2. At the top of the page, double-click the word "HOME" to select it.

3. If your Insert panel is docked above the document window, click the HTML tab at the top of the panel.

   If your Insert panel is docked on the right side of the screen, or if it is floating as a separate panel, choose HTML in the menu at the top of the panel.

If the panel is in standard mode, use the menu at the top to access different categories of options.

If docked in tabbed mode, use the tabs at the top of the panel to access different categories of options.

4. Click the Hyperlink button in the HTML Insert panel.

The HTML Insert panel contains many of the common functions you use to create web pages. If a different Insert panel is showing, you can return to the HTML Insert panel by choosing HTML in the panel menu.

Note:

From this point on, we will leave our Insert panel docked on the right side of the workspace, immediately below the Files panel. Feel free to organize your workspace however you prefer.

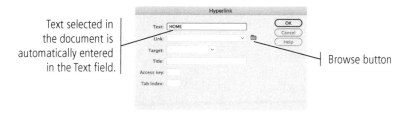

If docked in standard mode, buttons in the panel are identified by icon and name.

If docked in tabbed mode, hover your mouse over a button to find its name.

This word is selected.

5. In the Hyperlink dialog box, click the Browse button to the right of the Link field.

The text selected in the document appears in the Text field by default. (If an image is selected, this field defaults to be blank.)

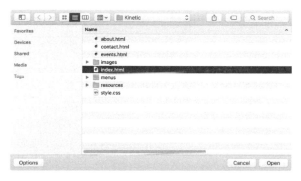

Text selected in the document is automatically entered in the Text field.

Browse button

6. Navigate to your WIP>Kinetic folder, select index.html, and click Open/OK to return to the Hyperlink dialog box.

In the Link field, you can either type the URL of a location outside the site you're building, or you can click the Browse button to select a file within the current site.

Note:

Remember, when commands are different for different operating systems, we list them as Macintosh/Windows.

The HTML Insert panel contains buttons for frequently used items. For example, to insert a hyperlink, simply click the corresponding button. (Some of the terms and functions in the following descriptions will make more sense as you use those tools to complete later projects.)

- **Div** inserts sections (divisions) in a page, which are useful for inserting blocks of content that you want to format independently from other blocks. You will work extensively with div tags in later projects.

- **Image** opens a dialog box where you can define the source for the image you want to insert.

- **Paragraph** surrounds each selected paragraph with <p></p> tags, which is the proper HTML structure for a paragraph of text.

- **Heading** is used to assign predefined HTML heading levels (h1 through h6) to selected text.

- **Table** inserts an HTML table into the page.

- **Figure** inserts a properly structured HTML figure, including the appropriate tags for the figure and the figure caption.

- **Unordered List** creates a bulleted list from the selected paragraphs; each selected paragraph is automatically tagged as a list item.

- **Ordered List** creates a numbered list from the selected paragraphs; each selected paragraph is automatically tagged as a list item.

- **List Item** creates a new list item at the location of the insertion point. No ordered or unordered list is created to surround the list item.

- **Hyperlink** opens a dialog box where you can create text or image links to another file, either in the same website or in an external website.

- **Header**, **Navigation**, **Main**, **Aside**, **Article**, **Section**, and **Footer** add the related HTML5 tags to the page. You have the option to determine exactly how the tags are applied in relation to selected text, as well as defining an ID or class attribute for the resulting tag.

- **Meta** opens a dialog box where you can define a variety of page head information. When you type specific values in the name and content fields, the appropriate information is added to the page head using the following structure:

  <meta name="test" content="123">

- **Keywords** opens a dialog box where you can define keywords in the page head. The keywords are added using the following structure:

  <meta name="keywords" content="words">

- **Description** opens a dialog box where you can define a text-based description to the page head. The description is added using the following structure:

  <meta name="description" content="Text">

- **Viewport** offers a way to better control the appearance of a page on mobile devices. It sets the width of the visible area of a web page on a user's device to match the width of the device screen.

- The **Script** button can be used to add code from an external file, which will be used by the browser to perform an action when the page is accessed.

- The **Email Link** button opens a dialog box where you can create links to email addresses.

- **HTML5 Video** inserts a video element, which allows a video file to be played directly in an HTML5 page without the need for external browser plugins.

- **Canvas** inserts a canvas element, which is a container for graphics that are created directly in the page using scripts.

- **Animate Composition** places a defined Animate composition (OAM file) into the HTML page at the location of the cursor.

- **HTML5 Audio** inserts a audio element, which allows an audio file to be played directly in an HTML5 page without the need for external browser plugins.

- **Flash SWF** allows you to place a SWF file (created from a Flash animation). Keep in mind that SWF files require the Flash Player browser plugin to function properly.

- **Flash Video** allows you to place an FLV file, which is a video format created from Flash professional. Again, this format requires the Flash Player browser plugin to function properly.

- **Plugin** embeds a specific user-defined plugin file into the page.

- **Rollover Image** opens a dialog box where you can define the default image, as well as a different image that will appear when a user's mouse cursor enters into the image area.

- **iFrame** inserts an iFrame element, which allows you to embed one document into another.

- **Horizontal Rule** inserts a solid line across the width of the page. This can be useful for visually separating sections of text.

- The **Date** button inserts the current date and time. In the resulting dialog box, you can choose the date format, as well as an option to update the date and time whenever the file is saved.

- **Non-Breaking Space** adds a special character that prevents a line break from appearing between specific words in a paragraph.

- **Character** is used to insert special characters, such as copyright symbols and foreign currency characters.

7. **Open the Target menu and choose _self.**

   This option determines where the linked file will open:

   - **_blank** opens every linked file in a new, unnamed browser window.
   - **new** creates a new browser window with the name "_new". Every link assigned the _new target will open in that same _new browser window.
   - **_parent** is relevant if a page includes nested frames; this option opens the link in the frame or window that contains the frame with the link.
   - **_self** opens the link in the same frame or browser window as the link. This is the default behavior if you do not choose an option in the Target menu.
   - **_top** opens the link in the same browser window, regardless of frames.

8. **In the Title field, type Kinetic Bistro home page.**

   The Title field defines text that appears when the cursor is placed over the link text. Defining a descriptive title for links can help a page achieve better search engine results.

Note:

You can use the Access Key field to define a keyboard shortcut for the link and use the Tab Index field to specify the number of times a user needs to press the Tab key to select the link.

9. **Click OK in the Hyperlink dialog box to create the link.**

10. **Click the Split button in the Document toolbar to review both the design and code views at one time.**

    A web page is basically a page full of code. A browser reads the code to determine how to treat various elements of the page. HTML code largely revolves around tags, which tell a browser how to interpret specific objects on the page.

    A hyperlink is identified by the **a** element, which starts with the opening **<a>** tag; the link destination and target are defined as attributes of that tag (**href="index.html" target="_self"**). After the link text, the closing tag (**</a>**) identifies the end of the link.

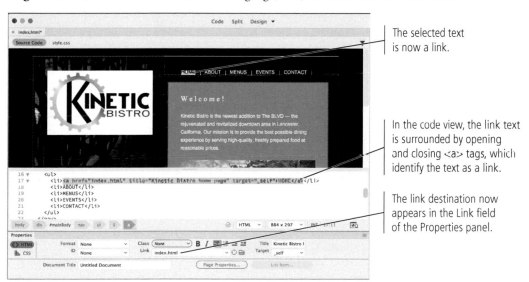

The selected text is now a link.

In the code view, the link text is surrounded by opening and closing <a> tags, which identify the text as a link.

The link destination now appears in the Link field of the Properties panel.

11. Select the word "ABOUT" at the top of the page.

12. Click the Browse for File button to the right of the Link field in the Properties panel.

If you don't see the Properties panel, choose Window>Properties. The Properties panel's primary purpose is to review and change the properties of the selected HTML element (such as a heading, paragraph, or table cell).

The word ABOUT is selected.

Browse for File button

13. In the resulting dialog box, select **about.html**, and then click Open/OK.

The link destination now appears in the Link field of the Properties panel.

14. Select the word "MENUS" at the top of the page.

15. Expand the **menus** folder in the Files panel.

You should expand and collapse Files panel folders as necessary, depending on your available screen space. We will not repeat instructions to collapse or expand folders unless it is necessary to perform a specific function.

16. Click the Point to File button in the Properties panel, hold down the mouse button, and drag to **menus/menu1.html** in the Files panel.

The word MENUS is selected.

Point to File button

17. **Select the word "EVENTS" at the top of the page.**

18. **Macintosh: Press the Shift key, then click the selected text and drag to events.html in the Files panel.**

    You have to press the Shift key, and then click and drag to the link destination. If you try to click and drag before pressing the Shift key, this technique will fail.

    Windows: Use any method you already learned to link the word "EVENTS" to the events.html file in the site root folder.

    The Shift-drag method does not work on the Windows operating system.

Note:

You can remove a link by selecting the linked text or object by simply deleting the text from the Link field in the Properties panel.

19. **Use any method you just learned to create a link from the word "CONTACT" to the contact.html file.**

20. **In the Document toolbar, click the arrow to the right of the Design button and choose Live from the menu to turn on the Live view.**

    In the Live view, you can accurately see how the CSS will be rendered by web browsers.

21. In the Design window with the Live view active, click once to select the footer paragraph at the bottom of the page.

When the Live view is active, clicking an object in the document window shows the Element Display, which shows the active HTML element. (If an element has a defined ID or class attribute, those also appear in the Element Display. You will learn about IDs and classes in later projects.) In this case, you can see that the selected element is a **p** element — in other words, it is a paragraph.

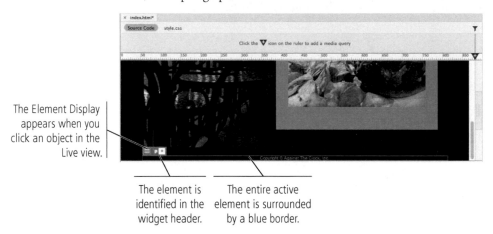

The Element Display appears when you click an object in the Live view.

The element is identified in the widget header.

The entire active element is surrounded by a blue border.

22. Double-click the text in the selected paragraph to place the insertion point.

You can now place the insertion point and edit text directly in the Live view. (You might have to look closely to see the insertion point in this case.)

Double-clicking places the insertion point inside the active element.

The orange border identifies the element where the insertion point is placed.

23. Double-click and drag to select the words "Against The Clock, Inc." within the active paragraph.

In the Live view, the Quick Property Inspector shows options related to the selected text. You can use the B and I buttons to apply the **<strong>** and **<em>** tags (respectively). You can also click the Hyperlink button to define a link destination for the selected text.

Quick Property Inspector

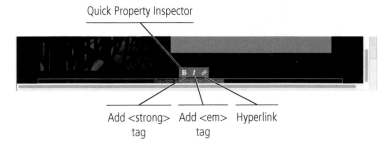

Add <strong> tag

Add <em> tag

Hyperlink

Note:

The strong and em tags are explained in Project 2: Digital Book Chapter.

24. **In the Quick Property Inspector, click the Hyperlink button. In the resulting Link field, type** http://www.againsttheclock.com **as the link destination.**

Dreamweaver can't help you create an external URL link because it's outside the site definition. You have to simply type or paste the address into the Link field.

An external **URL link** must begin with the "http://" protocol, followed by the domain name and, if relevant, the folder path and file name of the page to which you are linking.

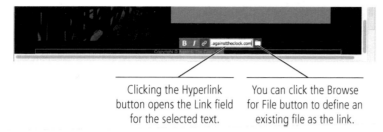

Clicking the Hyperlink button opens the Link field for the selected text.

You can click the Browse for File button to define an existing file as the link.

25. **Click anywhere else in the workspace to finalize the hyperlink you defined in Step 24.**

26. **In the Document toolbar, click the arrow to the right of the Live button and choose Design from the menu to turn off the Live view.**

You should become familiar with the process of turning the Live view on or off. We will not continue to repeat these specific instructions as you move throughout the projects in this book.

27. **Choose File>Save to save your changes, then continue to the next exercise.**

Note:

To minimize the repetitive work required, we already defined this link for you on the other pages in the site. In a professional environment, you would need to add this link to every page in the site.

 COPY AND PASTE LINKS

Rather than manually creating the same links on every page, you can now simply copy and paste them from one page to another.

1. **With** index.html **open (from the Kinetic site) in the regular Design view, click in any of the text links to place the insertion point.**

The insertion point is the location where text will appear if you type.

2. **Review the Tag Selector below the document window.**

The Tag Selector, located in the status bar of the document window, shows the nesting order of HTML tags (the "path of tags") based on the current selection or the current location of the insertion point.

Note:

You will work more extensively with tags beginning in Project 2: Digital Book Chapter.

Insertion point

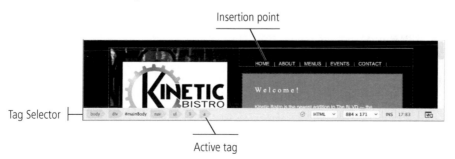

Tag Selector

Active tag

3. **Click the <ul> tag in the Tag Selector.**

   The **<ul>** tag identifies an unordered list, which is how this navigation structure was created; each link is a separate list item (using the **<li>** tag).

   Clicking a tag in the Tag Selector selects that HTML element and all of its content. In the document window, the associated content is highlighted.

   The entire unordered list (all of the links) is selected.

   Selected tag

4. **Choose Edit>Copy (or press Command/Control-C) to copy the selected content to the Clipboard.**

5. **Close index.html and open about.html.**

6. **Click to place the insertion point anywhere in the list of links at the top of the page, and then click the <ul> tag in the Tag Selector to select the entire unlinked list.**

   The selected list does not yet include links.

7. **Choose Edit>Paste (or press Command/Control-V) to paste the copied content from the Clipboard.**

8. **Place the insertion point in any of the links and review the Tag Selector.**

   The Tag Selector now shows the **<a>** tag for the current insertion point (in our example, the EVENTS link). The Properties panel also shows the destination of the active link.

   The pasted content includes the links.

9. **Save the changes to about.html and close the file.**

10. **Repeat Steps 6–9 to paste the copied content (the links) into all HTML pages in the site root level, as well as the two HTML pages in the menus folder.**

11. **Save and close any open file, and then continue to the next exercise.**

ADJUST RELATIVE LINK PATHS

A **path** is the route taken through the folder structure to link one page to another. By default, Dreamweaver uses **relative paths** when creating links (the application refers to this as "relative to the document"). The alternative is to create **absolute paths** ("relative to the site"); but unless your site is running on a web server, you can't test links that use absolute paths.

As an example, consider creating a link from index.html to about.html, both of which reside in the root folder (as shown in the figure to the right). In this case, the source and destination pages are in the same folder; the relative-path link simply states the file name of the destination page:

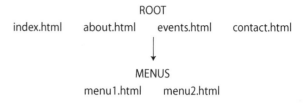

```
<a href="menu2.html">Link Text</a>
```

When you drill down into nested levels of folders, the source folder is not identified in the path; the link automatically works starting from the location of the link. To link from index.html to menu1.html, for example, you have to include the nested menus folder in the path:

```
<a href="menus/menu1.html">Link Text</a>
```

When the link is in an upward direction, the ../ notation says "go up one folder." To link from menu1.html to index.html in the site root folder means that the link needs to take the visitor up one folder level:

```
<a href="../index.html">Link Text</a>
```

Each step up in the folder structure requires another command to "go one step up" in the folder structure. If you had another level of nesting inside the menus folder, for example, a link would have to take the visitor up two folder levels to return to the main index page:

```
<a href="../../index.html">Link Text</a>
```

1. **With the Kinetic site open in the Files panel, open menu1.html.**

   In this exercise, you are going to adjust the various links so they work properly on all pages in the site.

2. **Double-click the word HOME at the top of the page to select that element.**

3. **In the Link field of the Properties panel, type ../ before the existing link. Press Return/Enter to finalize the change.**

Type **../** before the existing link.

4. **Repeat Steps 2–3 for the ABOUT, EVENTS, and CONTACT links.**

5. **Select the word MENUS at the top of the page.**

   In this case, the link is still a problem because it directs the browser to look for a folder named "menus" inside the same folder as the active page. You need to remove the folder part of the path to prevent an error if a user clicks this link from the menu1.html page.

   The active file is in the **menus** folder.

   This link would cause a browser to look for a menus folder at the same level as the active file.

6. **In the Link field of the Properties Inspector, delete menus/ (including the forward slash) from the existing link.**

   Delete the folder path from the existing link.

7. **Using any method you have learned, link "Lunch Menu" (in the main content area) to menu2.html and link "Dinner Menu" to menu1.html.**

   See "Accessing Page Content in the Menu Pages" (Page 47) for specific information about selecting the text in the main content area.

   Link this to menu2.html.   Link this to menu1.html.

8. **Repeat the process from Steps 1–7 to adjust the top links and add the necessary secondary links in the menu2.html file.**

9. **Save and close any open files, then continue to the next exercise.**

   You can save each file individually, or choose File>Save All to save all open files at once.

The files for this project were created using divs (using the opening and closing <div> tags), which are simply a way to identify and format parts or sections of a page.

(You will work with divs in Project 4: Museum CSS Layout.) Although you don't need to worry about the underlying page structure for now, you might see some unusual behavior when you try to select content in the main section the menu pages when the Live view is not active.

The area that holds the actual menu content has a fixed height, but both menus have more content than will fit into the defined size. When the page is viewed in a browser, the area includes a scroll bar for users to access the content that doesn't fit.

In Dreamweaver's regular Design view, however, this scrollbar doesn't appear. Instead, the first time you click, the entire div is selected and all of the contained text is highlighted.

Double-clicking inside the area again causes the page to jump down, showing the overflow content.

If you click a third time, you can place the insertion point inside the actual text, scroll up as necessary, and then select the link text at the top of the area.

Clicking once selects the entire div that contains the menu content:

Then double-clicking jumps the page down to show the overflow content:

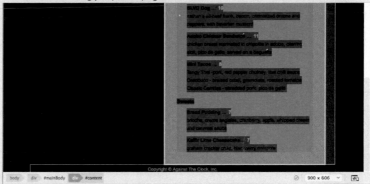

You can then click again to place the insertion point and select specific text:

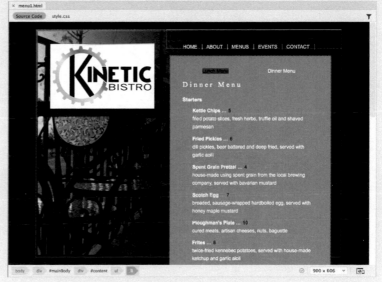

CREATE AN EMAIL LINK

Most websites include one or more external links (including email links), which require the appropriate protocol to tell the browser what type of link is present.

An **email link** requires the "mailto:" protocol, followed by the appropriate email address. This instructs the browser to open a new mail message with the defined address already in the To line.

1. With the Kinetic site open in the Files panel, open contact.html. Make sure the Live view is not active.

2. Select the words "info@kineticbistro.atc" in the main content area.

3. In the HTML Insert panel, click the Email Link button.

Selected text

4. Review the resulting dialog box.

If you select text before clicking the Email Link icon, the Text field is completed for you. Dreamweaver also recognizes that the selected text is an email address, so the Email field is filled in for you.

If the selected text is not recognized as an email address, the Email field defaults to the last address that was defined in the field.

5. Click OK to create the email link.

6. Review the link field in the Properties panel.

An email link must begin with "mailto:" followed by the address. When you use the Email Link dialog box, Dreamweaver automatically inserts the mailto: protocol.

Note:

You can access the same Email Link dialog box by choosing Insert>HTML>Email Link.

In many cases throughout this book, we use "[company].atc" as the domain of a site. Although at the time of writing, none of the domain names we use are real, new domains are registered every day. We use the fictitious ".atc" domain to avoid inadvertently using the domain name of a real company.

When you upload files to a server, you should use the accurate domain (.com, .gov, .edu, etc.) for the site you are building.

7. Save the file and close it, then continue to the next stage of the project.

Stage 3 Naming and Titling Documents

When a **web server** (a computer that stores and delivers web pages) receives a request for a folder but not a specific page, the web server delivers the default page for that folder — usually named index.html or index.htm. There is no practical difference between the two extensions; most web servers can serve files with either extension. (If you do not have an index file in that folder, the link will result in an error.)

To create links to the default page in a specific folder, you do not need to include the file name if you use the index naming convention. Both **www.kineticbistro.com/** and **www.kineticbistro.com/index.html** refer to the same page.

RENAME PAGES FOR SEARCH ENGINE OPTIMIZATION

Search engine optimization (SEO) is the process of improving the ranking of a web page on search engine results pages (SERPs). Search engines certainly use the content of a page for ranking purposes, but the names of folders and files also affect rankings.

Descriptive folder and file names improve usability; you can use **m/menu1.html** for the path to the dinner menu page, for example, but **/menus/dinner-menu.html** is much easier for visitors to understand — and will improve your search engine ranking.

In this exercise, you rename the menu pages to more accurately describe what is contained in the files. As with moving files, the application recognizes when a file name has been changed and knows that links to the page must be adjusted.

1. **With the Kinetic site open, click menus/menu1.html in the Files panel to select that file.**

2. **Click the selected filename again to highlight it.**

   This highlights the existing filename, excluding the extension.

Note:

You can also Control/right-click a file in the Files panel and choose Edit>Rename to rename a specific file.

3. **Type dinner-menu, then press Return/Enter. In the resulting dialog box, click Update to update all pages that link to this page.**

   Typing when the filename is highlighted replaces the previous file name. Pressing Return/Enter finalizes the change.

   As with moving files, Dreamweaver recognizes that all links to the renamed page need to point to the new file name.

4. **Repeat Steps 1–3 to rename menu2.html as lunch-menu.html.**

5. **Continue to the next exercise.**

Understanding Web File Naming Conventions

Because different servers run on different operating systems, the safest way to name pages is to use only characters that are guaranteed to work perfectly:

- a through z (use only lowercase letters)
- 0 through 9
- Hyphen (great-site.html)
- Underscore (great_site.html)

Consider everything else to be "illegal," including:

- Spaces
- Brackets of all kinds, including ( ), [ ], { }, and < >
- Symbols, including #, @, %, ~, |, *, and &
- Quotation marks, both double (" ") and single (' ')
- Slashes, both back slashes (\) and forward slashes (/)
- Commas, periods, question marks, and exclamation points
- Uppercase characters

Some designers use **CamelCase** — uppercase letters at the beginning of each word within a file name, such as UniversalStudios.html. The problem with mixing the lettercase is that some web server software is case-sensitive and some is not. Most Windows-based web server software is not case-sensitive, but UNIX- and Linux-based web server software is case-sensitive. Considering that many web servers run on UNIX- or Linux-based computers, it's best to use only lowercase file and folder names.

 CREATE DOCUMENT TITLES FOR INDIVIDUAL PAGES

Appropriate document titles are an important concern for both search engines and site visitors. While the document title does not appear within the body of a web page, it does appear in the title bar of the browser, as the default name of the page in the Bookmarks or Favorites list, and as the page name in search-engine results pages.

Page titles should be relatively short, around 70 characters or so to avoid their being truncated in various locations (such as a user's Bookmarks/Favorites list). You should separate the components of the title with some type of divider, such as a colon (:) or pipe (|) character.

In this exercise, you add document titles to the new pages to increase the pages' search engine rankings and improve usability for visitors who find the pages in search engines and bookmarks. You also learn to use the Find and Replace function, which can greatly reduce the amount of effort required to create all of the document titles.

1. **With the Kinetic site open in the Files panel, open index.html.**

2. **Click the Split button in the Document toolbar to show both the Code and Design views at one time.**

3. Examine the Document Title field in the Properties panel.

When you create a new page in Dreamweaver, the default title is "Untitled Document". That text appears in the Document Title field by default, and in the title element in the Code pane (wrapped in the opening and closing **<title>** tags).

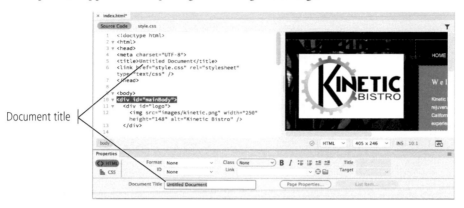

Document title

Note:

When you use the Split view, feel free to arrange the pane however you prefer. We arrange them as necessary to best suit what we are trying to show in our screen captures.

4. Choose Find>Find and Replace in Files.

This command opens the Find and Replace dialog box, which offers a number of options for searching and replacing specific text.

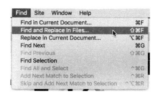

Note:

At least one file must be open to use the Find and Replace functionality.

5. In the Find field, type Untitled Document.

6. Make sure Entire Current Local Site is active in the [Find] In menu.

This option allows you to affect all files in the active site. You can also search only the current (active) document; all open documents; only files in a specific folder; or only selected files in the active site.

7. In the Replace field, type Kinetic Bistro | Lancaster, California | . (Include a space after the final pipe character.)

All pages in the site will include this block of text at the beginning of the document title. Further detail about individual pages will be added to the right of this information.

Unlike file names, document titles can use mixed lettercase and include spaces and other characters. However, you should avoid both single and double quotation marks.

Enter the text you want to find in this field.

Enter the text you want to change in this field.

Note:

Some experts disagree whether the company name should come before or after the specific page information in a title. However, putting the company name at the beginning of the page title can help with search engine results because the company name is an important keyword.

8. **Click Replace All. When prompted to confirm whether you want to proceed with this function, click Yes.**

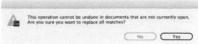

Like most applications, Dreamweaver has an Undo function that allows you to undo the most recently completed actions; however, this function only works if the document is open. Since you are using the Find and Replace function on the entire folder and not only on an open page, you are making changes in closed documents — which means you cannot use the Undo command.

After completing the Find and Replace function, Dreamweaver displays the results in the Search panel.

9. **Examine the title in the Properties panel and the Code pane again for the open file (index.html).**

As a result of the Find and Replace function, the document title has been changed. The same change has been made in all pages in the site. (Because the **title** tag of the open page is active in the Code pane, the Properties panel now shows only options for that active element.)

Note:

If you choose Find>Find/Replace in Current Document, a pop-up panel appears at the bottom of the document window with a fields to define the text you want to identify and/or change.

As soon as you enter text in the Find field of the pop-up panel, all instances of that text are highlighted in the Code pane. You can use the left- and right-arrow buttons to navigate through the various instances.

10. **Control/right-click the Search panel tab and choose Close Tab Group.**

11. **Click in the Code pane to make it active.**

Making a specific pane active is called "bringing it into focus."

12. **Click at the end of the existing page title to place the insertion point immediately before the closing </title> tag, then type Gourmet Casual Dining.**

You can edit the page title in the Document Title field of the Properties panel, or in the Code pane. Changes in either place are automatically applied to the other.

Type the new information immediately before the closing </title> tag.

13. **Save index.html and close it.**

Options in the Find and Replace dialog box allow you to conduct very specific and targeted searches.

The **[Find] In** menu determines where you want to perform the search. You can search only the current (active) document; all open documents; only files in a specific folder; only selected files in the active site, or all files in the current local site folder.

You can also use the **Tag** menu to limit where you want to search. For example, you can find the text "jpeg" only within an <img> tag and change those instances to the correct extension "jpg".

The **Find Previous** (◀) and **Find Next** (▶) buttons navigate to sequential instances of the text you enter in the Find field.

You can use the **Replace** button to change the active instance of text in the Find field, or use the Replace All button to change all instances.

Clicking the **Find All** button lists all instances of the search text in the Output panel. Double-clicking an item in the Output panel navigates to that instance in the document window.

Clicking the **Replace All** button changes all instances of the Find text to the Replace text. Changes are reported in the Output panel, but changes in files that are not currently open cannot be undone.

If you check the **Exceptions** option in the Find and Replace dialog box, clicking the Replace All button opens the Search panel with a list of each identified instance. You can use the checkboxes on the left to determine which instances will be changed, then click the Replace button in the panel to replace only certain instances.

Use these checkboxes to determine which will be changed.

Click Replace to change only selected instances.

You can also click the **Filters** button (▼) to define specific parameters for a search.

- **Match Case** limits the search to text that exactly matches the case of the text you want to find. For example, a search for Untitled Document will not find instances of "untitled document."

- **Use Regular Expressions** causes certain characters to function as operators, so that you can search for non-specific text.

  For example, when this option is not active, a search for the period character will identify actual period in the document.

  When Use Regular Expressions is checked, the period character is considered a wildcard that identifies any single character. A search for "p.p" would identify any instance where two ps are separated by one other character (pop, pap, puppy, etc.).

  Possible wildcard characters include:

.	Any character (except a newline character)
\d	Any digit (0-9)
\D	Any non-digit character
\w	Any alphanumeric character or the underscore
\W	Any character except an alphanumeric character or the underscore
\s	Any white-space character (space, tab, etc.)
\S	Any character except a white-space character
\t	Tab character

- **Match Whole Word** restricts the search to text that matches one or more complete words.

- **Ignore White Spaces** treats consecutive white space as a single space for the purposes of matching.

  For example, with this option selected, a search for My Portfolio would return instances of My Portfolio and My   Portfolio, but not MyPortfolio.

- **Find in Selected Text** (only available in the Find in Current Document mode) allows you to search only within text that is currently highlighted in the document window.

- **Search Text Only** (available only in the Find and Replace dialog box) allows you to search only text, ignoring any code within the text. When toggled off, your search will include the source code in the document as well.

14. **Open about.html. Using either the Code pane or the Document Title field in the Properties panel, add Hours of Operation to the end of the existing page title.**

15. **Save about.html and close it.**

16. **Repeat this process (Steps 14–15) to change the page titles of the remaining pages as follows:**

File	Title
contact.html	Address and Contact Information
events.html	Special Event Facilities
menus/dinner-menu.html	Dinner Menu
menus/lunch-menu.html	Lunch Menu

17. **Continue to the next exercise.**

 HIDE FILES FROM THE WEB SERVER

As you saw when you created the folders for the new site, not all of the new files are meant to be uploaded to the web server — specifically, the Photoshop file in the resources folder. (You should, however, store such files locally as source files or documentation for the work you completed.) Dreamweaver provides a very useful function — called **cloaking** — that allows you to prevent certain files from uploading. You can cloak an individual file; cloak all files with the same extension (for example, all native Photoshop files with the PSD extension); or cloak a folder, which also cloaks all files in that folder.

1. **With the Kinetic site open in the Files panel, open the Directory menu and click the Kinetic site name in the menu.**

    This opens the Site Setup dialog box for the selected site. You do not need to go through the Manage Sites dialog box to edit the settings for the active site.

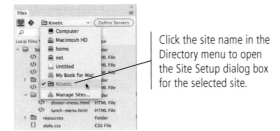

Click the site name in the Directory menu to open the Site Setup dialog box for the selected site.

2. **In the Site Setup dialog box, expand the Advanced Settings menu on the left side and click Cloaking to show the related options.**

3. **Make sure the Enable Cloaking check box is active.**

   When Enable Cloaking is checked, you can hide selected files and folders from a web server. You can also use the Cloak Files Ending With option to hide all files with the extensions that are listed in the field.

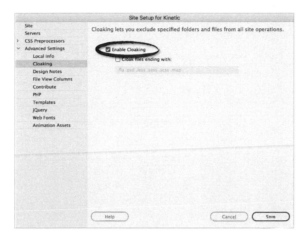

4. **Click Save to close the Site Setup dialog box.**

5. **In the Files panel, collapse all open folders and expand only the resources folder.**

6. **Control/right-click the resources folder and choose Cloaking>Cloak.**

   Notice the red slash through the resources folder icon and the icon for the file in the resources folder. The red slash refers to the cloaking function only; it does not prevent you from working with the files, adding more files, or deleting any of the existing files.

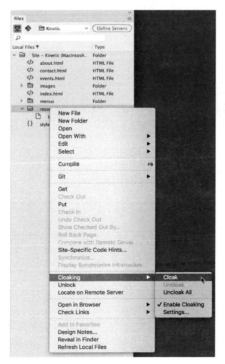

7. **Continue to the next exercise.**

EXPORT AND REMOVE THE SITE DEFINITION

To reduce the potential for confusion, it's a good idea to remove the defined sites of completed projects, leaving only the defined sites of current projects.

As stated in the Interface chapter, removing a site from Dreamweaver does not delete the actual files and folders from your computer; it simply removes them from Dreamweaver. Rather than removing a site, however, you can export a site definition file — which you can later import to restore the same settings and options you already defined (as you did in the Interface chapter when you imported the sf-arts site).

As you work through the projects in this book, you will export and remove site definitions for completed projects, so your site list remains manageable. You should get into this habit so you can quickly reinstate site definitions if necessary.

Note:

You can also cloak a specific file by Control/right clicking that file in the Files panel and choosing Cloaking>Cloak.

1. **With the Kinetic site open in the Files panel, choose Manage Sites at the bottom of the Directory menu.**

   You can access this menu even when the Files panel is in expanded mode.

2. **In the Manage Sites dialog box, choose the Kinetic site name, and then click the Export button.**

   This function creates a ".ste" file that stores the Dreamweaver site definition settings.

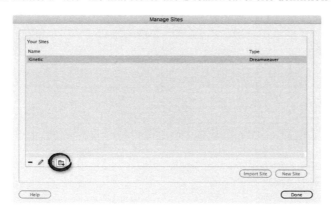

3. **Navigate to WIP>Kinetic and click Save.**

Macintosh users: The first time you open the Export Site dialog box, you might have to expand the dialog box to show all the navigation options.

Click here to expand the dialog box.

Note:

If you have defined server information including passwords, Dreamweaver asks if you want to include that login information in the site file.

If you are sharing site files with other users, you might want to exclude login and password information. Each user should have his or her own password and login information.

The Export Site dialog box defaults to the current site's root folder. You can restore the site settings by importing the site definition file from this location.

4. **In the Manage Sites dialog box, make sure Kinetic site is selected and click the "–" button to remove the site from the list.**

5. **Click Yes to the warning to confirm the removal of the Kinetic site definition.**

Remember, you are not deleting the files from the site; you are simply removing the site definition from Dreamweaver.

6. **At the bottom of the Manage Sites dialog box, click Done.**

DREAMWEAVER FOUNDATIONS

To make files available to other users, you must upload them to a server. When a user types your URL into a browser, the browser software retrieves the required files from a server and displays them for the user.

As a web designer, you should seriously consider signing up for a web hosting service, both for testing your work in progress, but also for displaying your completed work to potential employers. Many online companies offer hosting for a very low monthly fee, and some even offer a limited-time free trial for students.

Because we can't be sure what type of server you are using, the following discussion explains the process using a hosting company that provides web hosting services for a small monthly fee — a common use case.

Until you define a server for a specific site, the Files panel includes a Define Server button, which automatically opens the Servers pane of the Site Setup dialog box.

Clicking the Add New Server button opens a secondary window, where you define specific settings for your server.

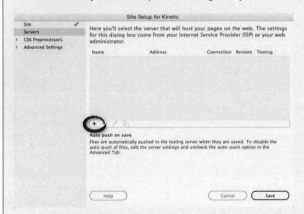

Our example, shown below, uses the information required by the specific hosting company we are using. You should consult your host's documentation to learn exactly what information you should enter in most of these fields.

Server Name simply identifies the host in Dreamweaver.

Connect Using determines the type of connection protocol. For most online hosting companies, you will choose FTP in this menu. If you are using a local server, consult your network administrator for the settings to use.

FTP Address is the hostname for your server. In many cases, the FTP host is the same as the server name. Check your hosting account documentation for your FTP hostname and account information.

Username and **Password** are the settings for your specific hosting account; consult your server documentation for the correct information to use. (If you are working on a shared computer, you might want to uncheck the Save option. However, you will have to retype your username and password every time you upload files.)

Root Directory is the location of the folder where you want the files to be placed. Some hosting providers require you to place public files inside a specific folder, such as public_html or www. When users navigate to your URL, they see the index page located in the designated folder.

Web URL is the actual URL with which users will access the site. This should generally not include any of the extra "public_html" or other folders that are included in the Root Directory field.

You can click the Test button to make sure you have the correct information. You must receive a message stating that Dreamweaver successfully connected to the web server. If a connection with the web server cannot be established,

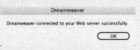

check your entries to make sure your Internet connection is active, and then try again.

Clicking Save in the Basic Server dialog box returns you to the Site Setup dialog box. The Remote Site option is toggled by default for the first server you define. You can also define a Testing server, which is used to manage files during development but is not available to the general public.

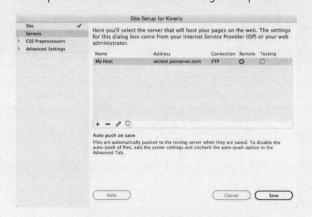

After you define a remote or testing server for a site, the Files panel includes a number of additional options.

A **Connect to Remote Server** establishes a connection with the defined remote server.

B **Get Files from Remote Server** copies the selected files from a remote server to the local folder.

C **Put Files to Remote Server** copies the selected files from the local folder to the remote server.

D **Synchronize with Remote Server** synchronizes files between the local folder and remote server so the same version appears in both places.

In the Synchronize menu you can choose to synchronize the entire site, or only selected local files.

In the Direction menu, you can choose how files will be synchronized:

- Put Newer Files to Remote uploads local files only if they are newer than same-named files on the remote site.

- Get Newer Files from Remote downloads remote files only if they are newer than same-named files on the remote site.

- Get and Put Newer Files moves files in whichever direction is necessary so that the latest version of each file is on both the remote and local site.

E **Expand/Collapse** shows both local files and the remote site (if one has been defined). The expanded Files panel has two panes; one displays the files on the remote or test server and one displays the local site files.

To collapse the panel back to its normal state, simply click the Collapse button.

When you click the Preview button in the Synchronize with Remote Server dialog box, Dreamweaver shows a list of all files that will be affected by the process.

When you upload files to the remote server, Dreamweaver keeps a log of affected files. The Background File Activity dialog box shows a list of each file, including any potential problems encountered during the transfer process. Clicking the Details button expands the dialog box and shows the progression of the synchronization.

When the synchronization process is complete, the local site files appear in the left side of the expanded Files panel (the remote site). Those files are now visible to any browser connected to the Internet.

1. The _____ extension identifies a Dreamweaver site definition file.

2. The _____ is the primary folder that contains all files and subfolders of a website.

3. The _____ is used to view and manage files that make up a site in Dreamweaver.

4. _____ is the process of improving a page's ranking in search engine results pages.

5. A(n) _____ is a path from one file to another, beginning from the current location and moving up or down through folder paths to the target image.

6. The notation _____ tells Dreamweaver to move up one folder from the current location.

7. The _____ shows the nested order of HTML tags to the currently selected object.

8. The _____ protocol is used to define an email link.

9. _____ is the process of hiding certain files in the site so they are not uploaded to the web server.

10. The _____ pane of the Site Setup dialog box defines the settings you need to upload site files through Dreamweaver's Files panel.

1. Briefly explain why it is important to define a Dreamweaver site file.

2. Briefly explain the importance of creating a site flowchart.

3. Explain three different methods for creating a link to a page in the current site.

Portfolio Builder Project

Use what you learned in this project to complete the following freeform exercise.
Carefully read the art director and client comments, then create your own design to meet the needs of the project.
Use the space below to sketch ideas; when finished, write a brief explanation of your reasoning behind your final design.

art director comments

Romana Place Town Homes is adding a photo tour to its website. The owner is fairly competent at building web pages, but is having trouble finalizing the new site. Your job is to finish what he started in a professional, organized manner.

To complete this project, you should:

❏ Import the site files into Dreamweaver (from the **Rentals_DW18_PB.zip** archive on the Student Files web page).

❏ Analyze the content of the different pages. Create a flowchart to map the direction of links from one page to another in the site.

❏ Organize the site folder into a clear, understandable structure.

❏ Create the links from one page to another throughout the entire site.

client comments

When I started working with our site files I noticed that none of the links exist anymore. I might have worked from an earlier version of the site files, but I'm not sure. Can you fix this for me? Other than the navigation in the middle of the pages, there are a number of other places where links are necessary:

• Users should be able to navigate between the different property pages without going back to the main Properties page.

• There should be a link to our main information email address (info@romanaplace.atc) on every page.

• The original design company's name in the footer should link to its website.

project justification

_____

_____

_____

_____

_____

_____

_____

_____

_____

_____

_____

_____

_____

_____

Project Summary

This project focused on two of the foundational elements of website design — organizing files and creating links. A well-organized site structure includes links that make it easy for users to navigate throughout the entire site. Dreamweaver makes it easy to manage the files in a site — renaming and moving them while maintaining the links between pages within the site. You also learned a number of ways to create links, whether to other pages in the site, to an external URL, or to an email address. The skills you used in this project will be required to complete virtually any site you create in Dreamweaver.

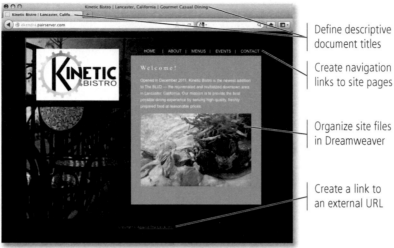

Define descriptive document titles

Create navigation links to site pages

Organize site files in Dreamweaver

Create a link to an external URL

Copy and paste a list of links

Create an email link

Adjust relative link paths to work on nested pages

Digital Book Chapter

In addition to application-specific books, Against The Clock Inc. (ATC) also has a series of "companion" titles that discuss the concepts underlying the use of digital software — basic design principles, type, color, and so on. You were hired to build an "excerpt" booklet of the companion titles, which ATC will use on its corporate website. Your task is to properly structure the content with HTML code.

This project incorporates the following skills:

❏ Adding text from external sources

❏ Working in both Design view and Code view to add appropriate HTML tags semantically

❏ Organizing content with appropriate heading tags

❏ Properly formatting block quotes and citations

❏ Adding special characters that work in HTML code

❏ Creating lists and tables within text-based content

❏ Attaching a CSS file to new pages

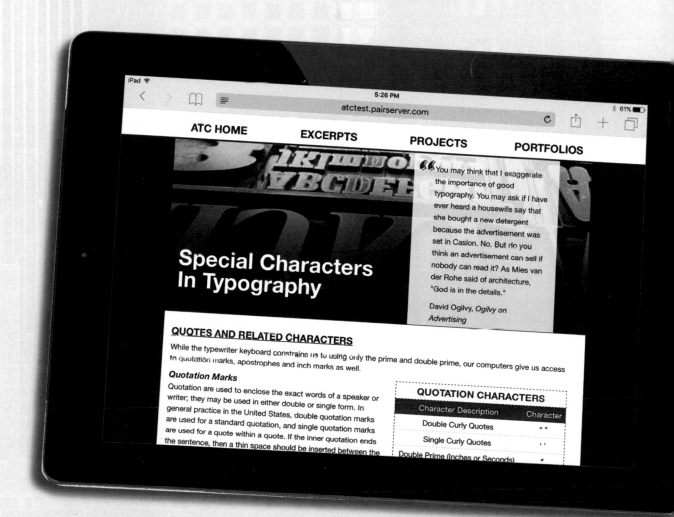

Project Meeting

client comments

We publish a series of books that are designed as companion titles to our application-specific training books (which is why it's called *The Companion Series*). The companion titles cover general topics that are important to graphic designers — basic design principles, color, writing, typography, and web design concepts — but don't quite fit into an application-specific book.

These books have been available for several years, but we haven't done any serious marketing of the titles. When we talk to people about *The Companion Series*, they ask, "Why haven't I heard about these books before?" We're hoping the sample chapters will help get the word out about these books and dramatically improve sales.

We want to be sure of two things: First, this web page needs to be instantly recognizable as part of our existing site, with the same layout and formatting. Second, the page must include searchable text.

art director comments

The publisher sent the text she wants to offer on the site. When you have this much text on a web page — which isn't uncommon — it's very important to format it with the proper structural tags. If you use Heading 2 because you think Heading 1 is too big, for example, you're causing problems for search engines and anyone with screen-reader software.

As you know, the client already has a corporate website. To create the new page, you can use the existing CSS file that defines the appearance of the various structural elements. Once you apply the correct structural tags to the text in the new pages, you can attach the existing CSS file. This will ensure that the existing format maps to the structural tags in your new page.

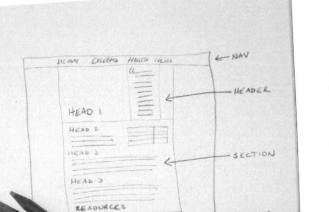

project objectives

To complete this project, you will:

- ❑ Paste text content from a text-only email
- ❑ Apply the appropriate heading and paragraph tags throughout the text
- ❑ Create block quotes and define quote citations
- ❑ Mark up abbreviations for improved usability and accessibility
- ❑ Use the correct HTML tags to show emphasis
- ❑ Add special HTML characters throughout the text
- ❑ Use a table to present well organized content
- ❑ Create ordered and unordered lists
- ❑ Attach an existing CSS file to the new page

Stage 1 Preparing the Workspace

In many web design jobs, you need to create new HTML files in addition to working with existing files. The first step in any new project, however, is to define the Dreamweaver site, so the application can accurately manage the various files and folders that make up the site. Once the site is defined, it's relatively easy to create as many new files as necessary to complete the job.

DEFINE THE ATC SITE

The procedure for defining the ATC site is essentially the same as it was for the Kinetic Site in Project 1: Bistro Site Organization.

1. Download **Chapter_DW18_RF.zip** from the Student Files web page.

2. Expand the ZIP archive in your WIP folder (Macintosh) or copy the archive contents into your WIP folder (Windows).

   This results in a folder named **Chapter**, which contains the files you need for this project.

3. From the Files panel, choose Manage Sites at the bottom of the Directory menu (or click the link if it is available).

4. In the Manage Sites dialog box, click the New Site button.

5. In the resulting Site Setup dialog box, type **ATC** in the Site Name field.

6. Click the Browse icon to the right of the Local Site Folder field, navigate to your **WIP>Chapter** folder, and click Choose/Select.

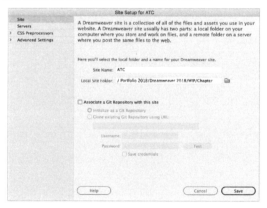

7. Click Save to accept the Site Setup definition.

8. In the Manage Sites dialog box, make sure the ATC site appears in the list of sites, and then click Done.

9. Continue to the next exercise.

CREATE A NEW HTML DOCUMENT

The content for the excerpt page was sent to you by the client in an email. You need to create a new HTML page and then move the supplied text into the page so you can apply the necessary HTML structure.

HTML was created as a coding language used to apply structure (paragraphs, headings, and lists) to online documents. By 1996, the modern methods of document markup had outgrown the inflexible HTML, so the extensibility concept from XML (eXtensible Markup Language) was added to HTML 4.01 and referred to as XHTML.

HTML5 is the current revision of the HTML standard and is the default document type in Dreamweaver CC. Officially published in 2014, HTML5 replaced both HTML 4 and XHTML.

1. **With the ATC site open in the Files panel, choose File>New.**

2. **In the New Document dialog box, choose New Document in the left pane and choose HTML in the Document Type list.**

   When you create a new HTML page, the Doc Type menu defaults to HTML5 — the current version of the standard.

3. **In the Title field, type Against The Clock | Special Characters in Typography.**

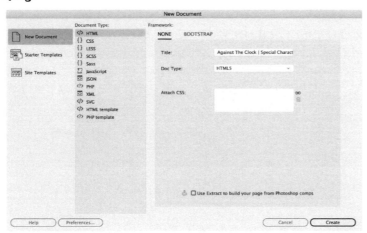

4. **Click Create to create the new blank file.**

5. If only the Design pane is visible, click the Split button in the Document toolbar.

Even though the document appears to be blank in Design view, it already contains some code in the background, which you can see in Code view.

Note:

Feel free to use whichever Split mode you prefer in your workspace.

6. Examine the code in the document window.

The first line — <!doctype html> — is the document type definition or DTD, which tells the browser what version of HTML is being used. For an HTML5 page — the default type in Dreamweaver CC — the doctype statement simply says "html" without a specific version number.

Content within the **head** element — between the opening **<head>** and closing **</head>** tags — is not visible to the user (except for the content enclosed in the **<title>** tags, which appears in the title bar of a browser, as the title of a bookmark, and as the text in search engine results). Visible web page content is created within the body section, between the opening **<html><body>** and closing **</body></html>** tags.

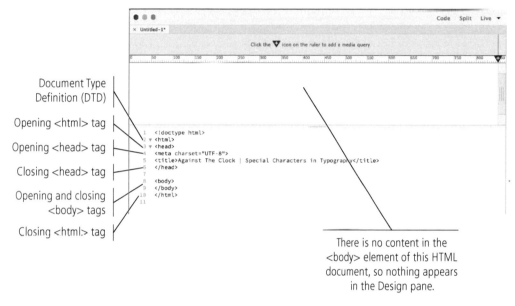

Document Type Definition (DTD)

Opening <html> tag

Opening <head> tag

Closing <head> tag

Opening and closing <body> tags

Closing <html> tag

There is no content in the <body> element of this HTML document, so nothing appears in the Design pane.

7. Choose File>Save As. Navigate to your WIP>Chapter folder (the root of the ATC site) as the target location and save the document as an HTML file named typography.html.

After the file is saved, it automatically appears in the Files panel.

8. Continue to the next stage of the project.

Stage 2 Working with Semantic Markup

Many people have difficulty structuring documents — including word processing files such as those created in Microsoft Word. Consider creating a heading; the user enters text, and then applies bold styling, increases the font size, and changes the text color. While this **local formatting** makes the text appear to be a heading, it is actually just a styled paragraph. Whether it is a web page, a PDF file, or a word processing document, a digital document should make use of available structures to enhance the document's usability. This is where HTML comes into play.

Properly structured HTML documents use tags semantically, to reinforce the meaning of the content and provide a wide range of benefits to users: they are more accessible, they load quickly in a browser, they reduce bandwidth costs for high-traffic websites, they achieve high search-engine rankings, and they are easy to style. As a web designer, you should take full advantage of these benefits by converting the unstructured or poorly structured documents you receive from clients into properly structured HTML documents. Dreamweaver makes it easy to do this, even if you don't understand a great deal of coding and code syntax.

PASTE TEXT CONTENT IN DESIGN VIEW

HTML is a coding language that defines the structure of the elements in a page; without HTML, the content between the opening and closing **<body>** tags would be completely unstructured. Web browsers depend on the structural markup of HTML to properly display a web page, so headings stand out from regular text and paragraphs are separated from one another. Without structure, all text on a page would appear as a single, large block of text.

Clients often supply content as plain text without structural markup (paragraph returns do not qualify as structure). When people read text that doesn't have structural markup, they are able to make logical inferences about the intended structure — for example, they can assume that a short block of text is a heading and a long block is a paragraph. Browsers, however, can't make assumptions; they require structure to correctly display content.

Although not all lines in a text document are paragraphs (some are headings and some are list items), marking each line as a paragraph provides a starting point that you can modify later.

> *Note:*
>
> *Web browsers (and Dreamweaver) ignore extra spaces between words and paragraph returns between lines of text. Properly displaying web page text requires structural markup.*

1. **With typography.html (from the ATC site) open in Split view, make the regular Design view active (turn off the Live view).**

2. **Double-click typography.txt in the Files panel to open that file.**

   Text (.txt) files only appear in Code view because there is no "design".

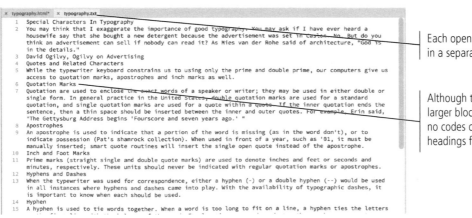

Each open file is accessible in a separate tab.

Although there are smaller and larger blocks of text, there are no codes or styles to separate headings from paragraphs.

3. **Choose Edit>Select All, and then copy the selected content to the Clipboard.**

   Choose Edit>Copy or press Command/Control-C to copy the selected text.

   Note:

   Press Command/Control-A to select all content in an open file or document.

4. **Close typography.txt.**

5. **In typography.html, click to place the insertion point in the Design pane, then paste the copied text into the Design pane.**

   If you pasted the text into the Code pane, the line-break characters would not be included. You will use those bits of codes in the next few steps to apply the proper structure to the paragraphs of text.

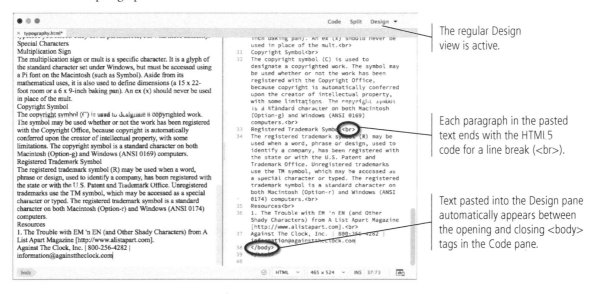

The regular Design view is active.

Each paragraph in the pasted text ends with the HTML5 code for a line break (<br>).

Text pasted into the Design pane automatically appears between the opening and closing <body> tags in the Code pane.

6. **Press Command/Control-A to select all the text in the Design pane, then choose Paragraph in the Format menu of the Properties panel.**

   An HTML paragraph is surrounded by opening **<p>** and closing **</p>** paragraph tags. Because the paragraphs of pasted text are separated by the code for a forced line break (**
**), the entire block of copy is treated as a single paragraph.

   When you apply the paragraph structure to the selected text, the entire block is surrounded by a single set of paragraph tags in the Code pane.

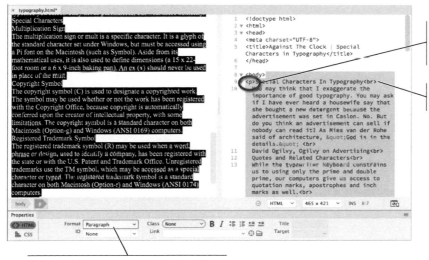

The entire selection is surrounded by a single set of paragraph tags.

The <br> tags are not removed or replaced.

Use this menu to apply one of the predefined structural tags to the selected text.

Note:

The Design pane shows text in the default font because you have not defined any other type formatting. Later in this project, you will attach a CSS file to change the formatting of various elements in the file.

7. **Choose Find>Find and Replace in Files.**

8. **Choose Current Document in the [Find] In menu.**

9. **In the Find, type `<br>`. In the Replace field, type `</p><p>`.**

   Do not press Return/Enter when typing in the Replace field because the dialog box will prematurely run the Find and Replace operation.

   Each line in the text currently ends with the line-break tag (`<br>`) when it should end with a closing paragraph tag (`</p>`). Each line should also begin with the opening paragraph tag (`<p>`), where nothing currently exists.

   Using the search and replace function, you can remove all of the line-break codes and place the necessary closing and opening paragraph tags in a single click.

Note:

You cannot undo a Find and Replace in documents that are not open. When doing a Find and Replace that includes files that aren't currently open, you might want to back up the site's root folder outside of Dreamweaver before continuing.

10. **Click Replace All.**

11. **Review the Search panel, and then close the tab group.**

Understanding Element Names, Tags, and Attributes

DREAMWEAVER FOUNDATIONS

The **element name** is the text that identifies the tag, such as meta, title, head, or body.

A **tag** consists of the element name surrounded by angle brackets, such as <html>, <head>, or <body>.

An **element** is the tag plus its containing content, such as the title element <title>Untitled Document</title>.

Container tags consist of an opening tag (<title>) and a closing tag (</title>). The closing tag is the same as the opening tag, with the addition of the initial forward slash. For example:

   <title>"Weather Forecast"</title>

Empty tags (<meta />) do not have a separate closing tag. In an empty tag, the closing forward slash appears with the closing angle bracket of the tag. For example:

   <img src="sun.gif" alt="sunny day" />

Attributes add properties to HTML elements. For example, the cite attribute of the <blockquote> tag allows you to identify the URL of a quotation. Attributes appear in the opening tag only; they consist of the attribute name and the attribute value in quotation marks (for example, attribute="attribute value").

When marking up a short quotation, you would type:

   <q cite="http://www.useit.com/alertbox/9710a.html">
   People rarely read web pages word by word.</q>

In this example, the attribute name is cite and the attribute value is http://www.useit.com/alertbox/9710a.html.

Most attributes are optional, such as the cite attribute of the <blockquote> tag. Some attributes are required, such as the alt attribute of the <img> tag, which describes an image for visually impaired visitors.

Some HTML attributes do not require an attribute value, such as the checked attribute that allows you to preselect a check box option.

12. Click the Refresh button in the Properties panel if necessary, then review the results in both panes of the document window.

In many cases, changes in the Code pane are automatically reflected in the Design pane. If the changes do not automatically take effect (as in the case of changing the page code using the Find and Replace dialog box), you can use several techniques to manually refresh the Design view:

- Click the Refresh button in the Properties panel.
- Press F5.
- Simply click in the Design pane bring it into focus (and refresh at the same time).

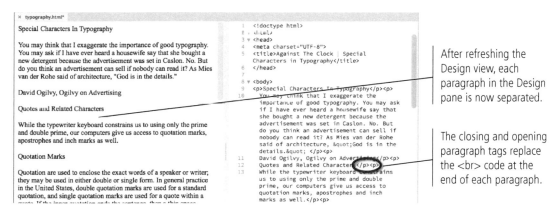

After refreshing the Design view, each paragraph in the Design pane is now separated.

The closing and opening paragraph tags replace the <br> code at the end of each paragraph.

13. Choose Window>Toolbars>Common to open the Common toolbar (if it is not already open).

14. Make sure the insertion point is placed in the Code pane. Click the Format Source Code button in the Common toolbar and choose Apply Source Formatting from the menu.

This command cleans up the code, moving the opening **<p>** tags to the beginning of each line of copy. Nothing changes in the Design pane when the tags are moved to the appropriate lines.

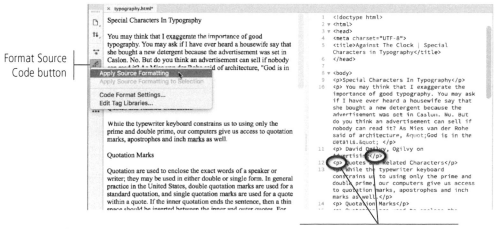

Format Source Code button

After applying source formatting, the opening paragraph tags are moved to the beginning of the lines.

15. Save the file and continue to the next exercise.

DREAMWEAVER FOUNDATIONS

You can use the Properties panel in HTML mode to view and modify a number of different properties for selected text:

- The **Format** menu contains the default HTML paragraph and heading styles. The Preformatted option lets you include more than one space between words and does not automatically wrap the contents.

- The **ID** menu contains the list of IDs defined in the page or the attached style sheet.

- The **Class** menu contains the list of defined style classes in the related CSS.

- The **Link** field displays the URL to which the selected text is linked. You can use the Point to File and Browse for File buttons to identify link targets.

- You can use the **B** and **I** buttons to apply the <strong> and <em> tags (respectively).

- The **Unordered List** button formats selected paragraphs as items in a bulleted list.

- The **Ordered List** button arranges the paragraphs in a numbered list.

- The **Remove Blockquote** button removes the indent (and blockquote tags) from selected paragraphs.

- The **Blockquote** button indents paragraphs, wrapping those paragraphs in the opening and closing <blockquote> tags.

- The **Title** field specifies the textual tool tip for a hypertext link.

- The **Target** menu determines where a linked file opens (new window, parent frame, etc.).

FORMAT HEADINGS IN DESIGN VIEW

Headings help readers find the information they need. For visual users, a heading is effective as long as it looks like a heading. This is not the case for visually impaired users who use screen-reading software; screen-reading software and some browsers enable users to skip forward and backward through headings. Also, when reviewing the content of a page and its relevance to a particular topic, search engine software uses headings and heading levels (among other criteria) to make evaluations. For these reasons, it is important to use properly structured headings rather than styled paragraphs.

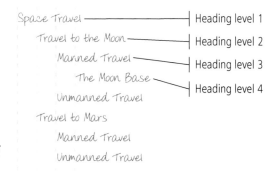

There are six predefined heading levels, **<h1>**, **<h2>**, **<h3>**, and so on to **<h6>**. Heading level 1 is the largest and most important; it should be used only once per page to describe the purpose or title of the web page. The rest of the headings can be used multiple times, but they should be used in a branch-like pattern or hierarchy.

Many new web designers complain that heading level 1 appears too large, so they apply heading level 2 or 3 instead. This is a mistake. In a later project, you will learn to use cascading style sheets (CSS) to define the appearance of different elements on a web page — including different levels of headings.

The special characters described in the text in this project are divided into related groups and subgroups. Your task is to determine which heading level is appropriate for each section. In professional situations, some client-supplied copy will be well-written and well-structured, enabling you to quickly determine appropriate heading levels (called **editorial hierarchy** or **editorial priority**). Other copy will be poorly structured and difficult to decipher; in such a case, you will need to contact the author for clarification or make a best-guess assessment yourself.

Note:

If you use a mouse with scrolling functionality, move the mouse cursor away from the Format menu before you try to scroll through the document window. If the cursor is over the Formatting menu, scrolling with the mouse wheel changes the menu selection.

1. **With typography.html (from your ATC site) open in Split view, click in the Design pane to place the insertion point in the first paragraph.**

   You should be working with the paragraph "Special Characters In Typography".

2. **In the Properties panel, open the Format menu and choose Heading 1.**

   In the Code pane, the opening and closing **<p>** tags automatically change to the **<h1>** tags that identify the paragraph as heading level 1.

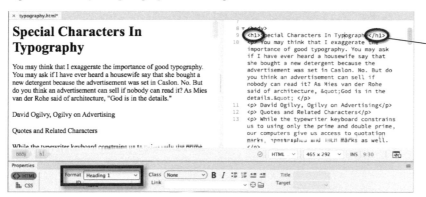

The <p> tags are replaced by the appropriate heading tags (<h1> and </h1>).

3. **Move the insertion point to the "Quotes and Related Characters" paragraph and use the Properties panel Format menu to apply the Heading 2 tag.**

   After choosing a format in the Properties panel, the Code pane shows that the **<p>** and **</p>** tags have been replaced with **<h2>** and **</h2>** tags, respectively.

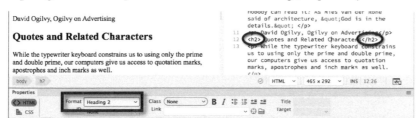

4. **Using the same technique from Step 3, format "Quotation Marks," "Apostrophes," and "Inch and Foot Marks" as Heading 3.**

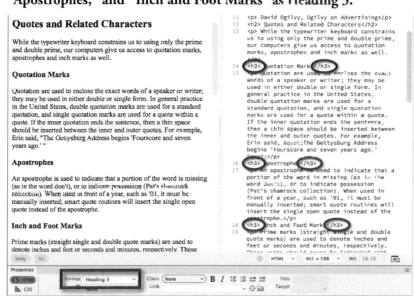

Note:

When you're working in Design view, you can apply paragraph structure and heading levels by choosing from the Format>Paragraph Format menu, or in the Heading menu of the HTML Insert panel.

Note:

You can also use keyboard shortcuts to apply common tags:

Paragraph
Command/Control-Shift-p

Heading 1
Command/Control-1

Heading 2
Command/Control-2

Heading 3
Command/Control-3

Heading 4
Command/Control-4

Heading 5
Command/Control-5

Heading 6
Command/Control-6

5. Apply heading levels to the rest of the document as follows:

Line Number in the Code pane	Content	Heading Level
20	Hyphens and Dashes	2
22	Hyphen	3
24	En Dash	3
26	Em Dash	3
28	Special Characters	2
29	Multiplication Sign	3
31	Copyright Symbol	3
33	Registered Trademark Symbol	3
35	Resources	2

6. Save the file and continue to the next exercise.

 FORMAT A BLOCKQUOTE AND INLINE QUOTE

The **blockquote element** formats a quotation as a block of text that is indented from the left and right margins, with extra white space above and below it. The blockquote element requires at least one paragraph element to be nested within it.

The **q element** defines a short quotation, commonly appearing inline with other text (called an "inline quote").

The **cite element** can be used to define the name of a work (book, painting, movie, etc.). This should not be confused with the cite attribute of the blockquote and q elements. The **cite attribute** defines the source of a quote; it does not have any visual effect in the browser window, but it can be used by screen-reading software.

1. With **typography.html** open in Split view, make the Design pane active. Select the first and second paragraphs immediately below the heading 1 text (from "You may think..." to "...on Advertising").

2. Click the Blockquote button in the Properties panel to apply the blockquote element to the selected paragraph.

In the Design pane, the blockquote has been indented from the left and right margins. The first **<p>** tag appears after the opening **<blockquote>** tag and the second closing **</p>** tag appears before the closing **</blockquote>** tag — the **<p>** tags have been nested within the **<blockquote>** tag.

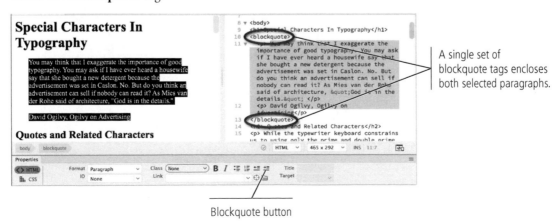

A single set of blockquote tags encloses both selected paragraphs.

Blockquote button

3. Select "Ogilvy on Advertising" at the end of the second paragraph in the blockquote.

Remember, the cite element defines the source of a quote. This is the actual title of a work, not the author's name.

4. Control/right-click the selected text in the Design pane and choose Wrap Tag from the contextual menu.

The Wrap Tag command opens the Quick Tag Editor, which allows you to temporarily work with code, while still working in Design view.

Note:

You can also open the Quick Tag Editor by pressing Command/Control-T.

5. Type cit.

As you type the code in the Quick Tag Editor, Dreamweaver provides Code Hints (a list of HTML tags) to assist you. As you type, the Code Hint list scrolls to the first HTML tag beginning with the letter "cit" — cite, which is the tag you want.

6. Press Return/Enter to choose cite from the list of tags.

When a Code Hint menu is visible, pressing Return/Enter applies the item that is highlighted in the list.

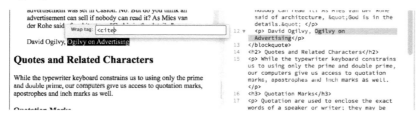

7. Press Return/Enter again to apply the cite tags to the selected text.

The default appearance of the cite element text is italic. As you can see in the Code pane, using the Quick Tag Editor automatically adds the appropriate opening and closing tags, wrapped around the text that you had selected (hence the menu command "Wrap Tag").

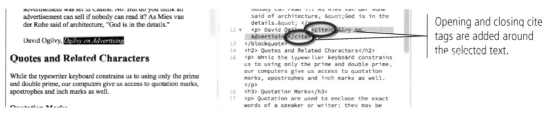

Opening and closing cite tags are added around the selected text.

8. In the Design pane, select the words "God is in the details." (including the period but not the quotation marks) at the end of the first paragraph in the blockquote.

9. **Control/right-click the selected text and choose Wrap Tag from the contextual menu.**

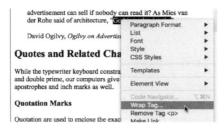

10. **In the Quick Tag Editor, type q. Press Return/Enter to accept the q tag, then press Return/Enter again to add the tag around the selected text.**

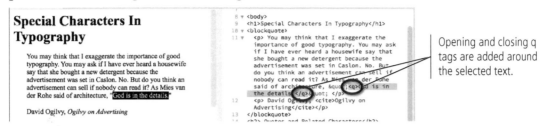

Opening and closing q tags are added around the selected text.

11. **Using the Document toolbar, turn on the Live view.**

As you can see in the Design pane, the q element adds quotation marks around the tag content. This means that the quotation marks included in the actual text are unnecessary.

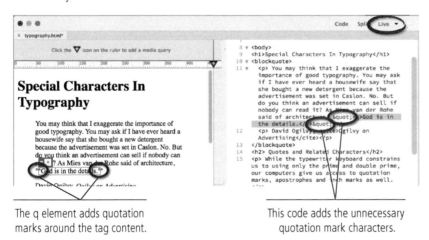

The q element adds quotation marks around the tag content.

This code adds the unnecessary quotation mark characters.

The current versions of Firefox, Safari, Opera, Chrome, and Internet Explorer automatically place quotation marks around q element text, eliminating the need to insert them as characters in the page content. However, different browsers use different types of quotes (straight quotes vs. curly quotes).

12. **In the Code pane, delete the code for the quote characters (") from around the "God is in the details." text.**

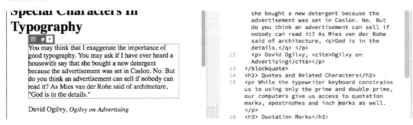

13. **Turn off the Live view, then save the file and continue to the next exercise.**

MARK UP ABBREVIATIONS IN CODE VIEW

Both abbreviations and acronyms are shortened forms of words or phrases. If you spell out the short form (such as HTML), it is an abbreviation. If you pronounce it like a word (such as NATO), it is an acronym.

HTML 4 includes two separate elements for these words — the **abbr** element identifies an abbreviation, and the **acronym** element identifies an acronym — but the acronym element has been deprecated (removed) in HTML5, so you should get into the habit of using the abbr element for both types of words.

The title attribute plays a useful role in the **abbr** element. Any text you insert into the title attribute — for example, the full text of the abbreviation or acronym — appears as a tool tip when you hover the mouse over the titled element. People who use screen-reader software also benefit from the title attribute because the software can be set up to read the title text in place of the abbreviation.

In this exercise, you will type directly in the Code pane, using Dreamweaver's code hints to add the necessary tags and attributes.

1. **With typography.html open, open the Preferences dialog box (in the Dreamweaver menu on Macintosh or the Edit menu on Windows).**

2. **Click in the left column to show the Code Hints preferences. On the right side of the dialog box, choose the After Typing "</" radio button**

Code hints display by default when you type code in Dreamweaver. You can use the Code Hints pane of the Preferences dialog box to control how code hints display.

The Close Tags options can be used to close tags automatically:

- If **After Typing "</"** is checked, the nearest open tag closes when you type the forward slash after the opening carat. This option is selected by default.

- If **After Typing the Open Tag's ">"** is checked, Dreamweaver automatically closes a tag as soon as it opens.

- Select **Never** if you don't want tags to close automatically.

You can disable code hints by deselecting the Enable Code Hints check box.

3. **Click Apply, then click the Close button to dismiss the Preferences dialog box.**

4. **In the Design pane, select "ANSI" in the paragraph following the Copyright Symbol heading.**

The text selected in the Design pane is also selected in the Code pane. This is a useful way to locate specific text in code (or vice versa).

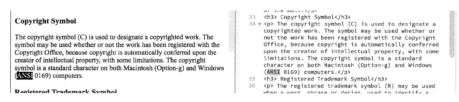

5. In the Code pane, click to place the insertion point before the ANSI text, and then type **<ab.**

The abbr tag is selected in the code hint list.

Copyright Symbol

The copyright symbol (C) is used to designate a copyrighted work. The symbol may be used whether or not the work has been registered with the Copyright Office, because copyright is automatically conferred upon the creator of intellectual property, with some limitations. The copyright symbol is a standard character on both Macintosh (Option-g) and Windows (ANSI 0169) computers.

Registered Trademark Symbol

```
33  <h3> Copyright Symbol</h3>
34  <p> The copyright symbol (C) is used to designate a
    copyrighted work. The symbol may be used whether or
    not the work has been registered with the Copyright
    Office, because copyright is automatically conferred
    upon the creator of intellectual property, with some
    limitations. The copyright symbol is a standard
    character on both Macintosh (Option-g) and Windows
    (<abANSI 0169) computers.</p>
35  <h3:  abbr
36  <p> The registered trademark symbol (R) may be used
    when a word  phrase or design  used to identify a
```

6. Press Return/Enter to accept abbr.

By pressing Return/Enter, you select the **<abbr>** tag. Once you add the tag, the insertion point flashes after the tag, where you can enter attributes of the new tag.

Copyright Symbol

The copyright symbol (C) is used to designate a copyrighted work. The symbol may be used whether or not the work has been registered with the Copyright Office, because copyright is automatically conferred upon the creator of intellectual property, with some limitations. The copyright symbol is a standard character on both Macintosh (Option-g) and Windows (ANSI 0169) computers.

Registered Trademark Symbol

```
33  <h3> Copyright Symbol</h3>
34  <p> The copyright symbol (C) is used to designate a
    copyrighted work. The symbol may be used whether or
    not the work has been registered with the Copyright
    Office, because copyright is automatically conferred
    upon the creator of intellectual property, with some
    limitations. The copyright symbol is a standard
    character on both Macintosh (Option-g) and Windows
    (<abbrANSI 0169) computers.</p>
35  <h3> Registered Trademark Symbol</h3>
36  <p> The registered trademark symbol (R) may be used
    when a word  phrase or design  used to identify a
```

7. Press the Spacebar, and then type t.

Inserting a space after the abbr element name within the tag prompts Dreamweaver to open code hints and present a list of valid attributes for the current tag.

Copyright Symbol

The copyright symbol (C) is used to designate a copyrighted work. The symbol may be used whether or not the work has been registered with the Copyright Office, because copyright is automatically conferred upon the creator of intellectual property, with some limitations. The copyright symbol is a standard character on both Macintosh (Option-g) and Windows (ANSI 0169) computers.

Registered Trademark Symbol

```
       of the mult </n>
33  <h3> Co  contenteditable
34  <p> The  contextmenu       is used to designate a
    copyrigh                   may be used whether or
    not the  onMouseOut        ered with the Copyright
    Office,  style             automatically conferred
    upon th  title             tual property, with some
    limitat                    ymbol is a standard
    charact  translate         (Option-g) and Windows
    (<abbr tANSI 0169) computers.</p>
35  <h3> Registered Trademark Symbol</h3>
36  <p> The registered trademark symbol (R) may be used
    when a word  phrase or design  used to identify a
```

8. Press Return/Enter to accept the title attribute.

When you select the attribute in the code hint list, Dreamweaver follows the attribute with =" " and places the insertion point between the two quotation marks, so you can immediately type a value for the attribute.

Copyright Symbol

The copyright symbol (C) is used to designate a copyrighted work. The symbol may be used whether or not the work has been registered with the Copyright Office, because copyright is automatically conferred upon the creator of intellectual property, with some limitations. The copyright symbol is a standard character on both Macintosh (Option-g) and Windows (ANSI 0169) computers.

Registered Trademark Symbol

```
       of the mult.</p>
33  <h3> Copyright Symbol</h3>
34  <p> The copyright symbol (C) is used to designate a
    copyrighted work. The symbol may be used whether or
    not the work has been registered with the Copyright
    Office, because copyright is automatically conferred
    upon the creator of intellectual property, with some
    limitations. The copyright symbol is a standard
    character on both Macintosh (Option-g) and Windows
    (<abbr title=""ANSI 0169) computers.</p>
35  <h3> Registered Trademark Symbol</h3>
36  <p> The registered trademark symbol (R) may be used
    when a word  phrase or design  used to identify a
```

9. Type **American National Standards Institute** between the quotation marks.

Attribute values must always be surrounded by quotation marks.

Copyright Symbol

The copyright symbol (C) is used to designate a copyrighted work. The symbol may be used whether or not the work has been registered with the Copyright Office, because copyright is automatically conferred upon the creator of intellectual property, with some limitations. The copyright symbol is a standard character on both Macintosh (Option-g) and Windows (ANSI 0169) computers.

Registered Trademark Symbol

```
       of the mult.</p>
33  <h3> Copyright Symbol</h3>
34  <p> The copyright symbol (C) is used to designate a
    copyrighted work. The symbol may be used whether or
    not the work has been registered with the Copyright
    Office, because copyright is automatically conferred
    upon the creator of intellectual property, with some
    limitations. The copyright symbol is a standard
    character on both Macintosh (Option-g) and Windows
    (<abbr title="American National Standards
    Institute"ANSI 0169) computers.</p>
35  <h3> Registered Trademark Symbol</h3>
36  <p> The registered trademark symbol (R) may be used
```

10. Move the insertion point to the right of the closing quotation mark and type > to close the tag.

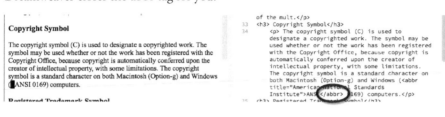

11. Move the insertion point to the right of the text "ANSI," then type </.

In opening tags, the HTML element name is specified between opening and closing angle brackets. In closing tags, the forward slash precedes the element name.

This step shows you another of Dreamweaver's code assistance functions, which is to automatically close the nearest unclosed tag when you type "</". In this case, Dreamweaver closes the abbr tag for you.

Note:

All current browsers display title text as a tool tip when the mouse hovers over the element text.

12. In the Code pane, click in the opening <abbr> tag to place the insertion point.

When the insertion point is placed in an opening tag in the Code pane, the application automatically highlights all code related to that tag — including the associated closing tag (in this case </abbr>). Notice, however, that text contained in the tag is not highlighted.

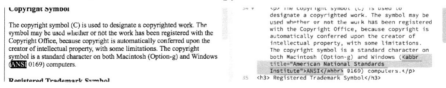

13. Select all of the code related to the ANSI abbreviation, including the contained text, then choose Edit>Copy.

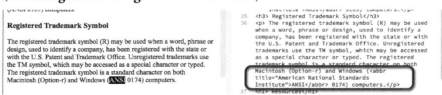

14. In the Code pane, highlight the instance of "ANSI" near the end of line 36. Choose Edit>Paste to replace the highlighted text with the copied code (including the abbr tags and title attribute).

15. Save the file, then continue to the next exercise.

DREAMWEAVER FOUNDATIONS

Code View Options

Code View options, which can be toggled on or off in the View menu, determine how code displays.

- **Word Wrap** ensures that code does not extend beyond the width of the window. This option only affects the appearance of code in the Code pane; it does not insert actual line breaks in the code or content.
- **Line Numbers** shows numbers to the left of each line.
- **Hidden Characters** displays characters such as line-break markers, which would not otherwise display.
- **Syntax Coloring** displays the code in defined colors.
- **Auto Indent** indents every new line of code to the same position as the previous line. A new line is inserted each time you press Return/Enter.

The three options at the bottom of the menu affect the font size only in the Code view; they have no effect on the font size in the Design pane.

Code Format Preferences

Code Format preferences allow you to specify rules that determine how the code is structured; the sole purpose of these rules is to make it easier for you to read code.

- **Indent With** indents the text within each tag so you can easily identify each block of code. You can indent by character spaces or by tabs.
- **Tab Size** specifies the number of spaces that each tab character contains. For example, if you type "4" in this box, each time you press the Tab key, four space characters are inserted.
- **Emmet** allows you to use a special type of shorthand when writing code. When this option is checked, pressing the Tab key expands the shorthand into the full HTML or CSS code.
- **Line Break Type** ensures the line breaks inserted by Dreamweaver are compatible with the operating system of the remote server on which your site will be hosted.
- The **TD Tag** option prevents a line break or white space from being inserted directly after a <td> (table cell) tag or directly before a </td> tag. Line breaks and white spaces within the tag cause problems in older browsers.
- **Advanced Formatting/Tag Libraries** opens a dialog box where you can define formatting options such as line breaks and indents for tags and attributes.
- **Minimum code folding size** determines how many lines must be included in a tag before that tag can be collapsed in the Code pane.

 FORMAT WITH STRONG AND EM ELEMENTS

Two HTML elements can be used to show emphasis — em and strong. The **em** element is used when light emphasis is needed, such as "you should go to your brother's game to support him." For stronger emphasis, use the **strong** element, such as "Don't touch the stove top, it is hot!"

Text marked up with the em element appears by default in italics; text marked up with the strong element appears in bold. Visually, it is the same as using the **<i>** and **<b>** tags (italic and bold, respectively), but the i and b elements are presentational — not structural — HTML. Screen-reader software changes the tone of voice when it finds em and strong element text, but not when it finds i and b element text.

Note:

Remember: b and i elements are for presentational purposes only, and strong and em elements are for structural purposes.

1. **With typography.html open, open the Preferences dialog box (Dreamweaver menu on Macintosh or Edit menu on Windows) and show the General category.**

2. **In the Editing Options group, make sure the "Use <strong> and <em>" option is checked.**

   When this option is checked, as it is by default, Dreamweaver inserts strong or em tags when you apply bold or italic styling (respectively) through interface menus or buttons.

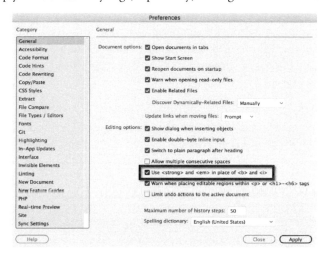

3. **Click Close to close the Preferences dialog box.**

4. **In the Design pane, scroll to the paragraph following the En Dash heading and select "not" in the fourth sentence.**

5. **Click the Bold button in the Properties panel.**

   There are no special attributes for the strong and em elements, so you can insert these elements with a single click.

6. **With the text still selected, examine the Tag Selector.**

   The selected text is formatted with the **<strong>** tag, not the **<b>** tag.

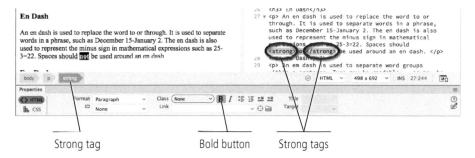

      Strong tag   Bold button   Strong tags

7. **In the paragraph after the Em Dash heading, select "more authority" in the third sentence and click the Italic button in the Properties panel.**

   The selected text is now formatted with the **<em>** tag.

      Em tag   Italic button   Em tags

8. **Save your changes and continue to the next stage of the project.**

Note:

As you work through this book, remember that preferences are accessed in the Dreamweaver menu on Macintosh and the Edit menu on Windows.

Stage 3 Working with Special Characters

HTML character entities are characters not directly available from your keyboard. HTML character entities can be specified in code either by name or by number. Using either method, the code begins with an ampersand (&) and ends with a semicolon (;).

- A named character entity uses a specific name for that character such as "©" for the © symbol and "™" for the ™ symbol. Some character names (such as "™") are not supported by all browsers; visitors using these browsers would see "™" in their browser window instead of the ™ symbol.

- Alternatively, you can specify a character using its numeric code, such as "¢" for ¢. (When using the numeric code, be sure to insert a "#" between the ampersand and the number.) All browsers support the numeric codes.

 INSERT SPECIAL CHARACTERS

In most cases, you don't need to worry about inserting the codes (named or numbered) for HTML character entities because you can select some of the most common characters from a list in the HTML Insert panel; Dreamweaver inserts the code for you.

This HTML Insert panel provides one-click access to many common structural elements — including common ones like various levels of headings, as well as headers, sections, and footers.

1. **With typography.html open in Split view, make the Design pane active. Select the hyphen between "December 15" and "January 2" in the paragraph below the En Dash heading.**

Selected text

2. **With the Insert panel in HTML mode, click the arrow button to the right of the Character button icon.**

   Your button icon might appear different than the one shown in our screen shot because the button reflects the last character inserted from this list. Simply clicking the button (label or icon) — not the arrow — inserts whatever character appears on the button.

3. **Choose En Dash from the pop-up menu.**

Use the menu to show HTML options in the Insert panel.

Click the arrow to open the Character menu.

Choose the appropriate character from the Character pop-up menu.

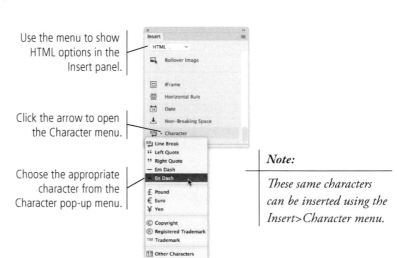

Note:

These same characters can be inserted using the Insert>Character menu.

4. Select the hyphen between "25" and "3" in the same paragraph.

En dashes are as wide as half an em dash. As you might have read in the text of this project page, en dashes are used to replace the word "to" or "through" or in mathematical expressions of subtraction.

5. In the HTML Insert panel, click the Character:En Dash button.

Because the button defaults to the last-used character, you can simply click the button to apply another en dash.

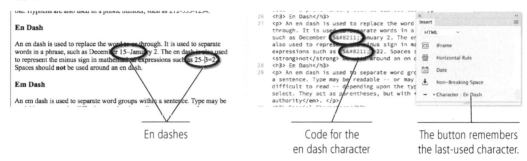

En dashes   Code for the en dash character   The button remembers the last-used character.

6. Use the same techniques from Steps 2–5 to replace both sets of double hyphens with em dashes in the paragraph after the Em Dash heading.

The em dash is as wide as the defined type size. This dash can be used to separate part of a sentence — an aside — from the rest of a sentence. Many authors do not know how to insert an em dash; instead, they use a regular hyphen or a pair of hyphens. As there are strict grammatical rules about when to use a hyphen, an en dash, and an em dash, you should consult a professional copy editor for the proper application of these characters.

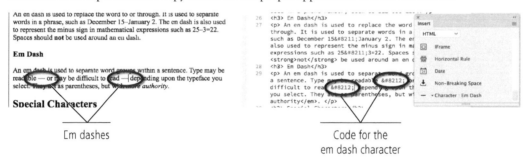

Em dashes   Code for the em dash character

7. Select the capital C in the first line after the Copyright Symbol heading. Use the Character menu in the HTML Insert panel to replace the letter with the Copyright character.

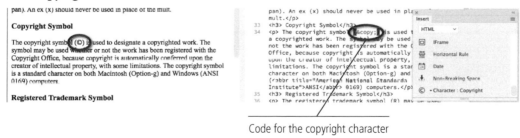

Code for the copyright character

8. **Select the capital R in the first line after the Registered Trademark Symbol heading. Use the Character menu to replace the selected letter with the Registered Trademark character.**

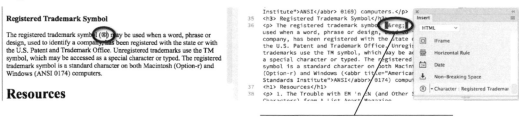

Code for the registered trademark character

9. **Select the capital TM in the same paragraph and use the Character menu to replace the selected letters with the Trademark character.**

In the Code pane, you can see that Dreamweaver creates this character using the numeric code because some browsers do not support the name for this character.

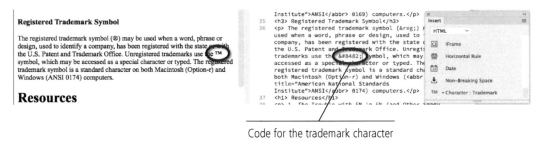

Code for the trademark character

10. **Save the changes to typography.html and continue to the next exercise.**

CREATE A TABLE OF QUOTE CHARACTERS

Common HTML tables that are used to present data or text information consist of only three components: a caption, table header cells, and table data cells.

A caption can be used to briefly describe the contents or purpose of a table. It generally appears at the top of the table. (You can use CSS to move the caption to another position, but many browsers offer poor support for these properties.)

Table data cells make up the majority of the cells in a table. The **<td>** tag is used to mark up the table data cells.

Table header cells, using the **<th>** tag, appear at the top or left (or both) of the table; they label the contents in the regular table cells. Think about a table of the days of the week across the top and the hours of the day down the left side. If the cell at the intersection of the second row and second column contained the text "Staff Meeting," you would know that the staff meeting was scheduled for Tuesday at 10:00 a.m.

The information in table header cells is very important for people using screen-reader software. For example, when they reach the Staff Meeting cell, they can prompt the software to read the headers associated with the cell. The screen-reader would report "Tuesday" and "10:00 a.m." Without proper cell markup, the software would not be able to report the day and time of the meeting.

Note:

When tables are used for layout components of a web page, they can become very complicated in structure, with tables within table cells (nested tables) and cells that have been merged with other cells. Tables should only be used to present tabular data.

1. With **typography.html** open in Split view, click in the Design pane to place the insertion point at the end of the first regular paragraph after the "Quotes and Related Characters" heading.

2. Click the Table button in the HTML Insert panel.

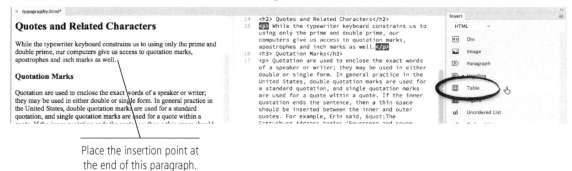

Place the insertion point at the end of this paragraph.

3. In the Table dialog box:
   - Set both the number of rows and number of columns to 2.
   - Delete any values in the Table Width, Border Thickness, Cell Padding, and Cell Spacing fields.
   - Choose the Top Header option.
   - Type **Quotation Characters** in the Caption field.

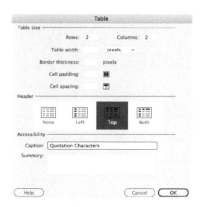

   Many Dreamweaver dialog boxes remember the last-used settings. If you or someone else used the Table dialog box before now, some of these fields might default to other values.

4. Click OK to create the table.

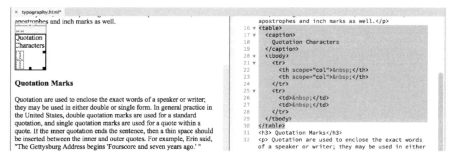

5. Click in the top-left table cell to place the insertion point, and then type **Character Description**.

6. Press Tab to move the insertion point into the top-right cell, and type **Character**.

7. **In the Code pane, review the code for the table you just created.**

- All content that makes up the table is enclosed in opening and closing **<table>** tags.

- The caption that you defined when you created the table is enclosed in opening and closing **<caption>** tags.

- The body content of a table is grouped together with opening and closing **<tbody>** tags. The <tbody> element must contain one or more <tr> tags.

- Each row in the table is enclosed in opening and closing **<tr>** tags.

- Each header cell is identified with opening and closing **<th>** tags. The **scope="col"** attribute identifies that column as information with the heading defined in the related cell.

- Each regular cell in the table is enclosed in opening and closing **<td>** tags. As you can see, each table row includes two <td> tags — one for each column in the row.

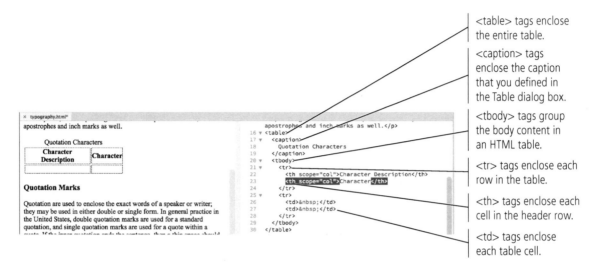

<table> tags enclose the entire table.

<caption> tags enclose the caption that you defined in the Table dialog box.

<tbody> tags group the body content in an HTML table.

<tr> tags enclose each row in the table.

<th> tags enclose each cell in the header row.

<td> tags enclose each table cell.

8. **Save the file and continue to the next exercise.**

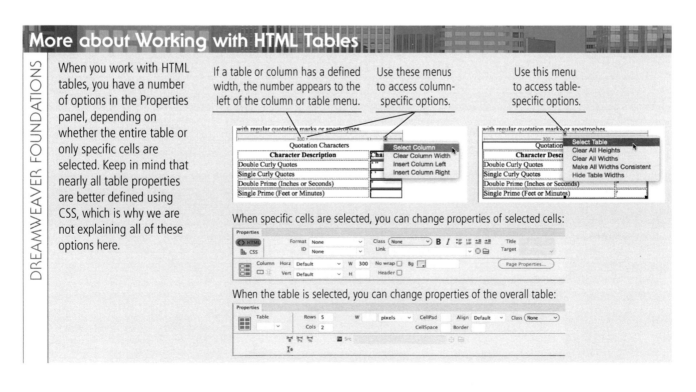

More about Working with HTML Tables

When you work with HTML tables, you have a number of options in the Properties panel, depending on whether the entire table or only specific cells are selected. Keep in mind that nearly all table properties are better defined using CSS, which is why we are not explaining all of these options here.

If a table or column has a defined width, the number appears to the left of the column or table menu.

Use these menus to access column-specific options.

Use this menu to access table-specific options.

When specific cells are selected, you can change properties of selected cells:

When the table is selected, you can change properties of the overall table:

USE THE INSERT OTHER CHARACTER DIALOG BOX

Although a few special characters are available directly in the Characters menu of the HTML Insert panel, there are many more characters available than those in the list. A number of common special characters are available in the Insert Other Character dialog box, which is accessed at the bottom of the Characters menu. Still others (many, in fact) are only available by typing the necessary code in the Code pane.

1. With **typography.html** open, click in the lower-left empty cell of the table that you created in the previous exercise. Type **Double Curly Quotes**.

2. Press Tab to move to the right cell, and then choose Left Quote from the Character menu in the HTML Insert panel.

3. Press Space, and then choose Right Quote from the HTML Insert panel Character menu.

   You might have to click after the left curly quote character to re-establish the insertion point before pressing the Space bar. This is a minor bug in the application.

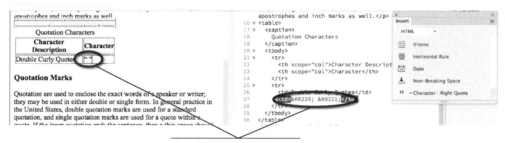

Numeric codes for the special characters are automatically added in the Code pane.

4. Press Tab to insert a new table row.

   Again, you might have to click after the right curly quote character to re-establish the insertion point before pressing the Tab key.

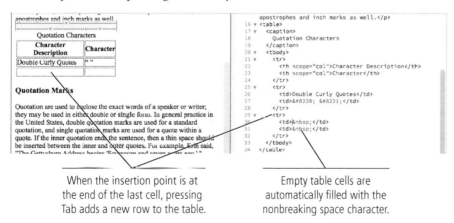

When the insertion point is at the end of the last cell, pressing Tab adds a new row to the table.

Empty table cells are automatically filled with the nonbreaking space character.

5. In the left cell, type **Single Curly Quotes**, then press Tab to move the insertion point into the right cell.

6. **Using the HTML Insert panel, open the Character menu and choose Other Characters from the bottom of the list.**

You can use the Other Characters option to find special characters that aren't included in the default list. This option opens the Insert Other Character dialog box, where you can select a specific character, or type the appropriate code in the field at the top of the dialog box.

7. **In the resulting dialog box, click the Single Left Curly Quote character and then click OK to insert that character into the active table cell.**

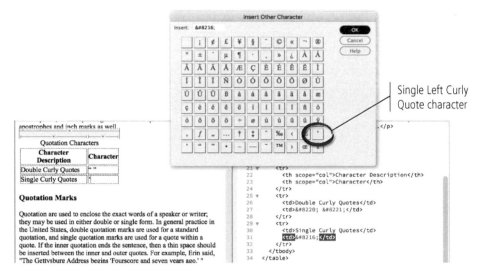

Single Left Curly Quote character

Note:

As you add content into the table, the column width changes to accommodate cell content. The specific appearance of the table will be determined by cascading style sheets when you attach an external CSS file later in this project.

8. **With the insertion point after the quote, press Space and then click the Character:Other Characters button to reopen the dialog box.**

In this case, the button remembers the last-used option (opening the dialog box) but not the last-used character. Clicking the button opens the Insert Other Character dialog box.

9. **Click the Single Right Curly Quote character and then click OK to insert that character into the table cell.**

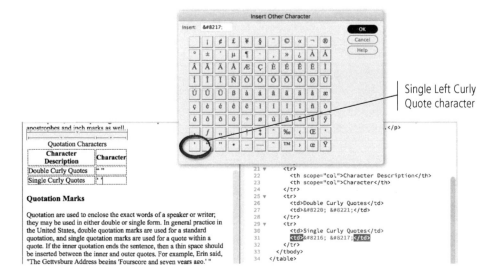

Single Left Curly Quote character

10. **Press Tab to insert another table row. Type** Double Prime (Inches or Seconds) **in the left cell of the new row.**

11. **Move the insertion point to the right cell of the new row, then click the Code pane to make it active.**

12. **In the Code pane, delete the code for nonbreaking space. Type** ″ **(with a capital P) and then refresh the Design view.**

    Remember: After typing in the Code pane, the Properties panel shows a Refresh button. You can click that button; press F5; or click in the Design pane to bring it into focus,

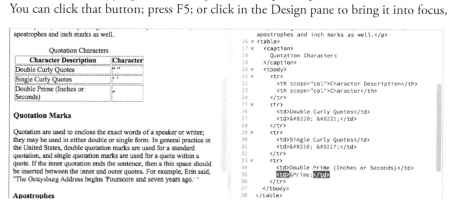

13. **Click in the Design pane to bring it into focus. Place the insertion point after the prime character, then press Tab to insert another table row.**

14. **Type** Single Prime (Feet or Minutes) **in the left column, then move the insertion point to the right cell.**

15. **Click the Code pane to make it active. Replace the nonbreaking-space code with** ′ **(with a lowercase p) and then refresh the Design view.**

    The single- and double-prime codes are almost the same; capitalization makes the difference between the two characters.

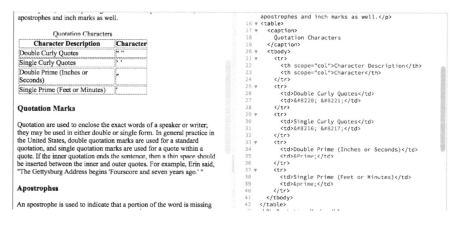

Note:

To find the necessary code for special characters, look for online sources such as http://www.w3schools.com/html/html_entities.asp.

16. **Save the file and continue to the next exercise.**

The multiplication sign is a seldom-used character; it doesn't even appear in the Insert Other Character dialog box. To insert this character, you can type code directly in the Code pane, or you can use the Insert field in the Insert Other Character dialog box.

There are many lists of HTML character entities on the Internet. Use your favorite search engine to search for "HTML characters." Some web pages have more characters than others; for very unusual characters, you might need to check a few sites until you find the code you need. Also, make note of both the name and the numeric code because some browsers support one but not the other (test both in your browser).

1. **With typography.html open in Split view, use the Design pane to scroll to the paragraph following the Multiplication Sign heading.**

2. **Select the letter "x" between 15 and 22.**

3. **Click the Code pane to bring it into focus, and then delete the selected letter "x".**

4. **Type &tim and press Return/Enter to choose × from the code hint list.**

   The code hints help you insert named character entities, but not numeric character codes.

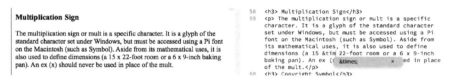

5. **Refresh the Design view.**

6. **In the Design pane, compare the appearance of the mult (multiply) character and the letter "x".**

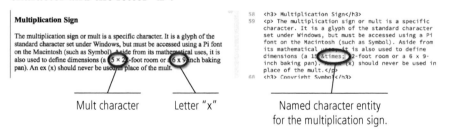

Mult character   Letter "x"   Named character entity
                                    for the multiplication sign.

7. **Select the letter "x" between 6 and 9 in the same sentence.**

8. **In the Code pane, replace the selected character with × and then refresh the Design view.**

   This is the numeric code for the mult character. Dreamweaver's code hints for character entities in Code view do not support numeric codes for characters.

Character code for the
multiplication sign.

Note:

The current versions of Firefox, Safari, Opera, and Chrome all support both the named and numeric character codes. Older versions, however, might show the characters "×" instead of the actual mult character.

9. **Save the file, then continue to the next stage of the project.**

Stage 4 Creating Lists

There are two common types of lists: ordered (numbered) lists and unordered (bulleted) lists. The two types are very similar in structure. In this stage of the project, you will create an ordered list of references and an unordered list that becomes navigation links in the final web page.

CREATE AN ORDERED LIST OF WEB RESOURCES

Ordered lists are commonly called numbered lists, although they are not always numbered. You can use Roman numerals (i, ii, iii or I, II, III) or letters (a, b, c or A, B, C).

The purpose of ordered lists is to show a sequence of steps or hierarchical order. If these purposes do not apply to the content of a list, you should use an unordered (bulleted) list instead.

1. **With typography.html open, click in the Design pane to place the insertion point in the numbered paragraph at the bottom of the page (under the Resources heading).**

2. **Click the Ordered List button in the Properties panel.**

   The **<ol>** tags surround the entire ordered list, identifying where the list starts and ends. Each list item within the list is surrounded by **<li>** tags.

   In the Design pane, the list as a whole is indented from the left edge of the page, and the space between list items is reduced. These presentation properties clearly identify that the text is part of a list, and not part of a regular paragraph.

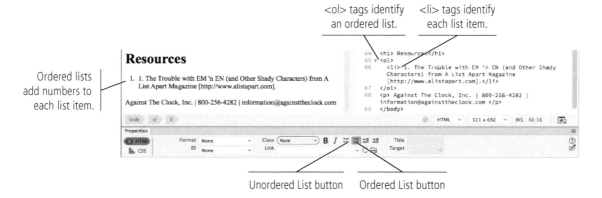

Ordered lists add numbers to each list item.

<ol> tags identify an ordered list.

<li> tags identify each list item.

Unordered List button   Ordered List button

3. **Delete the redundant number from the text at the beginning of the list item.**

   One of the presentation properties of an ordered list is that each list item is automatically numbered. If you receive content from an outside source, the number might already be typed at the beginning of each list item (as is the case in this project); you should remove the original number from the text of each list item.

4. **Click at the end of the text in the numbered list item and press Return/Enter.**

   When you press Return/Enter at the end of a list item in the Design pane, Dreamweaver automatically creates a new numbered list item for you. (You have to work in the Design pane to automatically add the new list item. Pressing Return/Enter in the Code pane simply adds white space in the code.)

5. Type HTML entities and other resources at W3schools.com. as the new list item, but do not press Return/Enter.

6. In the first list item, select the URL in the square brackets and cut it to the Clipboard (Edit>Cut or Command/Control-X).

7. Delete the two square brackets and the space before them.

8. Select "A List Apart Magazine," click in the Link field of the Properties panel, paste the copied URL, and press Return/Enter.

A link is identified by **<a>** tags. The **href** attribute defines the link destination, or the page that will open when a user clicks the link text.

9. Click to place the insertion point in the link (in the Design pane).

Placing the insertion point removes the highlighting that was applied to the text in the previous step. You can now see the default presentational properties of the <a> tag — blue, underlined text.

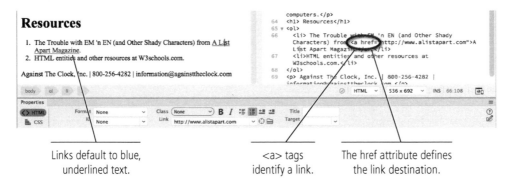

Links default to blue, underlined text.

<a> tags identify a link.

The href attribute defines the link destination.

10. In the second list item, make "W3schools.com" a link to http://www.w3schools.com.

11. Save the file and continue to the next exercise.

CREATE AN UNORDERED LIST OF NAVIGATION LINKS

A navigation bar is simply a list of links. It is common practice among web design professionals to mark up a navigation bar as a list of links; after CSS has been applied, however, the list takes on an all-new appearance. In this exercise, you use the unordered list format to create a navigation bar.

1. **With typography.html open, place the insertion point at the end of the last list item in the Resources section in the Design pane.**

2. **Press Return/Enter twice.**

   Pressing Return/Enter once creates the next list item — in this case, #3.

   If you press Return/Enter again (before typing anything else), Dreamweaver recognizes that you want to escape from the ordered list, deletes the last empty list item, and moves the insertion point into an empty paragraph below the ordered list.

3. **Click the Unordered List button in the Properties panel.**

   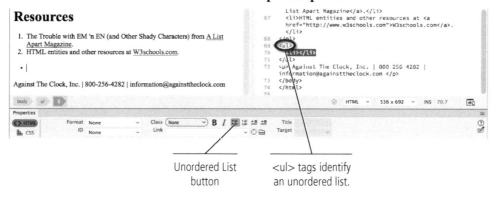

   Unordered List button

   `<ul>` tags identify an unordered list.

4. **Add four list items: ATC Home, Excerpts, Projects, and Portfolios. Press Return/Enter after each item, but not after the final list item.**

5. **Highlight the words "ATC Home" in the Design pane. In the Properties panel, type # in the Link field, the press Return/Enter to finalize the new link.**

   Using the # character in the Link field turns the selected text into a link without defining a specific destination. For the purposes of this project, the important thing is that the text of each list item be tagged as a link.

6. **Repeat Step 5 for each item in the list.**

7. **Save the changes and continue to the next stage of the project.**

Stage 5 Attaching an External CSS File

As you might have noticed, we paid particular attention to the tags that were applied to various structural elements through this project. Rather than simply accepting the default presentational properties, you can use cascading style sheets (CSS), which contain instructions that tell a browser how to format those various elements.

As you complete the rest of the projects in this book, you will work extensively with CSS to format both pages and specific page content. In this project, you are going to attach the client's existing CSS file to your page, so the appearance of your page matches the rest of the client's website.

ADD TAGS AND ELEMENT IDS

Although we will not discuss the finer details of CSS at this point, the following exercises will make more sense if you understand that a CSS file includes **selectors** (rules) that define the appearance of different tags. For the formatting to correctly map to content, you need to apply the appropriate tags to various elements.

In HTML 4, the div element was commonly used to identify different areas or divisions of a page. The ID attribute was attached to various div elements to clearly identify different areas — for example, div#header, div#nav, and div#footer. HTML5 includes header, nav, section, and footer elements that allow the same kind of page structure without the need to define and identify multiple divs on a page.

1. **With typography.html open in Split view, click and drag in the Design pane to select the level 1 heading and the blockquote.**

2. With the Insert panel in HTML mode, click the Header button.

HTML5 includes a number of elements that identify common elements of web pages. This button adds the **<header> </header>** tags to identify the header element.

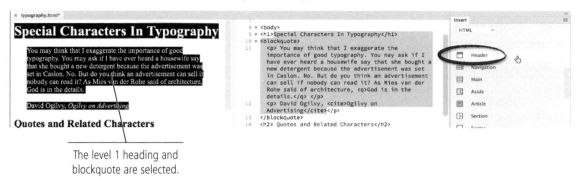

The level 1 heading and blockquote are selected.

3. In the resulting dialog box, choose Wrap Around Selection in the Insert menu, then click OK.

You can use the Insert dialog box (in this case, the Insert *Header* dialog box) to determine where the new element will be placed in relation to the selection. The Insert menu defaults to Wrap Around Selection because content is currently selected in the document. You can also use this dialog box to define a class or ID attribute for the resulting element.

4. Click once anywhere in the previously selected text to place the insertion point.

The boundaries of the header element are marked by a thin gray or dotted line in the Design pane. (If you don't see this border, you can turn on CSS Layout Outlines in the View>Visual Aids menu.)

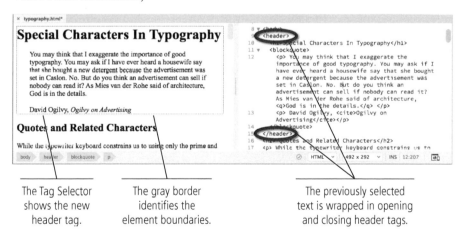

The Tag Selector shows the new header tag.

The gray border identifies the element boundaries.

The previously selected text is wrapped in opening and closing header tags.

5. **Switch to Design view and select all the text from the first level 2 heading (at the top of the page) to the last numbered list item under the "Resources" heading.**

   We used the regular Design view simply to make it easier to select the entire body of text; it isn't necessary, but it allows more of the actual document text to be visible in the document window than when working in the Split view.

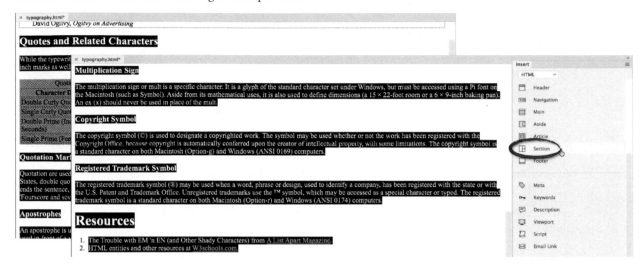

6. **Click the Section button in the HTML Insert panel. In the resulting dialog box, choose Wrap Around Selection in the Insert menu and then click OK.**

   The section element identifies (as you might imagine) a section of the page.

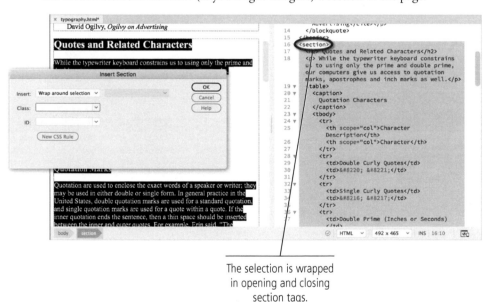

The selection is wrapped in opening and closing section tags.

7. **In the Design pane, place the insertion point anywhere in the unordered list near the bottom of the page. Click the <ul> tag in the Tag Selector to select the entire unordered list.**

8. **Click the Navigation button in the HTML Insert panel. In the resulting dialog box, choose Wrap Around Selection in the Insert menu, then click OK.**

The nav element identifies an area that includes navigation links.

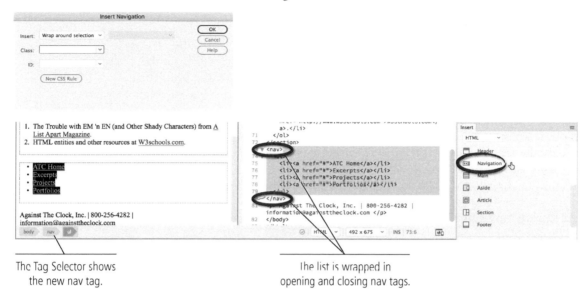

The Tag Selector shows
the new nav tag.

The list is wrapped in
opening and closing nav tags.

9. **In the Design pane, place the insertion point anywhere in the last paragraph. Click the <p> tag in the Tag Selector to select the entire last paragraph.**

10. **Click the Footer button in the HTML Insert panel. In the resulting dialog box, choose Wrap Around Selection in the Insert menu, then click OK.**

The footer element identifies the footer area of the page.

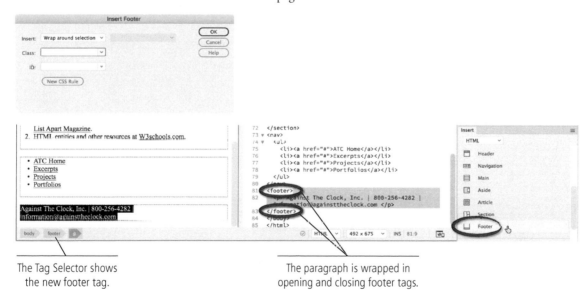

The Tag Selector shows
the new footer tag.

The paragraph is wrapped in
opening and closing footer tags.

11. **Save the file and continue to the next exercise.**

ATTACH THE CSS FILE

To make this page more visually pleasing to ATC site visitors — and to be consistent with the rest of the ATC site — you need to attach the CSS file already used for other pages in the client's site.

The CSS file, which is a set of instructions on how to display the web page, is separate from the HTML document. When a browser downloads an HTML file, it examines the code for external files required to display it, such as images and CSS files. The browser then downloads the external files and merges them into the display of the web page. In the case of a CSS file, the browser reads the instructions, and then applies the styles to the page.

After attaching the style sheet to the page, and depending on what the CSS file defines, you might see a dramatic difference in the appearance of the page. Not only will text styling change, but the layout will change too — even to the point of moving some page components to new locations.

1. **With typography.html open, turn on the Live view and hide the Code pane.**

   The Live view provides a more accurate view of how the page will render in an actual web browser. At this point, you can see that the file is little more than black text on a white background.

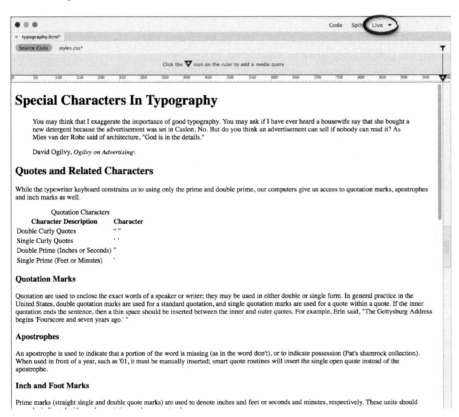

2. **Open the CSS Designer panel. Make sure the All button is active at the top of the panel.**

   Remember, all panels can be opened from the Window menu. If a panel is already available in the dock, you can click the relevant panel tab or button to show that panel.

3. **In the Sources section of the panel, click the Add CSS Source button and choose Attach Existing CSS File from the resulting menu.**

   If no CSS file is attached to an HTML file, you can also click the Add a CSS Source button in the Sources section of the panel.

Note:

For now, don't worry about the specifics of how the CSS file formats these elements. You will spend considerable time learning about CSS in the remaining projects of this book.

Add CSS
Source button

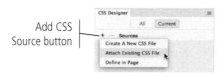

4. **In the Attach Existing CSS File dialog box, click the Browse button.**

5. **In the resulting Select Style Sheet File dialog box, navigate to styles.css in the root folder of the ATC site (WIP>Chapter). Click Open/OK to return to the Attach Existing CSS File dialog box.**

6. **Click OK in the Attach Existing CSS File dialog box to apply the CSS file.**

   As you can see in Design view, the main section of the page is clearly not formatted properly. The CSS Designer panel shows a number of selectors beginning with the # character. In the context of CSS, the # character at the beginning of the selector name identifies an ID selector, which can be used to distinguish one element from another on a single page.

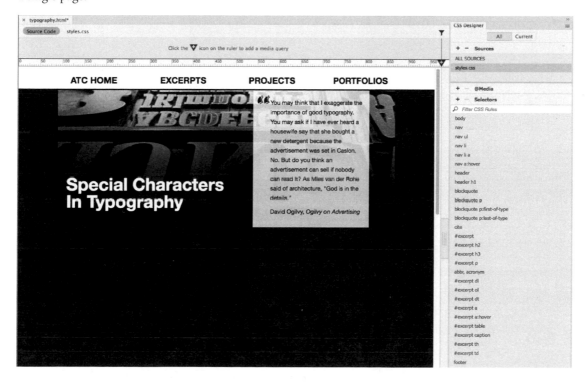

7. **In Design view, click to select the "Quotes and Related Characters" heading.**

8. **Using the Tag Selector, click the <section> tag to select the entire section element.**

9. **In the Properties panel, open the ID menu and choose excerpt.**

   This menu shows all available IDs that are defined in the attached CSS file. This method is an easy way to make sure that the ID you apply already exists in the attached CSS file.

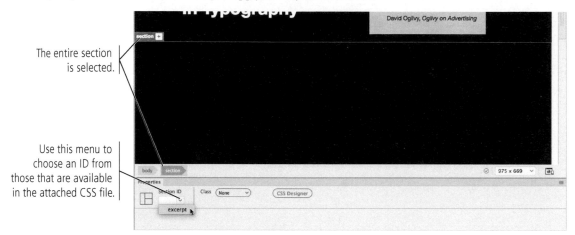

The entire section is selected.

Use this menu to choose an ID from those that are available in the attached CSS file.

By adding an ID attribute, you are uniquely identifying this section. The ID attribute has no effect on the structure of content, but simply identifies it for the purposes of CSS styling. This allows you to define different appearances for the same elements in different sections. For example, **<p>** tags in a section named "content" can have a different appearance than **<p>** tags in a section named "excerpt".

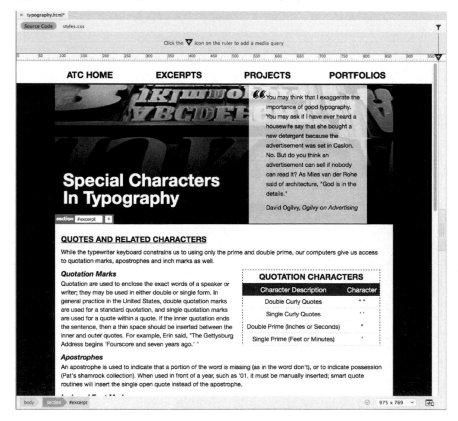

Note:

You will work extensively with CSS in later projects. For now, you should simply understand that the attached CSS file includes an ID selector named "excerpt" that defines the appearance of various elements within the section where that ID is applied.

10. **Save and close typography.html.**

11. **Choose Manage Sites from the bottom of the Directory menu in the Files panel.**

12. **In the Manage Sites dialog box, choose the ATC site name, and then click the Export button. Navigate to your WIP>Chapter folder and click Save to create the ATC.ste file.**

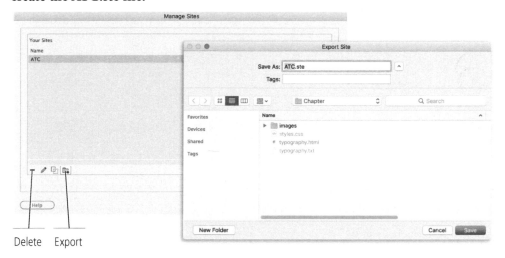

Delete   Export

13. **In the Manage Sites dialog box, remove the ATC site from the list and then click Done to close the Manage Sites dialog box.**

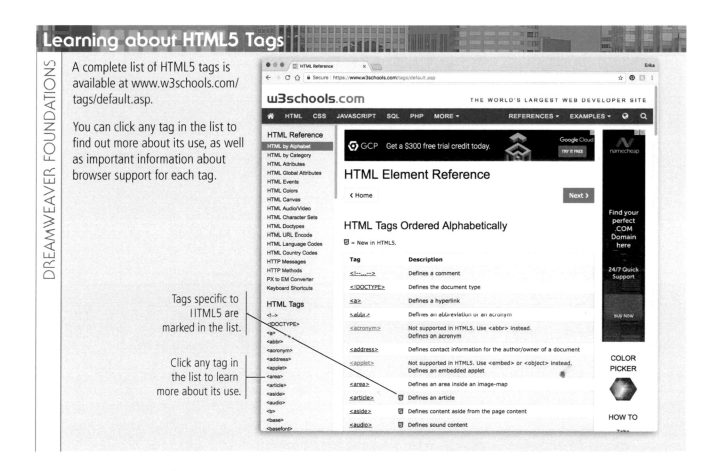

Learning about HTML5 Tags

DREAMWEAVER FOUNDATIONS

A complete list of HTML5 tags is available at www.w3schools.com/tags/default.asp.

You can click any tag in the list to find out more about its use, as well as important information about browser support for each tag.

Tags specific to HTML5 are marked in the list.

Click any tag in the list to learn more about its use.

1. The _____ tag marks up individual paragraphs in a story.

2. Each HTML page should have only one _____ element.

3. All visible content of a web page is contained within the opening and closing _____ tags.

4. _____ appear when you begin typing in the Code pane, showing a list of tags or elements that can be added at the current insertion point.

5. A(n) _____ tag includes both opening and closing tags, such as <title>text</title>.

6. A(n) _____ adds properties to HTML elements, such as the citation of a quote.

7. The _____ element is used to mark up text that is indented on the right and left, with extra white space above and below the affected text.

8. The _____ element is best used to mark up the short form of a phrase that is spoken as letters, such as HTML.

9. The _____ element identifies an individual item in an ordered or unordered list.

10. The _____ allows you to work temporarily with code, while still working in Design view.

1. Briefly explain the importance of properly structuring an HTML document.

2. Briefly explain the difference between an ordered list and an unordered list.

3. Briefly explain the importance of div tags for formatting an HTML page.

Portfolio Builder Project

Use what you learned in this project to complete the following freeform exercise.
Carefully read the art director and client comments, then create your own design to meet the needs of the project.
Use the space below to sketch ideas; when finished, write a brief explanation of your reasoning behind your final design.

art director comments

The owner of Against The Clock Inc. has received a number of positive comments — and new sales — because of the *Typography Companion* sample chapter that you created for her to post on her website. She would like to add another page with a sample from the *Color Companion* from the same series.

To complete this project, you should:

❏ Use the ATC site folder that you already created for the new page.

❏ Create a new HTML page and copy the text from **ColorCh3.txt** into the file. (The file is in the **Books_DW18_PB.zip** archive on the Student Files web page.)

❏ Mark up the page text with proper structural tags.

❏ Create header and footer elements and attach the same CSS file that you used in the type chapter.

client comments

We've had such a positive response from the type chapter that we also want to include a sample from the *Color Companion*. If we get the same increase in sales leads from this chapter, we'll probably go ahead and do online samples for all of our books.

In addition to the text file for the *Color Companion* chapter, we've sent you a PDF file of the printed chapter so that you can more easily see the different text elements — headings, lists, italics, special characters, and so on. You can just ignore the images and sidebars in the printed chapter; we don't need those in the online sample. There is, however, a table near the end of the file that we would like you to include in the online version.

At the end of the text file, we added in the glossary terms that we think are important for this chapter. There aren't any resources, so you can leave out that section.

project justification

_____
_____
_____
_____
_____
_____
_____
_____
_____
_____
_____
_____
_____
_____

Project Summary

No matter how you receive content for a web page, you will likely need to correct the formatting with the appropriate HTML tags. In this project, you learned how to use HTML tags and elements to semantically structure and mark up a document, so all visitors can successfully access and use a web page. You also learned that by applying ID attributes, <div> tags, and using CSS, you can turn a plain HTML document into a visually pleasing and highly structured web page.

The web pages that you create for clients will seldom be as text-intensive as this page, but now that you have a solid understanding of how to work with HTML structures, from both Design view and Code view, you are ready to format any content you receive from a client — regardless of its condition.

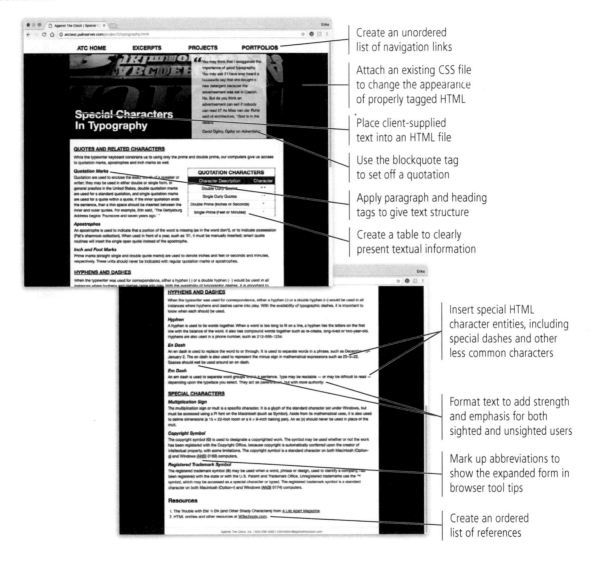

Create an unordered list of navigation links

Attach an existing CSS file to change the appearance of properly tagged HTML

Place client-supplied text into an HTML file

Use the blockquote tag to set off a quotation

Apply paragraph and heading tags to give text structure

Create a table to clearly present textual information

Insert special HTML character entities, including special dashes and other less common characters

Format text to add strength and emphasis for both sighted and unsighted users

Mark up abbreviations to show the expanded form in browser tool tips

Create an ordered list of references

Arts Council Website

The client is the director of a nonprofit guild, sponsored by the city government, with the goal of promoting artistic and cultural activities in the local community. Your job is to implement the client's new website design, based on the approved design that was created in a Photoshop file.

This project incorporates the following skills:

❑ Using various methods to add static images into a web page

❑ Assigning alt tags to images for improved usability

❑ Manipulating images in a web page

❑ Extracting content and styles from a native Photoshop file

❑ Working with CSS to define various element properties

Project Meeting

client comments

We want our new site to be very basic, highlighting the three main projects of the council — the summer arts festival, kids' workshops, and adult classes.

There will be a lot more information about each of our programs on secondary pages, but we haven't finished writing and gathering the content for those yet.

We have approved the final design comp we saw last week, so we want to get started on the home page as soon as possible. I sent our logo file to the art director, as well as three photos that will be featured on the home page.

art director comments

We've been working on the design for this project for several weeks, and the client just approved the layout comp that our artist created in Photoshop.

I assigned the HTML structural composition to another web designer, but she has other projects that need to take priority, so your job is to complete the home page. Once you're finished, you'll hand it off to a developer to create the secondary pages and the required interactive elements when the client provides the content.

A few of the images you need have been saved in the project folder, but some of the assets you need are only available in the Photoshop file. Fortunately, you can use Dreamweaver to access what you need to complete the project in a relatively short time.

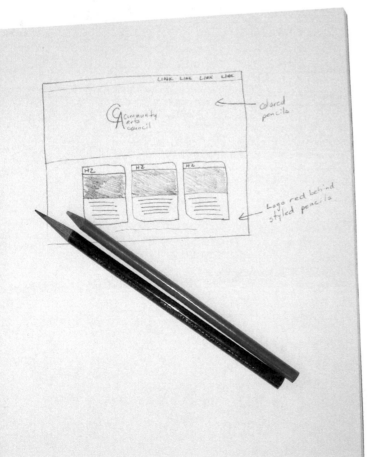

project objectives

To complete this project, you will:

- ❏ Use multiple techniques to add images to web pages
- ❏ Resize images to fit page areas
- ❏ Resample images to reduce download time
- ❏ Load a Photoshop file into your Creative Cloud account
- ❏ Extract text, images, and styles from a supplied Photoshop file
- ❏ Use CSS to control the appearance of various page elements

Stage 1 Placing Static Foreground Images

Important note: This project requires an individual user subscription to the Adobe Creative Cloud service. If your students are working on machines with a device license, they will not have access to the Extract functionality needed to complete the project. An alternate project, which does not require an individual user CC account, is available on the Instructor Downloads page.

As with many tasks, Dreamweaver offers a number of methods for inserting images into an HTML page. The variety of available options means you can choose whichever method best suits your personal working style and space. Before you begin placing objects in a page, however, you should understand the basics of images that will be used for web design.

Image Bit Depth

Bit depth refers to how many bits define the color value of a particular pixel. A **bit** is a unit of information that is either on or off (represented as 1 and 0, respectively).

- 1 bit has 2 states or colors

- 8 bits allow 256 possible colors (2^8 or $2\times2\times2\times2\times2\times2\times2\times2=256$)

- 24 bits allow 16,777,216 possible colors (2^{24}).

Image Formats

Four primary formats are used for images and graphics on the web:

- **GIF** (Graphics Interchange Format) is best used for graphics with areas of solid color, such as logos.

  The GIF format supports 8-bit color, or 256 possible values. To create the illusion or more possible colors, the format supports dithering, in which pixels of varying colors are interspersed in areas where colors transition from one to another.

  This format supports index transparency, in which specific colors in the image can be defined as transparent areas, as well as simple frame-by-frame animation. It is largely falling out of use in favor of the PNG format for graphics.

The GIF format supports 8-bit color and index transparency, which does not allow smooth color transitions or smooth fading of edges into a background.

The JPEG format supports 24-bit color but not transparency, allowing smooth color transitions but not fading of edges into a background.

- **JPEG** (Joint Photographic Experts Group). This format supports 24-bit color, is used primarily for continuous-tone images with subtle changes in color, such as photographs or other images that are created in Adobe Photoshop. In an RGB photograph, three color channels define how much of each primary color (red, green, and blue) makes up each pixel. Each channel requires 8 bits, resulting in a total of 24 bits for each pixel (called **true color**). The format does not support transparency.

The PNG-8 format supports 8-bit color and index transparency, which does not allow smooth color transitions or smooth fading of edges into a background.

The PNG-32 format supports 24-bit color and alpha transparency, allowing smooth color and transparency transitions.

  The JPEG format incorporates **lossy compression**, which means that pixels are thrown away in order to reduce file size. When areas of flat color are highly compressed, speckles of other colors (called artifacts) often appear, which negatively impacts the quality of the design.

- **PNG** (Portable Network Graphics) has two common variants, PNG-8 and PNG-32.

    PNG-8 has 8 bits, which means it can support 256 colors in an image. Although the PNG-8 format incorporates algorithms to better reflect color transitions and colors that are not included in the file's color table, it is still only an 8-bit color format so should not be used for true-color images such as photographs. Like the GIF format, it is more appropriate for logos and other graphics that do not use a large number of colors or smooth tone changes.

    PNG-32 supports 24-bit color, which means the format can be used for photographic and other images with a large range of color. PNG-32 also supports alpha transparency, in which each pixel can have a degree of transparency (the "alpha value") in addition to the three color channel values. In other words, PNG-32 supports smooth transitions from opaque to transparent. (The "32" designation comes from 24 bits for the color definition plus 8 bits for the transparency information.)

    Both variations of the PNG format use lossless compression, which means no image data is thrown away. This results in better-quality images, but also larger file sizes than can be accomplished using a lossy compression algorithm.

- **SVG (Scalable Vector Graphics)** are made up of mathematically defined lines called **vectors** (unlike **raster images**, which are made up entirely of pixels). Vector graphics are completely **scalable** without affecting their quality.

 ## REVIEW THE EXISTING PROJECT STATUS

This project involves working with files that have already been created by another designer. The best way to start this type of job is to evaluate the existing work before you jump in to complete the required tasks.

1. Download **Council_DW18_RF.zip** from the Student Files web page.

2. **Expand the ZIP archive in your WIP folder (Macintosh) or copy the archive contents into your WIP folder (Windows).**

    This results in a folder named **Council**, which contains the files you need for this project.

3. **Create a new site named Arts-Council, using the WIP>Council folder as the site root folder.**

    The procedure for defining this site is the same as for the sites you created in previous projects (except for the path, which is unique for every project). If necessary, refer to the first exercises in Project 1: Bistro Site Organization for more detailed instructions.

4. **With the Arts-Council site open in the Files panel, double-click index.html to open the file.**

5. Review the page contents in the Live view.

This is a fairly simple page, with several places marked to add various content. As you complete this project, you will use a number of techniques to place and manage images to add visual interest.

In the first stage of this project you will use a variety of techniques to add content that was provided with the basic HTML file. In the second stage of the project you will extract content from a Photoshop file that shows the finished and approved page design.

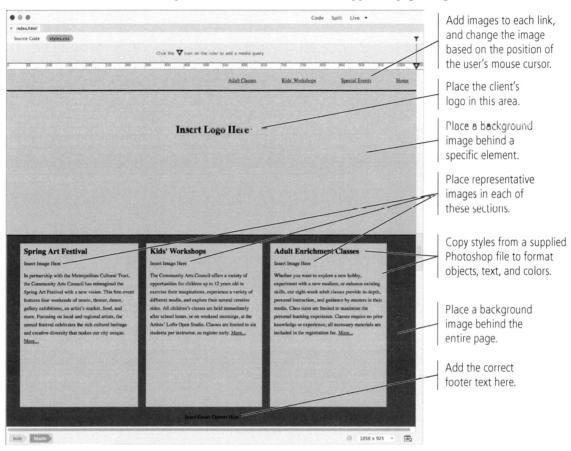

Add images to each link, and change the image based on the position of the user's mouse cursor.

Place the client's logo in this area.

Place a background image behind a specific element.

Place representative images in each of these sections.

Copy styles from a supplied Photoshop file to format objects, text, and colors.

Place a background image behind the entire page.

Add the correct footer text here.

6. Continue to the next exercise.

PLACE AN IMAGE IN THE REGULAR DESIGN VIEW

Dreamweaver provides many ways to insert images into web pages, one of which is to simply drag an image file from the Files panel to a specific location on the page. (This method only works in the regular Design view; you cannot drag an image from the Files panel when the Live view is active.) In this exercise, you will use this basic technique to place an image in the client's home page.

1. With index.html open (from the Arts-Council site folder), turn off the Live view to make the regular Design view active.

2. Click the Split button in the Document toolbar to show both the Design and Code views.

In this project we use the horizontal split view to maximize the line length that is visible in both panes. Feel free to use whichever method you prefer.

3. **In the Design view, select the words "Insert Image Here" in the left rectangle in the third row of the layout.**

4. **Delete the selected text from the Design view.**

   When you delete the placeholder text, the code for a nonbreaking space (** **) is automatically added as a placeholder inside the **<p>** tags.

The regular Design view is active. Live view is turned off.

The insertion point still flashes in the now-empty paragraph.

The Code pane shows that deleting the text from the Design pane does not delete the <p> tags.

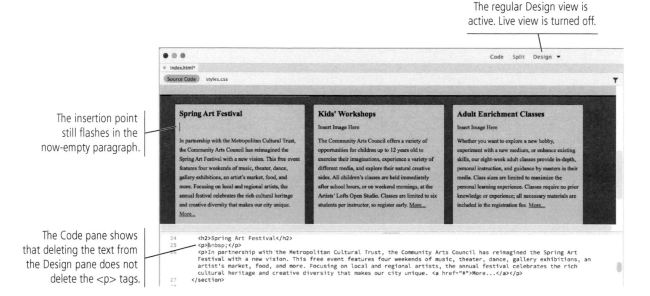

5. **In the Files panel, expand the site images folder and review the contents.**

   These four images have been provided by the client. You will insert them in various places on the client's new home page.

6. **Click the file festival.jpg in the Files panel and drag to the empty paragraph (where you deleted the text in Step 4).**

   When the regular Design view is active, you can drag any image from the Files panel to a specific position in the layout. (This method does not work when the Live view is active.)

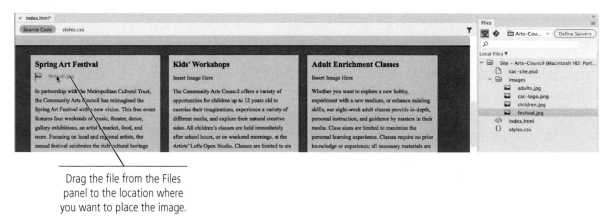

Drag the file from the Files panel to the location where you want to place the image.

7. **With the image selected in the Design view, type Spring Arts Festival link in the Alt field of the Properties panel. Click the image in the Design pane to finalize the change.**

8. **With the placed image selected in the Design pane, examine the Tag Selector and the Code pane.**

   The **<img>** (image) tag appears inside the opening and closing **<p>** tags.

   Some attributes of the **<img>** tag are automatically populated based on information saved in the image file:

   - The **src** attribute defines the file name and location of the image.

   - The **width** and **height** attributes are automatically populated based on the file's physical dimensions.

   - The **alt** attribute is the alternate text; this is the text that appears in place of an image if image display is disabled in a browser, or that is read by screen-reader software. The alt text is also indexed by search engines, which allows them to show your site's images in the search engine image gallery.

   When you place an image, Dreamweaver automatically creates an empty alt attribute in the <img> tag; if you do not add text in the Alt field of the Properties panel (or directly in the Code pane), the attribute remains empty.

Note:

The alt attribute is commonly misnamed the alt tag; it is not an HTML tag but an attribute of a tag.

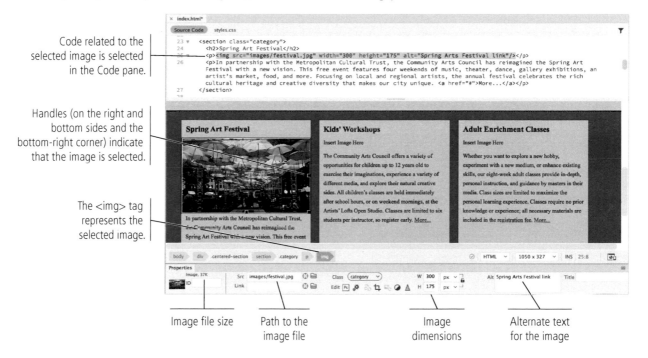

Code related to the selected image is selected in the Code pane.

Handles (on the right and bottom sides and the bottom-right corner) indicate that the image is selected.

The <img> tag represents the selected image.

Image file size   Path to the image file   Image dimensions   Alternate text for the image

9. **Save the file and continue to the next exercise.**

PLACE AN IMAGE WITH THE INSERT PANEL

In the last few upgrades to the software, the Dreamweaver Live view has been significantly enhanced. You can now access many of the editing features that were previously only available in the regular Design view, so you can immediately see the results in the document window. In this exercise, you will use the buttons in the HTML Insert panel to add a new image element to the page in the Live view.

1. **With index.html open, click the Design button in the Document toolbar to close the Code pane, then make the Live view active.**

2. **Click once to select the "Insert Image Here" paragraph in the middle rectangle in the third row of the layout.**

   When the Live view is active, clicking an object in the document window shows the Element Display. The blue tag shows the specific element, as well as any ID or class attributes that have been defined for that element. In this case, you can see that the selected element is a **p** element — in other words, it is a paragraph.

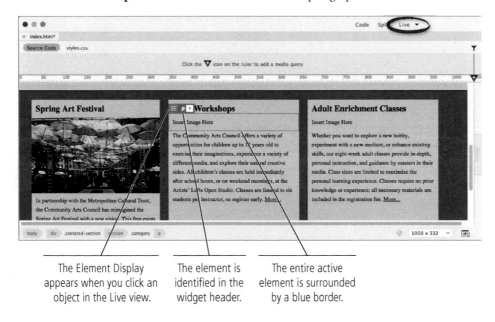

The Element Display appears when you click an object in the Live view.

The element is identified in the widget header.

The entire active element is surrounded by a blue border.

3. **Double-click the text in the selected paragraph to place the insertion point.**

   Remember, you can place the insertion point and edit text directly in the Live view.

Double-clicking places the insertion point inside the active element.

The orange border identifies the element where the insertion point is placed.

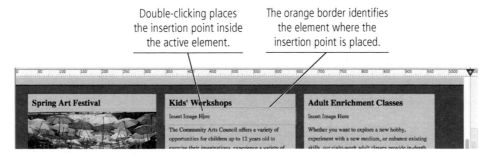

4. **Click and drag to select all the words in the active paragraph element.**

5. **Press the Delete key to remove the selected text from the Design pane.**

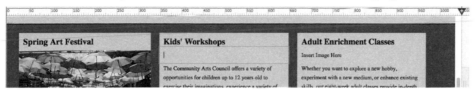

6. **Click away from the active element to exit the text-editing mode (unplace the insertion point).**

   You cannot use the Insert panel buttons when the insertion point is placed in the Live view. When you click away from the element to unplace the insertion point, the actual element — in this case, the p (paragraph) element — becomes the active selection.

7. **Open the Insert panel and, if necessary, switch the panel to the HTML options.**

8. **With the p element selected, click the Image button in the HTML Insert panel.**

   Because an element is selected in the Live view, clicking this button results in the Position Assistant over the selected element, which you can use to determine where the image will be placed relative to the selected element — Before, After, or Nest inside. (The Wrap option is not available in this case because you can't wrap an image around another object.)

Note:

You can also choose Insert>Image.

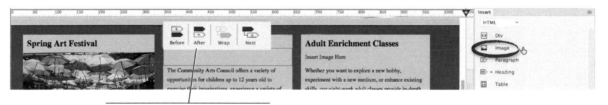

Use these buttons to place the image relative to the selected element.

9. **Click the Nest button in the Position Assistant.**

   You want to place the image inside the paragraph, so you are using the Nest option.

10. **In the Resulting dialog box, navigate to the file children.jpg (in the site images folder) and click Open/OK.**

11. **With the image selected in the Design pane, click the Edit HTML Attributes button on the left side of the Element Display.**

12. **Type Kids Workshops link in the alt field and press Return/Enter to finalize the new alt attribute.**

    You can use this pop-up window to change various attributes of a placed image without using the Properties panel or Code pane.

    Click here to open the HTML
    Attributes pop-up window.

13. **Press the ESC key to close the HTML Attributes pop-up window.**

No image handles
are available when
the Live view is active.

14. **Save the file and continue to the next exercise.**

DRAG AND DROP AN IMAGE FROM THE INSERT PANEL

When the Live view is active, you can drag a button from the HTML Insert panel to place a new element in the page; on-screen guides determine where the element will be placed. In this exercise, you will use this method to place an image in the page.

1. **Make sure index.html is open and the Live view is active.**

2. **Select and delete the words "Insert Image Here" from the right rectangle in the third row of the layout.**

3. **Click away from the empty element to unplace the insertion point.**

4. **Click the Image button in the HTML Insert panel and drag to the empty paragraph element.**

   When you drag elements within, or into, the Live view, visual indicators identify where the element you drag will be placed when you release the mouse button. A green two-headed arrow indicates that the dragged element will be placed in line with other elements; the line shows exactly where (before or after) the element will be placed. A blue rectangle inside another element indicates that the dragged one will be placed inside of the element to which you drag (referred to as **nesting**).

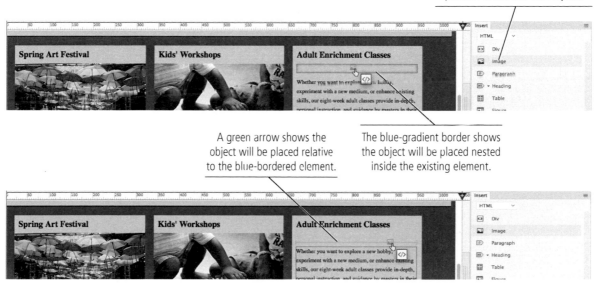

Drag the Image button to a specific position in the Live view layout.

A green arrow shows the object will be placed relative to the blue-bordered element.

The blue-gradient border shows the object will be placed nested inside the existing element.

5. **When a blue border appears inside the paragraph element, release the mouse button.**

6. **In the resulting Select Image Source dialog box, navigate to `adults.jpg` (in the site `images` folder) and click Open/OK.**

   Using the drag-and-drop method, you have to determine which image you want to place when you release the mouse button.

7. Using the pop-up HTML attributes window, define Adult Classes link as the alternate text for this image.

8. Save the file and then continue to the next exercise.

 ## INSERT AN IMAGE WITH THE ASSETS PANEL

The Assets panel allows you to sort the various assets in a site by type rather than by their location within the site folder structure. It also offers yet another way to insert an image into a web page. In this exercise, you will use the Assets panel to add the client's logo to the page.

1. With index.html open, make sure the Live view is active.

2. Select and delete the words "Insert Logo Here" in the second row in the layout, then click away from the element to unplace the insertion point.

3. Open the Assets panel (Window>Assets). On the left side of the Assets panel, click the Images button to show all images in the site.

The Assets panel displays a thumbnail of the selected image at the top of the panel.

4. Click the Refresh Site List button at the bottom of the Assets panel to make sure all images are visible.

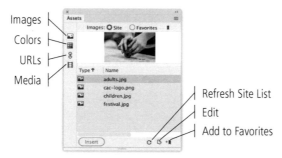

Note:

Do not double-click the image in the Assets panel or Files panel to insert it. Double-clicking an image in either panel prompts Dreamweaver to open the file in an image-editing application.

5. Select cac-logo.png in the panel.

6. **With the empty header element selected from Step 2, click the Insert button at the bottom of the Assets panel.**

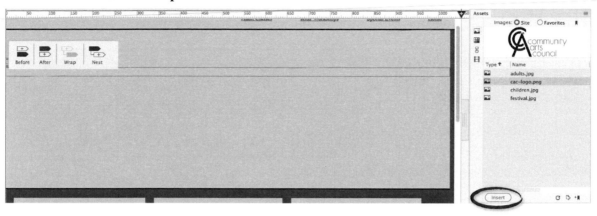

You can also drag an image from the Assets panel to the layout. If the Live view is active, on-screen guides identify where the dragged image will be placed. If the regular Design view is active, simply drag from the panel to a location indicated by the flashing insertion point.

7. **Click the Nest button in the resulting Position Assistant.**

8. **Define Community Arts Council as the alternate text for the placed image.**

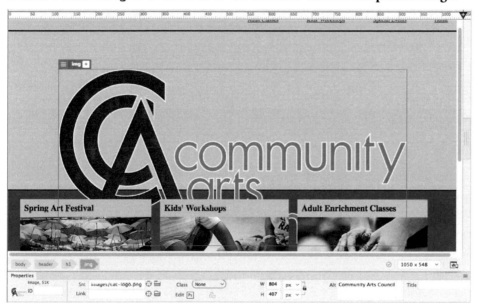

9. **Save the file and continue to the next exercise.**

RESIZE AND RESAMPLE AN IMAGE

As you can see in the Live view, the placed logo is much too large to fit in the defined space. In this exercise, you will adjust the image to fit the space.

1. **With index.html open, turn off the Live view.**

   When the Live view is active, you can only use the Properties panel to change the dimensions of a placed image.

2. **Click the placed logo to select the image (if necessary).**

   When the Live view is not active, the bottom center, right center, and bottom-right corner of a selected image show control handles, which you can drag to resize the height of the placed image. (You might not be able to see the right edge of the image depending on the size and arrangement of your workspace.)

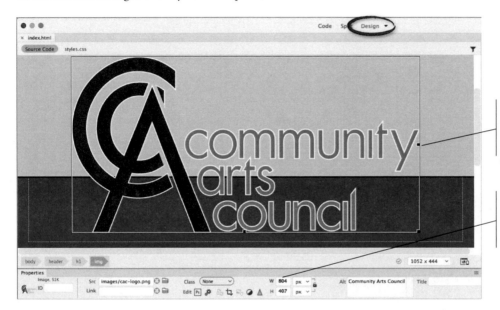

You can drag the image handles to resize the image in the document window.

You can use the W and H fields to change the image dimensions.

3. **In the Properties panel, make sure the lock icon to the right of the W and H fields is locked. If the icon is unlocked, click it to make it locked.**

   When the icon is locked, changing one dimension applies a proportional change to the other dimension; in other words, changes to the image dimensions maintain the original width-to-height aspect ratio.

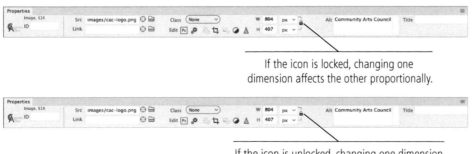

If the icon is locked, changing one dimension affects the other proportionally.

If the icon is unlocked, changing one dimension has no effect on the other dimension.

4. **Highlight the current value in the W field. Type 550, then press Return/ Enter to finalize the change.**

In the Properties panel, the image dimensions appear in bold, indicating that the image has been resized.

Two additional buttons are now available to the right of the W and H fields. Clicking the **Reset to Original Size button** restores the original image dimensions regardless of how many times you have changed the image size in the page or in the Properties panel.

Clicking the **Commit Image Size button** changes the placed image file to match the current image dimensions on the page.

Note:

You can usually reduce an image without losing quality, but enlarging an image beyond its original size can result in a significant loss of image quality.

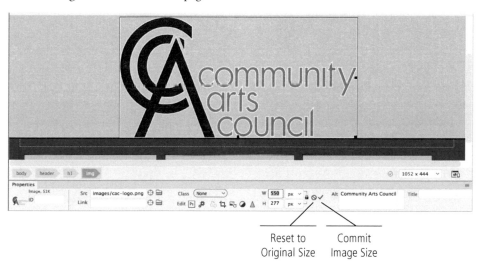

Reset to Original Size   Commit Image Size

5. **Click the bottom-right image handle, press Shift, and drag up and left. When the H field shows the height of 250, release the mouse button.**

If an image extends outside the edge of the element in which it is placed (as is the case for this logo), you will not be able to use the control handles to resize the image. Instead, you have to use the Properties panel.

You can drag any of the handles to resize the image in only one direction (by dragging the side handles) or in both directions at once (by dragging the corner handle).

Keep in mind that manually resizing the image using these handles does not honor the Lock icon in the Properties panel. If you drag either of the side handles, or the corner handle without pressing Shift, the lock icon in the Properties panel is automatically unlocked. By pressing Shift while dragging the corner handle, you constrain the resizing process and maintain the image's original aspect ratio.

Note:

Pressing Shift while dragging a side handle does not maintain the image's aspect ratio. You have to Shift-drag the corner handle to resize the image proportionally.

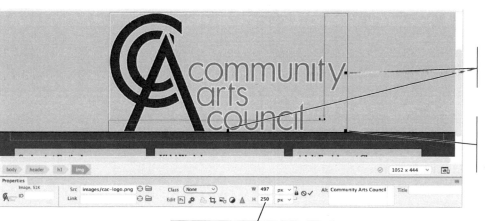

Drag a side handle to change only one dimension.

Drag the corner handle to change both dimensions at one time.

The Properties panel shows the adjusted size when you drag the handles.

6. **In the Files panel, expand the images folder if necessary.**

7. **Control/right-click the cac-logo.png file, and choose Edit>Duplicate from the contextual menu.**

   It's a common mistake to insert a large image into a web page, and then simply resize the image to take up less space on the page. The problem with resizing is that, while the image *appears* smaller, the file size ("weight") remains the same. Users might need to wait a considerable length of time to download the large image file.

   Instead of simply resizing, you should also resample any resized images to include only the necessary data. **Resampling** discards pixels (while downsizing), so the specified dimensions of the image are the actual dimensions of the image. This reduces the weight of the image, which reduces the download time for your visitors.

   In the next few steps, you are going to resample the image that you placed into the index.html page. However, you should understand that resampling in Dreamweaver permanently changes the image file. Before you make this type of change permanent, it is a good idea to create a copy of the file, so you can still access the original if necessary.

8. **In the Files panel, click the original cac-logo.png file once to select it, then click the file name again to highlight the file name.**

   Make sure you don't rename the one that has "Copy" in the file name; that file is the original-size logo. You want to rename the image file that you placed into the header and decreased to a smaller physical size.

9. **At the end of the current file name, type -small, then press Return/Enter to finalize the new file name.**

   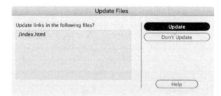

10. **In the resulting dialog box, click Update to update the link in index.html to the new file name.**

11. With the image selected on the page, click the Commit Image Size button to the right of the W and H fields.

Resample   Commit Image Size

Note:

You could also click the Resample button to accomplish the same effect.

12. Click OK to acknowledge the warning.

As we explained earlier, resampling in Dreamweaver permanently changes the image file; the resized dimensions become its (new) actual size. After resampling, the Reset to Original Size button is no longer visible, and the Resample button is not available.

Note:

If another user clicked the "Don't show me this message again" option, you won't see this warning.

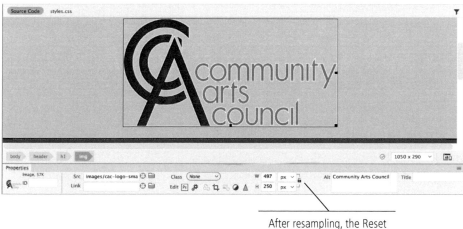

After resampling, the Reset Size button no longer appears.

13. Save the file and continue to the next stage of the project.

The Image Properties Panel in Depth

When an image is selected in the document window, the Properties panel not only displays properties (attributes) of the image, but also provides access to a number of image-related functions.

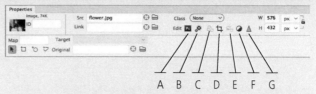

A B C D E F G

A. Edit opens the image file in its native application. GIF, JPG, and PNG files open in Photoshop (assuming you have that application).

B. Edit Image Settings opens a dialog box where you can change a variety of options for the selected file format. You can also use the Format menu to change the format of the selected image; if you change the format, you will be asked where you want to save the new file.

C. Update From Original can be used to make sure an inserted Photoshop image in the HTML file is the most recently saved version of the image.

If you insert a native Photoshop (PSD) file into a page, Dreamweaver converts it to a file that is appropriate for web browsers; the Edit Image Settings dialog box automatically appears, so you can define the settings for the generated image.

When you place a native Photoshop file, Dreamweaver stores a link to the original file.

The actual image in the page is converted to a web-friendly format.

The original link to the PSD file is also maintained; if the PSD file is changed, Dreamweaver notifies you that the image must be updated to the most recent version.

An icon appears in the top-left corner of a placed Photoshop file. Moving your mouse over the icon shows whether the image reflects the most-recently saved version of the Photoshop file.

Original asset modified

Images Synced

Although Dreamweaver is not an image-editing application, you can use it to perform some basic image-editing functions. These tools can't replace Adobe Photoshop, but they are well suited for making quick adjustments to an image from directly within the Dreamweaver application.

D. The **Crop tool** can be used to remove unwanted areas of an image. When you click the Crop tool, the lighter area shows the area that will be included in the cropped image; you can drag any of the eight handles around the edge of the crop area to change the area. Pressing Return/Enter finalizes the crop; pressing ESC cancels the crop and restores the original image.

Drag any of the handles to change the area that will be included in the cropped version.

The lighter area shows what will remain after the crop has been applied.

E. The **Resample tool** changes the number of pixels in an image to exactly match the size of the selected instance in the page. This has the same effect as clicking the Commit Image Size button after resizing an image in the Design pane.

F. Brightness and Contrast can be used to change those properties in a selected image.

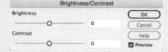

G. The **Sharpen** option can be useful for restoring some detail after resizing/resampling (especially upsizing). Keep in mind, however, that oversharpening can often produce worse results than what you start with.

Remember: All of the Dreamweaver image-editing tools permanently modify the edited file. If you use any of the image-editing buttons, you see a warning that the changes permanently affect the file (unless someone has checked the Don't Show ... option in the dialog box). Always keep a backup image, so if you over-edit, you can replace the backup image and start over.

Stage 2 Extracting Photoshop Assets

The "look and feel" of a website is often created in an image-editing application such as Adobe Photoshop, while the structure and code are created in Dreamweaver. Using the Extract tools that are part of an individual-user subscription to the Adobe Creative Cloud, integrating assets that are defined in Photoshop is now far easier than ever before.

✍ VERIFY YOUR ADOBE ID IN DREAMWEAVER

In the next exercise you are going to use the Extract tools that are part of your Adobe Creative Cloud subscription services. For that process to work, you must have an active internet connection and be signed in to your Creative Cloud account in Dreamweaver.

Important note: For the Extract functions to work properly, your user ID must be associated with a paid individual-user Creative Cloud subscription account. This service is not available if you have only a free Adobe ID, and is not available if you are using a computer that has a device license instead of an individual-user license.

In this exercise, you will verify that you are signed in to your Adobe Creative Cloud account.

1. **In Dreamweaver, open the Help menu.**

2. **If you see an option to Sign In, skip to Step 5.**

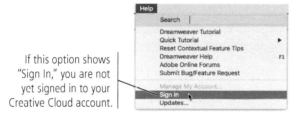

If this option shows "Sign In," you are not yet signed in to your Creative Cloud account.

3. **If you see an option to Sign Out, verify that the listed email is the Adobe ID linked to your Creative Cloud account.**

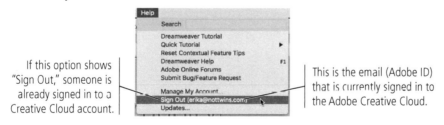

If this option shows "Sign Out," someone is already signed in to a Creative Cloud account.

This is the email (Adobe ID) that is currently signed in to the Adobe Creative Cloud.

4a. **If the email address listed in the Help menu is yours, continue to the next exercise.**

4b. **If the email in the menu is not yours, choose the Sign Out option. Read the resulting message and then click Sign Out.**

If you sign out of any Adobe CC application, this message informs you that you are also signing out of *all* Adobe CC applications.

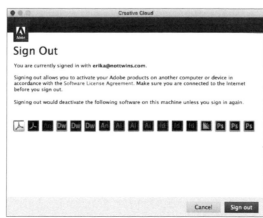

5. **In Dreamweaver, choose Help>Sign In.**

6. **Read the message in the resulting dialog box, then click Sign In Now.**

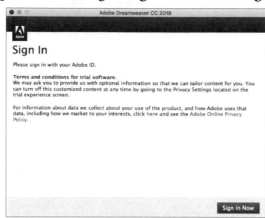

7. **In the Sign In screen, enter your Adobe ID and password, then click Sign In.**

8. **Read the message in the final screen, then click Continue.**

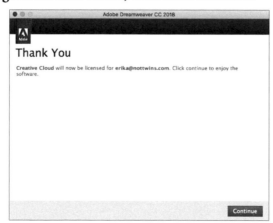

9. **Continue to the next exercise.**

LOAD A PHOTOSHOP FILE INTO YOUR CREATIVE CLOUD ACCOUNT

The structure of this web page, which you saw as gray rectangles when you first opened the index.html page, was defined in Dreamweaver using CSS. The overall design, however, was created in an Adobe Photoshop file that was provided with the resource files for this project. In this exercise, you will upload the provided Photoshop file to your Creative Cloud account so that you can extract the assets that are defined in that file.

1. **With the Arts-Council site open in the Files panel, open the file index.html if it is not already open**

   A file must be open in Dreamweaver before you can access the Extract panel functionality.

2. **Using the Document toolbar, activate the Live view and hide the Code pane (if necessary).**

3. **Choose Window>Extract to open the Extract panel.**

   If this is the first time you (or someone else) has used the Extract panel, you see the introductory version of the panel shown on the left, with links to a tutorial on the panel's functionality. After using the panel the first time, you see the version on the right.

Note:

Throughout the rest of this project (and in the rest of this book), we tell you what panels to use at various points. Our screen captures show only the panels most relevant to the immediate discussion. Feel free to arrange the workspace in any way that best suits your working environment.

The Creative Cloud Extract service offers an in-app method for accessing the images, text, colors, and styles that have been created in a Photoshop file directly in Dreamweaver — which makes it relatively easy to translate a designer's vision into a functioning web page.

4. **Click the Upload PSD button in the top-left corner of the introductory Extract panel, or in the middle of the standard Extract panel.**

5. **In the resulting navigation dialog box, navigate to the `cac-site.psd` file in your WIP>Council folder.**

This file was created by another designer. It includes the images and text that you need to complete the client's new home page. It also shows the formatting that should be used for various elements, such as the applied font and type sizes, element backgrounds, and colors.

6. **Click Open.**

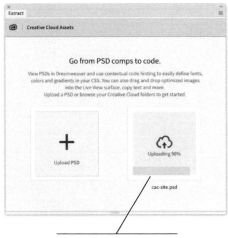

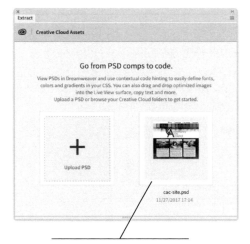

The new thumbnail shows the progress of the upload.

When the upload is complete, a thumbnail of the file appears.

7. **When the upload process is complete, double-click the cac-site.psd thumbnail in the Extract panel.**

This opens the file in the Extract panel, which means you can now access the various file assets — images, type styles, etc. — directly in Dreamweaver.

8. **Click the bottom-left corner of the Extract panel and drag to expand the panel as large as possible so you can clearly see the elements in the file.**

Change the view percentage of the preview in the panel.

Drag the corner of the panel to make it larger (if possible).

Note:

Files that you upload are stored in your Creative Cloud account; you can manage those files using the Assets>Files tab of the Adobe Creative Cloud app.

Note:

You can click the Creative Cloud icon in the top-left corner of the panel to return to the list of uploaded files.

9. **Continue to the next exercise.**

EXTRACT TEXT AND IMAGES FROM A PHOTOSHOP FILE

The Photoshop file that you uploaded in the previous exercise defines the appearance and content of the various elements in the HTML page. In this exercise you will extract content that will be required to complete the web page design in Dreamweaver.

1. **With index.html open from the Arts-Council site, make sure the Live view is active.**

2. **With the Photoshop file that you uploaded in the previous exercise open in the Extract panel, move your mouse cursor different areas of the preview.**

   In the Extract panel, a black border identifies distinct elements (layer content) in the Photoshop file. As you move your mouse cursor over various parts of the preview, you can see which element would be selected if you click.

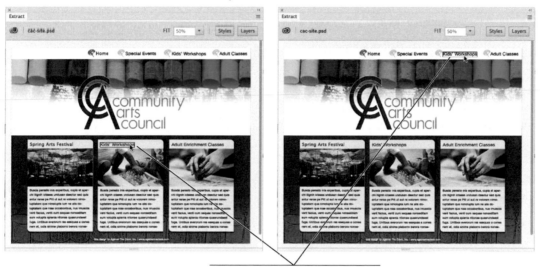

Move the mouse cursor over different
elements to highlight the layer content.

3. **Click the text element in the bottom row of the preview to select it.**

   When you select a specific element in the panel preview, a pop-up window presents options that can be extracted for the selected element.

Click an item to open
a window with extract
options for the
selected layer content.

4. **Click the Copy Text button in the pop-up window.**

5. **In the document window, select and delete the words "Insert Footer Content Here" from the bottom rectangle in the layout.**

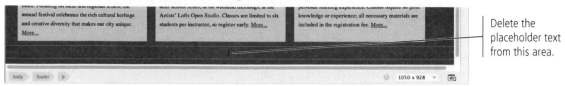

Delete the placeholder text from this area.

6. **With the insertion point in the now-empty paragraph, choose Edit>Paste (or press Command/Control-V).**

Paste the copied text from Step 5 in this area.

7. **Click the Layers button in the top-right corner of the Extract panel.**

These buttons allow you to review all the layers and layer groups that have been saved in the Photoshop file. You can expand layer groups to review the sublayers in those groups, show or hide individual layers, and select specific layers to more easily extract the information they contain.

8. **Click the sketch layer in the list to select it.**

When you select a layer, the available extract options appear in a pop-up window (just as when you selected a specific element in the preview image).

As the preview suggests, this image should be added as the background image for the entire page. Rather than copying the image's dimensions, you are going to extract the image from the Photoshop file into the site's images folder so you can use the image directly in Dreamweaver.

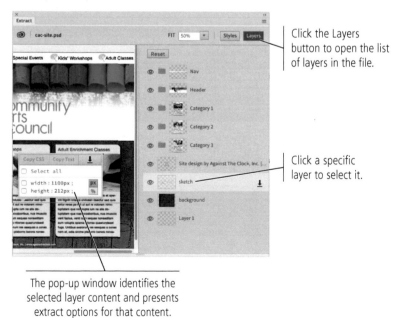

Click the Layers button to open the list of layers in the file.

Click a specific layer to select it.

The pop-up window identifies the selected layer content and presents extract options for that content.

9. **Click the Extract Asset button either on the layer list or on the pop-up window.**

10. **In the resulting pop-up window, click the Browse for Folder button to the right of the Folder field. Navigate to the images folder in your WIP>Council folder, then click Open/Select Folder.**

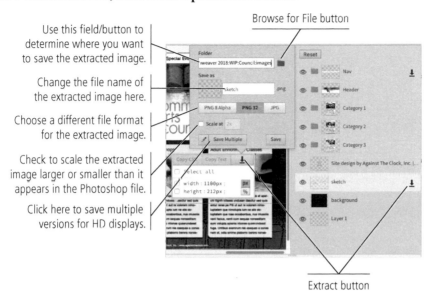

Use this field/button to determine where you want to save the extracted image.

Browse for File button

Change the file name of the extracted image here.

Choose a different file format for the extracted image.

Check to scale the extracted image larger or smaller than it appears in the Photoshop file.

Click here to save multiple versions for HD displays.

Extract button

Note:

You can also drag an image from the Extract panel to the document window. When you release the mouse button, the file is extracted using the default settings and the image is placed at the location to which you drag.

11. **Make sure the PNG 32 button is active, then click Save.**

    This layer is semi-transparent, allowing the background layer color to show through the image pixels. To incorporate that transparency into the extracted image, you must use the PNG 32 format (the default format).

    When the Extract process is complete, you see a message that the asset has downloaded successfully.

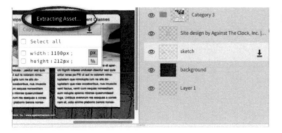
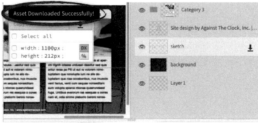

12. **Click the folder icon to the left of the Nav layer to expand that layer.**

    The layer group includes a text layer and an image layer for each navigation link. The "fade" icon should be the default image for each navigation link; the "full" icon should appear when the user's mouse moves over that link. For now you need to extract the required images so you can later use CSS to define the link backgrounds and change the image from "fade" to "full" when the user's mouse cursor moves over a specific link.

Click a folder icon to expand or collapse a layer group and view the sublayers.

13. Repeat Steps 8–11 to extract the palette-full and palette-fade images as PNG 32 files into the site **images** folder.

14. Click the folder icon to collapse the Nav folder, then click the folder icon to expand the Header folder.

15. Click to select the pencils layer, then click the Extract button for that layer.

16. In the resulting pop-up window, click the Browse for Folder button to the right of the Folder field. Navigate to the **images** folder in your WIP>Council folder, then click Open/Select Folder.

Note:

You only need to extract one copy of the palette-fade image from the Photoshop file.

17. Choose the JPG option and set the Optimize slider to 90.

    This image does not require transparency, so you can use the JPG format that allows compression (which can be important for reducing the size of background images.) The Optimize slider defines the quality level of the resulting image; higher values result in better quality but less compression.

18. Click Save to extract the file.

19. In the Files panel, expand the **images** folder. If you don't see the three extracted files, click the Refresh button at the bottom of the panel.

20. Save the HTML file and continue to the next exercise.

FORMAT THE PAGE BODY

In the previous exercise you extracted text from a Photoshop file and placed it into your HTML page. You also extracted images from a Photoshop file, one which you will use in this exercise to define the appearance of the overall page background.

1. **With index.html open and the Live view active, click to select the word "Home" link at the top of the document.**

2. **Review the Tag Selector in the bottom-left corner of the document window.**

   The Tag Selector shows the "path of tags", or the nested order of tags to the active selection.

\<body\>	identifies the basic page, where all visible content is contained
\<nav\>	identifies the HTML nav element
\<ul\>	identifies an unordered list element
\<li\>	identifies a list item element
\<a\>	identifies the selected link element

   It is important to understand the nested nature of tags — especially how that nested structure relates to CSS. A specific elements can be affected by any selector in its path of tags. The **body** element contains all visible elements on the page; the body selector in CSS, then, also affects all visible elements on the page.

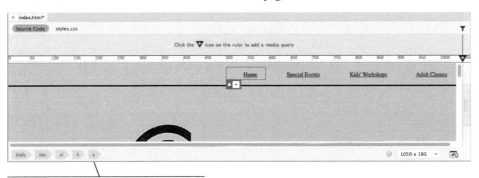

The Tag Selector shows that this a element is nested inside a number of other elements.

3. **Open the CSS Designer panel (Window>CSS Designer).**

   The CSS Designer panel is divided into four sections:

   - **Sources** lists the locations and files containing CSS styles that affect the active site.

   - **@Media** lists media queries, which can be used to define different styles depending on the size of the device being used to display a site.

   - **Selectors** are the items that define the properties of specific elements. If you have an object selected in the Design pane, only selectors related to the active selection appear in the list. When a specific selector is active in the panel, the relevant Source and Media options appear bold in those sections of the panel.

   - **Properties** are the rules that define the specific appearance of the selector for which they are defined.

   You can click and drag the lines between sections in the panel to expand a specific section. Clicking a section heading minimizes that section, so only the heading is visible in the panel; you can click a minimized section heading to re-expand that section. (The + and – buttons on the left side of each section heading are used to add or remove items from the panel; these buttons do not collapse or expand the various section.)

   If you expand the width of the CSS Designer panel far enough, the Properties section moves to the right, creating a second column within the panel.

4. **If necessary, click the All button at the top of the panel.**

The CSS Designer panel defaults to Current mode, in which the panel show only selectors related to the element that is selected in the document window. If you click the All button at the top of the panel, all selectors in the CSS file appear in the Selectors list.

5. **Click the body selector in the Selectors section of the panel.**

For the sake of readability, we identify selector names in red in the exercise steps.

Selectors beginning with a # character are **ID selectors**. These apply only to the element that is identified with the matching **ID attribute**. It is important to realize that an ID can only apply to a single element on the page.

Selectors beginning with a . (period) character are **class selectors**. These apply to any element that has the matching class attribute. A single **class attribute** can be applied to multiple elements on the same page, which means you can define the same properties for various elements at the same time.

Selectors that do not begin with a # or . character are HTML **tag selectors**. These apply to the specific HTML elements that match the selector name. For example, the section selector applies to all section elements on the page, regardless of any applied ID or class attributes. The section element is enclosed in the opening and closing **<section></section>** tags.

The body selector applies to the body element (the overall page background), which is enclosed in the opening and closing **<body></body>** tags. All visible elements are contained within the body element.

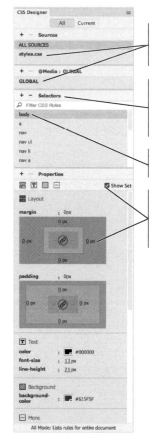

The source and media query of the active selector appear in **bold**.

All selectors related to the active selection in the Design pane are listed in the Selectors section.

The active selector is highlighted in the list.

When Show Set is checked, only defined properties appear in the Properties section.

6. **In the Properties section of the panel, uncheck the Show Set option.**

When the Show Set option is checked in the Properties section of the panel, only defined properties appear in the Properties pane. If this option is not checked, all available properties are listed; properties that appear grayed out are not defined for the active selector.

When Show Set is not checked, the Properties section shows all options that can be defined for the active selector.

7. **With the Photoshop file that you uploaded open in the Extract panel, click the Styles button in the top-right corner of the Extract panel.**

   The Styles list shows all fonts, colors, and gradients that are used in the Photoshop file.

   As you can see, the file uses only one font (HelveticaNeue), although every font size is listed separately. Rather than defining the font of each element separate element in the HTML page, you can define a font for the body element that will apply to every element contained in that body — in other words, everything you can see on the page.

8. **Expand the HelveticaNeue font if necessary, then click the 13px option to show where that type size is used in the design.**

   When you select a specific font size in the list, you see the font-family and font-weight properties that apply to the selected size.

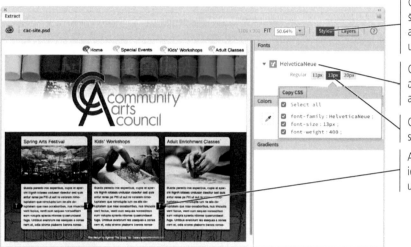

Click the Styles button to show the fonts, colors, and gradients that are used in the Photoshop file.

Click to expand the font and show the sizes that are used in the design.

Click to select a specific font size.

Arrows in the preview identify the elements that use the selected font size.

9. **With the body selector selected in the CSS Designer panel, click the Text button at the top of the Properties section to show those properties in the panel.**

   When Show Set is not checked, the Properties section includes a large number of options that can be defined for the active selector. You can simply scroll through all of the available options, or you can use these buttons to quickly jump to specific categories of properties.

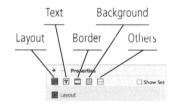

10. **Click the space to the right of the font-family property to open the menu of available font stacks. Choose the option that includes Helvetica Neue and ends with "sans-scrif."**

    A **font stack** (also called a **font family**) is a sequence of fonts that can be used to display content. When a browser opens a page, it goes through the various fonts in the list until it finds one that can be used on the active device. If none of the fonts in the list are available on a user's computer, the text will be displayed in the default font that is defined for the style at the end of the list — in this case, whatever the user chose as the default sans-serif font on the computer being used.

11. **Review the index.html file in the Live view.**

Because every visible element on the page is contained within the HTML **body** element, text in every element now adopts the new font family.

12. **In the Extract panel, click the red swatch in the Colors section of the list, and note the color value in the pop-up window.**

When you select a specific element in the Styles list, arrows in the preview image identify which elements use the selected color. The color definition appears highlighted in a pop-up window.

Click the Styles button to show the fonts, colors and gradients that are used in the Photoshop file.

Click a color swatch to show the color definition.

Arrows in the preview identify the elements that use the selected color.

13. **With the body selector selected in the CSS Designer panel, click the Background button at the top of the Properties section.**

14. **Click the existing background-color value to highlight it, then type rgb(157, 34, 66) — the value you noted in Step 12 — as the new color. Press Return/Enter to finalize the new background-color value.**

You might be able to copy and paste the color value from the pop-up window in Step 12 to the CSS Designer panel in Step 14. However, there is a bug in the software that prevents users on certain operating systems from using the copy-and-paste method.

Click the Background button to jump to those options.

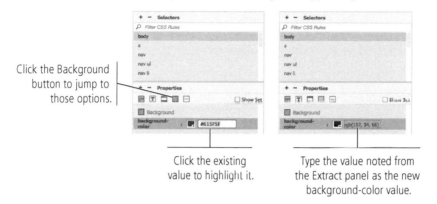

Click the existing value to highlight it.

Type the value noted from the Extract panel as the new background-color value.

After finalizing the new background color, you can see the background color in the bottom half of the page. The top half of the page still appears gray because the **nav** and **header** elements — which are nested inside the body element — in this file have defined background colors.

This is a very important point: CSS selector rules apply until they are overridden by another value. The CSS Designer panel lists selectors in the order they appear in the CSS file. The body selector is first in the list, so it is also first in the CSS file. The nav and header selectors appear after the body selector, so background-color values for those selectors override the background-color value in the body selector.

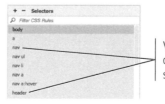

Values in later selectors override values in selectors higher in the list.

15. Look at the top of the document window.

Although you made changes that affect the appearance of the index.html file, the document tab does not show an asterisk — in other words, the HTML document has not been changed. You do not need to save it before continuing.

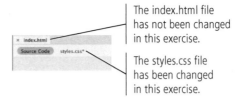

The index.html file has not been changed in this exercise.

The styles.css file has been changed in this exercise.

All changes in this exercise were made to the CSS file that is linked to the open HTML file. The Related Files bar below the document tab shows an asterisk next to styles.css, indicating that the CSS file has been changed and so should be saved.

16. Click styles.css in the Related Files bar, then choose File>Save.

When you click one of the related files in the bar, the document window automatically switches to Split view and the file you clicked is displayed in the Code pane.

Clicking one of the related files opens the Split view and shows relevant code in the Code pane.

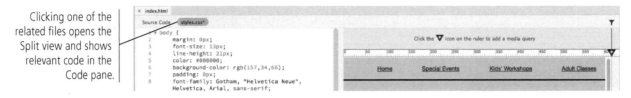

17. Click Source Code in the Related Files bar to return to the main HTML file.

Clicking the Source Code button restores the active page's HTML code to the Code pane.

Clicking Source Code reverts the Code pane to the HTML file's code.

18. Click the Live button in the Document toolbar to close the Code pane, then continue to the next exercise.

FORMAT ELEMENT BACKGROUNDS WITH EXTRACTED STYLES

As you can see in the Extract panel, different elements on the page should have different background properties — white background color, an applied drop shadow, and rounding on various corners. In this exercise you will extract settings from the Photoshop file to properly format the backgrounds of various elements in the page.

1. With index.html open and the Live view active, click the Layers button in the Extract panel to show the list of layers in the uploaded file.

The designer of this file provided meaningful names for the various layers in the file, so you can easily see which layer translates to which element in the HTML page. As a general rule, you should use meaningful names when you define elements in a file — whether layers in a Photoshop file or elements in an HTML file.

2. **Click the folder icon to expand the Nav folder, then click to select the nav-bkg layer.**

When you click the layer in the Extract panel, a pop-up window shows the aspects of this element that you need to apply to the related element in the HTML page. Any properties and styles applied in the Photoshop file that can be translated to CSS are listed in the pop-up window.

Because Photoshop does not incorporate settings that accurately map to element size and positioning, the width and height properties are not checked by default.

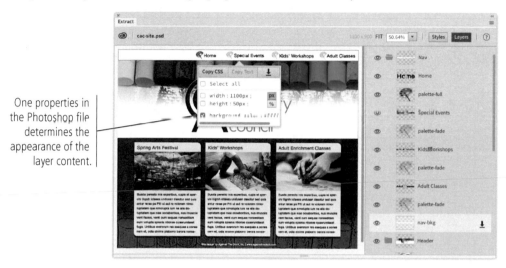

One properties in the Photoshop file determines the appearance of the layer content.

3. **With the background-color property selected in the list, click the Copy CSS button in the top-left corner of the pop-up window.**

4. **In the CSS Designer panel, Control/right-click nav in the Selector list. Choose Paste Styles in the contextual menu for the header element.**

Remember, you want to apply these settings to the header element on the page, so you are pasting the copied properties into the header HTML tag selector in the CSS file.

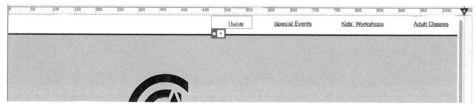

5. **Repeat Step 4 to paste the same copied style into the header selector.**

6. Click in the document window to select the element containing the words "Spring Art Festival."

The Tag Selector and the Element Display show that this text is an h2 element. The Tag selector also shows that it is in a section element that has a defined class attribute (.category).

This h2 element is inside a section element
with the class attribute "category".

7. Click in the document window to select the words "Kids' Workshops" in the middle rectangle of row three.

Again, the Tag Selector shows that this is an h2 element, which is in a section element that has the same defined class attribute as the first section element in the same row.

Each section element in this row has the same class attribute, which means you can change the background properties of all three sections by changing properties in the related class.

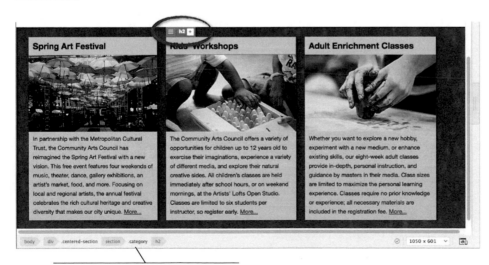

This h2 element is inside a section element
with the class attribute "category".

8. **In the Layers pane of the Extract panel, expand the Category 1 layer group and select the category-bkg sublayer.**

9. **Click the Copy CSS button in the pop-up window for the selected layer.**

10. **Control/right-click the .category selector in the CSS Designer panel and choose Paste Styles in the contextual menu.**

   Because the .category class is applied to all three sections in the row, the pasted properties now apply to all three elements.

11. **Choose File>Save All.**

   This command saves all files that are related to the active site, including the CSS file that you have been editing by defining CSS properties.

12. **Continue to the next exercise.**

DEFINE BACKGROUND IMAGES

The approved layout includes two separate background images — one for the overall page and one for only the area behind the logo. In this exercise you will use the assets you extracted earlier to create the required background images.

Note:

Every element in an HTML file can have distinct background settings.

1. **With index.html open and the Live view active, click to select the body selector in the CSS Designer panel.**

2. **Navigate to the Background options, then click to Browse button to the right of the url option.**

   The CSS Designer panel provides available properties whenever possible. In this case, you have to define a file, so you are presented with a text field and a Browse button, which you can use to define the image you want to use as the background.

   Click the Browse button for the url option.

3. **Navigate to the Arts-Council site images folder, select sketch.png, and click Open/OK.**

   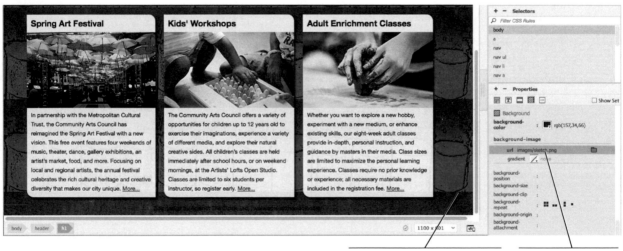

   By default, background images tile both horizontally and vertically.

   The defined value now appears in the panel.

4. **Click the no-repeat button for the background-repeat option.**

   Unless you specify otherwise, a background image will repeat (tile) across and down until the background of the element is completely filled with the background image.

   The CSS **background-repeat** property has four options: repeat (the default), repeat-x (horizontally only), repeat-y (vertically only), and no-repeat (the background image appears only once in the top-left corner of the element).

   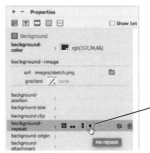

   The background-repeat options are available as buttons.

   Again, the panel provides the available options; the button icons suggest the values that will be defined. If you hover your mouse cursor over a button, a tool tip positively identifies the button.

5. **Click the "%" option for the first background-position value (X), and choose center from the pop-up menu.**

In this case, the panel offers a menu with the available values for this property.

The CSS **background-position** property allows two values: X (horizontal) position and Y (vertical) position. The panel lists both on the same line, X then Y.

You can define positions relative to the containing element (left, right, etc.) or use specific measurements such as "5 pixels" to position a background image.

Remember, these properties define the horizontal (X) and vertical (Y) positions of the background image *relative to the containing element*.

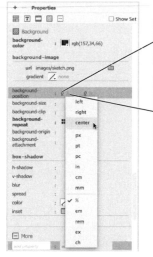

Click the number and type to define a specific numeric value.

Click the measurement to open a menu to change the active unit of measurement or to choose a fixed position relative to the document.

6. **Click the "%" option for the second background-position value (Y), and choose bottom from the pop-up menu.**

You can now see that the background image is attached to the bottom of the file, and does not repeat.

Depending on your monitor width, however, you might notice that the image is only 1100 px wide; if your document window is large enough, you can see that the background image might not extend the entire width of the page.

The background image is only 1100 pixels wide at the default setting.

7. **With the body selector active in the CSS Designer panel, click the background-size value and choose contain from the pop-up menu.**

The **background-size** property defines the size of background images.

- If you do not define a specific background size, the image will simply display at its actual size. The same result can be achieved using the **auto** value.

- You can define a specific value using a variety of measurement units. You can also use two values to define both the width and height.

   background-size: 400px 600px [width height]

   Instead of specific values, you can use percentages. In this case, the background image appears as a percentage of the container.

   background-size: 80% 100% [width height]

- The **cover** value scales the background image as large as necessary completely fill the container. If the image has a different aspect ratio than the container, some parts of the background image will be cut off.

- The **contain** value scales the image to the largest possible size so that the entire image fills the container. If the image has a different aspect ratio than the container, some areas of the container will not be filled by the background image unless you tile it.

In this case, the contain value scales the image so that it fills the width of the document window, regardless of the required scaling.

8. **In the document window, click to select the logo in the middle of the page.**

The second background image needs to appear only in the area behind the logo. The Tag Selector shows that this image is placed in the h1 element, which is nested inside the header element.

9. **In the CSS Designer panel, click to select the header selector. In the properties section of the panel, move the mouse cursor over the background-color property.**

When the cursor moves over a specific property, two icons appear to the right of the defined value. You can click the Disable CSS Property icon to disable the property (the code stays in the CSS file, but is disabled using comments), or click the Remove CSS Property icon to permanently delete the property's code from the selector.

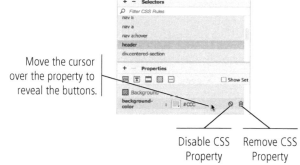

Move the cursor over the property to reveal the buttons.

Disable CSS Property   Remove CSS Property

10. **Click the Remove CSS Property button for the background-color selector.**

Now that the header selector has no defined background color, you can see the background image of the body selector in the header area.

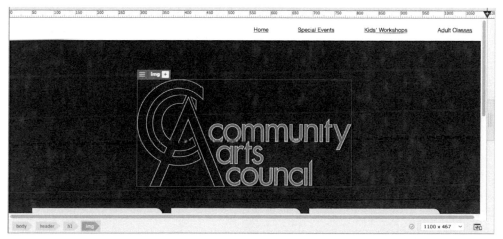

11. Using the CSS Designer panel, define **pencils.jpg** as the background image for the header selector, using the following rules:

> **background-size:** cover
>
> **background-repeat:** none

The header element has a fixed height, but it can be narrower or wider depending on the size of the document window. Using the cover value for the **background-size** property, the image will enlarge or shrink to fill the available window width.

12. Choose File>Save All, then continue to the next exercise.

FORMAT TEXT WITH EXTRACTED STYLES

The site design is nearly complete, but you still need to adjust a number of text elements based on what you see in the approved Photoshop file. In this exercise you will define properties for the h2 and footer elements to match what you see in the Extract panel.

1. With **index.html** open, make sure the Photoshop file you uploaded is open in the Extract panel.

2. In the Extract panel, click the "Spring Arts Festival" text to reveal the CSS for that element.

3. **In the pop-up window, uncheck the font-family property, then click the Copy CSS button.**

You already adjusted the body selector to format all text in the page with the Helvetica Neue font family, so you don't need to include this property in the nested elements.

Uncheck the
font-family property.

4. **Click the "Spring Art Festival" text in the document window to select that element.**

5. **Click the Current button at the top of the CSS Designer panel.**

When Current mode is active, the Selectors list shows only selectors that relate to the active element (what is selected in the document window). This is very useful for finding only and exactly what you need, especially if you are working with a large list of selectors.

Current mode is active.

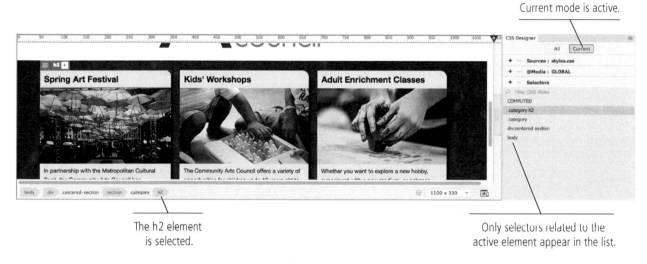

The h2 element
is selected.

Only selectors related to the
active element appear in the list.

6. **Control/right-click the .category h2 selector in the CSS Designer panel and choose Paste Styles in the contextual menu.**

The styles you copied in Step 3 (color, font-size, and font-weight) are pasted into the .category h2 selector. Because all three of the sections use the .category class, the h2 elements in each section now show the pasted formatting.

7. **Repeat the process from Steps 2–6 to change the formatting of the footer p selector to match what you see in the Extract panel.**

   Again, you do not need to copy the font-family property.

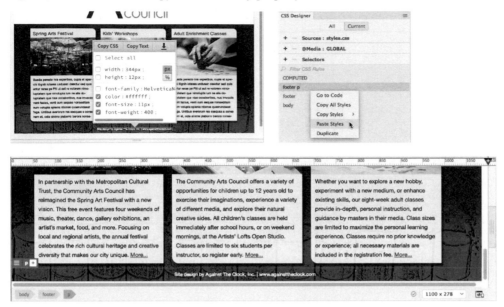

8. **Choose File>Save All, then continue to the next exercise.**

FORMAT LINKS WITH DESCENDENT SELECTORS

The final required tasks for this project involve formatting links in various areas of the page. In this exercise you will work with **descendant selectors** (also called **compound selectors**) which allow you to define properties that affect very specific elements.

1. **With index.html open, review the various links on the page.**

   Two different areas include links: navigation links in the nav element and "More..." links in the category sections.

These links should appear in black, with no underline.

These links should appear bold, using in the logo color, with no underline.

2. In the Extract panel, click the "Adult Classes" text to show the CSS for that element. Uncheck the font-family property, then click the Copy CSS button.

3. In the Design view, click to select the "Adult Classes" text. In the CSS Designer panel, Control/right-click the a selector and choose Paste Styles.

The **a** selector affects all links on the page, so all links now show the pasted properties.

All links now show the adjusted color, font-size, and font-weight properties.

4. In the Properties section of the panel, uncheck the Show Set option (if necessary) and then click the Text button to scroll to those properties.

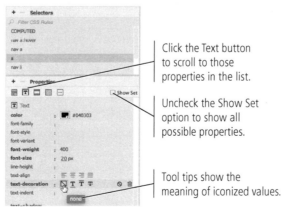

Click the Text button to scroll to those properties in the list.

Uncheck the Show Set option to show all possible properties.

Tool tips show the meaning of iconized values.

5. **Locate the text-decoration property and click the none button.**

Because this selector applies to all links in the page, the links in the nav element and the three category sections are no longer underlined.

The underline property has been removed from all links on the page.

6. **Click to select the word "More" in one of the category sections.**

In Current mode, the CSS Designer panel shows two **a** selectors that affect the selected element: the basic **a** selector and the **.category p a** selector.

You already saw that changes to the basic **a** selector affected the links in the category sections — in this case, making the text in these links too large for their context.

The **.category p a** selector is called a **compound selector** or **descendant selector**. It applies only to links (using the <a> tags) which are in paragraph elements (using the <p> tags) in an element that uses the "category" class. Links in other elements are not affected by the properties in this selector, so you can use this selector to adjust the size and color of only links in these sections.

7. **With the .category p a selector selected in the CSS Designer panel, navigate to the Text formatting options in the Properties section of the panel.**

8. **Click the empty space to the right of the font-size property and choose px from the menu. Type 13 in the resulting field, then press Return/Enter to finalize the change.**

9. **Open the font-weight menu and choose bold.**

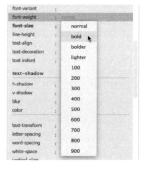

10. **Click the swatch for the color property to open the color picker.**

    The **background-color** property affects the background of an element. The **color** property affects the color of text in the element.

11. **Choose the Eyedropper tool in the bottom-right corner of the color picker.**

12. **Move the mouse cursor over the red background color (above the background image), then click to sample that color as the new color.**

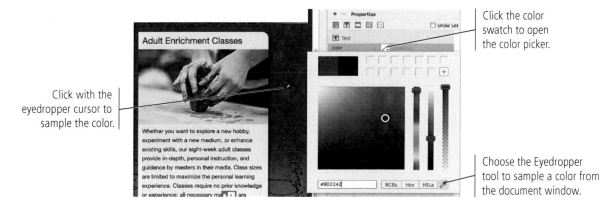

Click with the eyedropper cursor to sample the color.

Click the color swatch to open the color picker.

Choose the Eyedropper tool to sample a color from the document window.

13. Press Return/Enter to finalize the new color for all links on the page.

Because you edited the compound selector, the changes in Steps 7–12 only affect links in the .category sections; other links on the page are not affected.

14. Choose File>Save All, then continue to the next exercise.

Understanding Hexadecimal Color Codes

The RGB color model describes colors using values for red, green, and blue respectively. Each color can be assigned a value from 0 (none of that color) to 255 (full strength of that color), for a range of 256 values.

Black has zero values for all three colors, so it is represented as 0, 0, 0. White has full values for all three colors, so it is represented as 255, 255, 255. The hexadecimal system is a numeric system that uses 16 numerals from 0–9 plus A–F (11 is represented by A, 12 by B, up to 15 by F). Since 256 = 16 × 16, in hexadecimal code, 256 = F × F.

The range of 256 values for each color is from 0 to FF (by convention, the first 16 values from 0 to F are given a leading zero: 00 to 0F). Since RGB requires a value for each of the three colors, you will see hexadecimal color values such as #EE04F3, #40896C, and #E843A0.

When both digits for a particular color value are the same, you can abbreviate the code to only three digits. For example, the full code for black is #000000, but it can be abbreviated to #000.

In web design, the hexadecimal color code must be preceded by the "#" sign (called the hash, pound, or octothorpe character). By convention, the letters should be uppercase, but neither Dreamweaver nor browsers differentiate between #EE04F3, #ee04f3, or #eE04f3.

DEFINE BACKGROUND IMAGES FOR NAVIGATION LINK STATES

As you saw in a previous exercise, one advantage of CSS is that you can define different background properties for every identified element. In this exercise, you will use this capability to create a background image for each link in the nav element, and change that background image based on the position of the user's mouse cursor.

1. **In the open index.html file, click to select any of the links in the nav element.**

2. **In the CSS Designer panel, select the nav a compound selector.**

3. **In the Background category of properties, define palette-fade.png (from the main site images folder) as the background image url.**

    As we explained earlier, a background image repeats (tiles) across and down until the background of the element unless you specify otherwise. Each link in the nav element shows the background image tiled down and across, originating in the top-right corner.

Click to jump to the Background options.

4. **Choose no-repeat for the background-repeat property.**

5. **Choose right in the background-position (X) menu, and choose center in the background-position (Y) menu.**

    Remember, you have to click the "%" option for the background-position value to open the pop-up menu.

6. **Select the nav a:hover selector in the CSS Designer panel. In the Text properties, open the Color Picker and then use the Eyedropper cursor to change the color property to the red background color.**

    The **:hover** pseudo-class selector defines the **mouseover state** for a particular link, which determines what happens when the user moves the mouse cursor over the link.

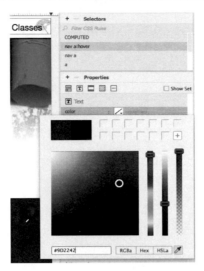

7. **In the Background properties, define the following settings:**

url:	**images/palette-full.png**
background-repeat:	**no-repeat**
X background-position:	**right**
Y background-position:	**center**

8. **With the Live view active, move your mouse cursor over the navigation links to test the hover effect.**

    The **:hover** pseudo-class is a dynamic effect that Dreamweaver's Design pane cannot display unless the Live view is active.

As you move your mouse cursor over a link, the :hover pseudo-class is activated.

9. **Save all files, then close index.html.**

10. **Export a site definition named Arts-Council.ste into your WIP>Council folder, and then remove the Arts-Council site from Dreamweaver.**

    If necessary, refer back to Project 1: Bistro Site Organization for complete instructions on exporting a site definition or removing a site from Dreamweaver.

1. The _____ attribute of the <img> tag is required to make images accessible for all web users.

2. The _____ attribute defines the specific file that will appear in the <img> tag location.

3. The _____ property of CSS can be used to tile a single background image horizontally, vertically, or both throughout the entire document window.

4. _____ is the process of cutting out/off portions of an image.

5. The _____ format supports continuous-tone color but not transparency; it is best used for photographs.

6. The _____ format supports index transparency but not a large gamut of color; it is best used for graphics and artwork.

7. In CSS, a(n) _____ selector defines the appearance of specific HTML tags such as <body> or <header>.

8. In CSS, a(n) _____ selector begins with a # character and defines the appearance of the one element on the page that has the matching attribute.

9. In CSS, a(n) _____ selector begins with a . character and defines the appearance of all elements on the page that have been identified with the matching attribute.

10. In CSS, a(n) _____ selector defines the appearance of specific elements within other specific elements on the page, such as nav a.

1. Briefly describe three image file formats that might be used on the web, including advantages and disadvantages of each.

2. Briefly explain the importance of resampling, relative to resizing images in Dreamweaver.

3. Briefly explain the advantages to using CSS to define background colors and images.

Portfolio Builder Project

Use what you learned in this project to complete the following freeform exercise.
Carefully read the art director and client comments, then create your own design to meet the needs of the project.
Use the space below to sketch ideas; when finished, write a brief explanation of your reasoning behind your final design.

art director comments

You have been hired by the National Aeronautics and Space Administration (NASA) to design a new home page as the entry point to a site that presents general information of interest to the public at large.

To complete this project, you should:

❏ Use the same basic layout structure that you used in this project to create the new NASAview site home page.

❏ Find or create a logo treatment for the new site. Include that logo on every page in the site.

❏ Find or create icons to use as the "hover" treatment for links in the navigation area.

❏ Identify and download images you want to use from the NASA on the Commons web page (https://www.flickr.com/photos/nasacommons).

client comments

We want to create a new website called NASAview, which should be a simple, easy-to-navigate site that includes only the most common things that the general public finds of interest.

The main page should eventually include links to secondary pages for each of the three site categories:

• About NASA

• History of U.S. Space Travel

• Upcoming Events and Exhibits

We haven't written the text content yet, so just use placeholder text for the headings and body copy.

NASA images generally are not copyrighted, although we occasionally use copyrighted material by permission. Those images are marked copyright with the name of the copyright holder; please don't use those images in the new site design.

project justification

_____
_____
_____
_____
_____
_____
_____
_____
_____
_____
_____
_____
_____
_____

When you prepare the design for a site, you need to determine which images will carry content (they must be placed in the foreground using the **<img>** tag), and which images will appear in the background. Appropriate alt text — which enables visually impaired visitors, users who have disabled the display of images, and search engines to use the content of your pages — is required for all foreground images.

Dreamweaver also provides image-editing tools that enable you to crop, resize, resample, and sharpen images. Although these tools do not replace full-featured image-editing applications such as Photoshop, the Dreamweaver tools enable you to complete simple editing tasks quickly and easily, without requiring another application.

The Extract utility, available to individual-user Creative Cloud subscriptions, provides an easy interface for translating Photoshop page comps into functional HTML and CSS code. By editing various CSS properties, you have virtually unlimited options for controlling the appearance of different sections of a page.

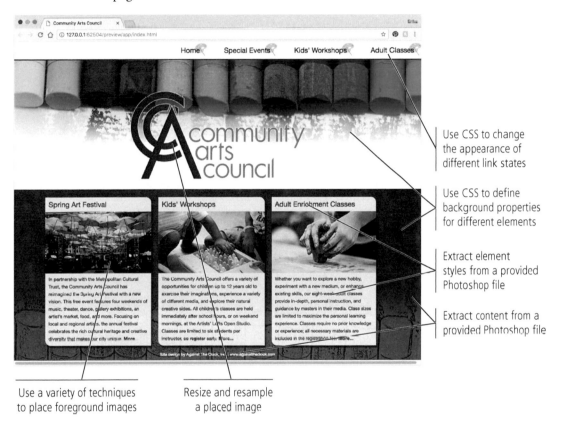

Use CSS to change the appearance of different link states

Use CSS to define background properties for different elements

Extract element styles from a provided Photoshop file

Extract content from a provided Photoshop file

Use a variety of techniques to place foreground images

Resize and resample a placed image

Museum CSS Layout

The Getty Foundation hired you to build a new website to provide area visitors with information about the various art collections being displayed at their facilities. The client wants a website that can be quickly and easily updated and modified. In addition, the site should project a consistent look and style across all pages. To fulfill these requirements, you will create (CSS) and apply a cascading style sheet for the website.

This project incorporates the following skills:

❏ Creating and linking an external CSS file

❏ Understanding the CSS box model

❏ Creating a layout with HTML elements

❏ Working with templates to improve workflow and maintain consistency

❏ Editing CSS rules to adjust the page layout

❏ Defining HTML tag selectors, ID selectors, and compound selectors to control the appearance of page content

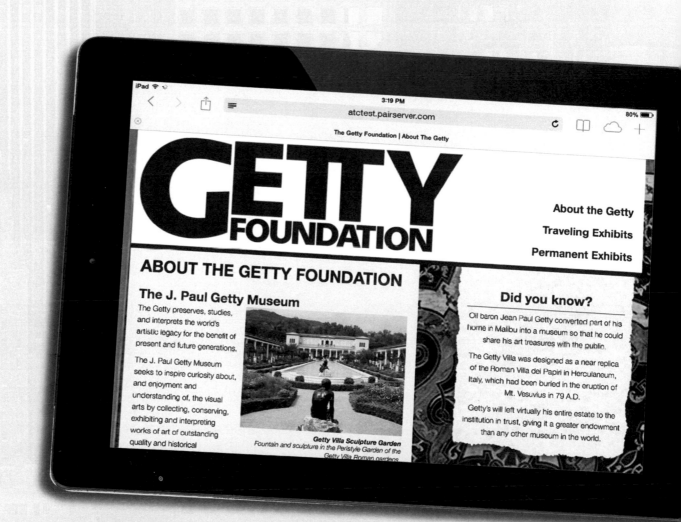

client comments

We want to create a new website to provide a brief description of permanent and traveling exhibits at our museums.

We have a site already, but we can't figure out how it was built, so it's extremely difficult to change even a comma. We called the site designer, but he can't work us into his schedule for more than a month — and we don't have the time to wait.

The new site should be very easy to manage and, more importantly, easy to change — whether it's a comma or the entire site layout.

art director comments

When a site is properly designed, the HTML file stores the page content, while the cascading style sheet (CSS) file defines the appearance of page elements. This makes it easier to find and change content, since the HTML code isn't cluttered with formatting instructions.

You're also going to use template files, which are an excellent tool for maintaining consistency across multiple pages of a site. The template defines the overall page structure, including common elements such as navigation links and editable areas where content varies from one page to another. If you make changes to common elements in the template file, those changes automatically appear in pages where the template is applied.

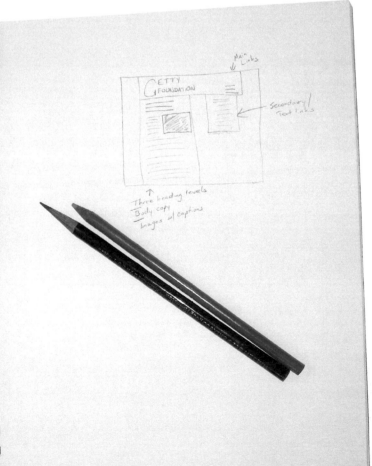

project objectives

To complete this project, you will:

- ❑ Create and link an external CSS file
- ❑ Create ID selectors
- ❑ Create a layout with HTML elements and CSS selectors
- ❑ Use the float property to control nested elements
- ❑ Use margins and padding to affect element placement
- ❑ Define properties for the body tag
- ❑ Create a template file
- ❑ Define named anchors
- ❑ Create figure tags to contain images and captions
- ❑ Define HTML tag selectors
- ❑ Create compound tag selectors
- ❑ Create pseudo-class selectors

Stage 1 Creating Layouts with Style Sheets

A **cascading style sheet** (CSS) is a collection of formatting rules that controls the appearance of different elements in a web page. Formatting instructions are stored in **rules**, which consist of two parts: a **selector** (basically, naming the element to be formatted) and **attributes** (such as font, color, width, height, etc.) that will be applied to the selected element.

The following example shows the proper syntax for a CSS rule; **p** is the selector, **font-size** is the attribute, and **14px** is the attribute value:

```
p {
    font-size: 14px;
}
```

There are three types of styles: inline, embedded (or internal), and external. To make the best use of styles, you should have a clear understanding of these different types — including when each is best suited to a specific goal.

An **inline style** applies directly and instantly to an individual element within a tag, affecting only that single element of the HTML page. For example, if you apply a font size and color to a paragraph, the inline style looks like this:

<p style="font-size: 10px; color: blue">Paragraph content goes here.</p>

An **embedded or internal style sheet** is added directly in an HTML page, within style tags; this type of style affects only the particular HTML page in which it is placed. The following code for an embedded style sheet includes a style that defines the formatting of all h1 elements:

```
<style type="text/css"
<!--
h1 {
    font-size: 24px;
}
-->
</style>
```

Note:

The set of <!-- and --> tags prevents a few older browsers from displaying the style rules.

An **external style sheet** is saved as a separate file (with the extension ".css"). HTML files include links to the external CSS files, which are uploaded to the web server along with the website pages. External CSS files offer several advantages:

- A single CSS file can be attached to multiple HTML pages at one time, applying the same rules to elements in different pages. Changes to the styles affect all HTML pages that are linked to that CSS file, which makes it easier to maintain consistency across all pages in a site.

- Different types of styles can control the appearance of general HTML elements; specific individual elements that are identified with a unique ID attribute; all elements that are identified with a specific class attribute; and even elements only within a certain area of a page.

- External styles separate page formatting (CSS) from structure and content (HTML). This helps to reduce file size and server processing time, as well as making it easier for designers and coders to more easily find exactly what they are looking for.

In this exercise, you will import the client's provided files, then create the HTML and CSS files that you need to complete the project.

1. Download **Museum_DW18_RF.zip** from the Student Files web page.

2. Expand the ZIP archive in your WIP folder (Macintosh) or copy the archive contents into your WIP folder (Windows).

   This results in a folder named **Museum**, which contains the files you need for this project.

3. Create a new site named **Museum**, using the WIP>Museum folder as the site root folder.

4. With the Museum site open in the Files panel, choose File>New. Using the New Document dialog box, create a new, blank HTML5 page.

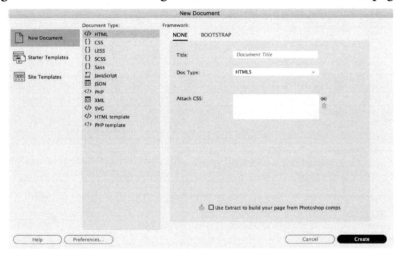

5. Choose File>Save. Save the new page as an HTML file named **design.html** in the root folder of the Museum site.

6. With **design.html** open, open the CSS Designer panel. Make sure the All button is active at the top of the panel.

7. **In the Sources section of the panel, click the Add CSS Source button and choose Create a New CSS File.**

   You can also create a new CSS file in the New Document dialog box. Simply choose CSS in the Document Type window and click Create.

Add CSS Source button

8. **In the resulting dialog box, type museum-styles.css in the File/URL field.**

   The name you define will be used for the new CSS file that is created. By default, the CSS file is placed in the root folder of the active site; you can click the Browse button if you want to create the file in another location.

9. **With the Link option selected, click OK to create the new CSS file.**

   museum-styles.css is now related to design.html.

   museum-styles.css is added to the site folder.

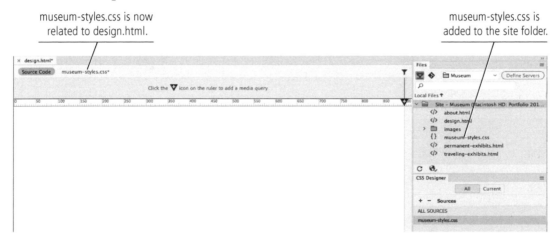

10. **Click the Split button in the Document toolbar, and review the page source code.**

    Using the Link option, the CSS file is connected to the HTML page using the **<link>** tag in the HTML page's header information. When a user opens the HTML page, the browser merges the instructions in the linked CSS file with the information in the HTML file to present the final page design.

    The <link> tag attaches the museum-styles.css file to the HTML file.

11. **Choose File>Save All, then continue to the next exercise.**

    The Save All command saves any open HTML page, as well as any linked files such as the CSS file that you created in this exercise.

DEFINE A NEW ELEMENT AND TAG SELECTOR

HTML includes a large number of elements that are specifically designed to create common page elements — headers (usually) at the top of the page, footers at the bottom, navigation (nav) areas with lists of links, and so on. In this and the next exercise, you are going to use several of these elements to create the basic page structure for the museum's website.

1. **With design.html open, make sure the Split view is active and the Live view is turned off.**

   You are going to work in the regular Design view in this exercise. In later exercises, you will use other methods in the Live view to add elements to the page.

2. **Click the Header button in the HTML Insert panel.**

3. **In the resulting dialog box, click the New CSS Rule button.**

   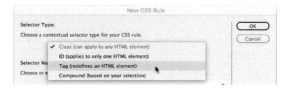

4. **Choose Tag in the Selector Type menu.**

   In the New CSS Rule dialog box, you can define the type and name of a selector, as well as where to create the rule (in the attached external CSS file or embedded in the active HTML file).

   A tag selector applies to all elements using that tag, such as every paragraph that is structured with <p> tags.

5. **Choose header in the Selector Name menu.**

   When you choose Tag in the Selector Type menu, the Selector Name menu includes a large number of available HTML tags. You can open the menu and choose the tag you want, or simply type the tag name in the field.

   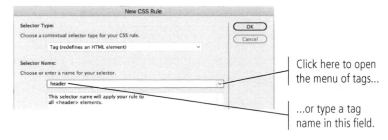

   Click here to open the menu of tags...

   ...or type a tag name in this field.

5. **In the Rule Definition menu (at the bottom of the dialog box), choose museum-styles.css.**

If you choose This Document Only, the resulting CSS style will be created in the active HTML file's header information; the style will not be available for other files in the site.

Because you want to use these styles in multiple files, it is best to place them in the separate CSS file and link each HTML file to that file.

6. **Click OK to open the CSS Rule Definition dialog box.**

This dialog box includes nine categories of options. Many properties that can be saved in a CSS rule are available in the various panes of this dialog box.

7. **Click Background in the Category list. Type #FFF in the Background-color field, or click the related swatch and use the pop-up color picker to define white as the background color.**

Click a category to view the related options.

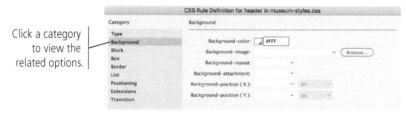

8. **Click Box in the Category list. Type 930 in the Width field, and make sure px (pixels) is selected in the related menu.**

If you do not define a specific width or height, elements fill the containing element horizontally; their height expands automatically as content is added.

9. **In the Padding area, leave the Same for All option checked. Type 10 in the Top field, and make sure px is selected in the related menu.**

10. **In the Margin area, uncheck the Same for All check box. Type 0 in the Top and Bottom fields, and make sure px is selected in the related menus.**

11. **Type auto in the Left and Right fields.**

The **auto** value allows the element to be centered within its parent container (in this case, the body element of the HTML page).

12. Click OK to return to the Insert Header dialog box.

13. Make sure At Insertion Point is selected in the Insert menu, then click OK to return to the HTML page.

Different options are available in this menu depending on what is selected in the document. Because nothing exists in the file yet, the insertion point is assumed to be placed at the beginning of the document body — that is where the new element will be added.

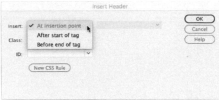

After clicking OK, the new element is automatically added to the page; placeholder content is added inside the element. The top edge is slightly indented because Dreamweaver automatically adds several pixels of padding around the content of a new page. (Some browsers do the same.)

In the document tab, an asterisk indicates that the HTML file has been edited. In the Related Files bar, an asterisk indicates that the museum-styles.css file has been edited.

In the CSS Designer panel, the Selectors section shows the new header selector.

14. Review the page code in the Code pane.

Adding elements adds to the page's HTML code. Those elements, however, are very short — they simply identify each element and add some placeholder content. In the page code, there is no mention of background images, borders, or other attributes that make up the page layout. Those attributes are controlled by editing the selectors applied to each element within the CSS file.

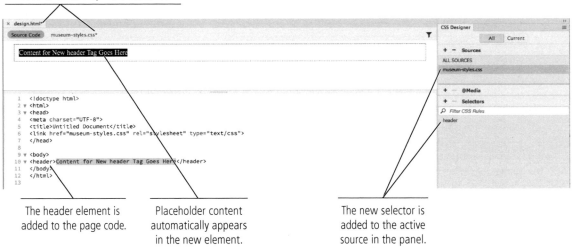

The asterisks tell you the files have been modified since they were last saved.

The header element is added to the page code.

Placeholder content automatically appears in the new element.

The new selector is added to the active source in the panel.

15. In the Design pane, click the edge of the header element to select it.

When an element is selected in the regular Design view, you can see various aspects of the CSS box model in the design pane. If you don't see the margin area, make sure CSS Layout Box Model is toggled on in the View>Design View Options>Visual Aids menu.

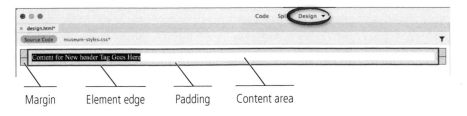

Margin   Element edge   Padding   Content area

16. **In the Related Files bar, click museum-styles.css to show that file in the Code pane.**

Clicking the CSS file name in the Related Files bar automatically switches the document window to Split mode if the Code pane is not already visible; the CSS file code is displayed in the Code pane.

You can now see the code for the new rule you defined. Properties and values for the selector are contained within curly brackets; each property is separated by a semicolon.

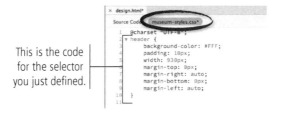

This is the code for the selector you just defined.

17. **Choose File>Save All, then continue to the next exercise.**

DRAG AND DROP TO CREATE NEW ELEMENTS

Dreamweaver's Live view enables a drag-and-drop method of adding elements to a page. On-screen prompts allow you to define exactly where you want elements to exist, making it easy to create the proper code using only visual tools. In this exercise you use the Live view to add a footer element, then define the CSS for that element separately.

1. **With design.html open, show the page source code in the Code pane and turn on the Live view.**

2. **Click the footer button in the HTML Insert panel and drag onto the Live view.**

3. **When a green line appears below the header element, release the mouse button.**

When you drag to add elements in the Live view, visual indicators identify where the new elements will be added in relation to existing elements. A thin blue line highlights the active element, and the green double-headed arrow determines whether the new element will be added above or below the highlighted element.

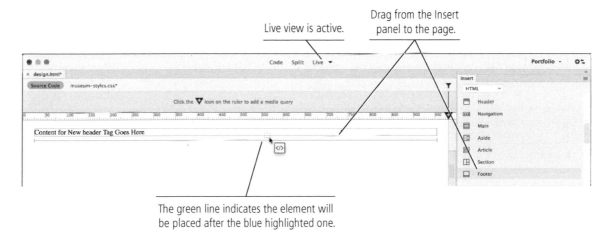

Live view is active.

Drag from the Insert panel to the page.

The green line indicates the element will be placed after the blue highlighted one.

When you release the mouse button, the new footer element appears in the Design pane after the previously selected header element. The box model that you saw in the regular Design view does not appear when the Live view is active; only the element boundary is visible as a thin blue line when the element is selected.

4. **Make sure the CSS Designer panel is displaying the All mode.**

   Current mode must be turned off to add new selectors using the panel.

5. **In the CSS Designer panel, click to select museum-styles.css in the Sources section.**

6. **Click the Add Selector button in the Selectors section of the panel.**

   Clicking this button automatically creates a descendant selector, with the entire path to the currently selected element. In this case, the new footer element is inside the body element (i.e., the body element is the immediate parent of the footer element), so "body footer" is the default selector name.

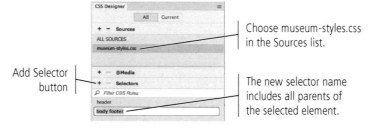

Choose museum-styles.css in the Sources list.

Add Selector button

The new selector name includes all parents of the selected element.

   This type of descendant selector allows you to define different settings for the same type of element in different areas of the page. Since you will only use one footer element in the client's design, the parent is not necessary in this selector name.

7. **Press the Up Arrow key once to remove the parent ("body") from the selector name, then press Return/Enter to finalize the new name.**

   Depending on the active selection, the selector name might have more than one parent in the path to the active tag. Each time you press the Up Arrow key, the first parent in the list is removed.

Note:

You can also press the Down Arrow key to add the parents back into the selector name.

8. **In the Properties section of the panel, show the Layout properties and make sure the Show Set option is not checked.**

9. **Double-click the width value to highlight the field. Type 100%, then press Return/Enter to finalize the new value.**

When you type values for a CSS selector, do not include a space between the value and the unit of measurement.

If you use percentage as the width measurement, you are defining the element's width as a percentage of the width of its parent container. In this case, the footer element will occupy the same horizontal width as the overall page (the body element).

Click to jump to Layout properties.

Double-click a value to access the field.

Press Return/Enter to finalize the new value.

10. **Define 10px top and bottom margins.**

11. **Show the Text properties in the CSS Designer panel. Locate the text-align property and choose the center value.**

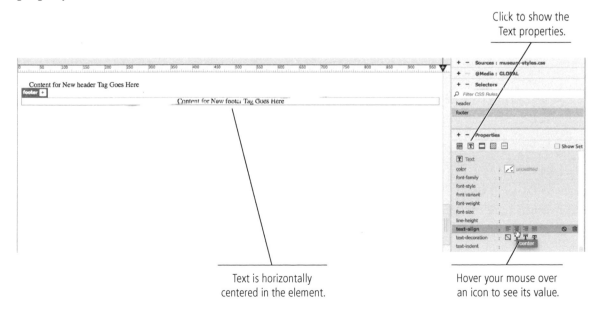

Click to show the Text properties.

Text is horizontally centered in the element.

Hover your mouse over an icon to see its value.

12. **Choose File>Save All, then continue to the next exercise.**

DEFINE A SELECTOR WITH AN ID ATTRIBUTE

Elements such as the ones you already added are the basic building blocks of an HTML page. You can use ID attributes to differentiate elements of the same type, which allows you to define different properties for different same-type elements. In this exercise, you define and identify a div element, then create a CSS selector that applies to only that unique element.

1. **With design.html open and the Live view active, click the div button in the HTML Insert panel and drag onto the Live view.**

   A **<div>** tag is simply a container, identifying a division or area of a page. Although the HTML5 elements such as header and section have largely replaced the div element in modern design, you can (and will) still find uses for a non-specific container. In this case, you are creating a div element simply as a parent container for the two main content areas of the page (which you will create later).

2. **When a green line appears between the two existing elements, release the mouse button.**

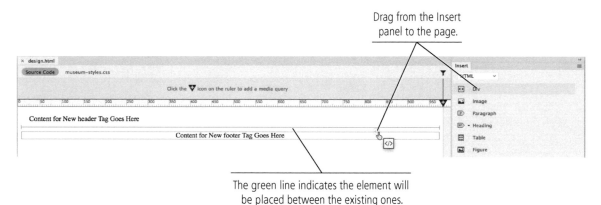

Drag from the Insert panel to the page.

The green line indicates the element will be placed between the existing ones.

3. **With the new div selected in the Design pane, click the + button in the Element Display.**

   The div element is a fairly generic container. If you define CSS for the basic div tag, your changes would affect every div element on the page. Instead, you are going to assign this element a unique ID attribute to better identify it in the page and CSS code.

Note:

Each element on a page can have a different identity (defined using the ID attribute), and each ID can be used only once on a page.

Click the + button to open the Class/ID field.

4. **In the resulting field, type #page-content, then press Return/Enter.**

   ID selectors always begin with a # character; make sure you type it in the field when you assign the new ID attribute.

Note:

CSS Selector names are case-sensitive.

Type an ID or class attribute in the field.

5. **Make sure museum-styles.css is selected in the resulting Select a Source menu, then press Return/Enter.**

Dreamweaver recognizes that a CSS selector does not yet exist for this ID, so it will create one for you. You are asked to determine where the new selector should be saved.

Choose where to save
the new selector.

6. **In the CSS Designer panel, click to select the new #page-content selector.**

7. **At the top of the Properties section, make sure the Show Set option is <u>not</u> checked.**

8. **Click the Layout button to jump to those properties in the panel.**

9. **Double-click the width property value to access the field, then type 950px as the new value.**

10. **In the Margin settings, make sure the Lock icon is not active, then define the following margins:**

Top:	**0px**
Left:	**auto**
Bottom:	**0px**
Right:	**auto**

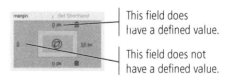

The lock is not active.   The lock is active.

When the Lock icon is active, all four fields are connected and have the same value; changing any one of the values applies the same setting to the other three. If you want to define different values for different sides, you have to turn off the lock option.

Remember, setting the right and left margins to auto centers the element horizontally in its parent container.

When no setting has been defined for a property that has a numeric value, the fields in the CSS Designer panel appear to show "0" (zero). However, you have to actually highlight the field and press Return/Enter to intentionally define the 0px value for that property. If a "0" value does not show a unit of measurement, it has not been defined for the active selector.

This field does have a defined value.

This field does not have a defined value.

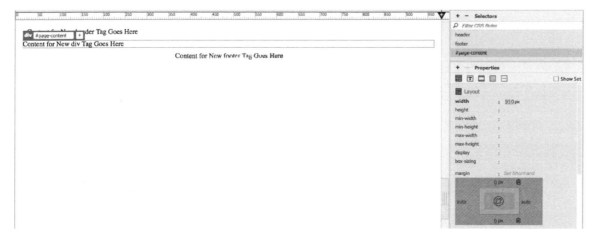

11. **At the top of the Properties section, click the Border button to jump to those properties in the panel.**

12. **Click the Top tab to define border options for only the top edge.**

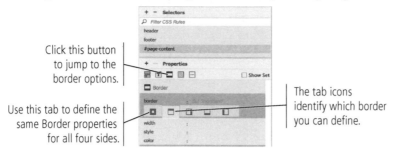

Click this button to jump to the border options.

Use this tab to define the same Border properties for all four sides.

The tab icons identify which border you can define.

13. **Define the border-top width property as 8 px.**

The width menu here functions in the same way as the width menu that you used to define the box width: click the value and choose px from the menu, then type the value in the resulting field.

14. **Open the style menu and choose solid.**

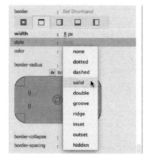

15. **Click the color swatch to open the Color picker. Type #54210F in the hexadecimal value field, then press Return/Enter to finalize the new border color.**

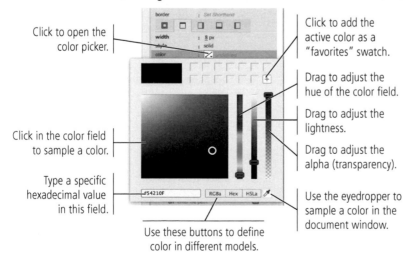

Click to open the color picker.

Click in the color field to sample a color.

Type a specific hexadecimal value in this field.

Use these buttons to define color in different models.

Click to add the active color as a "favorites" swatch.

Drag to adjust the hue of the color field.

Drag to adjust the lightness.

Drag to adjust the alpha (transparency).

Use the eyedropper to sample a color in the document window.

16. **Show the museum-styles.css file in the Code pane.**

All three defined options for the border-top property (width, style, color) are combined into a single property statement.

The border properties are combined in a single line.

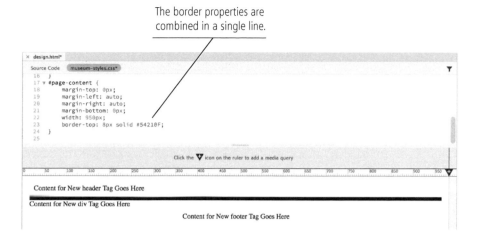

17. **Choose File>Save All, then continue to the next exercise.**

Understanding CSS Shorthand

In many cases, you will define more than one value for the same CSS property. In the previous exercise, for example, you defined the width, style, and color of the border-top property. In the Code pane, you can see that all three values are combined into a single CSS statement:

    border-top: 8px solid #54210F;

This type of combining properties into a single line is referred to as **shorthand**. Without shorthand, you would require three separate lines in the selector:

    border-top-width: 8px;

    border-top-style: solid;

    border-top-color: #54210F;

Combining the three properties into a single line saves space and makes the overall CSS code less complex.

The CSS Designer panel includes a number of Set Shorthand fields that allow you to define properties without interacting with the panel's various menus and field.

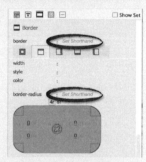

Keep in mind, if you decide to type in the Set Shorthand fields, most CSS property:value pairs have very specific rules; you must use the proper syntax to accurately define those values. (For example, do not include a space between a number and unit of measurement.)

The CSS Designer panel offers a lot of flexibility for creating and managing selectors. In this exercise, you will define several new selectors, which will later apply to new elements when you add them to the layout.

1. **With design.html open, click museum-styles.css in the Sources section of the CSS Designer panel.**

2. **In the Selectors area of the panel, click the Add Selector button.**

3. **With the new selector's name highlighted, type n.**

   You don't have to accept any part of the default name for a new selector; you can simply type while the name is highlighted to change the selector name.

   When you type a new selector name in the panel, Dreamweaver automatically presents a menu of known selectors that match the characters you type. In this case, a large number of tag names include the "n" character; "nav" is highlighted because it is the first name that begins with the character you typed.

A menu presents a list of known selectors that match what you type.

Note:

Your changes in the following steps do not affect the HTML files; you are only changing the CSS file that is linked the HTML file.

4. **With nav selected in the menu, press Return/Enter to accept the selected menu item, then press Return/Enter again to finalize the new selector.**

5. **In the Properties section of the panel, define a 200px width value and 10px padding on all four sides.**

Note:

There are hundreds of available CSS properties. http://w3schools.com/ cssref/css_selectors.asp is an excellent source of information about each property — including proper names, browser compatibility, and possible values.

6. **Click the Add Selector button again. Type #main-copy as the new selector name, then press Return/Enter to add the new selector.**

7. **Define the following settings for the new selector:**

width:	500px
min-height:	200px
padding (all four sides):	20px
margin-right:	50px

By default, elements collapse to the smallest possible height required to contain their content. By setting the **min-height** property, you prevent an element from collapsing entirely if you delete all the element's content.

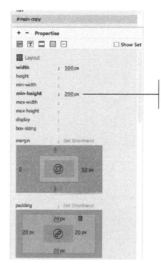

Define the min-height property for this selector.

Note:

Remember: ID selectors always begin with the # character.

8. **Repeat this process to create another new ID selector named #sidebar, using the following properties:**

width:	350px
min-height:	200px

9. **Show the museum-styles.css file in the Code pane.**

Because you selected museum-styles.css in the Sources section of the panel, the new selectors are added to that file. You can see the new selectors in the Code pane as long as the museum-styles.css file is showing in that pane.

Nothing has been added to the HTML file, as you can see in the Design pane. The asterisks show that the CSS file has been modified, but the HTML file has not changed.

Note:

Elements also expand as high as necessary to display all their content unless you define a specific height and restrict the overflow content.

design.html has not been modified.

museum-styles.css has been modified.

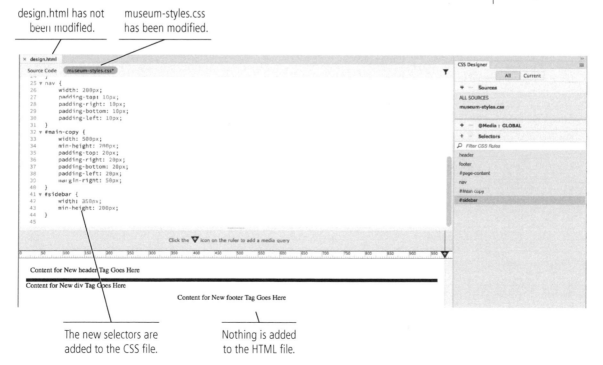

The new selectors are added to the CSS file.

Nothing is added to the HTML file.

10. Click in the Code pane to make it active, then choose File>Save.

The Save command (and its shortcut, Command/Control-S) saves the active file wherever the insertion point is placed. By clicking in the Code pane to place the insertion point in the museum-styles.css file, you are saving the CSS file and not the HTML file. (The HTML file did not change in this exercise.)

11. Continue to the next exercise.

 CREATE AND MANAGE NESTED ELEMENTS

The Museum site's basic page structure requires three additional elements, which will be nested inside the ones you already created. In this exercise, you use several techniques for creating nested elements.

1. With design.html open, show the page source code in the Code pane.

2. In the HTML Insert panel, click the Navigation button and drag into the document window. When a blue border outlines the header element, release the mouse button.

If you drag an element into an existing element, a heavy blue border identifies the active element. The new element will be nested inside the highlighted one.

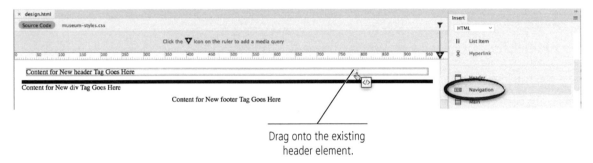

Drag onto the existing header element.

3. Review the page's source code in the Code pane.

Nested container elements should always appear before other content in the containing element. As you can see, Dreamweaver properly places the nav element code before the header element's placeholder text.

Because you defined width and padding properties for the nav selector in the previous exercise, those properties automatically apply to the newly placed nav element.

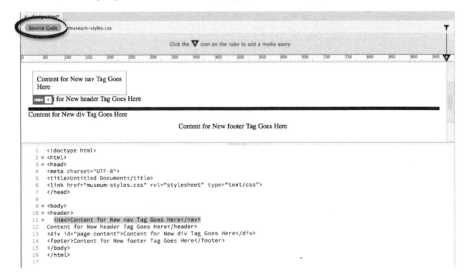

4. **Click the Section button in the HTML Insert panel and drag into the document window. When the mouse cursor is not over any existing element, release the mouse button.**

If you drag an element into an empty area of the page (below other elements), the body element is highlighted. The new element will be added at the top of the page hierarchy.

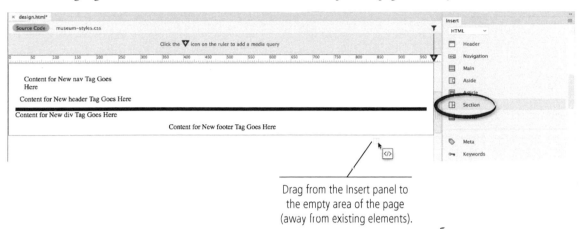

Drag from the Insert panel to the empty area of the page (away from existing elements).

As you can see in the Design pane, the element is added above the existing header element. The page code shows the position of the new section element, at the beginning of the element hierarchy.

The new section element is added to the page, above the header element.

5. **Click the Add Class/ID button (the + button) in the Element Display. In the resulting field, type #.**

The resulting menu shows all available selectors that match the characters you type. (Remember, ID selectors always begin with the # character.)

You can use the Arrow keys to navigate items in the resulting menu, or double-click an option in this menu to accept it.

The menu presents IDs that match your typing.

6. Click #main-copy in the menu to apply that ID to the active element.

Remember, the #main-copy selector defines a width of 500px and minimum height of 200px, so the section element now shows those dimensions in the document window.

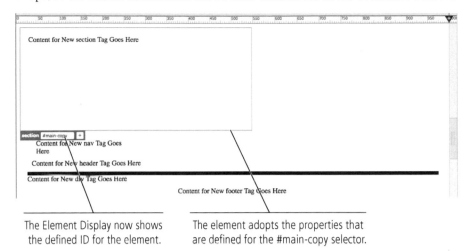

The Element Display now shows the defined ID for the element.

The element adopts the properties that are defined for the #main-copy selector.

7. Open the DOM panel (Window>DOM).

DOM is short for document object model. The DOM panel shows the overall structure of elements in your document. The elements appear in the same order as what you see in the document window. You can simply review your page content, or drag items in the panel to rearrange the various elements.

8. In the DOM panel, drag the section#main-copy element onto the div#page-content element. When you do not see a green line in the panel, release the mouse button.

When you drag elements in the panel, a green line shows where the element you are dragging will be placed in the hierarchy. If you want to nest one element into another, make sure the intended parent is highlighted but no green line appears.

When you release the mouse button, you can see the section#main-copy element has moved into the div#page-content element.

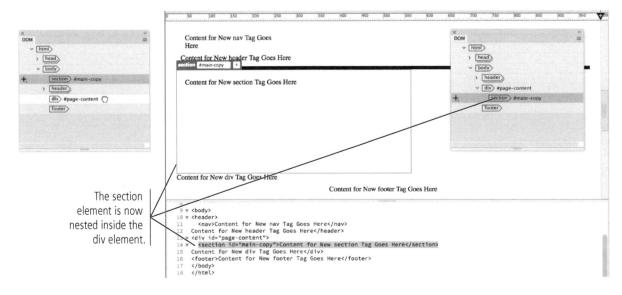

The section element is now nested inside the div element.

9. **Click to select the nested section element in the DOM panel.**

10. **Click the + button to the left of the section element and choose Insert After in the pop-up menu.**

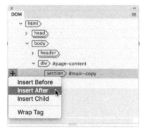

11. **With the word "div" highlighted, type sec.**

   The new element defaults to be a div element, but you can type a different element name in the field to change it.

   As you type, code hints present a list of options that match the characters you type. As soon as you type the "c", "section" is the only available option in the menu.

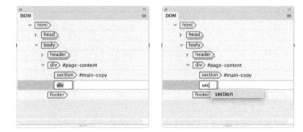

12. **Press Return/Enter two times to finalize the new element as a section instead of a div.**

13. **Double-click to the right of the section tag in the panel. In the resulting field, type #, then select #sidebar from the pop-up menu. Press Return/Enter to finalize the new section ID.**

   The menu shows all available selectors that match the characters you type. You can use each ID only once on any given page; because the #main-copy ID has already been used on this page, it is no long available and does not appear in the list.

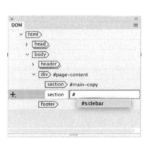

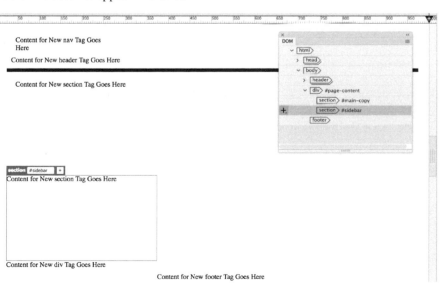

14. In the Code, select and delete the placeholder content in the page-content div.

This div exists to contain the other two elements, so you don't need the placeholder text.

If you delete the text in the Live view, Dreamweaver leaves a nonbreaking space character in place of the deleted text. By deleting the text in the Code pane, you avoid the unwanted character.

```
 9 ▼ <body>
10 ▼ <header>
11       <nav>Content for New nav Tag Goes Here</nav>
12   Content for New header Tag Goes Here</header>
13 ▼ <div id="page-content">
14     <section id="main-copy">Content for New section Tag Goes Here</section>
15     <section id="sidebar">Content for New section Tag Goes Here</section>
16 ▼ Content for New div Tag Goes Here</div>
17   <footer>Content for New footer Tag Goes Here</footer>
18   </body>
19   </html>
20
```

Select and delete this
placeholder text.

15. Choose File>Save All, then continue to the next exercise.

CONTROL ELEMENT FLOAT POSITION

The nav element should appear on the right side of the header element. Inside the div#page-content element, the main-copy section and sidebar section should appear in the same "row." As you can see in your current layout, several elements do not yet appear in the correct position.

Nested elements automatically align based on the horizontal alignment properties of the containing element. If no specific alignment is defined, the nested elements align to the left side of the container and each appears in sequential order.

1. With design.html open, show only the Design view and turn off the Live view.

When the Live view is turned off, visual aids make it easier to see the boundaries of various elements on the page.

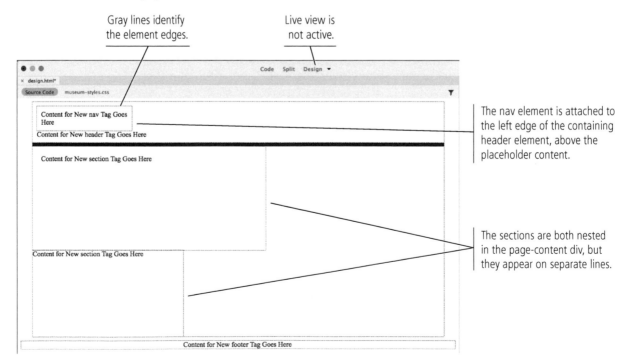

Gray lines identify
the element edges.

Live view is
not active.

The nav element is attached to the left edge of the containing header element, above the placeholder content.

The sections are both nested in the page-content div, but they appear on separate lines.

2. Click the Current button at the top of the CSS Designer panel to turn that mode on.

3. Click the edge of the nav element in the document window to select it.

When Current mode is active, the panel shows only selectors that affect the active selection in the document. In this case, the active element is contained inside the header element, so the selected element can be affected by both the header and nav selectors.

4. With the nav selector selected in the CSS Designer panel, check the Show Set option in the Properties section.

When Current mode is active, the panel shows only selectors related to the active selection.

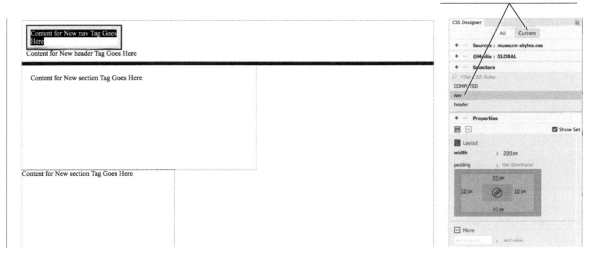

5. Click in the Add Property field at the bottom of the Properties section and type **flo.**

You can use the "More" section of the panel to add any new property to the active selector. (Many are not available in the other sections of the panel.) Simply type the property name to add the property you want.

Type in the field to show available properties with the characters you type.

Choose a specific property in this menu to add it to the selector.

Typing in the field presents a menu of all available properties that contain the characters you type. You can also use the arrow keys to navigate the resulting menu, and press Return/Enter to add the highlighted property.

6. Click float in the resulting menu to add it as a new property.

After you define the property you want to add, the secondary menu presents the possible values for that property.

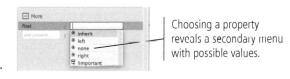

Choosing a property reveals a secondary menu with possible values.

7. Click right in the menu of values to select it.

The CSS **float** property allows you to intentionally attach an element to the left or right edge of the containing element, and allows other content to sit beside or wrap around that element. This gives you greater flexibility when creating complex layouts.

The nav element now properly aligns on the right side of its immediate parent container (the header element).

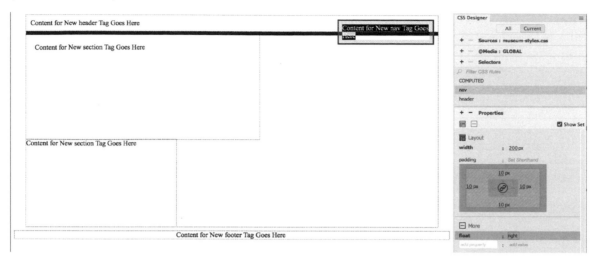

8. Repeat the process from this exercise to define float values as follows:

> **#main-copy**   **float:left**
>
> **#sidebar**   **float:right**

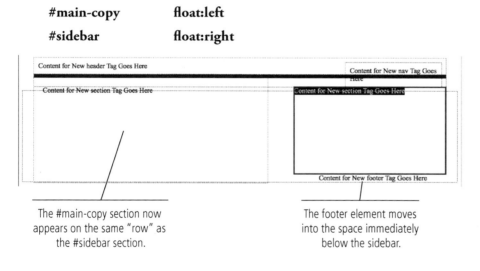

The #main-copy section now appears on the same "row" as the #sidebar section.

The footer element moves into the space immediately below the sidebar.

Note:

You will fix the issue with the nav element height in the next exercise.

9. **Assign the left float value to the footer selector.**

   When the footer element had no defined float property, it moved into an unpredicted position to the right of the main-copy section; to solve the problem, you are assigning a specific float property to the footer element to attach it to the left edge of its parent container (the body element).

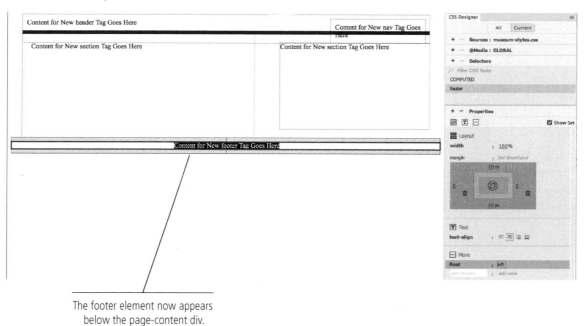

The footer element now appears below the page-content div.

10. **Choose File>Save All, then continue to the next exercise.**

WORK WITH THE CSS BOX MODEL

When you design layouts using CSS, think of any element as a box made up of four parts: margin, border, padding, and content. The object's overall size — the amount of space it occupies on the page — is the sum of the values for these four properties:

- The **margin** is outside the box edges; it is invisible and has no background color. Margin does not affect content within the element.

- The **border** is the edge of the element, based on the specified dimensions.

- The **padding** lies inside the edge of the element, forming a cushion between the box edge and the box content.

- The **content** lies inside the padding. When you define the width and height for an element, you define the content area.

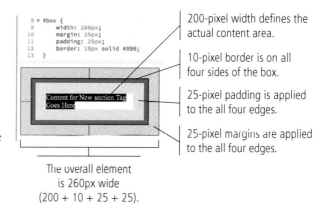

200-pixel width defines the actual content area.

10-pixel border is on all four sides of the box.

25-pixel padding is applied to the all four edges.

25-pixel margins are applied to the all four edges.

The overall element is 260px wide (200 + 10 + 25 + 25).

1. With **design.html** open, make sure the Live view is turned off.

2. Drag the file **getty-logo.png** (from the site **images** folder) into the header element. Using the Properties panel, define **The Getty Foundation** as alternate text for the placed image.

   Unless you define otherwise, HTML elements always expand to whatever height is necessary to show all content. When you place this image, the header element automatically expands to the height necessary to accommodate the logo.

Note:

Remember, to define alternate text, you can select the image in the Design pane and then type in the Alt field of the Properties panel.

3. Select and delete the placeholder text from the header element.

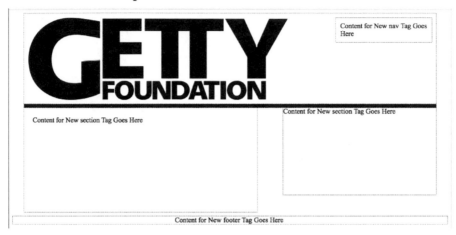

4. Delete the placeholder text from the nav element, then type the following in the nav element:

   About the Getty [Return/Enter]

   Traveling Exhibits [Return/Enter]

   Permanent Exhibits

5. In the CSS Designer panel, use the Add Property field to define a **50px** margin-top value for the nav selector.

   As you can see from the gray element edges, the increased top margin aligns the bottom edge of the nav element to the bottom edge of the placed logo.

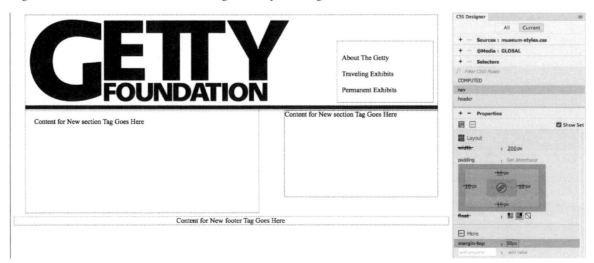

6. **Click to select the section#sidebar element in the layout.**

7. **With the #sidebar selector active in the CSS Designer panel, uncheck the Show Set option and navigate to the Background properties.**

8. **In the background-image options, define `parchment.png` (from the site images folder) as the background image, and choose the no-repeat option.**

   Some users will see the bottom edge of the parchment in the sidebar (as shown in our screen shot here), while others might see the edge cut off. The next few steps illustrate the problem of relying solely on the regular Design view when working with CSS.

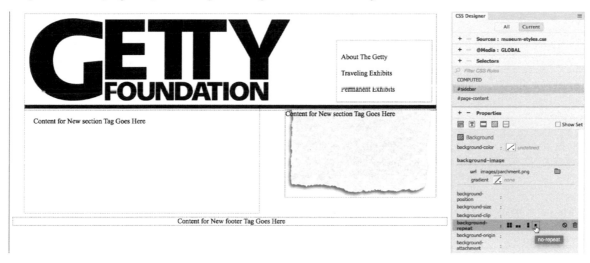

9. **Turn on the Live view.**

   Although the regular Design view makes it easier to see the CSS layout structure (including the element boundaries), it does not always accurately depict CSS. When the Live view is active, you get a better idea of exactly what will appear when a browser renders the CSS.

   As you can see, the parchment image is bluntly cut off at the bottom of the section#sidebar element. Background images default to begin at the top-left corner of their containing element.

   This section element has a defined min-height property, so it will always be at least 200px high — but it will expand as high as necessary to contain the element content. Since you don't know exactly how high the element will be, you can avoid the cutoff problem by changing the positioning of the background image.

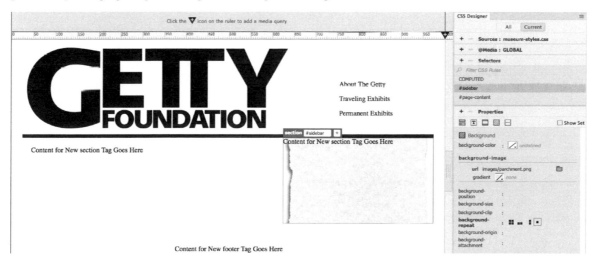

10. **Choose center in the first background-position menu, and choose bottom in the second background position menu.**

These settings tell the browser to align the bottom edge of the background image to the center bottom edge of the container. The torn-off edge of the parchment will always appear at the bottom, even when the element expands to contain various content.

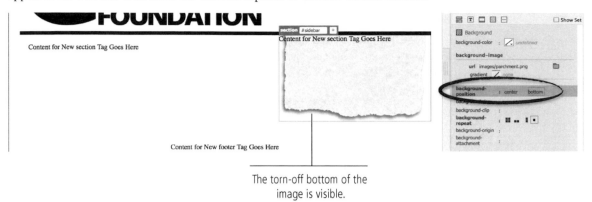

The torn-off bottom of the image is visible.

You might notice another problem. Placeholder content in the section#sidebar element runs directly into the element edge. In the CSS box model, padding defines a distance at which content exists from the element edge; you can use this property to fix the problem.

11. **Define the following padding values for the #sidebar selector:**

padding-top:	10px
padding-right:	30px
padding-bottom:	30px
padding-left:	30px

The background image extends into the padding area because the padding is part of the actual element area. Margin values are added outside the element; background images do not extend into the margin area.

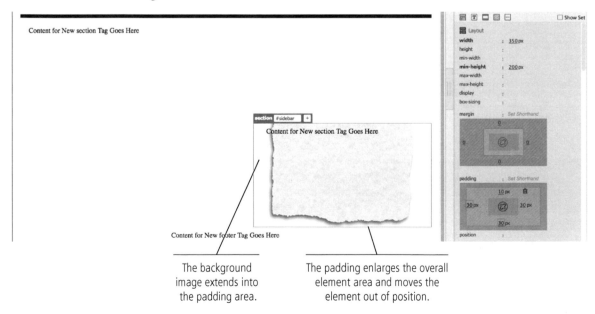

The background image extends into the padding area.

The padding enlarges the overall element area and moves the element out of position.

It is important to realize that both padding and margins affect the overall size of the element. The section#sidebar element is now 410 pixels wide (350 defined width + 30 left padding + 30 right padding). With that width, it no longer fits on the same "row" as the section#main-copy element.

12. Subtract 60 from the width value of the #sidebar selector.

To change the existing property values, simply click the value to highlight it and then type the new value.

When you change margins and/or padding, you often have to make a proportional change to the width and/or height properties if you want the element to occupy the same overall space. After changing the width, the section#sidebar element moves back into place.

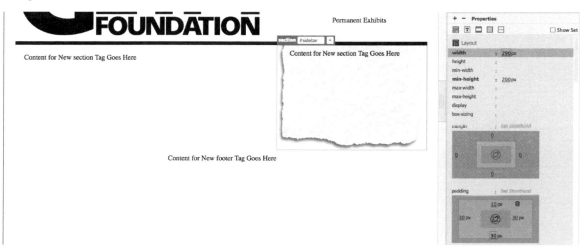

13. Click to select the section#main-copy element in the layout.

14. In the CSS Designer panel, make sure #main-copy is selected and show the Background properties.

15. Click the background-color swatch to open the color picker, then choose the Eyedropper tool in the bottom-right corner.

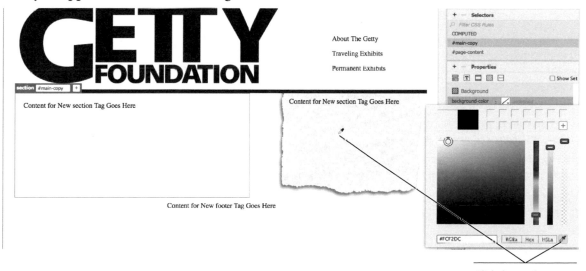

Click the eyedropper to sample color from an existing page element.

16. **Move the cursor over a medium-yellow shade in the parchment image. Click to select the color, then press Return/Enter to finalize the new background-color property.**

17. **Choose File>Save All, then continue to the next exercise.**

 DEFINE PROPERTIES FOR THE <BODY> TAG

The **<body>** tag surrounds all visible content in a web page. Because **<body>** is an HTML tag, you have to create a tag selector to define properties for the body element.

1. **With design.html open, click All at the top of the CSS Designer panel to turn off the Current mode.**

2. **Click museum-styles.css in the Sources section of the CSS Designer panel, then click the Add Selector button in the Selector section of the panel.**

3. **Type body as the new selector name, then press Return/Enter two times to finalize the selector.**

4. **In the Layout properties, click to highlight the Set Shorthand field for the margin property. Type 0px, then press Return/Enter to finalize the new value.**

   When you define values for a CSS property, do not include a space between the number and the unit of measurement.

5. **Turn on the Lock icon in the center of the padding proxy to make all four padding values the same. Highlight the top padding field and type 0px to define a zero-pixel padding.**

   Because you linked all four padding fields by clicking the Lock icon, changing one value changes the other three, as well.

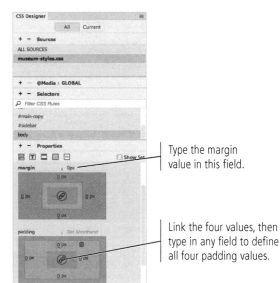

Type the margin value in this field.

Link the four values, then type in any field to define all four padding values.

6. **Review the new selector in the code of the museum-styles.css file.**

The margin, which you defined using the Set Shorthand field, only occupies one line; the **margin** property without specific sides defined applies to all edges of the element.

The various fields in the Properties panel defined separate properties for each margin (**padding-top**, **padding-right**, **padding-bottom**, and **padding-left**).

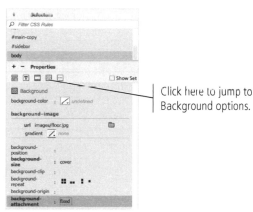

```
Source Code    museum-styles.css*
58 ▼ body {
59        margin: 0px;
60        padding-top: 0px;
61        padding-right: 0px;
62        padding-bottom: 0px;
63        padding-left: 0px;
64   }
65
```

7. **With body still selected in the Selectors section of the panel, define the following Background properties for the body selector:**

background-image:	floor.jpg
background-size:	cover
background-attachment:	fixed

Click here to jump to Background options.

As we explained in Project 3: Arts Council Website, the **background-size** property defines the size of background images.

The **background-attachment** property determines whether a background image moves when the page scrolls. By default, background images scroll with the page. When you define the **fixed** value, the background image remains in place even when the rest of the page scrolls in front of it.

8. **In the Text options, define the following properties for the body selector:**

font-family:	Gotham, Helvetica Neue, Helvetica, Arial, sans-serif
font-size:	14px
font-weight:	300
line-height:	22px

Click the value and choose from the available list of font families.

The **font-family** list defines fonts that will be used to display the text, in order of availability.

The **font-weight** property defines how thick characters should be displayed. Numeric values from 100 to 900 (in hundreds) define this option from thin to thick; 400 is approximately normal.

The **line-height** property defines the distance from one line of text to the next in a paragraph.

9. **Review the results in the Design pane.**

Web browsers have default values (which can differ) for many elements, including the body element. By specifying padding and margins of 0, you are standardizing these settings or negating any default values (called "normalizing"), so all browsers will render the body element the same way.

By this point you should begin to understand the concept of nested tags. The **<body>** tag is the parent of the tags it contains. Properties of the parent tag are automatically inherited by the child (nested) tags.

In this case, the font family, size, weight, and line height you defined for the **<body>** tag are automatically applied to content in the nested elements.

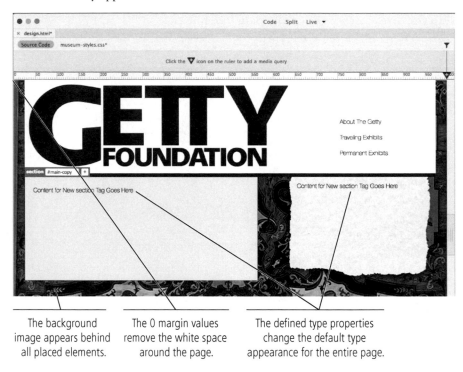

The background image appears behind all placed elements.

The 0 margin values remove the white space around the page.

The defined type properties change the default type appearance for the entire page.

10. **Save all files, then continue to the next stage of the project.**

Stage 2 Working with a Template

Using a template file (with the ".dwt" extension), you can create common page elements only once, rather than recreating them every time you add a new page to a site. If you modify a template, pages based on the template are updated to reflect the same changes.

When you create a Dreamweaver template, you indicate which elements of a page should remain constant (non-editable; locked) in pages based on that template, and which elements can be changed.

CREATE A TEMPLATE

When all pages in a site will have the same basic layout, you can save the common elements as a template, and then apply the template to all pages. This workflow makes it much faster and easier to maintain consistency and complete the project.

Following the same logic, keep in mind that the museum-styles.css file in this site is attached to the design.html file — which will become the template. Any pages created from the template file will also be attached to the museum-styles.css file, so changes made in the museum-styles.css file will affect pages created from the template.

1. **With design.html from the Museum site open, turn off the Live view.**

    You can't create a template while the Live view is active.

2. **In the nav element, create links for each paragraph as follows:**

About The Getty	Link to about.html
Traveling Exhibits	Link to traveling-exhibits.html
Permanent Exhibits	Link to permanent-exhibits.html

3. **Select and delete the placeholder text in the main-copy and sidebar section elements.**

    Because you defined a minimum height for the #main-copy and #sidebar selectors, the elements do not entirely collapse in the page layout.

4. **In the CSS Designer panel, make the footer selector active. In the Properties section of the panel, show the Text properties and define the text color as white (#FFF).**

    It's important to realize that layout development is an ongoing evolutionary process; as you continue to work, new issues will pop up. You can always add properties to or remove properties from specific selectors, edit the values of specific properties, and add new selectors as necessary to meet a project's needs.

5. Replace the placeholder text in the footer div with the following:

   Site design by Against The Clock, Inc.

6. Choose File>Save All.

Before creating the template file, you should save the changes you just made to the HTML and CSS files.

6. Choose File>Save As Template.

7. In the Save As Template dialog box, make sure Museum is selected in the Site menu.

8. In the Description field, type Museum Site Template.

The description is only relevant in Dreamweaver; it will not appear in any page based on the template. (You can modify the template description by choosing Modify>Templates>Description.)

Note:

You can also create a template from the active page by choosing Insert>Template Objects>Make Template.

9. Click Save to save the active file as a template.

The extension ".dwt" is automatically added on both Macintosh and Windows.

10. Click Yes in the resulting dialog box.

The template is saved in a Templates folder, which Dreamweaver automatically creates for you in the local root folder of the Museum site. To ensure that all images and links function properly, you should allow Dreamweaver to update the link information as necessary.

The template is automatically added to the site in a new Templates folder.

Your template contains the layout structure you created in the first stage of this project. However, after converting the document into a template, all parts of the page become non-editable. Until you define an editable region, you won't be able to add page-specific content to any pages based on this template.

Do not move your templates out of the Templates folder or save any non-template files in the Templates folder. Also, do not move the Templates folder out of your local root folder. Doing so causes errors in paths in the templates.

11. Show the page source code in the Code pane.

12. Change the Document Title to The Getty Foundation.

When you define a title in a template file, that title is automatically applied to any page attached to the template. You are adding the basic information in the template, so you can then simply add page-specific information in each attached file.

As you can see in the Code pane, the <title> tag is contained in special tags that define it as an editable region. This means that the title can be edited independently on any page that is attached to the template file.

These tags identify the editable region.

13. In the Design pane, click to place the insertion point in the main-copy section, then click section#main-copy in the Tag Selector to select the entire element.

14. Click the Editable Region button in the Templates Insert panel.

You can also choose Insert>Template>Editable Region.

Click the section#main-copy tag
to select the entire element.

15. Type Page Content in the resulting dialog box and then click OK.

When pages are created from this template, the editable regions will be the only areas that can be modified.

16. In the Design pane, click the blue Page Content tag above the editable region.

In the Design view, editable areas are identified with a blue tag and border; these are for design purposes, and will not be visible in the resulting HTML pages. If you don't see a blue tag with the Page Content region name, open the View>Visual Aids menu and choose Invisible Elements to toggle on that option.

Clicking this tab selects the entire editable template object; this makes it easier for you to see the related code in the Code pane.

Click the tab to select the entire editable region.

The editable region code surrounds only the main-copy section.

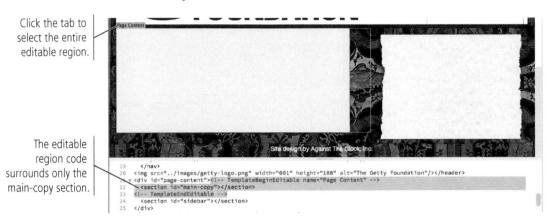

The new editable area was added around the selected section element. Because you want the main-copy *and* sidebar sections inside the editable area, you have to edit the page code.

17. In the page code, move the closing code of the editable region (<!-- TemplateEndEditable -->) to be after the closing tag of the section#sidebar element. Refresh the Design view and review the results.

When something is selected in the Code pane, you can click the selected code and drag to move that code to a new position. Alternatively, you can cut (Command/Control-X) the relevant code from its original location, move the insertion point to another position, and then paste (Command/Control-V) the cut code into place.

The editable area now contains the two nested sections, but not the surrounding div#page-content element.

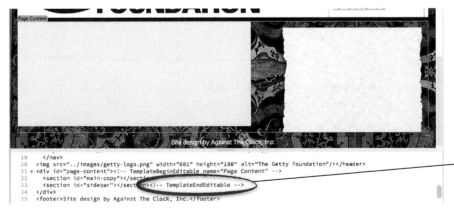

Move the ending code of the editable area after the closing tag of the section#sidebar element.

18. Choose File>Save All, close the template file, and then continue to the next exercise.

Unlike other applications, you do not have to use the Save As command to rewrite a Dreamweaver template. You can simply choose File>Save or press Command/Control-S.

APPLY THE TEMPLATE TO EXISTING PAGES

Templates can be applied to existing HTML pages, basically wrapping the template around the existing content. You simply map existing page content to editable regions in the template. After the template is applied, you can begin to make whatever changes are necessary based on the actual content in the files.

1. **In the Files panel, double-click the Museum site name in the Directory menu to open the Site Setup dialog box for the active site.**

   Remember, this technique opens the Site Setup dialog box for the selected site and allows you to skip the Manage Sites dialog box.

   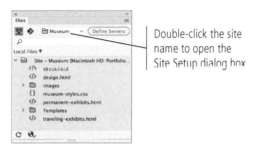

   Double-click the site name to open the Site Setup dialog box

2. **Expand the Advanced Settings options and click Templates in the category list to show the related options.**

3. **Make sure the Don't Rewrite option is checked.**

   When you saved the template file, it was placed in a folder named Templates. Links from this template file to images or other pages must first go up from the Templates folder to the root folder (e.g., **../images/getty-logo.png**).

   When this template is attached to a page in the root level of the site, the same link would not be accurate. For example, the path from about.html in the root folder to the same image would simply be **images/getty-logo.png**. If this check box is not active, the links on pages where the template is attached would not work properly.

4. **Click Save to close the Site Setup dialog box.**

5. **Using the Files panel, open about.html from the root folder of the Museum site.**

   Each file in the site contains two areas of content — the primary page copy, and a list of links to help users navigate through the long blocks of text. The two sections are already tagged with ids (#main-copy and #sidebar) that match the ones you used in the template file. This will direct the appropriate elements of the provided pages to appear in the defined areas of the template.

6. **Choose Tools>Templates>Apply Template to Page.**

7. **In the Select Template dialog box, make sure Museum is selected in the Site menu.**

   Since this is the active site, the menu should default to the correct choice.

8. **Click design in the Templates list to select it, and make sure the Update Page... option is checked at the bottom of the dialog box.**

9. **Click Select to apply the template to the open page.**

   In the Inconsistent Region Names dialog box that appears, you have to determine where to place the named regions of the open file relative to the editable regions in the template you selected.

10. **In the resulting dialog box, click the Document body (in the Name column) to select it. In the Move Content to New Region menu, choose Page Content.**

    Remember, "Page Content" is the name you assigned to the template's editable region. The page body (named "Document body" by default) will be placed into the "Page Content" editable region when the template is applied to the page.

This refers to content within the <body> section of the HTML page to which you are attaching the template.

Use this menu to map file content to an editable region in the template file.

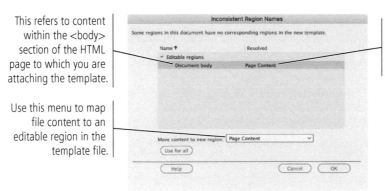

This is the name assigned to the editable region in the template file.

Note:

You can choose Nowhere in the Move Content... menu to exclude specific content in the newly "templated" page.

11. **Click OK to finalize the process.**

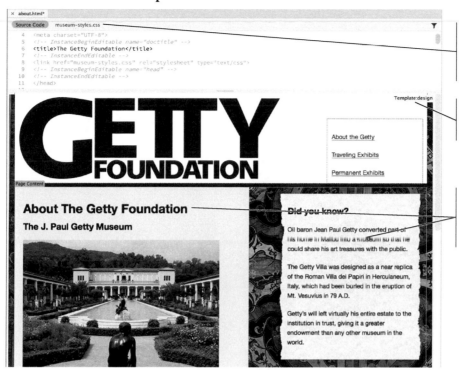

Because the template is linked to museum-styles.css, that file is also attached to this HTML page.

This tag identifies the template that is applied to the HTML file.

Content defined with ID attributes in the original HTML file is moved into the correct location in the template.

12. **Click the Split button to show the page code (if ncessary), and scroll to the top of the code.**

    Although you did not specifically define it as an editable area, the <title> tag of each page is always editable, even when attached to a template file.

13. **In the Code pane, add the text | About The Getty (including a preceding space) to the end of the existing document title.**

Note:

If you move the cursor over areas other than an editable region, an icon indicates that you can't select or modify that area. You can modify only the editable region.

TION ®

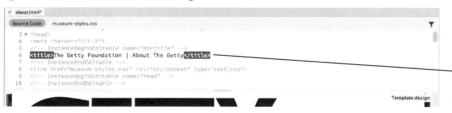

The title element in the page head is automatically an editable region.

14. **Save the file and close it.**

15. Repeat this process to attach the design.dwt template to the two remaining pages in the site. Define appropriate page title information to each page.

16. Save and close any open files, and continue to the next stage of the project.

DREAMWEAVER FOUNDATIONS

The Insert>Template Menu Options

Template objects consist primarily of different types of regions. These options are available in the Templates Insert panel or the Insert>Template submenu:

- **Make Template** converts an HTML file into a template, automatically prompting you to save the HTML file as a template.

- **Make Nested Template** inserts a template in a page created from an existing template.

- **Editable Region** creates areas of a template that you can modify in pages using the template. (You can change the highlight color of editable template regions in the Highlighting pane of the Preferences dialog box.)

- **Optional Region** defines a section of the page that will be shown or hidden depending on the content being presented.

- **Repeating Region** creates a section of template content that you can easily duplicate (primarily used in tables and lists).

- **Editable Optional Region** combines the Optional Region functionality with the Editable Region functionality. If the Editable Optional Region is shown, the content within the region can be modified.

- **Repeating Table** creates both a table and repeating regions simultaneously. Selecting a repeating table object opens the standard table dialog box for defining rows within a repeating region.

Creating a New Page from a Template

In addition to attaching a template to an existing page, you can also create a new HTML page from an existing template.

You can use the Assets panel (Window>Assets) to show all templates that are available in the current site. Control/right-clicking a specific template file opens a contextual menu, where you can choose New from Template.

This results in a new untitled HTML file containing all the content that is defined in the template, with the template already attached to the HTML page. Any changes in the template file will apply to files created from the template.

Pages can also be created from a template using the New Document dialog box (File>New). Choose Site Templates in the left column of the New Document dialog box, select your site in the middle column, and then choose the template you want to apply in the right column.

The Tools>Templates Menu Options

Commands in the Tools>Templates submenu are useful when you want to make changes to pages based on a template.

- **Apply Template to Page** applies a template to the current HTML page.

- If you don't want a page to be based on a template, **Detach from Template** separates the page from the template. Non-editable regions become editable, but changes in the template no longer reflect in the page.

- **Open Attached Template** opens the template attached to a page.

- The **Check Template Syntax** option enables the software to automatically check code syntax in the template.

- **Update Current Page** updates a page if the template on which it is based is modified.

- You can use the **Update Pages** option to manually update all pages based on the template.

- **Export without Markup** exports an entire site to a different location by detaching all pages from templates on which they are based.

- Use **Remove Template Markup** to convert an editable region to a non-editable region.

- The **Description** is simply a textual explanation of the selected file, which does not appear in the page body.

- **New Entry After** or **Before Selection.** You can use these options to add repeated elements, such as rows of a table, in a repeating regions.

- Use **Move Entry Up** or **Down** to move a repeating element up or down.

- You can use **Make Attribute Editable** to make a specific attribute of an HTML tag editable in template-based pages.

Editing a Design Template

When you make changes to a template and save the template file, Dreamweaver recognizes the link from the template to pages where that template is attached. You are automatically asked if you want to update those pages to reflect the new template content.

The resulting Update Pages dialog box shows the progress of updating linked files. When you see the "Done" message, you can click Close to dismiss the dialog box.

Stage 3 Using CSS to Control Content

The first stage of this project focused on building a layout with properly structured HTML; in the second stage, you created a template file to more easily apply the defined layout to multiple pages. Although defining structure is a significant part of designing pages, it is only half the story — professional web design also requires controlling the content in pages.

In this stage of the project, you will complete a number of tasks required to present the client's information in the best possible way:

- Define CSS to format HTML elements, including headings, paragraphs, and links.

- Create a list of links for users to jump to different parts of a page.

- Define CSS to format the rollover behavior of links throughout the site.

- Define CSS to format specific elements only in certain areas of the page.

- Create and format figures and captions within the copy of each page.

 ## DEFINE HTML TAG SELECTORS

In addition to the **<body>** tag that encloses the page content, properly structured pages use HTML tags to identify different types of content. As you already know, CSS uses tag selectors to format HTML tags such as paragraphs (**<p>**), headings (**<h1>**, **<h2>**, etc.), links (**<a>**), and so on.

1. **Open permanent-exhibits.html from the Museum site root folder, and turn on the Live view.**

   When you are editing CSS to define the appearance of page content, it's a good idea to work in the Live view so you can see an accurate representation of the CSS rendering.

2. **In the CSS Designer panel, select museum-styles.css in the Sources list and then click the Add Selector button in the Selectors section.**

3. **Type h1 as the selector name, then press Return/Enter twice to finalize the new selector name.**

   This tag selector defines properties for any h1 element — in other words, content surrounded by the <h1> </h1> tags. Tag selectors do not require a # character at the beginning of the name; only the actual element name is required.

4. In the Properties section of the panel, define the following properties for the h1 tag selector:

margin:	0px (all four sides)
color:	sample the color of the client's logo
font-size:	30px

Note:

Remember, the CSS color property defines the color of text.

Content block elements such as headings and paragraphs have default top and bottom margins equivalent to the current text size. It is common to modify some or all of these margins with CSS. By defining margins of 0 for <h1> tags, any subsequent paragraph or heading's top margin will determine the spacing between the elements.

The first paragraph in the text — which is formatted with the <h1> tag — is affected by the new selector definition.

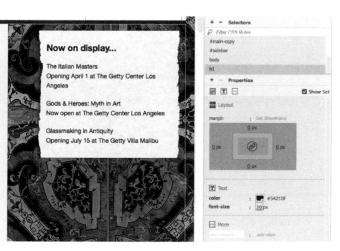

This is the h1 element.

5. Create another tag selector for the <h2> tag, using the following settings:

margin-top:	30px
margin-bottom:	5px
color:	sample the color of the client's logo
font-size:	24px

Note:

We have the Show Set option turned on in our screen shots to reinforce the properties you should define in each step.

The margin settings for h2 elements are not yet apparent because the <h3> margins are still ambiguous.

5. **Create another tag selector for the <h3> tag, using the following settings:**

margin-top:	0px
margin-bottom:	15px
font-style:	italic
font-weight:	400

Margin settings for h2 elements are
now apparent because the <h3>
margins have been clearly defined.

6. **Create another tag selector for the <p> tag, using the following settings:**

margin-top:	0px
margin-bottom:	10px

Paragraphs in all areas of the page
are affected by the p selector.

8. **Add another tag selector for the <a> tag, using the following settings:**

color:	sample the color of the client's logo
font-weight:	bold
text-decoration:	none

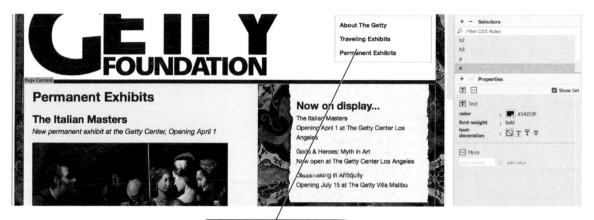

Links no longer have the default
blue underline appearance.

9. **Choose File>Save All, then continue to the next exercise.**

CREATE NAMED ANCHORS

Documents with large blocks of copy — like the ones in this site — often benefit from named anchors, which mark specific locations on a page that can be linked from other locations within the same page or from other pages. Instead of forcing the reader to search for the information by scrolling or other means, you can create a hyperlink that points to the exact location of the information. Clicking the anchor link moves that anchor to the top of the browser window.

1. **With permanent-exhibits.html open, turn off the Live view (if necessary) and show the page source in the Code pane.**

   Selecting text and creating links can be a bit easier in the regular Design view.

2. **In the Code pane, click to place the insertion point immediately after the opening <h2> tag for the first h2 element.**

Place the insertion point after
the opening <h2> tag.

3. Type the following code:

```
<a name="masters"></
```

As soon as you type the "/" character, Dreamweaver automatically closes the last unclosed container tag — in this case, the <a> tag.

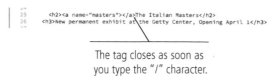

```
25      <h2><a name="masters"></a>The Italian Masters</h2>
26      <h3>New permanent exhibit at the Getty Center, Opening April 1</h3>
```

The tag closes as soon as you type the "/" character.

4. Refresh the Design pane.

When the Live view is not active, a named anchor appears in the page as a small anchor icon. These icons are not visible in the Live view or in the browser.

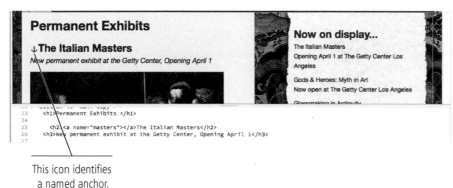

```
23      <h1>Permanent Exhibits </h1>
24
25      <h2><a name="masters"></a>The Italian Masters</h2>
26      <h3>New permanent exhibit at the Getty Center, Opening April 1</h3>
27
```

This icon identifies a named anchor.

5. Repeat this process to add named anchors to the other h2 elements on the page. Use gods and glassmaking as the names of the related anchors.

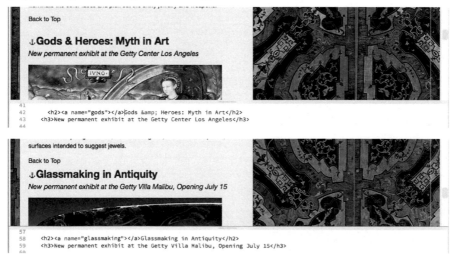

```
41
42      <h2><a name="gods"></a>Gods &amp; Heroes: Myth in Art</h2>
43      <h3>New permanent exhibit at the Getty Center Los Angeles</h3>
44
```

```
57
58      <h2><a name="glassmaking"></a>Glassmaking in Antiquity</h2>
59      <h3>New permanent exhibit at the Getty Villa Malibu, Opening July 15</h3>
60
```

6. In the Design pane, highlight the words "The Italian Masters" in the section#sidebar element.

7. **Click the Hyperlink button in the HTML Insert panel.**

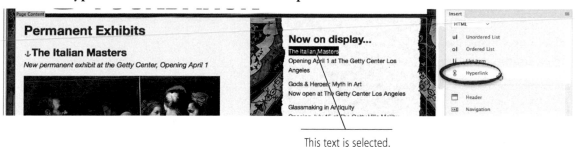

This text is selected.

8. **In the Hyperlink dialog box, open the Link menu and choose #masters.**

This menu includes all named anchors; each anchor name is preceded by the # character.

9. **Click OK to close the dialog box and create the new anchor link.**

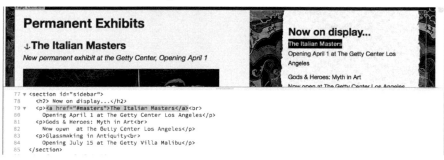

10. **Repeat Steps 6–9 to create links for the other two items in the section#sidebar element:**

Link Text	Link Target
Gods & Heroes: Myth in Art	gods
Glassmaking in Antiquity	glassmaking

11. In the Code pane, place the insertion point immediately after the opening `<h1>` tag near the top of the page.

12. Define a new named anchor as follows:

```
<a name="top"></a>
```

To help the reader return to the link list from any section of the page, it is good practice to include a link to the top of the page at the end of each section.

Add the named anchor after
the opening `<h1>` tag.

13. Select the words "Back to Top" above the second `<h2>` element. Create a link to the #top named anchor.

Note:

To reduce the amount of repetitive work required to complete this project, we have already created the named anchors and links in the provided traveling-exhibits.html file.

14. Repeat Step 13 to link the remaining two "Back to Top" paragraphs to the #top anchor.

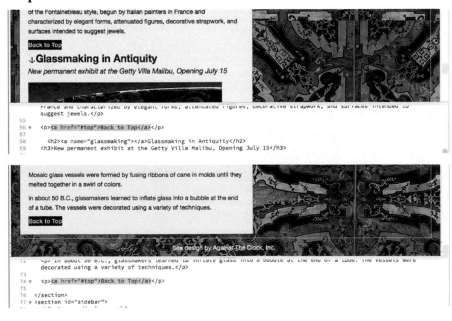

15. Save the file and continue to the next exercise.

CREATE A PSEUDO-CLASS SELECTOR

A **class selector** is used when the same style needs to be applied to more than one element in a page. Unlike an ID attribute, which is used only once per page, a class attribute can be used to repeat the same style throughout the page.

As you should remember from the previous exercise, controlling the default appearance of link text is accomplished with the <a> tag selector. To affect the rollover behavior, you have to define **pseudo-classes** (or variants) of the <a> selector. Four common pseudo-classes important to the appearance of links are:

- **a:link** refers to a hyperlink that has not yet been visited.

- **a:visited** refers to a hyperlink that has been visited.

- **a:hover** refers to a hyperlink when the mouse pointer is hovering over the link.

- **a:active** refers to an active hyperlink (in other words: when the link is clicked before the mouse button is released).

1. With **permanent-exhibits.html** open, turn on the Live view and hide the code pane.

2. Select **museum-styles.css** in the Sources section of the CSS Designer panel, then click the Add Selector button.

3. With the new selector name highlighted, type **a:hover**.

4. Define the following property for the new selector:

    color: sample a light brown color
                   from the background
                   image

Note:

For them to work correctly in all web browsers, these pseudo-class selectors should appear in the following order in the CSS file:

   a:link

   a:visited

   a:hover

   a:active

5. With the Live view active, test the rollover property of the links in various sections of the page.

The a:hover selector changes the color of the links in all areas of the page.

6. Choose File>Save All, close the HTML file, then continue to the next exercise.

CREATE A FIGURE AND FIGURE CAPTION

The figure element is used to define content such as illustrations or photos that are related to the copy. The figure element is a container that can include a nested figcaption element describing the figure, which means the image and caption can be treated together as a single unit.

1. **Open about.html and make sure the Live view is active.**

2. **Click to select the image near the top of the section#main-copy element.**

3. **Click the Figure button in the HTML Insert panel.**

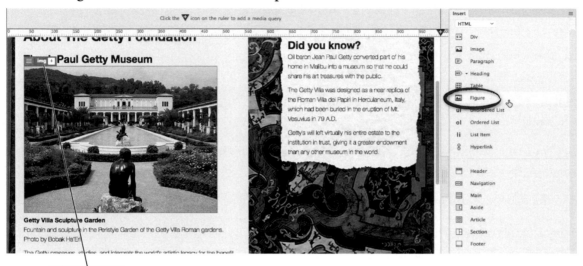

The img element
is selected.

4. **Choose Before in the Position Assistant.**

For some reason, the Wrap option is not available in this case. You have to use a workaround to move the image into the proper position inside the figure tags.

Note:

To minimize repetitive work, we created the figure and figcaption tags for you in the traveling-exhibits.html and permanent-exhibits. html files.

5. **Click to select the image again, then open the DOM panel.**

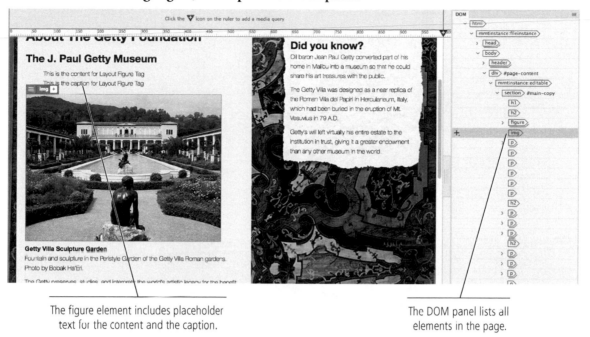

The figure element includes placeholder text for the content and the caption.

The DOM panel lists all elements in the page.

6. **In the DOM panel, click the arrow to expand the figure element.**

7. **In the panel, click the img tag and drag onto the figure element. When you don't see a green line, release the mouse button.**

This moves the img element into the figure element; in other words, the img element becomes nested inside the figure element.

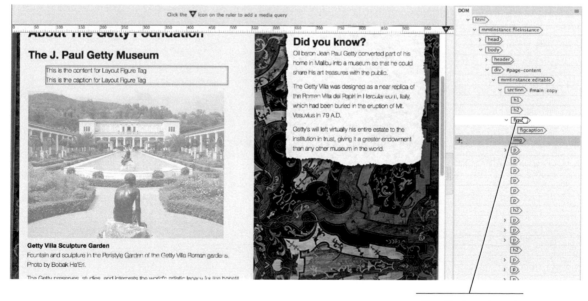

Drag the img element onto the figure element.

8. In the Design pane, click to select the paragraph immediately below the image (beginning with Getty Villa...").

9. In the DOM panel, drag the selected paragraph onto the figcaption element.

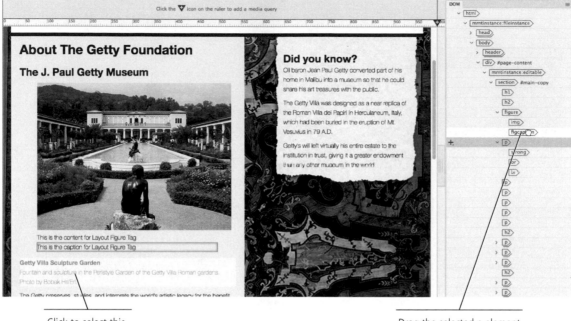

Click to select this paragraph element.

Drag the selected p element onto the figcaption element.

10. In the Code pane, review the code related to the figure element.

As you can see in the code, the img element is nested inside the figure element. The figcaption is also nested inside the figure element, which allows you to treat the image and caption as one unit by editing the figure element.

Placeholder text remains in the code.

```
25
26 ▼    <figure><img src="images/villa.jpg" alt="Getty Villa Sculpture Garden" width="450" height="338">This is the content
       for Layout Figure Tag
27 ▼      <figcaption>
28 ▼         <p><strong>Getty Villa Sculpture Garden</strong><br>
29            Fountain and sculpture in the Peristyle Garden of the Getty Villa Roman gardens.<br>
30            Photo by Bobak Ha'Eri.</p>
31          This is the caption for Layout Figure Tag</figcaption>
32      </figure>
33    <p> The Getty preserves, studies, and interprets the world&rsquo;s artistic legacy for the benefit of present and
       future generations </p>
```

11. Using the Code pane, delete the placeholder text that was included in the figure and figcaption elements.

```
25
26 ▼    <figure><img src="images/villa.jpg" alt="Getty Villa Sculpture Garden" width="450" height="338">|
27 ▼      <figcaption>
28 ▼         <p><strong>Getty Villa Sculpture Garden</strong><br>
29            Fountain and sculpture in the Peristyle Garden of the Getty Villa Roman gardens.<br>
30            Photo by Bobak Ha'Eri.</p>
31          </figcaption>
32      </figure>
33    <p> The Getty preserves, studies, and interprets the world&rsquo;s artistic legacy for the benefit of present and
       future generations.</p>
34      <p> The J. Paul Getty Museum seeks to inspire curiosity about, and enjoyment and understanding of, the visual arts
```

12. Using the CSS Designer panel, define a new tag selector named **figure** with the following settings:

width:	300px
margin-top:	0px
margin-right:	0px
margin-bottom:	10px
margin-left:	10px
float:	right

Because the figcaption is nested inside the figure element, it is also affected by the width and float values you defined here.

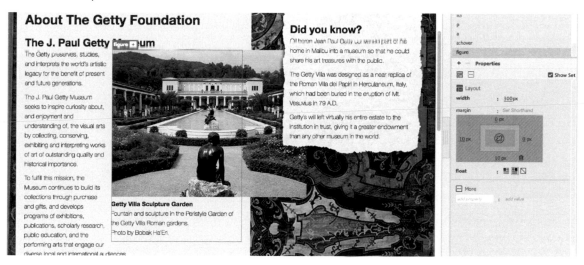

13. Using the CSS Designer panel, define a new tag selector named **figcaption** with the following settings:

font-style:	italic
font-size:	12px
line-height:	15px
text-align:	right

14. Choose File>Save All, then continue to the next exercise.

CREATE DESCENDANT SELECTORS

Three items remain in the list of known formatting requirements:

- Images in the main-copy section should not extend past the edge of the containing section element.

- The sidebar text should be centered, and a border should appear below the h2 element in that section.

- Navigation links in the header area should be larger, and should align to the right edge of the nav container.

Each of these items refers to content in a specific area of the page. To meet these requirements without affecting similar tags in other areas, you need to define **descendant selectors** (also called compound selectors) to format certain elements only within a specific area.

1. **With about.html open, click to select the image in the section#main-copy element.**

2. **Select museum-styles.css in the Sources section of the CSS Designer panel, then click the Add Selector button to the left of the Selectors heading.**

   When an element is selected in the page layout, the new selector automatically adopts the name of the active insertion point, including all tags in the path to the active insertion point.

   This compound or descendant selector specifically identifies where the properties will be applied: in this case, all img elements that exist in a figure element, which is in an element with the #main-copy ID attribute.

3. **Define the following properties for the new #main-copy figure img selector:**

width:	300px
height:	auto

   If you defined settings for the basic img element, you would affect all images on the page — including the logo at the top of the page. You are using a descendant selector here because you only want to affect images in the main-copy section.

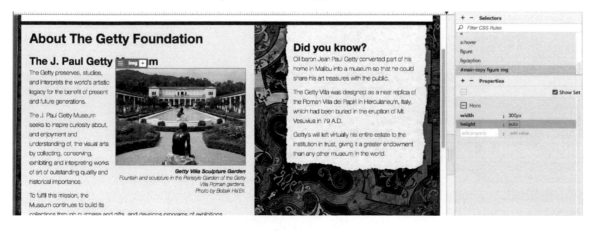

4. **Click the Add Selector button again. With the new name highlighted, type #sidebar p, then press Return/Enter two times to finalize the new name.**

It is not necessary to first place the insertion point or select an object to create a descendant selector. You can simply type the appropriate selector name.

5. **Define the following settings for the #sidebar p selector:**

   text-align: center

6. **Create another descendant selector named #sidebar h2 using the following settings:**

padding-bottom:	10px
text-align:	center
border-bottom-width:	thin
border-bottom-style:	solid
border-botom-color:	sample the brown color in the client's logo

6. **Create another descendant selector named nav p using the following settings:**

margin-top:	20px
font-size:	20px
text-align:	right

7. **Save all files (File>Save All) and close them.**

8. **Export a site definition named Museum.ste into your WIP>Museum folder, and then remove the Museum site from Dreamweaver.**

If necessary, refer back to Project 1: Bistro Site Organization for complete instructions on exporting a site definition or removing a site from Dreamweaver.

fill in the blank

1. The _____ tag is used to attach an external CSS file to an HTML file.

2. A(n) _____ is the formal name of a CSS rule.

3. A(n) _____ style sheet stores CSS rules in a separate file, which can be linked to multiple HTML pages.

4. Click the _____ button in the CSS Designer panel to create a new CSS files or define an existing external CSS file that should be used for the active page.

5. A(n) _____ selector type is used to control unique div elements.

6. A(n) _____ selector type is used to format specific HTML tags.

7. A(n) _____ selector type can be used to format specific tags only within a certain div.

8. The _____ property can be used to attach an object to the right or left side of the containing object.

9. The _____ property exists inside the container; background properties of the container extend into this area.

10. The _____ exists around the container; background properties of the container do not extend into this area.

short answer

1. Briefly explain two reasons why CSS is the preferred method for creating a web page layout.

2. Briefly explain the difference between external, embedded, and inline styles.

3. Briefly explain how padding, margin, and border properties relate to the CSS box model.

Use what you learned in this project to complete the following freeform exercise.
Carefully read the art director and client comments, then create your own design to meet the needs of the project.
Use the space below to sketch ideas; when finished, write a brief explanation of your reasoning behind your final design.

art director comments

You have been hired by the local chapter of the Girls & Boys Club of America to design a web page featuring the programs that are available to local community. The club director wants the site to be easily navigable, and attractive to both children and their parents.

❏ Download the client-supplied resources in the **Club_DW18_PB.zip** archive on the Student Files web page.

❏ Create a cohesive site design for all pages in the site.

❏ Create individual pages for each category that is defined by the client.

❏ Find one main image that supports the message of each page on the site. Look for public-domain images to minimize costs (try unsplash.com).

client comments

Our group serves thousands of children in the local community, especially during the summer when school is not in session. We serve children from all demographics, and we encourage kids to build relationships regardless of social or economic status.

We don't want to present too much information on any one screen, so we'd like each program to be featured on its own page. In addition to the Home page, we want individual pages for:

– Personal Development program

– Summer Tutoring program

– Overnight Adventure program

– VolunTeen Enrichment program

– Career Mentoring program

project justification

_____

_____

_____

_____

_____

_____

_____

_____

_____

_____

_____

_____

_____

_____

Project Summary

Cascading style sheets offer tremendous flexibility when you are designing the look and feel of a website. By linking multiple HTML files to a single external CSS file — with or without an HTML page template — you can experiment with options by altering the CSS selectors and immediately seeing the effect on all linked pages. In addition to this flexibility, CSS is also compliant with current web design standards, which means pages designed with CSS are both search-engine and accessibility-software friendly.

By completing this project, you have worked with different types of selectors to control both the layout of an HTML page and the formatting attributes of different elements on different pages in the site. The site structure is entirely controlled by the selectors in the linked CSS file, so you could change the appearance of the entire site without ever touching the individual HTML pages. And the inverse is also true — you can change the content of individual pages without affecting the site structure.

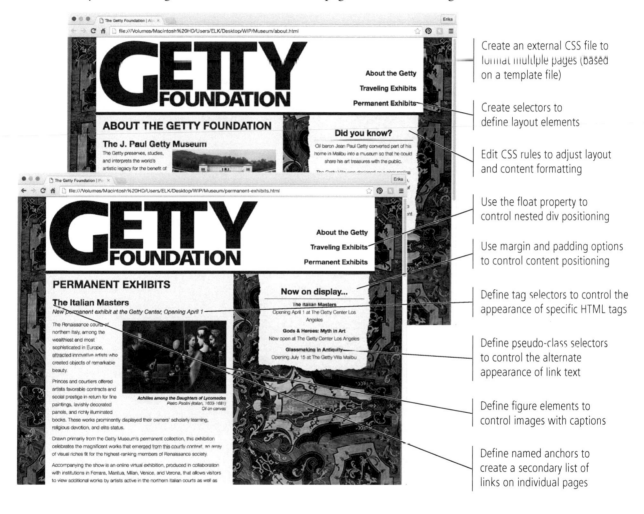

Create an external CSS file to format multiple pages (based on a template file)

Create selectors to define layout elements

Edit CSS rules to adjust layout and content formatting

Use the float property to control nested div positioning

Use margin and padding options to control content positioning

Define tag selectors to control the appearance of specific HTML tags

Define pseudo-class selectors to control the alternate appearance of link text

Define figure elements to control images with captions

Define named anchors to create a secondary list of links on individual pages

Music Festival CSS Site

Your client promotes a long-running music festival that takes place every year in the California desert. Your job is to finalize the existing pages in the site and add a simple form that users can submit to join the client's email list.

This project incorporates the following skills:

- ❏ Working with CSS classes
- ❏ Manually editing CSS code
- ❏ Making an editable attribute in a template
- ❏ Working with the float and clear properties
- ❏ Creating an iframe element
- ❏ Creating and formatting form fields

client comments

The working files that we've seen so far are on the right track, but the pages still need some fine-tuning.

We want a different feature image to appear behind the main content area on every page in the site.

The images on the food pages aren't the same size; we'd like them to be consistent, so the pages don't look so messy.

Also, we need to be able to update the festival schedule page frequently, but we don't want to have to deal with the whole site structure. Can you set it up so we can edit one simple page and have our changes show up on the site?

Finally, we want a form that users can submit to get updates about new vendors, performers, and so on. It doesn't need to be complicated, just name and email address, and we'd also like to know how users heard about the festival.

art director comments

The basic site design has already been created using a Dreamweaver template and CSS styles. You need to modify the existing template and CSS files where necessary to meet the client's first two goals.

The third objective is fairly easy to accomplish using an iframe, which will feed one HTML page into another when a browser calls the containing page. You will, however, need to apply a couple of simple workarounds when it comes to formatting the elements in the included page.

The final goal is the form. Again, Dreamweaver makes this very easy to accomplish. This doesn't need to be a large form, and you can use built-in tools to create everything you need.

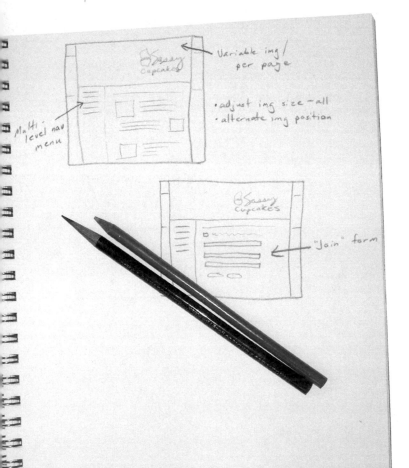

project objectives

To complete this project, you will:

- ❑ Create class selectors to place background images
- ❑ Make an editable attribute in a template
- ❑ Control float and clear properties
- ❑ Search page code to apply classes
- ❑ Apply multiple classes to elements
- ❑ Insert one HTML page into another
- ❑ Create a form element and form fields
- ❑ Apply CSS to form fields

Stage 1   Working with Classes

As you complete this project, keep the following points about CSS in mind:

- **Tag selectors** define properties for a specific HTML element; all content on the page with that tag is affected. For example, properties in the a tag selector format every instance that is marked with **<a>** tags (all links on the page).

- **ID selectors** define properties for an element that has been named with a specific ID. In the page code, the ID is applied as an attribute of the relevant tag, such as **<section id="header">**.

    It is important to remember that each ID can only be applied once on a particular page, which means each element can be uniquely addressed. ID selector names begin with the # character, such as **#header**.

- **Compound selectors** (also called **descendant selectors**) define properties for a specific HTML element only within a defined path, such as **section#header a** to format all **a** elements (links) only within a section with the ID attribute of "header".

- **Pseudo-classes** define properties for alternate states of an element, such as the **a:hover** pseudo-class, which defines the appearance of a link when the mouse cursor hovers over that link.

You should also understand the nested nature of CSS properties (and HTML in general). Tags in a page contain other tags, creating a nested structure that is a type of **parent-child relationship**. Nested tags (the children) inherit properties from their containing (parent) tags; tags at the same level of nesting are referred to as **siblings**. Consider the following example:

```
<body>

    <header>

    <section id-"main">

        <article id="right">

    <footer>
```

Any properties that you define in the **body** tag selector automatically apply to all content on the page, because the **<body>** tag is the parent of all the nested elements. You can override those settings in a specific element by defining different properties for a specific ID.

If you define (for example) a different font size for the **#main** ID selector, the new font size will override the font-size properties in the **body** tag selector for the **<section id="main">** tag. The same font size is also inherited by its child (**<article id="right">**), but not by its siblings (**<header>** and **<footer>**).

REVIEW EXISTING SITE FILES

When you start any new project — especially one where some of the work is already done — you should begin by analyzing the existing files and then determine what work needs to be completed. You will then be better able to create a plan to efficiently accomplish the necessary work.

1. Download **Voices_DW18_RF.zip** from the Student Files web page.

2. Expand the ZIP archive in your WIP folder (Macintosh) or copy the archive contents into your WIP folder (Windows).

   This results in a folder named **Voices**, which contains the files you need for this project.

3. Create a new site named **Voices**, using the WIP>Voices folder as the site root folder.

4. In the Files panel, expand the Templates folder and then open the **design.dwt** file in the regular Design view.

   Although the applied CSS might not render properly in the regular Design view, many Live view options are not available when working with Dreamweaver template files.

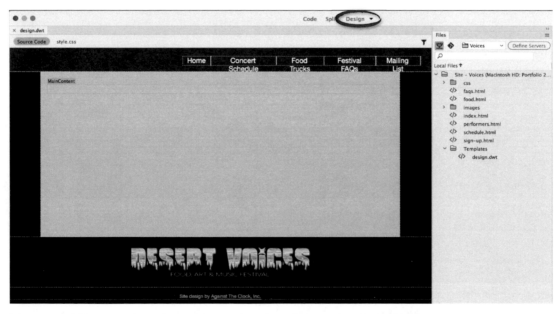

This site includes a number of pages that are based on this template. You should notice that there is only one editable area (named "MainContent"), where all page-specific text and images are placed.

A CSS file (named style.css) is attached to the template, which means it defines properties for all pages that are attached to the template.

To complete this project you need to accomplish a number of tasks:

1. Add a page-specific background image to the main area of the page.

2. Format the content on individual pages to meet aesthetic requirements.

3. Link the "Performers" file to the schedule page that appears in the site.

4. Create a form so users can sign up to receive information via email.

5. Continue to the next exercise.

Note:

The index.html file in this project has a slightly different layout, so that file is not based on the template file.

CREATE A CLASS SELECTOR TO PLACE BACKGROUND IMAGES

A **class selector** defines properties for any element that is marked with that class. Classes offer a number of advantages over other kinds of selectors:

- A class can be applied multiple times on a single page, unlike an ID selector which can be applied only once on a page.

- A class can be applied to different HTML tags on the same page, which means you can apply the same class to (for example) an **h2** element and an **img** element.

- A class only applies to specific elements where you attach it, unlike a tag selector that affects all same-tagged elements on the page. For example, an **h2** tag selector affects all **h2** elements on the page; a class selector can be applied to only specific **h2** elements without affecting other **h2** elements on the page.

- You can apply more than one class to a single element, which means you can define classes to perform very specific tasks, and then apply only and exactly what you need to a specific element.

Note:

The one primary disadvantage of classes, however, is that they must be intentionally and manually attached to every element where you want those properties to apply.

1. With the **design.dwt** template open in the regular Design view, show the CSS Designer panel in All mode.

2. Select style.css in the Sources section of the panel, then click the Add Selector button in the Selectors section of the panel.

   Remember, to add a new selector in the CSS Designer panel, you must first select the source where you want to add the style. We will not continue to repeat these instructions every time you need to add a new selector in this project.

Note:

Feel free to work in either Design view or Split view. We will tell you when you need to work in the Code pane, and when you need to change to a specific view.

3. With the new selector name highlighted, type **.bkgFaqs**. Press Return/Enter to finalize the new selector name.

   Class selector names always begin with a period.

4. Make sure Show Set is not checked, then click the Background button at the top of the Properties section to jump to those options in the list.

5. Define the following options for the new selector:

background-image URL:	**images/backgrounds/back-faqs.jpg**
background-size:	**cover**

   The Related Files bar above the document window shows that the style.css file has been changed. However, nothing has changed in the open template file. Classes do not affect a page until they are intentionally applied to one or more elements.

Add Selector button

6. **If the new selector does not appear at the bottom of the list in the CSS Designer panel, click the new class selector and drag it to the bottom of the list.**

New selectors are automatically added below the previously selected item (yours might have been in a different location than ours). You can reorder them by simply dragging in the panel.

Although this step isn't strictly necessary, it is a good idea to keep your styles organized to make them easier to navigate.

Nothing has changed in the page file.

The style.css file has changed.

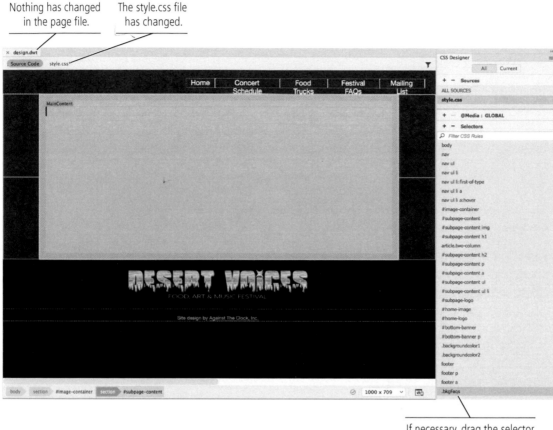

If necessary, drag the selector to the bottom of the list.

7. **Click to place the insertion point in the MainContent area.**

8. **In the Tag Selector, click to select the section#image-container element.**

The insertion point is placed in the paragraph element in the editable template region.

The editable region is nested inside a section element that defines the gray background color.

The primary parent, section#image-container, will contain the background images.

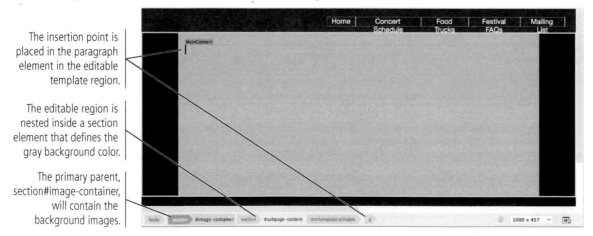

9. **In the Properties panel, open the Class menu and choose bkgFaqs.**

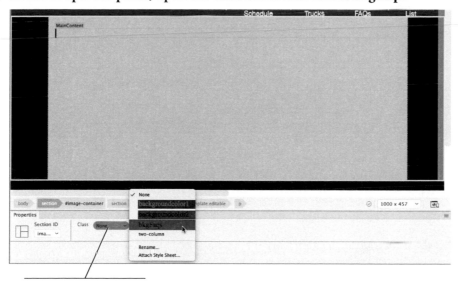

Use this menu to apply a
class to the active selection.

After applying the class, you can see the background image that is defined by the class inside the selected element.

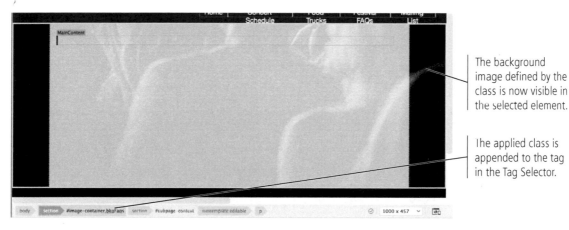

The background image defined by the class is now visible in the selected element.

The applied class is appended to the tag in the Tag Selector.

10. **Choose File>Save to save the template file. When prompted, update all files linked to the template. When the Update Pages dialog box shows the process is done, click the Close button.**

11. **Click style.css in the Related Files bar to show that file's code, then choose File>Save.**

In this exercise, you changed both the page and the attached CSS file, so you need to save both files.

Click style.css to open
that file in the Code
pane, then save the file.

12. **Continue to the next exercise.**

MANUALLY EDIT CSS CODE

The class selector you created in the previous exercise defines a background image for the header element. Remember, though, you need to apply different images to the same element on each page. In this exercise, you will define additional classes that you will apply in the next exercise.

1. **With design.dwt open, click the Code button in the Document toolbar. If necessary, click style.css in the Related Files bar to show that file instead of the template page source code.**

2. **Scroll to the bottom of the code and review the class selector that you created in the previous exercise.**

   The selector code appears at the bottom of the file because you dragged it to the bottom of the list in the CSS Designer panel. The order of selector code in the CSS file matches the order you see in the CSS Designer panel.

   CSS code uses the following syntax:

   >   name {
   >   property:value;
   >   }

3. **Click and drag from the line number for line 187 to the number for line 190.**

   Clicking a line number selects the entire line of code.

   > Click and drag over the line numbers to select entire lines of code.
   > ```
   > 187 ▾ .bkgFaqs {
   > 188        background-image: url(../images/backgrounds/back-faqs.jpg);
   > 189        background-size: cover;
   > 190 }
   > ```

   Rather than using the CSS Styles panel, you are going to simply copy and paste the required code, then make the necessary changes in each version.

4. **Choose Edit>Copy (Command/Control-C) to copy the selected code.**

5. **Click at the beginning of Line 191 to place the insertion point, then choose Edit>Paste (Command/Control-V).**

   This results in two .bkgFaqs selectors; you will change the selector name and background-image URL of the duplicate in the next few steps.

6. **Review the Files panel.**

   The name of each HTML file gives you an idea of what each page contains. Because you will use a different class to change each page's header background, you should use similarly indicative class names to make your work easier later.

7. **In line 191 of the Code pane, change the class name to .bkgFood.**

8. **In line 192, select and delete the code that defines the image path. Leave the closing semicolon in place.**

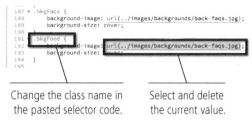

Change the class name in the pasted selector code.

Select and delete the current value.

9. **Type u to open the Code Hints menu.**

   When you work directly in the Code pane, Dreamweaver provides code hints related to the current context. As soon as you type the letter u, the Code Hints menu shows the only matching available option — the url() attribute of the background-image property.

10. **Press Return/Enter to accept the highlighted option in the Code Hints menu.**

    Again, Dreamweaver provides significant help when you are working directly in the Code pane. As soon as you accept the url() attribute, the application moves the cursor inside the parentheses and presents a menu of possible values. The Browse option at the top of the menu is highlighted by default.

11. **Press Return/Enter to accept the Browse option in the Code Hints menu.**

    You can also double-click Browse in the menu to open the navigation dialog box.

12. **In the resulting navigation dialog box, select back-food.jpg (in the site's images>backgrounds folder) and click Open/OK.**

Note:

You can also manually type the required file name in the CSS code. If you choose to use this option, make sure the file names you type match exactly what you see in the Files panel. Capitalization matters!

13. **In the Code view, move your mouse over the new image path.**

    This technique allows you to preview a specific image directly in the Code view.

14. Repeat this process to add two more class selectors, using the following information:

Class name	Background Image
bkgSchedule	back-schedule.jpg
bkgSignup	back-mailing.png

Note:

You don't need a class for performers.html. Later in this project, you are going to place it into schedule.html, which will already have the required background image.

```
186   }
187 ▼ .bkgFaqs {
188       background-image: url(../images/backgrounds/back-faqs.jpg);
189       background-size: cover;
190   }
191 ▼ .bkgFood {
192       background-image: url(../images/backgrounds/back-food.jpg);
193       background-size: cover;
194   }
195 ▼ .bkgSchedule {
196       background-image: url(../images/backgrounds/back-schedule.jpg);
197       background-size: cover;
198   }
199 ▼ .bkgSignup {
200       background-image: url(../images/backgrounds/back-mailing.jpg);
201       background-size: cover;
202   }
```

15. Save the CSS file and then continue to the next exercise.

MAKE AN EDITABLE ATTRIBUTE IN A TEMPLATE

You need to apply different background images to the header element for each page in this site. However, the section element in the template where the background image is defined is not an editable area, which means you can't select it to apply the necessary class in pages where the template is applied.

To solve this problem, you can define an editable attribute in the template. This allows you to change only that attribute on each page.

1. With **design.dwt** open, turn on the Split view and show the page source code in the Code pane.

2. Click to select the section#image-container element in the layout.

In the Code pane, the code related to the active selection is also highlighted. The first line of the highlighted code shows the opening section tag, along with the applied class attribute. In the next few steps, you are going to make the class attribute editable in pages that are attached to this template.

The .bkgFaqs class is applied to the selected element.

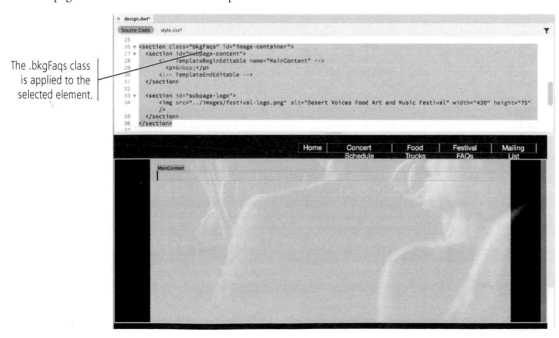

3. **Choose Tools>Templates>Make Attribute Editable.**

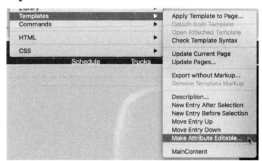

4. **In the resulting dialog box, make sure CLASS is selected in the Attribute menu, then check the Make Attribute Editable option.**

   All attributes of the selected tag are available In this menu (in this case, only CLASS is applied so it is the only one available).

5. **Click OK to apply the change.**

   When you make an attribute editable in a template, the previously defined value is removed from the page code. In the Design view, the background image is no longer visible in the template.

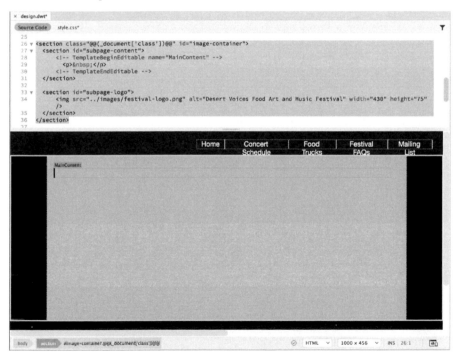

6. **Save the template file, updating linked pages when asked.**

7. **Close the Update Links dialog box, then close the template file.**

8. **Using the Files panel, open the faqs.html file and turn on the Live view.**

Because you are now working with a regular HTML file and not editing the template, you can switch back to the Live view for a better preview of your changes.

As you can see, this file still shows the background image as defined in the .bkgFaqs class. You do not need to modify the template attribute for this file.

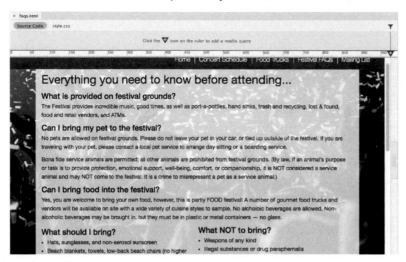

9. **Open the file food.html.**

This file also shows the background image as defined in the .bkgFaqs class, because that class is still defined in the template file (even though you made it an editable attribute).

10. **In the CSS Designer panel, select style.css in the Sources list to show all selectors that are available in that file.**

In the next few steps, you will need to type these exact class names to change the attribute values for individual pages in the site. By displaying the selectors in the CSS Designer panel, you can see exactly what you need to type.

11. **Choose Edit>Template Properties.**

The resulting dialog box shows all editable properties of the applied template. In this case, the class attribute (of the header element, even though this information is not presented in the dialog box).

12. In the Class field at the bottom of the dialog box, type the name of the class you want to apply (bkgFood).

Unfortunately, Dreamweaver does not provide you with a menu of available class names; you have to type the exact class name (without the opening period).

Note:

Click away from the class field to see the changed value in the top section of the dialog box.

13. Click OK to apply the change.

Even though the section#Image-container element is not selectable or editable on the page, the background image defined in the bkgFood class now appears in the section#image-container element.

14. Save the file and close it.

15. Repeat the same process to change the class for the other two secondary pages:

File name	Class
schedule.html	bkgSchedule
sign-up.html	bkgSignup

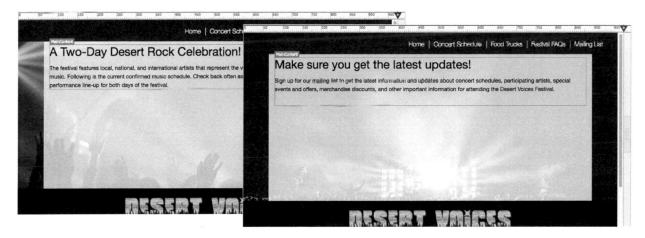

16. Save and close any open files, then continue to the next exercise.

The Float property of CSS defines how an element attaches to its container and how other elements appear in relation to the floating element.

- If you define a left float value, the floating element attaches to the left edge of its container; other content wraps around the right edge of the floating element.

- If you define a right float value, the floating element attaches to the right edge of its container; other content wraps around the left edge of the floating element.

- If you define a none float value, the element does not float; other content does not wrap around the non-floating element.

1. **Open the file food.html and make sure the Live view is active. Scroll through the page if necessary and review the contents.**

   Each listing includes a photo and a brief description. If you look closely, however, you will notice that the images are not uniform in size. Rather than manually editing each image, you are going to define a class that controls the size of each image where that class is applied.

   As a general rule, you should avoid scaling images without resampling in Dreamweaver because the web server still has to transmit all of the file data for the original-size image.

   In this case, the required scaling is very slight, and would not require users to download huge amounts of unnecessary data. As a "best practice," however, it would be better to edit the actual image files in an image-editing application such as Adobe Photoshop.

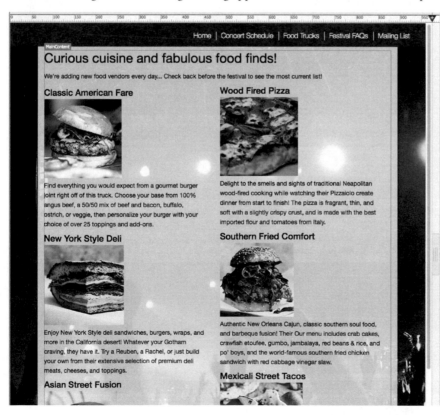

2. Using the CSS Designer panel, create a new class selector named **.img150px**. Define the following properties:

width:	150 px
height:	150 px
margin-left:	0 px
margin-right:	10 px
float:	left

Note:

All of the food images in this site are square, so you are not changing their aspect ratio.

3. **Click the first food image to select it. In the Properties panel, open the Class menu and choose img150px.**

   This menu provides the same options as the contextual menu for a specific tag in the Tag Selector. You can apply any class that is available in the attached CSS file to the selected object.

Note:

Any changes you make in the right side of the panel automatically change the related selector properties.

As you can see, the selected image resizes slightly. Because you defined the float:left property, other content is able to wrap around the right edge of the image.

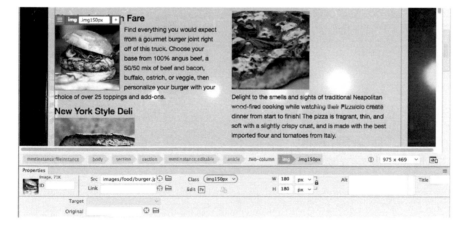

4. **Choose Find>Find and Replace in Files.**

   Remember, this command opens the Find and Replace dialog box.

   As we explained previously, classes only work when you intentionally apply them to selected elements. This can be very time consuming when you need to apply the same class to a large number of elements.

   Whenever you face a repetitive task, it is a good idea to look for a way to automate the process. In this case, you are going to use the Find and Replace function to apply the same class to all img elements on this page.

5. **Click the Advanced option at the top of the dialog box.**

   Dreamweaver is a web design application, so the Find and Replace dialog box includes options for easily performing exactly the kind of task you need to complete — assigning a single class to multiple elements on multiple pages.

   The Advanced Find and Replace options allow you to search for specific tags, with or without specific attributes.

   Click the Plus button to add a Search parameter.

   Click the Minus button to remove a Search parameter.

   Use this menu to define parameters of the search.

6. **Choose Current Document in the Find In menu.**

7. **Click the [any tag] field to the right of the Find In menu and type img.**

   You are going to search for any img tag in this document. You can also use the menu attached to the search field to scroll through a list of every available option.

8. **If anything appears immediately below the Search menus, click the Minus button (–) to remove those parameters from the search.**

9. **Open the Action menu and choose Set Attribute (if it is not already selected).**

10. **Type class in the Search field, then choose img150px in the To field menu.**

   By searching for a specific tag, you can locate all <img> tags at once. Using the Action menu, you can easily apply the selected class (img150px) as an attribute to all <img> tags in all open documents.

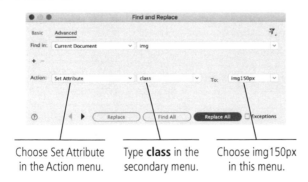

   Choose Set Attribute in the Action menu.   Type **class** in the secondary menu.   Choose img150px in this menu.

11. **Click Replace All, read the resulting message, then click OK.**

   Remember, all but one of these files are based on a template. The client's logo, which is placed in the near the bottom of the page, is an image, so it uses the <img> tag. However, because the logo is not an editable region, the Find and Replace function is not able to add the attribute for the logo. This is why the logo is outside the editable template region — to protect it from changes, even inadvertent ones that would have been made by this type of Find and Replace.

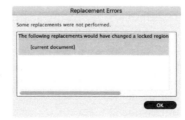

12. Review the Search panel, then close the tab group.

When you use the Find and Replace dialog box, the Search panel automatically opens to show the results of the process.

13. Review the results of the replacement.

14. Choose File>Save All, then continue to the next exercise.

DREAMWEAVER FOUNDATIONS

CSS Mode of the Properties Panel

You can easily make changes to CSS rules using the options in the CSS mode of the Properties panel:

- Targeted Rule shows the CSS rule applied to the current selection. You can also choose a different target rule in the attached menu, or choose New CSS Rule from the menu to create a new selector.

- Edit Rule opens the CSS Rule Definition dialog box for the targeted rule.

- CSS Designer opens the CSS Designer panel and displays properties for the active selection.

- Font, Size, and Color change the associated options in the targeted rule.

- The Font Style and Font Weight menus define the font-style and font-weight properties (respectively).

- Align Left, Align Center, Align Right, and Justify change the text-align property of the targeted rule.

As we explained in the beginning of this project, some professionals define very specific classes to accomplish only a defined goal. This method can make it easier to understand the purpose of various classes, especially after you return to a project you created a long time ago, if you work on files created by another user, or if you hand off your site files to another designer.

Using this technique, however, often requires multiple classes applied to the same element. Fortunately, Dreamweaver makes that process relatively easy. In this exercise, you will create a new class that assigns the float:right property, then apply that class to every other image in the list of food vendors.

1. **With food.html open and the Live view active, click style.css in the Related Files bar to show that file in the Code pane.**

   As you know, you can use the CSS Designer panel to edit the properties associated with a specific CSS selector. Once you are comfortable with the basic concepts of CSS, you might find it easier to work directly in the Code pane to make necessary changes.

   When you write code, you must follow the proper rules of **syntax** (the formal structure or "grammar" required in code). Dreamweaver Code Hints facilitate writing and changing code; hints make it easier to create the proper syntax and ensure that your code functions as expected.

2. **In the Code pane, scroll to the end of the existing code. Place the insertion point in the first empty line and type:**

   ```
   .imgFloatRight {
   ```

3. **Press Return/Enter.**

   When you press Return/Enter, Dreamweaver automatically adds the required closing bracket to the code.

   ```
   210  }
   211 ▼ .imgFloatRight {
   212
   213  }
   ```

4. **Type flo .**

   As soon as you begin typing, the Code Hints menu presents options that match the characters you type.

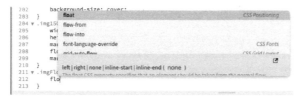

5. **With the float property highlighted in the menu, press Return/Enter to add that property to the selector code.**

   Code Hints are invaluable for creating the proper code syntax. If you don't know the exact name of a property, you can use the Code Hints menu to find exactly what you need.

   After you add a specific property to the selector code, Dreamweaver automatically adds the required colon and shows the default value options in a secondary Code Hints menu.

   ```
   206    height:
   207    margin-
   288    float: left
   209    margin-
   210  }       none
   211 ▼ .imgFloatR
   212    float:   right
   213  }
   ```

6. **Choose right in the resulting Code Hints menu, then type a semicolon at the end of the line.**

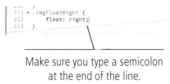

Make sure you type a semicolon
at the end of the line.

7. **With the Live view active in the Design pane, click to select the image under the "New York Style Deli" heading.**

8. **Click the Add Class/ID button in the Element Display.**

   The Element Display appears at the top of the selected element.

Note:

Click the menu button on the left side of the Element Display to edit HTML properties of the selected img element:

9. **In the resulting field, type .i and then click .imgFloatRight in the menu to apply that class.**

   As soon as you type in the field, Dreamweaver presents a list of available options that match the characters you type.

10. **Click Source Code in the Related Files bar to show the page source in the Code pane.**

    In the code for the selected **<img>** tag, you can see the two classes are listed inside the quotes for the class attribute.

    If you remember, the **img150px** defined a float:left property. Because the **imgFloatRight** class comes second — it is later in the nesting order — the float:right property overrides the previous float value.

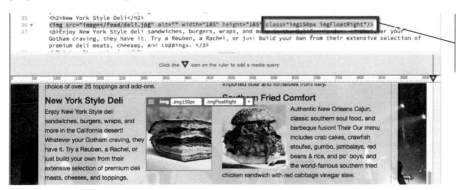

The class attribute for the <img> tag includes two values inside the quotes, separated by a space.

11. Using the same technique, apply the imgFloatRight class to the Southern Fried Comfort image.

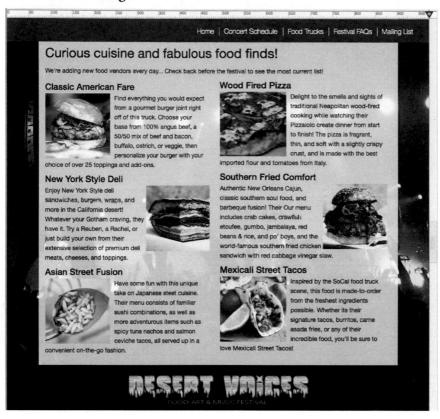

12. Choose File>Save All, close the food.html file, then continue to the next exercise.

INSERT ONE HTML PAGE INTO ANOTHER

The client wants to be able to easily update the schedule without interacting with the entire site, so the master schedule is being managed in a simple file named performers. html. (This scenario is not uncommon in professional web design.)

Rather than copying and pasting the content from one file to another, in this exercise you will create an iframe element to load one HTML file inside another. When a browser calls the page, the web server reads the link and delivers the linked file as part of the parent page.

1. Open schedule.html and make sure the Live view is active.

2. Click to select the paragraph element after the heading.

3. Click the iframe button in the HTML Insert panel, then click the After button in the Position Assistant.

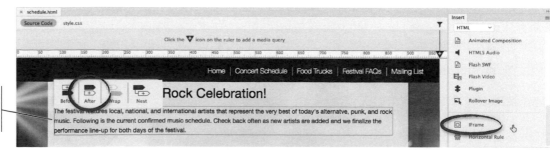

You are adding the iFrame element after this paragraph.

4. Show the page source in the Code pane.

The iframe element appears after (below) the previously selected paragraph element in both the Code and Design panes. At this point is has no content because you have not yet defined the iframe's source.

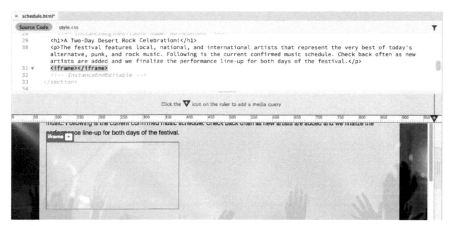

5. Place the insertion point before the closing ">" of the opening tag. Press the spacebar once to open the Code Hint menu.

6. Type src, and press Return/Enter to accept src in the Code Hint menu.

Accepting the menu option automatically places the required =" " characters in the code for you and opens the Code Hint menu with the Browse option already highlighted.

7. When the second Code Hints menu appears, press the down-arrow key until performers.html is highlighted, then press Return/Enter.

After defining the src attribute for the iframe element, you can see the defined file's content inside the iframe when the Live view is active.

The iframe element is commonly used to display entirely external websites (such as a displaying a Twitter or Facebook feed), styles that apply to the parent page are not inherited by the child page in the iframe element.

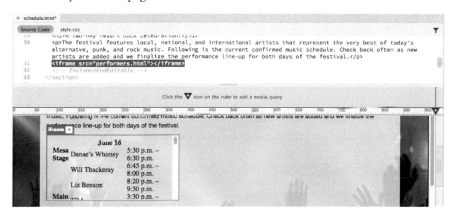

8. **Using the CSS Designer panel, define a new tag selector named iframe using the following settings:**

width:	750px
height:	350px
border:	0px

An iframe is still an HTML element, which means you can format its basic appearance using CSS selectors.

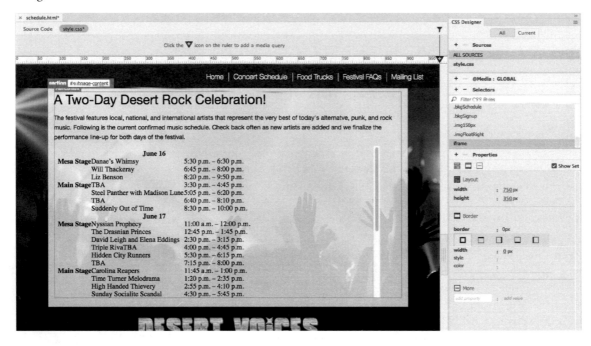

9. **Open performers.html.**

The source page in this iframe is not linked to style.css, because you don't want some of the attributes applied to the embedded page (such as the background color of the overall body element). Instead, you are going to link the update page to a second CSS file that contains only the styles you need for those elements.

10. **In the CSS Designer panel, click the Add CSS Source button and choose Attach Existing CSS File.**

11. **Click the Browse button in the resulting dialog box. Navigate to style-performers.css (in the site's css folder) and click Open to return to the Attach Existing CSS File dialog box.**

12. Choose the Link option, then click OK to attach the CSS file to the performers.html file.

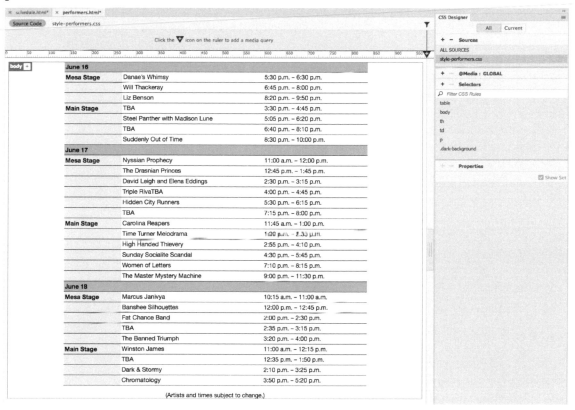

13. Save and close performers.html.

14. Turn the Live view off and back on, then review the iframe content.

At times your changes do not reflect unless you first toggle the Live view off and on.

Note:

To simplify this exercise, we provided the second external CSS file for you. In a professional environment, you would probably have to determine the appropriate styles and create the file yourself.

15. Save and close all files, then continue to the next stage of the project.

Stage 2 Creating Online Forms

Online forms are used to collect user information, and then transfer that information to web servers. Surveys, electronic commerce, guest books, polls, and membership applications all make use of online form technologies. While well-designed forms are easy to use, poorly designed forms prove troublesome for both users (who complete the forms) and web server managers (who access user data). Fortunately, Dreamweaver makes it easy to create robust yet understandable forms — simplifying and streamlining the interaction between users and web servers.

Web-based forms are composed of a series of **form objects** (also referred to as **form fields**). Different types of form objects have different purposes, and they gather different types of information. Basically, all form objects allow users to enter data; each object type facilitates a distinct format of data input. You can use Dreamweaver to create a number of different form objects, including text fields, radio buttons, check boxes, menus, and buttons.

It is important to realize that processing a submitted form requires some type of script. These contain instructions to identify the user's data and then perform tasks based on that data. You can write your own scripts, and many hosting providers offer sample form-processing scripts (as well as instructions on how to implement those scripts when you build a form).

CREATE A FORM ELEMENT

A form element is a distinct element of a web page; it is the container for all form objects. As a container, the form element ensures that different form objects are related to one another, which makes it possible to combine all of the form information as a single submission. A form's Submit button identifies all related form objects and collects the information they contain in a single string.

1. **Open sign-up.html from the Voices site root folder.**

2. **With the Live view active, click to select the paragraph element after the heading.**

3. **Open the Insert panel and show the Form options.**

4. **Click the form button in the Form Insert panel, then click the After button in the Position Assistant.**

Show the panel in Form mode.

You are adding the form element after this paragraph element.

4. **In the Properties panel, type `register` in the Form ID field and type `mailto:info@voices` in the Action field. Leave the remaining fields at their default values.**

The form ID creates a unique name for the form you are creating. This will be useful later when you apply CSS to format the various form elements.

The **mailto:** protocol in the Action field is one method of receiving data without using a script. When a user submits the form, the user's default email client opens and creates a message with the form data. This is not a particularly reliable method for receiving form data, but it suits the purpose if you are gathering generic information; however, it is not suitable for gathering sensitive information such as credit card numbers.

Note:

You use the mailto protocol in this exercise because we cannot be certain that everyone has access to the same script on a specific type of server.

We are intentionally using an incomplete email address here to avoid conflicts with any actual websites.

The form tag now includes the defined #register ID attribute.

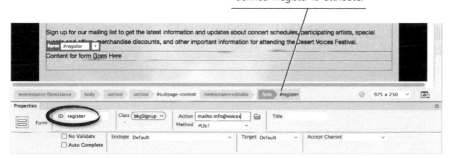

5. **Save the file and continue to the next exercise.**

The Form Properties Panel in Depth

The Form Properties panel allows you to control the options related to a specific form area.

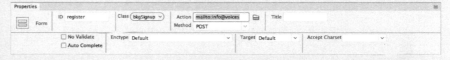

- **Form ID** is a unique name that identifies the form for scripting or CSS formatting.
- **Action** specifies the page or script that will process the form data, essentially determining what should be done with the form content.
- **Class** allows you to apply a class selector (from a CSS style sheet) to the form.
- **Method** determines how the browser and web server present the form data to the application that processes the form (the action page):
  - **Default** uses the browser's default settings to send the form data to the server. According to W3C specifications, the default method for forms is GET.
  - **GET** attaches form data to the URL of the action page that processes the form data. This method limits the amount and format of data that can be passed to the action page.
  - **POST** sends the form data as a standard input to the action page. This method does not impose any limits on the passed data.

- **No Validate** adds the HTML5 novalidate attribute to the form tag, so the form is not automatically validated when the form is submitted.
- **Auto Complete** sets the HTML5 autocomplete attribute to "on" when checked; this allows the form to autofill based on a user's settings.
- **Enctype** (short for "encoding type") specifies the format in which the data will be sent to the server so the server software can interpret the input correctly. The default is application/x-www-form-urlencoded. The text/plain enctype is used for email replies. If a file is being uploaded with the form, multipart/form-data must be used.
- **Target** defines the window or frame in which the server displays the action page's response (data) to the form.
- **Accept Charset** defines character encodings that are to be used for the form submission. Common values include UTF-8 (Unicode) and ISO-8859-1 (for the Latin alphabet).

CREATE FORM TEXT FIELDS

Text fields, defined with the **<input>** tag, are the fundamental building blocks of almost all online forms. HTML5 adds a number of field types and attributes to the <input> tag, which makes it easy to define special fields such as email addresses, phone numbers, and passwords.

Dreamweaver incorporates these options directly in the Insert Form panel. Keep in mind that not all browsers support all HTML5 input types and other options. If a user's browser does not support certain options, the special fields will behave as regular text fields.

Note:

A text area is similar to a standard text field, but intended for larger amounts of text, such as multiple sentences or paragraphs.

1. **With sign-up.html open, turn off the Live view.**

   It can be easier to create form fields in the regular Design view. You can always toggle on the Live view to see how the fields appear in the rendered page.

2. **Display the Split view and show the page source in the Code pane.**

3. **Select and delete the placeholder text that was added when you inserted the form element.**

   If the Live view is turned off, a red outline identifies the boundary of the newly inserted form. (If you don't see this outline, choose View>Visual Aids>Invisible Elements.)

4. **Click the Text button in the Form Insert panel and drag into the existing form element.**

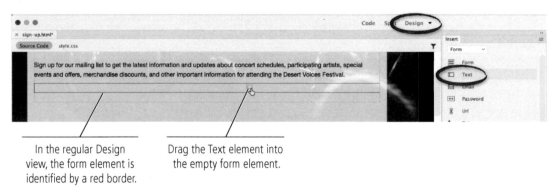

In the regular Design view, the form element is identified by a red border.

Drag the Text element into the empty form element.

5. **Review the Code pane.**

   When you insert a form field, Dreamweaver automatically creates a field and a field label.

   In the Code pane, the **<input>** tags define the text field and **<label>** tags define the text field's label. The field name that you defined is used as both the **name** and the **id** attribute of the **<input>** tag. In the code for the **<label>** tag, the name of the text field is assigned to the **for** attribute — basically defining which text field this is the label *for*.

The <label> tag defines the field label.

The <input> tag defines the text field.

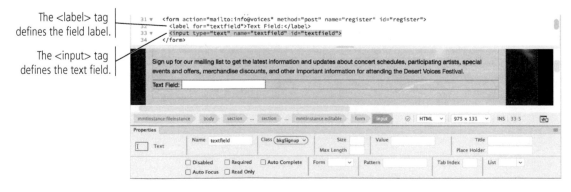

6. **In the Properties panel, change the Name field for the selected field to firstname. Press Return/Enter to finalize the new name.**

In the Code pane, you can see that this changes both the name and ID attributes of the <input> tag, as well as the for attribute of the <label> tag.

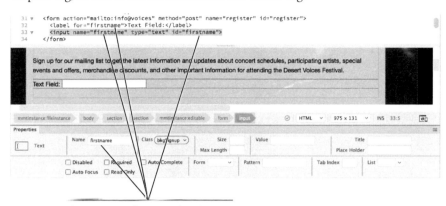

The new name becomes the <input> tag's name and ID attribute, as well as the for attribute of the <label> tag.

7. **With the field still selected in the Design pane, check the Required option in the Properties panel.**

Because you checked the Required box in the Properties panel, the HTML5 **required** attribute is added to the <input> tag. This attribute is a boolean attribute; it is either true or false. It does not need an actual value in quotation marks; its presence in the tag indicates that the attribute is "true" — in other words, this field is required.

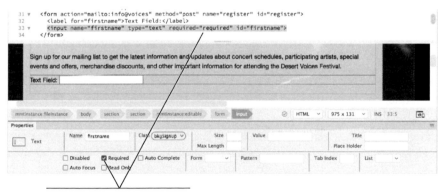

The required attribute is added, which means the field must be filled in to submit the form.

Note:

Later in this project you will use CSS to format the various fields and labels in this form.

8. **In either pane of the document window, change the field label text to First Name:.**

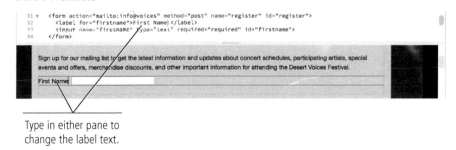

Type in either pane to change the label text.

9. **In the Design pane, place the insertion point after the existing text field, then press Return/Enter to create a new paragraph.**

When you press Return/Enter, the line with the first text field (and its label) is automatically tagged as a paragraph; the **<label>** and **<input>** tags are now surrounded by opening and closing **<p> </p>** tags.

The <label> and <input> tags are now surrounded by opening and closing paragraph tags.

10. **Insert another text field at the insertion point, using `lastname` as the field name and `Last Name:` as the label text. Make the field required.**

Note:

You have to select the actual text field in the document window to change properties in the Properties panel.

Note:

On mobile device browsers that recognize the email type attribute, bringing this type of field into focus causes the on-screen keyboard to show the "@" and ".com" options.

11. **Create a new paragraph after the lastname text field, then click the Email button in the Form Insert panel. Use the Properties panel to make the field required.**

An <input> tag with the **email** type attribute is automatically validated when the form is submitted on HTML5 browsers. Keep in mind that email field validation only looks for the correct pattern of characters (e.g., xxx@xxx.xxx). This validation does not check to see if the user's entry is an actual, working email address.

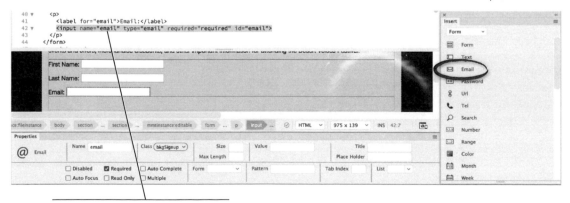

The new field has "email" as the type, name, and ID attributes of the <input> tag and "Email:" as the label text.

12. **Save the file and continue to the next exercise.**

DREAMWEAVER FOUNDATIONS

Most of the options in the Form Insert panel create input elements (using opening and closing <input> tags); the button text in the Form Insert panel determines the type attribute of the resulting input element.

We describe the most common input element — the textfield — first. However, for ease of use, we then list the other types of elements in alphabetical order rather than the order they appear in the Form Insert panel.

Keep in mind that many of these form-object types were added in HTML5, which means they are not yet uniformly supported. If a browser does not support a specific type, the field will simply appear as a regular text field. (HTML5-specific options are noted in **blue**.)

For more information about which browsers support different options, check http://www.w3schools.com/html/html_form_input_types.asp.

Text. This creates an input element with the "textfield" type attribute; users can enter alphanumeric content in the field. In the Properties panel, you can define a number of attributes for a textfield input element:

- **Auto Complete** defines a field that will be automatically filled in with information that is stored somewhere on the user's computer.

  This attribute requires a value of on or off. Because you can control this attribute for an entire form and for individual fields in a form, you can prevent certain fields in an autocomplete form from being included:

      <input type="email" name="email"
      autocomplete="off">

- **Auto Focus** defines a field that is automatically in focus when the form loads.

  This attribute is a boolean value, which means it is either true or false. If true, the autofocus attribute is added to the <input> tag:

      <input type="email" name="email" autofocus>

- **Disabled** defines a field that cannot be modified by the form user. You can use disabled fields to include required, developer-defined information with the form submission. This attribute is a boolean value; if true, the disabled attribute is added to the <input> tag:

      <input type="email" name="email" disabled>

- **Form** can be used to define which form an element is related to. (HTML5 allows you to place form fields outside the boundaries of the actual form element.)

- **List** can be used to call an existing list, which you define somewhere on the page using the datalist element; each item in the list is created as an option element inside the opening and closing <datalist> tags:

      <datalist id="list1">
          <option value="Item 1">
          <option value="Item 1">
      </datalist>

  (The datalist element does not need to be defined within the form element to be applied to a specific form field.)

- **Max Length** is the maximum number of characters that can be entered in the text field.

- **Pattern** defines a regular expression that is the pattern of characters that must be used in a field.

  Regular Expressions are based on JavaScript syntax, which is beyond the scope of this book. The site *html5pattern.com* includes a library of common patterns that have already been created by experienced users; you can copy the necessary pattern code from that site and paste them into Dreamweaver.

- **Place Holder** defines text that appears inside a field when the form first loads. You can use this to provide hints or other advice (such as the expected content).

- **Read Only** defines a field that cannot be modified by the user. This is a boolean value; if true, the readonly attribute is added to the <input> tag:

      <input type="email" name="email" readonly>

- **Required** defines a field that must be filled in for the form to be submitted. This is a boolean value; if true, the required attribute is added to the <input> tag:

      <input type="email" name="email" required>

- **Size** is the number of characters that are visible in the field. (You can also use CSS to define the width property of a field, using any unit of measurement that is supported by CSS.)

- **Tab Index** is order in which a field is selected if a user presses the tab key to move through fields in a form.

- **Title** defines text that appears in a tooltip when the user's mouse moves over a field.

  If you define both value and placeholder attributes for the same field, the value appears in the field when the form opens:

  When a user deletes the existing value, the placeholder attribute content appears in the form field:

  Text Field: This is the placeholder

- **Value** defines an initial value that appears in the field when the form loads. This attribute is actually transmitted when the form is submitted.

Button. This creates a basic button element. You can change the button's name/ID and value in the Properties panel and use scripting to cause the button to do something.

Checkbox. This creates an input element with the "checkbox" type attribute. A checkbox has only two possible values — selected or not selected.

Checkbox Group. A checkbox group is simply a group of checkboxes with the same name attribute. When you click the Checkbox Group button in the Form Insert panel, a dialog box opens where you define the items in the group. (To add more than the default two options, you have to use the + button above the Label field.)

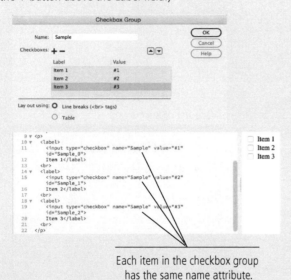

Each item in the checkbox group has the same name attribute.

Color. This creates an input element with the "color" type attribute. When a user clicks the field, a browser-specific color picker allows the user to select a color.

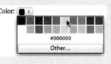

Date. This creates an input element with the "date" type attribute. In addition to the attributes that can be defined for a textfield input element, you can also use the Properties panel to define the following attributes:

- **Min** and **Max** values are the minimum possible date and the maximum possible date, respectively.

- **Step** defines the legal interval for the field.

Users can select a specific date from the pop-up selector. If you have defined a step attribute for the field, legal values are white; in this example, the step value of 3 means only every third day is a legal value:

Date Time. This creates an input element with the "datetime" type attribute. Users can select a date and time based on the Coordinated Universal Time or UTC clock (also known as Greenwich Mean Time or Zulu Time).

In the Properties panel, you can define the same properties as for the date input element. You can also define the time zone for the value, min, and max attributes — for example, UTC+06:00.

Date Time Local. This creates an input element with the "datetime-local" type attribute. This field allows users to select a date and time (with no time zone).

Email. This creates an input element with the "email" type attribute. Users should enter an email address in this field.

In addition to the same attributes that you can define for a textfield input element, you can also check the **Multiple** option in the Properties panel to allow users to enter multiple values in the field (separated by a comma). This attribute is a boolean value; if true, the multiple attribute is added to the <input> tag:

<input type="email" name="email" multiple>

On supporting mobile browsers, bringing an email-type field into focus adds the "@" and ".com" options to the on-screen keyboard.

Fieldset. This button creates a fieldset element by wrapping field objects with opening and closing <fieldset> tags. Fieldsets can be used to combine multiple form fields into a group; you can define a legend (using <legend> tags) for the grouped form objects.

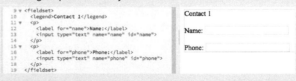

File. This creates an input element with the "file" type attribute. A file field is simply a text field with an attached Browse button, which allows users to select a file and upload it to your server. (If you include a file field in your form, the selected file uploads to the server using the POST method; you cannot use the GET method.)

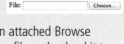

Hidden. This creates an input element with the "hidden" type attribute. The field does not appear in the browser window; you can use these in scripts to pass information that is transparent to the form user.

Image Button. This creates an input element with the "image" type attribute. The selected image functions as a submit button for the defined form.

Label. This button creates opening and closing <label> tags at the location of the insertion point. If something is selected when you click this button, the label tags wrap around the existing selection.

Month. This creates an input element with the "month" type attribute. Users can choose a specific month from the pop-up selector.

Number. This creates an input element with the "number" type attribute. Users

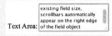

can click the field's arrows to increase or decrease the number in the field. In the Properties panel, you can define all the same attributes as for a textfield input element. You can also define Min, Max, and Step values, which have the same function as for a date input element.

Password. This creates an input element with the "password" type attribute. Content entered in this field appears as asterisks or bullets (dots).

Radio Button. This creates an input element with the "radio" type attribute. A radio button has a yes-or-no value — it is either selected or not selected.

Radio Button Group. A radio group is simply a group of radio buttons with the same name attribute. When you click the Radio Button Group button in the Form Insert panel, a dialog box opens where you define the items in the group.

(Unlike a checkbox group, which allows multiple selections, users can select only one option in a radio group.)

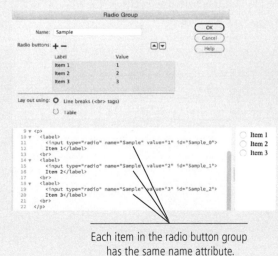

Each item in the radio button group has the same name attribute.

Range. This creates an input element with the "range" type attribute. Users can drag a slider to define specific value.

Properties for this kind of field are the same as those for the textfield and number types of field.

Search. This creates an input element with the "search" type attribute. This field behaves like a textfield type element.

Tel. This creates an input element with the "tel" type attribute. This type of field is intended to be used to gather users' phone numbers

Text Area. This creates a textarea element, which is simply a multi-line text field. In the Properties panel, you can define:

- **Rows** and **Cols**, or the number of rows and columns that are visible in the area

- **Max Length**, or the maximum number of characters that can be entered in the area.

- **Wrap**, or how text should be displayed inside the field.

Time. This creates an input element with the "time" type attribute. Users can enter the time in a specially formatted field.

Url. This creates an input element with the "url" type attribute. The value of the url field is automatically validated when the form is submitted. On supporting mobile browsers, the bringing a url-type field into focus adds the ".com" option to the on-screen keyboard.

Week. This creates an input element with the "week" type attribute. Users can select a specific week from the pop-up selector.

CREATE A MENU FIELD

Menus and lists display a set of options from which users can select one or more responses. These two types of form fields have the same basic underlying structure, but with different appearances and purposes.

A basic menu shows a single option; when a user clicks the menu, the menu opens (drops down) and more options appear. With a standard menu field, users can choose only a single response from the available options. The menu closes when the user chooses a response, displaying only the selected option.

1. With **sign-up.html** open, create a new empty paragraph after the email field in the existing form.

2. Drag the Select button from the Form Insert panel to the new empty paragraph.

   A menu or list object is created using the **<select>** tag.

3. In either panel of the document window, change the field label to **How did you hear about the Desert Voices Music Festival?**.

4. Click the select field in the Design pane to select it, then use the Properties panel to change the field name to **source**.

Menus and lists are created with the <select> tag.

5. With the field selected in the Design view, click the List Values button in the Properties panel to define the selections that will appear in the menu.

6. **Macintosh users:** Click the first field in the Item Label column to place the insertion point.

   Windows users do not need to click in the field because the insertion point is already in place when you open the dialog box.

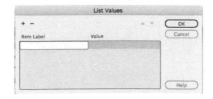

Note:

When working with a select element, you can use the Size option in the Properties panel to define the size attribute, which controls how many items will be visible in the form field when displayed in the browser.

7. Type **Social Media** as the first item label. Press Tab to move to the Value column and type **social**.

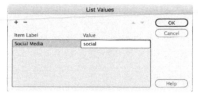

8. **Press Tab again to move to the second line of the Item Label field.**

   Each line in the dialog box represents a new list/menu option. When the insertion point is within the last item value, pressing Tab adds a new list item. Alternatively, you can simply click the "+" button above the Item Label column to add a new list item (or click the "–" button to remove the currently selected list item).

9. **Type Radio Ad as the item label, press Tab, and type radio as the item value.**

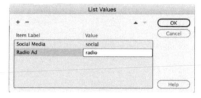

10. **Repeat Steps 8–9 to add four more list items:**

Item Label	Value
Email	email
Website Ad	web
Newspaper	paper
Friend	friend

11. **After typing the Friend value, press Tab to add a final list item.**

12. **Type -Select- in the Item Label field and leave the Value field blank.**

13. **Click the Up Arrow button (above the Value column) until the -Select- option appears at the top of the list.**

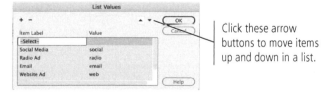

Click these arrow buttons to move items up and down in a list.

14. **Click OK to add the list values to the menu field in the form.**

15. In the Properties panel, choose -Select- in the Selected list.

In the Design pane, the width of the placed menu expands to accommodate the longest option in the list.

The Code pane shows that each item in the defined list has been created as an **option** element within the opening and closing **<select>** tags. The first option (-Select-) element includes the **selected** boolean attribute, which means that option is automatically selected in the menu when the page opens in a browser.

Note:

If you check the Multiple option in the Properties panel, the multiple attribute is added to the <input> tag; users can select more than one option in the list.

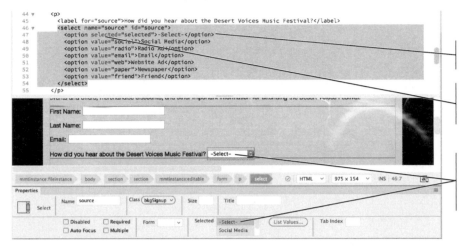

List items are defined in <option> tags.

The default option has the **selected** attribute defined.

Clicking an item in this list changes the default option in the menu object.

16. Save the file and continue to the next exercise.

CREATE A CHECKBOX

Individual **checkboxes**, which have an on or off state, are commonly used to indicate agreement. A **checkbox group** is simply a group of checkboxes with the same name; when the user submits a form, the value of each selected box is sent as the value for that field name.

1. With sign-up.html open, create a new empty paragraph before the label of the first text field (First Name) but within the form object.

You can place the insertion point before the label, then press Return/Enter to add the new paragraph within the form object.

2. Drag the Checkbox button from the Form Insert panel into the new empty paragraph.

3. In either pane of the document window, change the field label to Yes! Send me the latest news about the Desert Voices Music Festival!.

4. **Select the field (the actual checkbox) to make it active. In the Properties panel, change the field name to `agree` and make the field required.**

In the Properties panel, you can use the **Checked** option to determine whether a checkbox object is already selected when the form first displays. By default, the checkbox is not selected.

The **Value** field defines the value that will be sent to the server when the form is submitted. For example, you can define a checked value of "A" for a form object named "Checkbox1"; if the user checks that box, information will be sent to the server as Checkbox1=A. If you do not define a checked value, information will be sent to the server as Checkbox1=ON when the box is checked.

5. **Save the file and continue to the next exercise.**

 ## ADD SUBMIT AND RESET BUTTONS

Buttons perform an assigned task when clicked. The **Submit** button is crucial to any form, ensuring that the data is not sent to the server until the user chooses. The **Reset** button clears all entries in form objects and restores the form to its original (empty) state.

1. **With sign-up.html open, create a new empty paragraph after the select list in the form.**

2. **Drag the Submit Button button from the Form Insert panel into the new empty paragraph.**

An input element with the **submit** type attribute submits the form data to the server.

3. **In the Properties panel, type Sign me up! in the Value field.**

In the Properties panel, the **Name** field shows the ID of the button object; this is just a name used for CSS purposes; it does not control the button's behavior. The **Value** field defines the text that appears on the button.

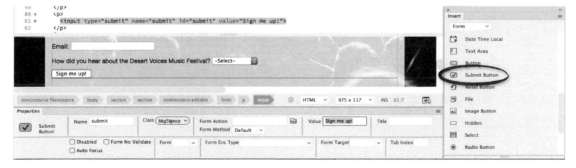

4. **Drag the Reset Button button from the Form Insert panel to the immediate right of the existing button.**

    An input element with the **reset** type attribute clears the entered data.

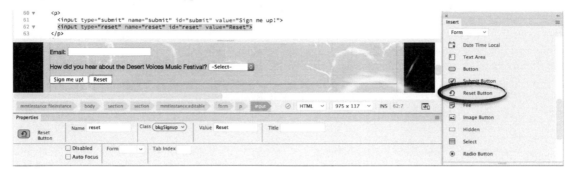

5. **Save the file and continue to the next exercise.**

 APPLY CSS TO THE FORM

To effectively format forms using CSS, you should remember that several HTML tags are used for most objects in the form:

- The **<form>** tag encloses the entire form.

- The **<input>** tag identifies each form object that allows user input. Different types of form objects are identified with the **type** attribute, such as:

    <input name="last" type="text" id="last" />
    <input type="reset" name="reset" id="reset" value="Reset" />

- The **<select>** tag creates drop-down menus and selection lists.

- The **<label>** tag creates the text that identifies form fields.

1. **With sign-up.html open, turn on the Live view.**

    It is a good idea to use the Live view to preview the accuracy of the CSS selectors and properties you define.

2. **In the Design pane, click to select the label for the checkbox field.**

3. **Click the Current button at the top of the CSS Designer panel to show only selectors related to the current insertion point.**

    The editable region where the form object is placed inside the section#subpage-content element. Each line in this form is also tagged as a paragraph element (using the **<p>** tag). So, the **#subpage-content p** selector controls the default appearance of form labels.

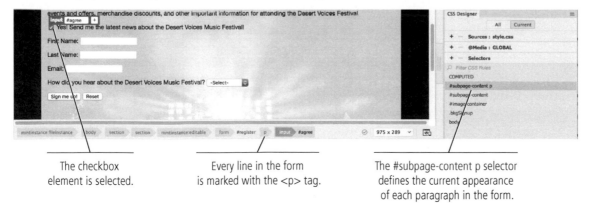

The checkbox element is selected.

Every line in the form is marked with the <p> tag.

The #subpage-content p selector defines the current appearance of each paragraph in the form.

4. **Click the <p> tag in the Tag Selector to select the entire paragraph, then choose Heading 2 in the Format menu of the Properties panel.**

After applying the Heading 2, the first line is now tagged with the **<h2>** tag instead of the **<p>** tag; the applied formatting is now defined by the **#subpage-content h2** selector.

CSS rules apply to content within a form object just as they do to content in a regular page area. The only difference is that you now have additional tags that can be defined to format specific form objects.

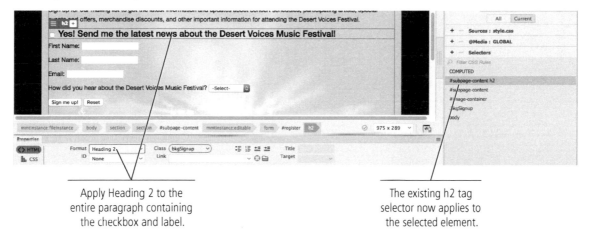

Apply Heading 2 to the entire paragraph containing the checkbox and label.

The existing h2 tag selector now applies to the selected element.

5. **In the CSS Designer panel, turn off the Current mode. Click the Add Selector button, then change the name of the new selector to input. Define the following properties for the new selector:**

width:	**100%**
margin-bottom:	**10px**
float:	**left**
clear:	**both**

This selector is a tag selector, defining properties for all **<input>** tags. The input objects are now attached to the left edge of the containing area.

The **clear** property defines where other floating content cannot wrap around an element. In other words, if you assign a right clear value to an **<img>** tag (for example), no other floating content can appear on the right side of that image. The clear property can have a value of left, right, both, or none.

Note:

Remember the principles of parent/child relationships: if you want to affect all text within a form (for example), you can define specific font properties for the <form> tag. Those properties would then be inherited by all objects in the form.

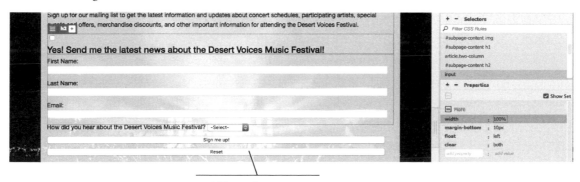

All input elements are affected by the new selector.

6. **Click the input selector in the CSS Designer panel.**

   When the Live view is active, clicking a selector in the CSS Designer panel highlights all items in the Live view that are affected by that selector. This makes it easy to identify elements that are affected by changing properties in the active selector.

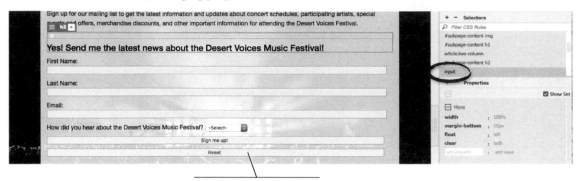

All related elements are highlighted in the Live view.

The input tag selector did most of the formatting work for you. You should notice a few issues that need to be addressed:

- The settings in the **input** tag selector also affected the actual checkbox object and both buttons.
- The settings in the **label** tag selector also affected the label of the checkbox.
- The buttons each extend the full width of the form, which is not necessary.

To override these selector properties in only certain elements, you will create a class selector.

7. **Create a new class selector named .noClear in the style.css file. Define the following properties:**

width:	**auto**
margin-right:	**10px**
clear:	**none**

   The auto value allows the object to occupy only what space is necessary (rather than the defined percentages in the **input** and **label** tag selectors).

8. **In the Design pane of the document window, click to select the checkbox object at the top of the form. Use the Element Display to add the .noClear class to the selected object.**

   Selecting the object in the Live view adds a checkmark to the box; this has no effect on the page code, it simply provides a reflection of what users will see in a browser window.

   There is not much apparent difference from applying the class, however, because you also need to apply the class to the checkbox label.

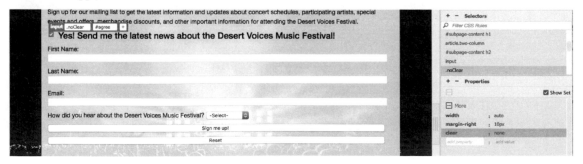

9. **Apply the noClear class to both buttons at the bottom of the form.**

Because the noClear class allows objects' width to automatically size, the two buttons no longer fill the width of the containing area; they again appear on a single line.

10. **Choose View>Live View Options>Hide Live View Displays.**

Toggling the Hide Live View Displays item hides the element highlighting that occurs when you click a selector in the CSS Designer panel, as well as the Element Displays that appear when you select an element in the Live view.

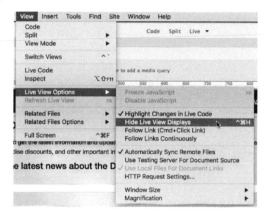

11. **Review the final form in the Live view.**

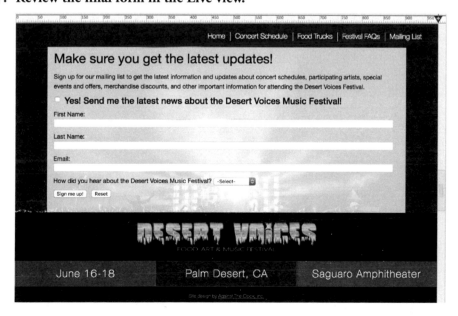

12. **Save the open HTML file and the style.css file, then close the HTML file.**

13. **Export a site definition named Voices.ste into your WIP>Voices folder, and then remove the site from Dreamweaver.**

Project Review

fill in the blank

1. A(n) _____ can be used to change the appearance of multiple elements on a single page, including elements of different types, once it is applied to those elements.

2. You can make a(n) _____ editable in a template to protect the container's contents in pages where that template is applied.

3. The _____ property can be used to prevent other floating objects from appearing on the same line as an element.

4. The _____ tag identifies a text field in a form.

5. The _____ type of text field displays entered text as asterisks or dots.

6. A(n) _____ can be used to place one HTML file into another.

7. A(n) _____ attribute has only two possible values: true or false.

8. The _____ tag creates the text that identifies form fields (including the text of checkboxes).

9. The _____ tag creates a selection list.

10. The _____ determines the text that appears on a Submit button.

short answer

1. Briefly explain the concept of a class in CSS.

2. Briefly explain the float CSS property.

3. Briefly explain the clear CSS property.

Portfolio Builder Project

Use what you learned in this project to complete the following freeform exercise.
Carefully read the art director and client comments, then create your own design to meet the needs of the project.
Use the space below to sketch ideas; when finished, write a brief explanation of your reasoning behind your final design.

You have been hired by the Green California Initiative, a non-profit organization dedicated to increasing the use of alternative energy sources in private homes. The group wants to create a simple web page to promote the benefits of home solar power and allow people to request more information.

❏ Download the **Solar_DW18_PB.zip** archive from the Student Files web page to access provided client files.

❏ Find or create artwork to support the client's message.

❏ Design a web page to present the client-supplied content in a clear, attractive manner.

❏ Create a form so users can request more information about installing solar power on their homes.

Our group does not sell anything or promote any specific company. Instead, we try to encourage people to consider the benefits of reducing energy consumption from the main power grid.

The new page will feature home solar power, which is a perfect source for Southern California homes with our abundant sunshine. The page needs to include our logo, a brief text explanation, and a short form with fields to:

– Gather contact information (name, mailing address, phone, and email address)

– Determine home size, household income, and average monthly electric bill

– Determine how users learned about Green California Initiative

– Determine how much interest each user has in installing alternative energy (use a 0–5 scale)

_____
_____
_____
_____
_____
_____
_____
_____
_____
_____
_____
_____
_____
_____
_____

In this project, you learned more about CSS selectors — specifically, using class selectors to control specific elements in a page. Because of the versatility of using classes, some professional web designers use only classes to define an entire site layout. You also learned several different techniques for editing CSS selectors, both in the CSS Designer panel and in the Code pane. Once you are familiar with all of the options, you can better determine which method suits your working style.

This project also expanded on your knowledge of Dreamweaver templates. You learned how to make only a specific attribute editable, allowing different options on individual pages while protecting placed content.

Finally, this project introduced the concept of HTML forms, including using CSS to control the appearance of various elements in a form.

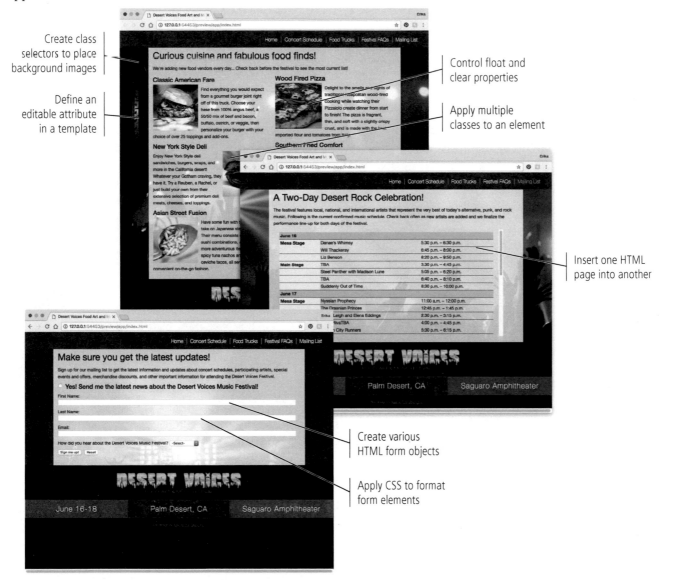

Create class selectors to place background images

Define an editable attribute in a template

Control float and clear properties

Apply multiple classes to an element

Insert one HTML page into another

Create various HTML form objects

Apply CSS to format form elements

Kayaking CSS3 Site

Your client, Clearwater Kayaking Outfitters, has hired you to create a new site that functions properly in all current browsers. They want to include two different articles on the site home page, as well as video and images from past trips.

This project incorporates the following skills:

❑ Using CSS3 selectors to add aesthetic appeal to page content

❑ Understanding and managing different browser requirements for HTML5/CSS3 options

❑ Adding web fonts to display page content with specific fonts

❑ Placing video into the page without the need for a browser plug-in

❑ Using CSS3 to create a simple photo gallery

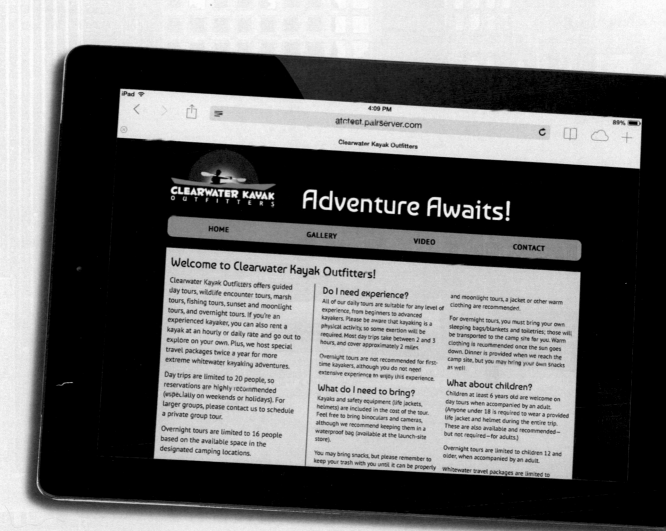

Project Meeting

client comments

Our site doesn't need to be complex, but it does require a few specific elements:

- A basic introduction and list of frequently asked questions

- A video from one of our recent trips

- A photo gallery to show a series of images from past trips and tours

We want to make it very easy for people to find the information they want. If possible, all of the important text — intro and FAQs — should appear directly on the home page.

The old site had embedded Flash files for video and slideshow, but too many people were complaining about not being able to see the content. We get a lot of traffic from people who are traveling, so we want our site to work on mobile devices.

art director comments

HTML5 and CSS3 are the perfect solution to the client's problem of files not working on mobile devices. Unfortunately, Dreamweaver hasn't completely incorporated HTML5 and CSS3 options into the user interface. You'll have to do some work in the page code to make this site work.

Fortunately, everything you already know about HTML and CSS code will make it easier to accomplish your goals. Tags are still tags and CSS selectors still function in the same general way. The difference is the tags that have been added to HTML5 and the new properties that are available in CSS3.

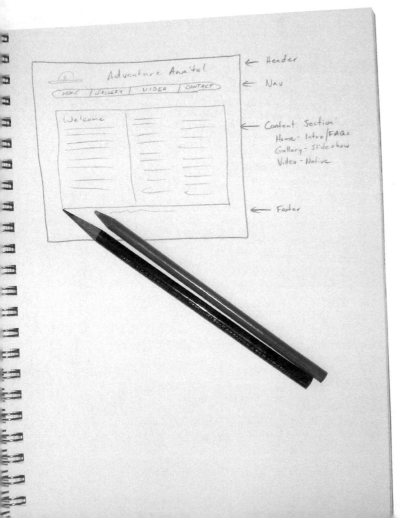

project objectives

To complete this project, you will:

- ❑ Add rounded corners to an element
- ❑ Define transparency for a background color
- ❑ Create multiple columns of text
- ❑ Define web fonts in Dreamweaver
- ❑ Apply web fonts to page elements
- ❑ Place a video in an HTML5 page
- ❑ Define video tag attributes
- ❑ Define absolute object positioning
- ❑ Use nth-of-type selectors

CSS3 includes a number of properties that give you considerably more creative control over the appearance of web pages. In this stage of the project, you will use several CSS3 properties to add visual appeal to the index page. (Because all files in the site are attached to the same CSS file, your changes in the CSS file will affect the appearance of all four pages in the site.)

Although you can use the CSS Designer panel to add many properties to a selector — including many of the more common CSS3 properties — you can also manually edit the code in a CSS file to add various selectors. You should become familiar with this technique because not all CSS properties are available in the panel. Much of your work in this stage of the project will be done directly in the Code pane.

DEFINE HTML ARTICLES

The HTML5 article element identifies individual articles in a page, just as you might find in a printed magazine. As with the section element, you can place multiple articles in a single page. This allows you to more easily define different CSS settings for different articles on the same page.

1. Download **Kayaking_DW18_RF.zip** from the Student Files web page.

2. **Expand the ZIP archive in your WIP folder (Macintosh) or copy the archive contents into your WIP folder (Windows).**

   This results in a folder named **Kayaking**, which contains the files you need for this project.

3. **Create a new site named Kayaking, using the WIP>Kayaking folder as the site root folder.**

4. **Open index.html from the site root folder. Turn off the Live view (if necessary).**

   In the next few steps, you are going to wrap tags around multiple elements at one time. This is much easier to accomplish when the Live view is not active.

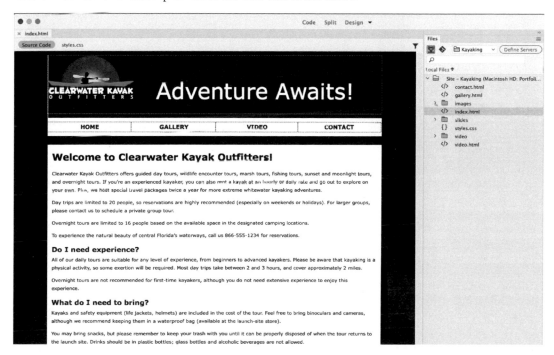

5. In the CSS Designer panel, review the selectors in the attached styles.css file.

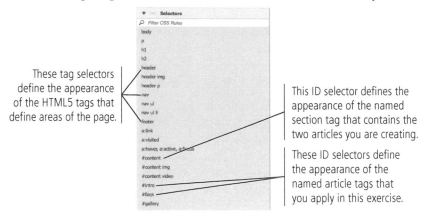

These tag selectors define the appearance of the HTML5 tags that define areas of the page.

This ID selector defines the appearance of the named section tag that contains the two articles you are creating.

These ID selectors define the appearance of the named article tags that you apply in this exercise.

6. In the Design pane, select the four paragraphs immediately after the h1 element ("Welcome to...).

7. Click the Article button in the HTML Insert panel.

8. In the resulting dialog box, make sure Wrap Around Selection is active in the Insert menu. Open the ID menu and choose intro from the list of available options, then click OK.

Remember: Any given ID can only be used once per page. The ID menu lists any unused IDs that have been defined in the active HTML file or its related CSS files. Because the #content ID has already been applied to the section element on this page, it does not appear in the menu.

The #intro selector defines a specific element width, so the following paragraphs move up and to the right of the now 200px-wide article#intro element.

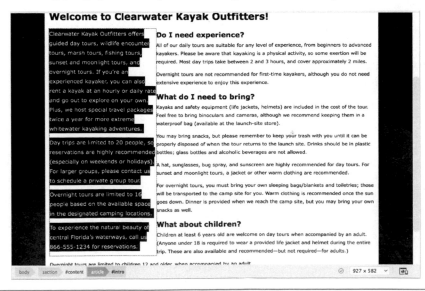

9. Select the remaining text in the page (beginning with "Do I need..." and ending just before the footer element).

10. Click Article in the HTML Insert panel. In the resulting dialog box, choose **faqs** in the ID menu, then click OK.

The #faqs selector also defines a specific width, with a right float value. The entire article moves to the right of the article#intro element, including content that flows below the bottom edge of the intro article.

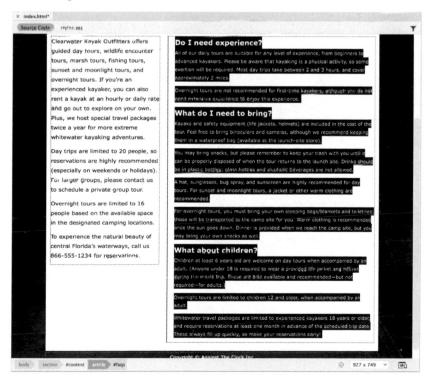

11. Save all files and continue to the next exercise.

ADD ROUNDED CORNERS TO AN ELEMENT

Using CSS3, rounded corners are very easy to define for any element. A navigation bar typically has a simple format. To change the appearance of the menu bar in this site, you can simply edit the CSS selectors applied to the various aspects of the menu. Keep in mind the following tags when you review the selectors:

      \<ul\> = unordered list   **\<li\>** = list item   **\<a\>** = link

1. **With index.html open, turn on the Live view.**

   Many of the CSS3 properties do not display properly in the regular Design view. You will use the Live view in these exercises so you can more accurately preview your ongoing work.

2. **Command-Option-click (Macintosh) or Alt-click (Windows) the "Home" link text to show the Code Navigator.**

   The Code Navigator lists all pieces of code related to the selected item. In this case, you see all CSS selectors (in the styles.css file) that affect the selected navigation link.

3. **If the Disable check box is not selected in the bottom-right corner of the Code Navigator, click the box to disable the indicator icon.**

   The Code Navigator icon can be distracting, depending on your workflow. We often find it easier to turn it off and use the modifier keys to access it only when necessary.

4. **Move your mouse over the nav item in the Code Navigator.**

   When you mouse-over an item in the Code Navigator, a pop-up window shows the properties that are defined in that selector.

> **Note:**
>
> *When the Code Navigator indicator is enabled, an icon*  *appears in the Design pane when you place the insertion point in a specific element and wait a moment. You can click the indicator icon to open the Code Navigator window.*

The dynamic links include pop-up windows that show the settings of the selected item.

This option should be checked.

5. Click the nav link in the Code Navigator.

The Code Navigator does more than simply list the relevant selectors; it also provides a dynamic link to all related code. This is an easy way to find the appropriate code for specific items — especially for files you did not create.

When you use the Code Navigator links, the document window automatically switches to Split view and the appropriate code file displays in the Code pane. The active selector is also selected in the CSS Designer panel. The Related Files bar above the document window shows which code file is active in the Code pane.

The selector you clicked is visible in the Code pane.

6. In the Code pane, place the insertion point at the end of the last property in the nav selector.

7. Press Return/Enter to add a new property to the selector.

8. Type border-r, then press Return/Enter to accept the border-radius property from the Code Hint menu.

As you type, the Code Hint menu scrolls to the available properties that match the characters you type. After you type border-r, the first option — border-radius — is automatically selected. Pressing Return/Enter adds that item to your code, including the required colon after the property name.

Note:

Moving forward, we will not include the complete instructions for using code hints to add specific CSS properties. You can use the menu to add the necessary code, or simply type the properties and values that you want to add.

The **border-radius** property defines the same corner radius for all corners of an element.

To understand the concept of corner radius, think of a rectangle with an imaginary circle on top of the corner; the point at which the sides of the rectangle meet the sides of the circle is the **corner radius**.

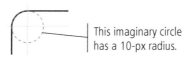

This imaginary circle has a 10-px radius.

9. **Type 10px; as the value of the new property.**

   This is the amount of rounding (the radius) that will be applied to all four corners of the nav element.

   When you type in the Code pane to define CSS properties and values, do not add a space between the value and the unit of measurement.

   Changes made in the code automatically reflect in the Design pane when the Live view is active. You should now see the rounded corners on the nav element.

Note:

You can define a different radius for each corner using the following properties:

border-bottom-left-radius

border-bottom-right-radius

border-top-left-radius

border-top-right-radius

10. **Save the styles.css file and then continue to the next exercise.**

    If the CSS file is visible in the Code pane, you can choose File>Save to save the CSS file. You can also choose File>Save All to be sure all related files are saved.

Using CSS3, you can define colors in a number of ways:

- Using a hexadecimal color code, such as #FF0066. Each couplet in the color value defines the red, green, and blue components of that color.

- Using a color name, such as "aqua" or "green." There are 147 defined color names in the HTML and CSS color specification.

- Using specific RGB values, in the following format:

  rgb(255, 0, 100)

  Each number in the parentheses defines the amount of red, green, and blue (respectively) — from 0 (none of a color) to 255 (all of a color) — that makes up the overall color. By combining various percentages of each color component, this method theoretically allows you to define any of the 16.7 million colors in the visible spectrum.

  This flexibility gives you considerably more color options than the basic web safe color list that was the standard in earlier generations of web design. Keep in mind, however, that colors still vary from one display to another. Although you can now define a much wider range of colors, you still can't guarantee that the color you want is the color users will see.

- Using RGBA values, which adds the alpha property to standard RGB color values in the following format:

  rgba(255, 0, 100, 0.5)

  The fourth parameter in the parentheses is the alpha value, which defines the color's transparency from 0.0 (fully transparent) to 1.0 (fully opaque).

Note:

Refer to http://www. w3schools.com/cssref/css_ colors.asp for a complete list of supported color names.

1. **With index.html open, make sure the Live view is active in the Design pane and styles.css is visible in the Code pane.**

2. **In the code for the nav selector, delete the existing value for the background property.**

   Leave the colon and space after the property name, and leave the semicolon at the end of the line.

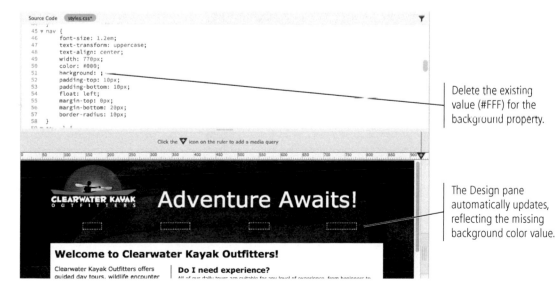

Delete the existing value (#FFF) for the background property.

The Design pane automatically updates, reflecting the missing background color value.

3. Type **rgba(255, 255, 255, 0.6)** as the new property value.

As soon as you type "rgb," the color picker appears so you can choose a color using the various sliders and fields. In this case, you are simply typing the color value you want.

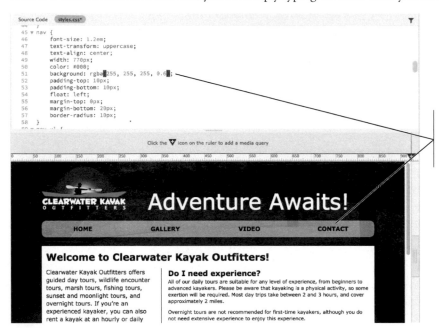

Note:

The Design view does accurately render semi-transparent color even when the Live view is not active.

The semi-transparent background color is rendered accurately in the Design pane.

4. Repeat this process to change the background-color property of the #content selector to **rgba(255, 255, 255, 0.8)**.

The nav and section#content elements have the same basic background color, but different alpha values. The background image and color are visible behind both elements, but the higher alpha value in the content element allows the text to be more legible.

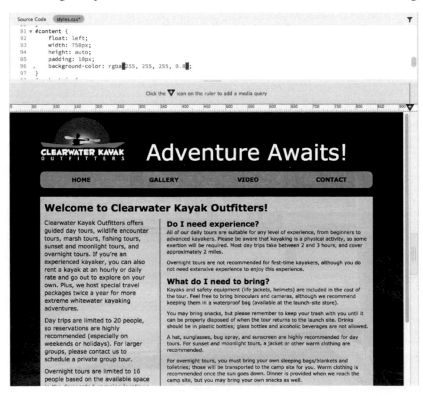

5. Save the styles.css file and continue to the next exercise.

CREATE MULTIPLE COLUMNS OF TEXT

As you have already seen, you can use different elements to create the appearance of multiple columns. In the index file you are currently building, the two article tags have unique id attributes; the selectors for those ids define width and float properties that make it seem like the page is laid out with two columns.

Using CSS3, you can also use the **column-count** property to define a number of columns within a single element. In this exercise, you will add this property to the #faqs ID selector to change the text layout only within the article element that is identified as the faqs article.

It is important to note that some CSS3 properties — including the column-count property that you use in this exercise — are not supported by all browsers. In these cases, you can sometimes use a workaround to define options that will work in various browsers.

Note:

Throughout this project, we are referring to the most current versions of these browsers; older versions might not support CSS3 properties. You can check whether a property is supported by different browsers at www.w3schools. com/cssref/css3_ browsersupport.asp.

1. **With index.html open, make sure the Live view is active in the Design pane and styles.css is visible in the Code pane.**

2. **Open the Code Navigator for the right article and click the #faqs link.**

3. **In the Code pane, place the insertion point at the end of the last property in the #faqs selector code and press Return/Enter to add a new line.**

4. **Type -moz-column-count: 2; then press Return/Enter.**

   The "-moz-" prefix at the beginning of the property name identifies that property for the Mozilla Firefox browser.

5. **On the next line, type -webkit-column-count: 2; then press Return/Enter.**

   The "-webkit-" prefix at the beginning of the property name identifies that property for the Safari, Opera, and Google Chrome browsers — and for the Dreamweaver Live view.

6. **On the next line, type column-count: 2;.**

   Without a vendor specific prefix, this property is supported by the Internet Explorer browser.

   When you add multiple properties in this manner, a browser will continue down the list until it finds one it understands; non-supported properties are ignored.

```
111 ▼ #faqs {
112     float: right;
113     width: 465px;
114     height: auto;
115     padding: 0px;
116     border-left: solid 1px #000;
117     margin-left: 15px;
118     padding-left: 15px;
119     -moz-column-count: 2;
120     -webkit-column-count: 2;
121     column-count: 2;
122 }
123 ▼ #gallery {
```

7. **Review the results in the Live view.**

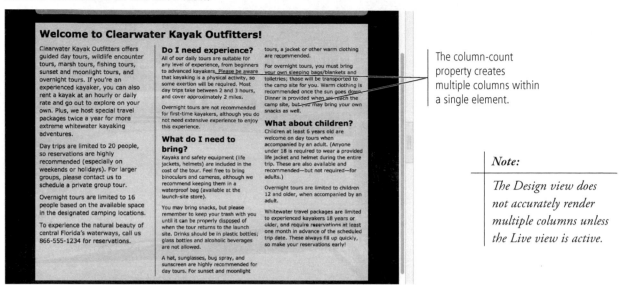

The column-count property creates multiple columns within a single element.

Note:

The Design view does not accurately render multiple columns unless the Live view is active.

8. **Save the styles.css file, then continue to the next stage of the project.**

Learning More about CSS3 Properties

In the first stage of this project, we focused on three different properties that highlight various issues you will encounter using CSS3 in Dreamweaver:

- Manually typing code into the CSS file to define CSS3 properties
- Using the Live view to preview CSS3 in Dreamweaver
- Using multiple vendor prefixes to define properties for different browsers

The three properties you used here are hardly exhaustive. In fact, it would be virtually impossible to create a project that included every available CSS3 property.

To learn more about specific CSS properties, including all of the properties that were added in CSS3, visit www.w3schools.com/cssref/default.asp. You can click any property in the list on the left to learn more, including examples and browser support information.

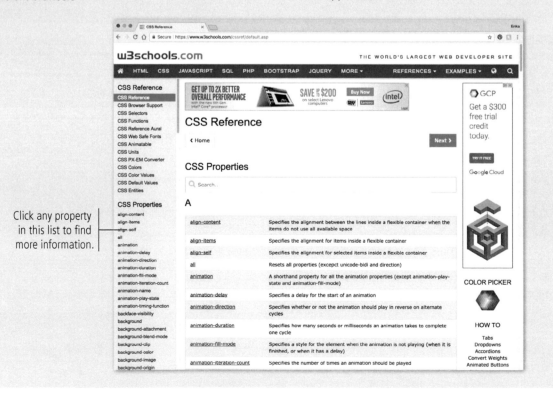

Click any property in this list to find more information.

Stage 2 Working with Web Fonts

Prior to CSS3, websites were limited to the fonts that were installed on a user's computer. When we design pages, we use font families to define a sequence of possible fonts to use, usually ending with a generic type of font like serif or sans-serif. Even those options weren't guaranteed because an individual user can customize a browser to display all type in (for example) Comic Sans regardless of the type of font a design defined.

The addition of web fonts in CSS3 now means that you can embed specific fonts into a web page; when a user opens your page, the exact fonts you define will be used in the browser. You do, however, have to include all of the formats that are required by different browsers. The current versions of all browsers support the Web Open Font Format (WOFF), TrueType Fonts (TTF), and OpenType Fonts (OTF). (Internet Explorer 9+ requires certain modifications for TTF/OTF to work properly.)

ACTIVATE ADOBE EDGE WEB FONTS

Many sources of web fonts are available on the Internet; some sources are free, some are free only for non-commercial use, and some require a fee just like high-quality fonts for print applications. Dreamweaver allows you to incorporate external web fonts in your sites, but also provides easy access to a library of web fonts that you can activate and apply in your sites.

1. **Choose Tools>Manage Fonts.**

   The default tab in this dialog box provides access to Adobe Edge Web Fonts. As the text at the top of the dialog box explains:

   > "Edge Web Fonts give you access to a library of web fonts made possible by contributions from Adobe, Google, and designers around the world. The fonts are served by Typekit, free for use on your website."

2. **On the left side of the dialog box, make sure none of the buttons are toggled on (dark).**

   You can use these buttons to filter the available fonts, showing only those that meet your selected criteria. If any buttons are dark (toggled on), click that button to toggle it off.

3. **Scroll through the list of available fonts, then click the Baumans font thumbnail in the list.**

   Clicking a font in the list adds a checkmark, which means it is now available for use in your version of Dreamweaver.

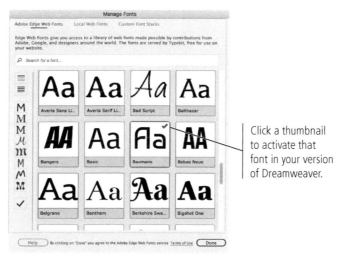

Click a thumbnail to activate that font in your version of Dreamweaver.

4. **On the left side of the dialog box, click the second button from the top.**

5. **Click PT Sans to activate that font.**

Fonts recommended for headings
Fonts recommended for paragraphs
Sans fonts
Serif fonts
Slab fonts
Script fonts
Blackletter fonts
Monospace fonts
Handmade fonts
Decorative fonts
Fonts previously added to the font list

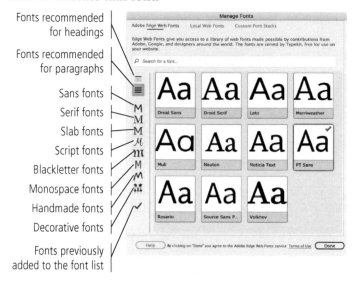

6. **Click the Custom Font Stacks option at the top of the dialog box.**

    A **font stack** (also called a **font family**) is a sequence of fonts that can be used to display content. When a browser opens a page, it goes through various fonts in the list until it finds one that can be used on the active device.

    Using web fonts, the page should theoretically only display content in the font you define. However, older browsers do not support web fonts, so you should still create a font stack to at least define the basic category to use if the web font is not available.

7. **In the Manage Fonts dialog box, scroll to the bottom of the Available Fonts window (if necessary).**

    Installed web fonts appear at the end of the Available Fonts list after the font categories.

8. **Select baumans in the list and then click the << button.**

9. **Select sans-serif in the Available Fonts list and then click the << button.**

    This font stack tells the browser:

    Use Baumans. If that font cannot be used,
        use the default sans-serif font that is defined by the user's browser.

Click the << button to add a font to a font stack.

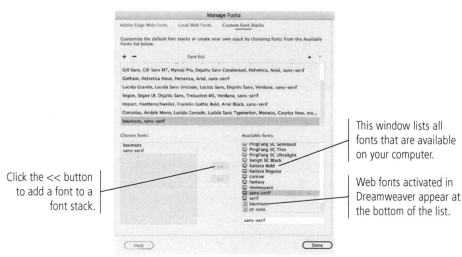

This window lists all fonts that are available on your computer.

Web fonts activated in Dreamweaver appear at the bottom of the list.

10. **Click the + button in the top-left corner of the dialog box to add a new font stack. Add pt-sans and sans-serif to the second custom font stack.**

Click the + button to
add a new font stack.

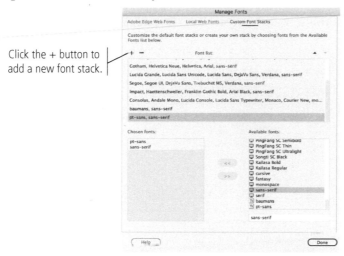

11. **Click Done to close the Manage Fonts dialog box, then continue to the next exercise.**

 ## APPLY WEB FONTS TO PAGE ELEMENTS

After web fonts are installed in Dreamweaver and defined in font stacks, you can apply those web fonts to page elements just as you would apply the built-in font stacks. In this exercise, you are going to apply the web fonts you just activated in various elements in the kayaking site.

1. **Make sure index.html (from the Kayaking site) is open and the Live view is active.**

2. **Click the Current button at the top of the CSS Designer panel to change the panel mode.**

   When the Current mode is active, clicking an element in the Design pane shows only selectors that are related to the element you click.

3. **Click the h1 element in the Design view.**

   Even when the Live view is active, you can still click a specific element to show the related selectors in the CSS Designer panel.

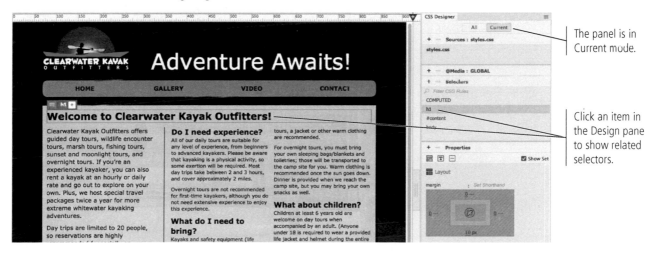

The panel is in Current mode.

Click an item in the Design pane to show related selectors.

4. **Click h1 in the CSS Designer panel Selectors list. In the Properties section of the panel, turn off the Show Set option if necessary.**

5. **Click the T button at the top of the Properties section to show text-related properties.**

6. **Open the font-family menu and choose baumans, sans-serif.**

Click this button to jump to text-related properties.

Choose your custom-defined font stack in the menu.

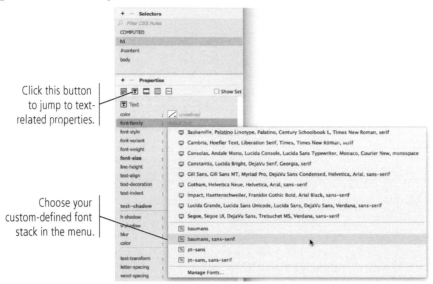

When you first apply a web font in a page, Dreamweaver might show a warning at the top of the document window that other properties have been modified so that the web font works to best advantage.

The web font appears when the Live view is active.

Click here to close the warning message.

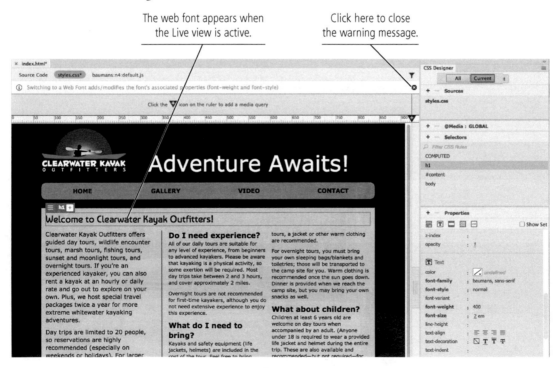

7. **If necessary, click the Close button on the warning message.**

8. **Display the page's source code in the Code pane and review the information in the <head> tag.**

Edge web fonts are served by Typekit servers, which deliver the appropriate font data to the browser when the page is loaded. When you add Edge web fonts to a page, Dreamweaver automatically adds the required scripts to the page's <head> element.

A JavaScript file that has been added to accurately render the baumans font.

Scripts are required for Edge web fonts to work properly.

9. **Repeat the process from Steps 2–5 to apply the baumans, sans-serif font family to the h2 selector and the header p selector.**

10. **Repeat the process from Steps 2–5 to apply the pt-sans, sans-serif font family to the body selector.**

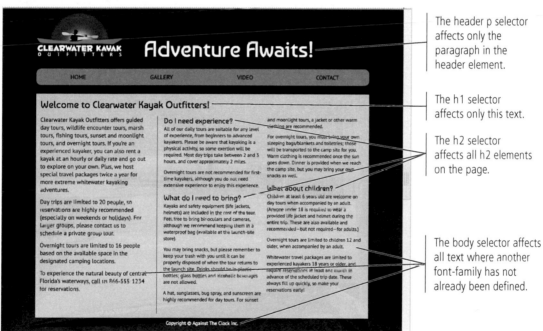

The header p selector affects only the paragraph in the header element.

The h1 selector affects only this text.

The h2 selector affects all h2 elements on the page.

The body selector affects all text where another font-family has not already been defined.

11. **Choose File>Save All. Read the resulting message, then click Update.**

You have defined web fonts in a CSS file that is linked to multiple HTML pages in the active site. Dreamweaver recognizes that the same script information must appear in each page's <head> tag, so you are asked if you want to update the necessary <script> tag in those files.

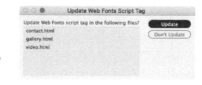

12. **When the process is done, click Close to close the Update Pages dialog box.**

13. **Close index.html, then continue to the next stage of the project.**

Accessing Local Web Fonts

In addition to Adobe Edge web fonts, you can also work with local web fonts — fonts that you have acquired from external sources and are available on your local machine.

Web fonts are available from a number of sources; the most important thing to remember is that different browsers and platforms require different font formats. High-quality web fonts should be available in each of these formats, typically distributed as a Webfont kit.

- Embedded OpenType (EOT)
- Web Open Font Format (WOFF)
- TrueType (TTF)
- Scalable Vector Graphics (SVG)

In Dreamweaver, you can use the Local Fonts tab of the Manage Fonts dialog box to locate web fonts and make them active in Dreamweaver.

If you click the Browse button for any of the available formats, you can navigate to the file on your local system. If multiple formats of the same font exist in the same folder, Dreamweaver automatically recognizes those files and loads

each into the Manage Fonts dialog box. The Font Name field is also automatically populated.

Before finishing the process, you have to check the box to agree that you have properly licensed the font you are adding. (Always respect the font license of whatever source you use to download web fonts.) Clicking Add makes the selected font available in Dreamweaver.

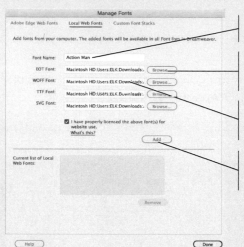

The font name is filled in based on font-file data.

Click any of the Browse buttons to locate a local web font file.

Dreamweaver automatically locates all files for the same font.

Click Add to make a local web font available in Dreamweaver.

Applying Local Web Fonts

Once a local web font is available in Dreamweaver, you can apply it to a specific selector, just as you did with the Edge web fonts in the previous exercise. Local web fonts appear in the Font-family menu, directly above the Edge web fonts and font stacks.

When you use a local web font, that font must be available to your users. In other words, the actual font files must be included in the files that you upload to a web server.

Dreamweaver automatically copies used local web fonts into your site root folder (in a folder named "webfonts").

An import statement is added to the CSS file where the web font is used, referencing a secondary CSS file that defines the location of the required web font files. (This secondary file is generated for you and placed in the same folder as the web font files.)

This folder contains all the fonts that are required for the local web fonts to work properly when the files are uploaded to a web server.

```
×  test.html
Source Code   styles.css*   stylesheet.css
1   @charset "UTF-8";
2   @import url("webfonts/Action_Man/stylesheet.css");
3 ▼ body {
4       font-family: "Action Man";
5   }
6
```

An import statement is added to the CSS file, referencing a secondary CSS file that defines the web font location.

```
×  test.html
Source Code   styles.css*   stylesheet.css
1 ▼ @font-face {
2       font-family: 'Action Man';
3       src: url('Action_Man-webfont.eot');
4       src: url('Action_Man-webfont.eot?#iefix') format('embedded-opentype'),
5           url('Action_Man-webfont.woff') format('woff'),
6           url('Action_Man-webfont.ttf') format('truetype'),
7           url('Action_Man-webfont.svg') format('svg');
8   }
```

The stylesheet.css file, which is generated for you, defines the location of the necessary web font files.

Stage 3 Adding Video in HTML5

One of the advantages of HTML5 is the ability to present multimedia files without the need for a plug-in. Using the <video> tag, you can define a source for video that will play directly in the page. There are currently three supported video formats for the <video> element: MP4, WebM, and Ogg. Different browsers support different formats when you use the HTML5 video tag:

Browser	MP4	WebM	OGG/OGV
Internet Explorer	✓	✗	✗
Chrome	✓	✓	✓
Firefox	✓	✓	✓
Safari	✓	✗	✗
Opera	✓	✓	✓

A number of free video converters are available on the Internet. To create the required files for this project, we used the Freemake Video Converter for Windows (www.freemake.com).

As you saw when you added web fonts in the last stage of this project, you can work around issues of non-standardization by defining multiple files to use in a given situation. In this stage of the project, you will create a video tag and define multiple sources to meet different browser requirements.

PLACE A VIDEO IN AN HTML5 PAGE

In this exercise, you are going to place a video file into an HTML page. Keep in mind that the <video> tag is specific to HTML5; if you open the page in an older browser that does not support HTML5, the video will not be visible.

1. **With the Kayaking site open in the Files panel, double-click the video.html file to open it. Make sure the Live view is active.**

2. **Click the Split button in the Document toolbar to show both the Code and Design panes.**

3. **In the Files panel, expand the video folder.**

   This folder includes three versions of the same video, which was saved in various formats to be compatible with different browsers.

Note:

The video you are using in this project, by Scott Dunsmuir, is in the public domain with no rights reserved. It was downloaded from The Internet Archive (www.archive.org), which is an excellent source of free imagery and video. However, be aware that individual files on this site have different use permissions and restrictions, determined by the creator; please respect the ownership and rights of the media you want to use in your work. We removed the audio from the original video to avoid violating the copyright of the artists who created the music.

4. Click the HTML5 Video button in the HTML Insert panel and drag to the Design view until a green line appears above the first p element on the page.

In the Live view, visual indicators show where the new element will be placed in relation to other elements on the page. The blue outline highlights the p element; the green line shows that the new element will be placed above the outlined p element.

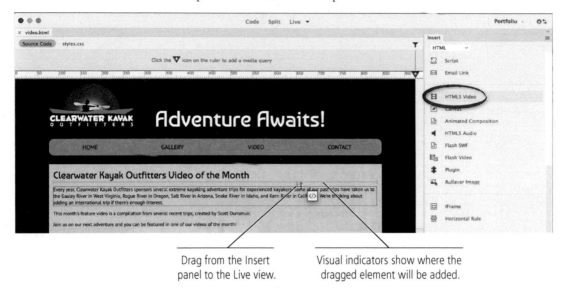

Drag from the Insert panel to the Live view.

Visual indicators show where the dragged element will be added.

At this point, the video object is simply a placeholder in the Design view. It is aligned to the right side of the containing element because the CSS video tag selector defines the right float property. The blue outline in the Design pane identifies the default measurements of a new video element.

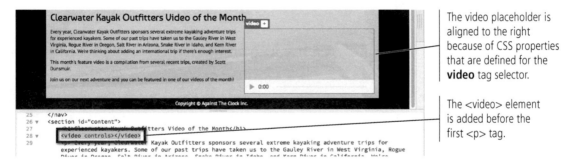

The video placeholder is aligned to the right because of CSS properties that are defined for the **video** tag selector.

The <video> element is added before the first <p> tag.

As you can see in the Code pane, the video element is added after the closing </h1> tag and before the first opening <p> tags. The current code is only the opening and closing tags (**<video controls></video>**).

The word **controls** is an attribute of the video element. Rather than requiring a specific value in quotation marks, many video tag attributes are boolean — they are either present or not; if they are present, they are considered to be true (i.e., active). When this attribute is included in the video tag, video controls will appear on top of the video object on the page.

Note:

*The **<video>** tag identifies a video that is placed on the page.*

Dreamweaver automatically adds controls when you place an HTML5 video object. If you don't want to include video controls, you can simply delete the word "controls" from the opening <video> tag.

5. Open the Properties panel.

Although you have added the video element to the page, you still need to define a number of other tags and attributes to allow the video to play on the page. This is accomplished in the Properties panel.

6. **With the video element selected in the Design view, click the Point to File button for the Source field and drag to the dunsmuir.mp4 file (in the site's video folder). Press Return/Enter to finalize the source path.**

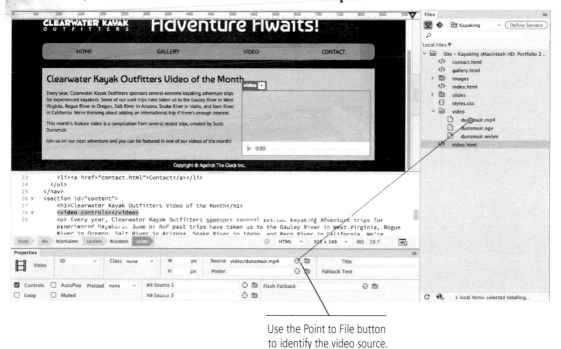

Use the Point to File button to identify the video source.

Dreamweaver recognizes that the source folder contains alternate file formats; the Alt Source 1 and Alt Source 2 fields are automatically populated with the other files.

In the Code pane, you can see three new lines have been added between the opening and closing **<video>** tags.

The HTML5 **<source>** tag is used to specify multiple media resources for the <video> tag. When a browser opens the page, it moves through the different <source> tags until it finds one it can use.

The **src** attribute of the <source> tag defines the location of the video file you are using.

The **type** attribute of the <source> tag defines the MIME type of the selected file. This information allows an individual browser to identify a file that it can use.

Note:

"OGV" is the correct extension for an OGG video file.

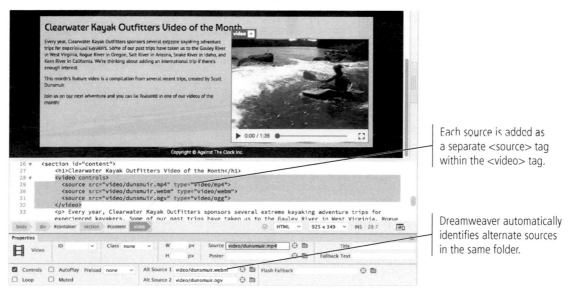

Each source is added as a separate <source> tag within the <video> tag.

Dreamweaver automatically identifies alternate sources in the same folder.

7. **In the Fallback Text field of the Properties panel, type:**

   Your browser does not support the HTML5 video tag. Please update to a current browser.

8. **Press Return/Enter to finalize the fallback text.**

   The paragraph is added to the page code after the <source> tags, but before the closing </video> tag. If a user's browser doesn't support HTML5, this fallback text statement will appear in place of the video.

Fallback text appears if the user's browser does not support the HTML5 video tag.

9. **In the Properties panel, choose auto in the preload menu.**

   The **preload** attribute determines when the video file is downloaded. Using the auto value, the video downloads as soon as the page opens. You can use the none value to prevent the video from loading until a user plays the video, or the metadata value to preload only the video's embedded metadata.

   preload="auto" allows the video file to download as soon as the page loads in a browser.

Video Tag Attributes

The <video> tag supports a number of attributes, which control the way the video object appears in the page.

- **autoplay** causes the video to start playing as soon as it is ready.
- **controls** adds video controls to the video object on the page.
- **height** defines the height of the video player (in pixels).
- **loop** specifies that the video will start over again, every time it is finished.

- **muted** specifies that audio output of the video should be muted.
- **poster** defines an image to be shown while the video is downloading or until the user hits the play button.
- **preload** determines when the video file should be downloaded.
- **src** defines the URL of the video file.
- **width** defines the width of the video player (in pixels).

Some of these attributes support values, which are added in quotes as you do for other attribute values. The autoplay, controls, loop, and muted attributes do not require specific values; simply adding the attribute to the opening video tag is sufficient.

10. In the Properties panel, type 320 in the W field and type 240 in the H field. Press Return/Enter to finalize the change.

These fields define the width and height (respectively) of the video object. In the Code pane, you can see the width and height attributes have been added to the opening <video> tag.

By defining specific height and width attributes, the video object will always appear at the correct size, even before the video has finished downloading.

Note:

We are telling you what dimensions to use for this video. In a professional project, you would have to determine the correct width and height for a specific video file.

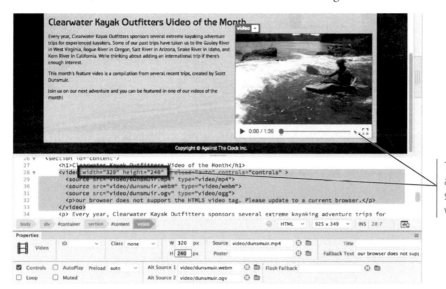

The width and height attributes define a specific size for the video object.

11. Use the controls in the Live view to review the video object.

When the Live view is active, you can see the first frame of the placed video. You can use the controls to play the video directly in the Design pane.

When Live view is active, use the controls to watch the video.

12. Save the file and close it, then continue to the next stage of the project.

Stage 4 Creating a CSS3 Image Gallery

As you might know, Flash animations are not supported on many devices — specifically, mobile devices that use the iOS operating systems (iPhones and iPads). Adobe also recently stopped supporting the Flash Player plug-in for all mobile devices, which means Flash-based animations will likely fall out of common use in favor of a more universally supported method of delivering animation and interactivity.

CSS3 includes a number of options that make it easier to create a basic image gallery without any external scripting. In this stage of the project, you are going to use special selectors to create and position image thumbnails across the top of the gallery area. You will then define hover behavior that enlarges each image when a user's mouse moves over the thumbnail, or when a user taps a thumbnail on a touch-enabled device such as a tablet.

DEFINE ABSOLUTE POSITIONING

Although you can use scripting to create interactive slideshows, you can also use CSS3 and HTML to create interesting galleries using only Dreamweaver's built-in tools. In this exericse, you are going to use CSS to resize images as thumbnails, and position them at specific locations in the containing section.

1. **Open the file gallery.html (from the Kayaking site root folder). Make sure the Live view is active.**

2. **Switch to Split view, and review the code in the <section id="gallery"> tag.**

    The gallery section includes eight images, each of which is simply placed in the section at its original size (740 px × 380 px); only the required alt attribute has been defined.

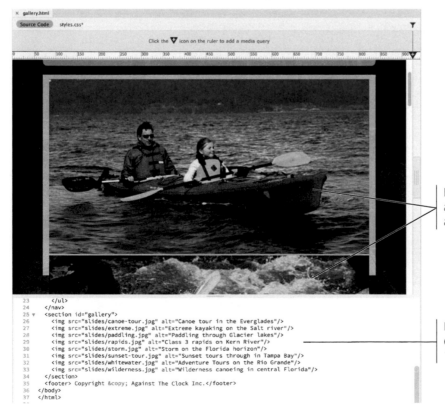

Note:

We are telling you the actual size of these images; in a real-world project, you would have to determine an image's size on your own.

By default, images simply appear in the order they are placed in the code.

Eight image elements exist inside the "gallery" section.

3. **Click styles.css in the Related Files bar to show that code in the Code pane.**

4. **Create a new line at the end of the existing code, then type:**

```
#gallery img {
    position: absolute;
    top: 10px;
    width: 80px;
    border: 3px solid #FFF;
}
```

The position property of CSS allows five possible values:

- **static.** This is the default value, which is applied if no other specific position value is defined. Elements appear in the order they are placed in the code (for example, image1, then image 2, and so on).

- **absolute.** This value defines a specific position relative to the first containing element that does not have static position. Consider the following code:

```
<body>
    <section id="gallery">
        <img src="slide1.jpg" />
    </section>
</body>
```

If CSS code for the <img> tag defines absolute position, it is positioned relative to the <section id="gallery"> only if the #gallery ID selector defines a position other than static. If the #gallery ID selector does not define another position value, the image element will be placed relative to the body element.

- **fixed.** This value allows you to define a position relative to the browser window, regardless of an elements nesting position.

- **relative.** This value allows you define an element's position relative to its default.

- **inherit.** This value means the element's position value is defined by the position value of its immediate parent (i.e., the containing element)

The #gallery img selector defines properties for all image elements within the div that is identified by the gallery ID. As you can see in the Design pane, the width and border properties change the size and border of each image.

Note:

You could define selectors and properties for this section using the CSS Designer panel, but it is sometimes easier to simply type in the Code pane.

Note:

If a selector does not include a position property value, the static position is considered to be applied by default.

Note:

Don't worry if the line numbers in your CSS code do not match what you see in our screen captures. The important point is that you add the same code exactly as we define it in the steps.

```
134 ▼ #gallery {
135     float: left;
136     width: 750px;
137     height: 448px;
138     background: rgba(255, 255, 255, 0.7);
139     padding: 10px;
140     text-align: center;
141 }
142 ▼ #gallery img {
143     position: absolute;
144     top: 10px;
145     width: 80px;
146     border: 3px solid #FFF;
147 }
```

Each image is resized and bordered based on the properties defined in the #gallery img selector.

Each image element has the defined absolute position (10 pixels from the top).

The immediate parent element (the gallery section) does not define a position other than static, so the image elements are placed relative to the body element.

You can also see the effect of the absolute position property — the images are positioned at 0px from the top of the page body. You did not define a left position value, so the left position value is assumed to be 0 for each image. The result is a stack of all eight image elements appearing in the same place; you can see only the last image in the stack because images appear by default in the order they are placed.

5. **Place the insertion point at the end of the last property of the #gallery selector and press Return/Enter to create a new line in that selector's code.**

As we explained, the **absolute** position value applies the defined position based on the last containing element that *does not have static position defined*. At this point, the <section id="gallery"> element that contains the gallery images does not have a defined position, which means the static position is considered to be defined.

6. **Type position: relative; in the new line.**

Because the gallery section now defines a position other than static, the contained image elements are now positioned relative to the gallery section. They are still placed one on top of the next because they all have the same absolute position.

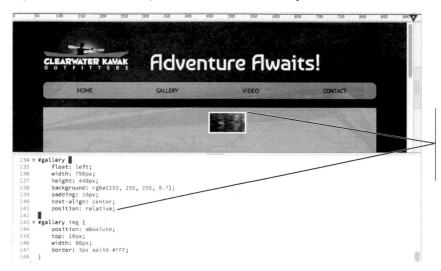

The non-static position allows the absolute position of contained image elements to be relative to the gallery section instead of the page body.

7. **Save all files and then continue to the next exercise.**

 ## WORK WITH NTH-OF-TYPE SELECTORS

At this point all eight images in the gallery occupy the same absolute position. In this exercise you will use CSS to change the absolute position of each image, so they do not all appear in the same spot.

1. **With gallery.html open, make sure the Live view is active.**

2. **At the end of the existing CSS file, define two new selectors:**

```
#gallery img:nth-of-type(1) {
    left: 10px;
}
#gallery img:nth-of-type(2) {
    left: 105px;
}
```

The **:nth-of-type** selector, new in CSS3, allows you to define properties of a specific instance of the defined element type.

Remember, you already defined images in the gallery section to have absolute position, at 10 pixels from the top of the containing element. In the code you just defined, you have now defined the absolute left position of the first — **img:nth-of-type(1)** — and second — **img:nth-of-type(2)** — image elements in the gallery.

Note:

Prior to CSS3, you would have to define unique IDs or classes for each image in the gallery to accomplish the same thing you are doing in this exercise.

The nth-of-type selectors define the position of the first and second image elements in the gallery section.

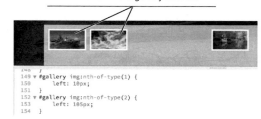

3. Add new selectors to define the position of the remaining images as follows:

```
#gallery img:nth-of-type(3) {
    left: 200px;
}
#gallery img:nth-of-type(4) {
    left: 295px;
}
#gallery img:nth-of-type(5) {
    left: 390px;
}
#gallery img:nth-of-type(6) {
    left: 485px;
}
#gallery img:nth-of-type(7) {
    left: 580px;
}
#gallery img:nth-of-type(8) {
    left: 675px;
}
```

Note:

:nth-of-class is a pseudoclass that modifies the #gallery img selector.

Do not include a space before or after the colon when you type the :nth-of-class selector names.

4. **Review the results in the Design pane.**

We switched to a vertically split document window to better show the entire gallery section and the related CSS code at the same time. Feel free to set up the interface and various panes however you prefer for working most efficiently.

5. **Save all files and continue to the next exercise.**

DEFINE HOVER BEHAVIOR

You now have a row of eight thumbnail images at the top of the gallery section. The final step is to define a CSS selector to control the appearance of each image element when the user's mouse hovers over a thumbnail.

1. **With gallery.html open, make sure the Live view is active.**

2. **At the end of the existing CSS file, define a new selector:**

   ```
   #gallery img:hover {
       width: 740px;
       height: 420px;
       top: 15px;
       left: 10px;
   }
   ```

3. **In the Design pane, move the mouse over the right thumbnail image.**

   As you should already know, the **:hover** selector defines behavior when a user's mouse moves over an element. In previous projects you used this method to define the appearance of link elements (<a> tags); however, it is not limited to link element. Here you are using it to enlarge and reposition the images when a user hovers over the thumbnails.

4. Move your mouse cursor over any thumbnail other than the right one.

If you look carefully at the enlarged image, you should notice that images to the right of the enlarged thumbnail overlap the enlarged image.

Each image exists in a theoretical "stack" based on the order it is placed in the code. An object's top-to-bottom position in a stack is referred to as its **z-index**. The first object has a z-index value of 0 (zero), then next object has a z-index of 1, and each successive object increases the z-index by 1.

Although you used absolute positioning to place the thumbnails at specific locations, you did not change their positions in the stack. Successive images still overlap previous images in the stack.

Successive images overlap the enlarged image.

5. In the CSS file, add a new line to the #gallery img:hover selector:

```
z-index: 99;
```

6. Review the results in the Design pane.

By increasing the z-index of the image affected by the hover behavior, you move it to the top of the stack so it is not overlapped by any of the other thumbnails.

7. Save all files and continue to the next exercise.

ADD A DROP SHADOW

As we have explained, CSS3 includes a number of properties that make it much easier to create visual effects that once required a complicated series of images cut apart in an image-editing application and reassembled in the HTML and/or CSS code. In this exercise, you are going to add a drop-shadow effect to the enlarged images to enhance those images and separate them from the smaller thumbnails.

1. With **gallery.html** open, make sure the Live view is active.

2. In the CSS Designer panel, locate and select **#gallery img:hover** in the Selectors section of the panel.

3. In the Properties section, of the panel, click the Background button to jump to those options.

4. Scroll to the box-shadow options and set the following values:

    h-shadow: 5 px

    v-shadow: 5 px

    blur: 3 px

    color: #333333

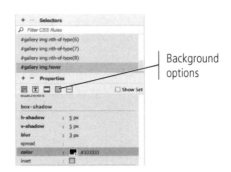

Background options

The box-shadow property has six possible values:

- **h-shadow** and **v-shadow** are the horizontal and vertical offset positions of the shadow. These are the only required values of the property

- **blur** is the blur distance of the shadow.

- **spread** is the size of the drop shadow.

- **color** is the color of the drop shadow.

- **inset** can be used to make the shadow appear inside the element.

5. In the Code pane, review the code for the **#gallery img:hover** selector.

The code for a drop shadow occupies a single line with each option as part of the overall property value. The various options appear in this order:

box-shadow: h-shadow v-shadow blur spread color inset;

```
173 ▼ #gallery img:hover {
174       width: 740px;
175       height: 420px;
176       top: 15px;
177       left: 10px;
178       z-index: 99;
179       -webkit-box-shadow: 5px 5px 3px #333333;
180       box-shadow: 5px 5px 3px #333333;
181 }
```

Although the current versions of each browser support the drop-shadow property, earlier versions of Safari and Chrome — and the Dreamweaver Design view — require the -webkit- prefixed statement to correctly render the element's drop-shadow.

6. In the Design pane, move your mouse over one of the thumbnail images.

7. Save all files and close them.

8. Export a site definition named Kayaking.ste into your WIP>Kayaking folder, and then remove the site from Dreamweaver.

1. A(n) _____ is a sequence of fonts that can be used to display content.

2. In CSS, the _____ prefix defines settings for the Google Chrome Browser, as well as Dreamweaver's Live view.

3. The _____ property format can be used to define transparency for a color in a CSS3 selector.

4. The _____ CSS3 property can be used to create rounded corners on all four corners of an element.

5. The _____ CSS3 property can be used to create multiple columns of text within a single element.

6. True or false: A web font is specific to the file that is open when it is installed in Dreamweaver. _____

7. The _____ in Dreamweaver must be used to preview the effects of applying a web font to a page element.

8. The _____ attribute of the video tag allows a video file to download as soon as the page containing the tag is opened.

9. Which position property value defines a specific position relative to the first containing element that does not have static position?

_____

10. The _____ property defines an object's top-to-bottom position in the object stack.

1. Briefly explain how to define a CSS3 property for multiple browsers.

2. Briefly explain how to define a <video> tag, including multiple formats for different browsers.

3. Briefly explain the nth-of-type pseudo-class.

Portfolio Builder Project

Use what you learned in this project to complete the following freeform exercise.
Carefully read the art director and client comments, then create your own design to meet the needs of the project.
Use the space below to sketch ideas; when finished, write a brief explanation of your reasoning behind your final design.

art director comments

You have been hired to create a new website for the Watermann Gallery, an art and history museum in Green Valley, Arizona. The director wants the site to be simple and functional, yet present the necessary information in an aesthetic manner appropriate for an art gallery.

- ❏ Download the client-supplied resources in the **Gallery_DW18_PB.zip** archive on the Student Files web page.
- ❏ Design a site that presents the client's information in a clear, well-organized manner.
- ❏ Read the client-supplied text to determine what type of background or supporting images might best enhance the site pages.

client comments

Our gallery has been completely renovated in the last year, and we're taking this opportunity to redesign our web page as well. We might want to add more pages to the site later, but for now we only want to present the most important points.

We've given you content for four pages:

- Home. This should include both the mission statement and the collections and exhibitions blurb. We've included a couple of images that you can use on this page, but you can also use other images that support our image.
- Current Exhibits. We have three rotating exhibits; we've given you three images for each exhibit, but you don't have to use all of them unless you think it works well.
- Calendar of Events. Find one or two images to tastefully illustrate this page.
- How to Help. Find one or two images to tastefully illustrate this page.

project justification

HTML5 is intended to adapt the underlying page code to better serve both the way designers work and the way users browse the Internet. Coupled with CSS3 selectors and embedded web fonts, you now have far greater creative control over the structure and appearance of web page content.

This project highlighted a number of issues you should understand when you work with HTML5. First, Dreamweaver is not yet optimized to apply many of the HTML5/CSS3 features through user interface components like the Properties panel or Insert bar; to successfully use some HTML5 features in Dreamweaver, you will sometimes be required to work directly in the page code.

Second, different browsers require different code for HTML5 to function properly; you should remember to verify your code and include the required variations so that your pages will work in as many current browsers as possible. Also, keep in mind that older browsers do not support HTML5/CSS3; over time we can expect older, non-HTML5 browsers to fall out of use, but until then, some users will not be able to see the content as you intend it to be displayed.

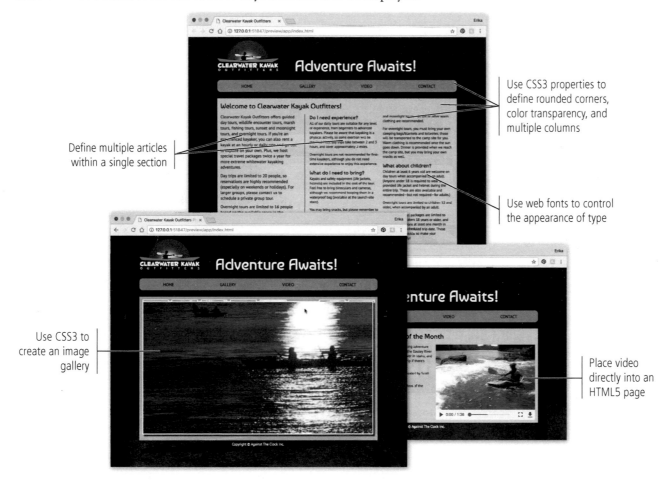

Define multiple articles within a single section

Use CSS3 properties to define rounded corners, color transparency, and multiple columns

Use web fonts to control the appearance of type

Use CSS3 to create an image gallery

Place video directly into an HTML5 page

jQuery Mobile Site

Your client, an up-and-coming photographer in the San Franciso area, wants to create a web site that is simple to access and navigate, regardless of the device being used. Your job is to implement the approved site design, using JavaScript to include multiple pieces of information on a single page.

This project incorporates the following skills:

❏ Creating a mobile-friendly site structure

❏ Creating and managing a jQuery user-interface object

❏ Defining a JavaScript Lightbox image gallery

client comments

I would like the site to work on as many devices as possible — desktop and mobile. I don't want it to be overly complicated; the site should be compact and easy to navigate.

The most important information to present is my current exhibits, contact information, and galleries with samples of my work. I've also sent you a brief "About Me" section of text, just because everyone else seems to include that. You don't need to make that prominent on the site, but it should be available for anyone who is interested.

Although I started by specializing in photographing people, I have recently been asked to do a series of pet photographs for a national magazine. To start with, I want galleries to show those two collections. I might eventually expand to include a couple of other collections, but I haven't made up my mind on that issue yet.

art director comments

I've already gotten the initial site layout approved by the client. She especially likes the plans for keeping all of the site content in only a few pages, with a simple user interface.

Overall, you only need three pages — a home page, a page with all of her text content, and a page with links to image galleries.

The text she supplied is relatively short, and I don't think it requires individual pages for each section. Instead, you can create a single "Info" page and use a JavaScript tabbed-panel object to consolidate all of the information into a single space. This will keep the site small and more manageable, so that users don't have to dig through multiple levels of navigation to find the information they want.

You can also use JavaScript to build image interactive galleries. The client has only submitted a few images so far, but she said she will be sending more at some point. For now, just build two galleries — one for her "portraits" collection and one for her "pets" collection.

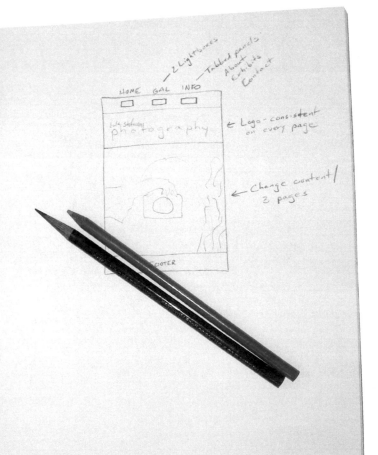

project objectives

To complete this project, you will:

- ❏ Create a basic site structure
- ❏ Define inline navigation links
- ❏ Control relative image size
- ❏ Create a jQuery tabbed panel object
- ❏ Add content to tab panels
- ❏ Change the tab CSS
- ❏ Learn about grouping CSS selectors
- ❏ Create a JavaScript Lightbox image gallery

Stage 1 Creating Mobile-Friendly Design

Recent statistics show that 54.32% of web users are accessing information on mobile devices (including tablets), compared to only 45.68 percent who are using a desktop computer.[1] We can expect these numbers to continue changing in favor of mobile devices, so designing sites that work properly on mobile devices is a required skill for web design professionals.

In this project you are going to create a simple page and site design that can present all of the client's information in a compact, easy-to-navigate structure that will work as well on mobile devices as it will on a desktop. (In Project 8: Bootstrap Responsive Page, you will learn how to create a site that changes based on the size of the device being used.)

CREATE THE BASIC PAGE STRUCTURE

1. Download **Photography_DW18_RF.zip** from the Student Files web page.

2. **Expand the ZIP archive into your WIP folder (Macintosh) or copy the archive content into you WIP folder (Windows).**

   This results in a folder named Photography, which contains the files you need for this project.

3. **In Dreamweaver, create a new site named Photography, using your WIP>Photography folder as the site root folder.**

4. **Choose File>New. Define the following settings in the right side of the dialog box, then click Create:**

Document Type:	HTML
Title:	Julia Stoferson Photography
DocType:	HTML5

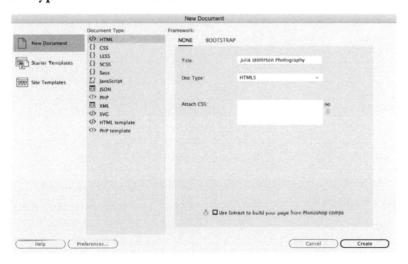

5. **Choose File>Save As. Save the file as design.html in your WIP>Photography folder.**

---

1 http://gs.statcounter.com/platform-market-share/desktop-mobile-tablet

6. **In the bottom-right corner of the document window, open the Display Size menu and choose iPhone 7 Plus.**

Open this menu to show predefined display sizes.

This menu includes a number of common device sizes. Choosing one of these options changes the document window to the size you choose, allowing you to better preview the space that is available on specific device displays. You can also use the two options at the bottom of the menu change the orientation of the display in the document window. Choosing Full Size restores your view to the entire visible area of the Design view.

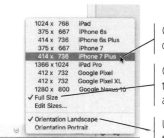

Choose one of the common display sizes in the menu.

Choose Full Size to display the page in the entire available Design view.

Use these options to change the display orientation.

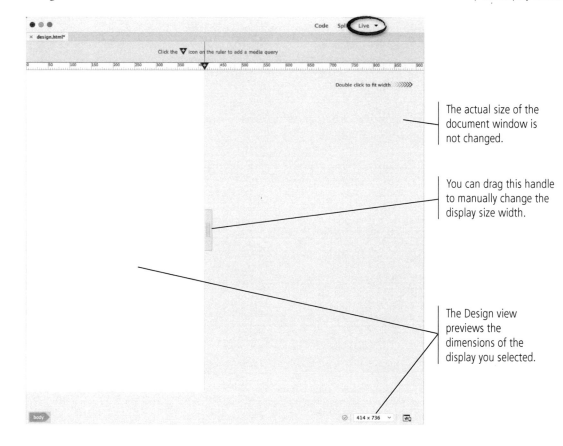

The actual size of the document window is not changed.

You can drag this handle to manually change the display size width.

The Design view previews the dimensions of the display you selected.

7. **With the Live view active, use the HTML Insert panel to add four elements to the page:**

> **Navigation**
>
> **Header**
>
> **Main**
>
> **Footer**

You can use the click-and drag method to add these elements, or click the related button and then use the Position Assistant to add each element after the previous one.

If you use the drag-and-drop method, remember that the green line indicates when you are placing one element immediately after an existing one. Simply dragging the buttons from the Insert panel to the document window without using the green lines will place each subsequent element at the top of the document stack, resulting in the elements in reverse order from what you see here.

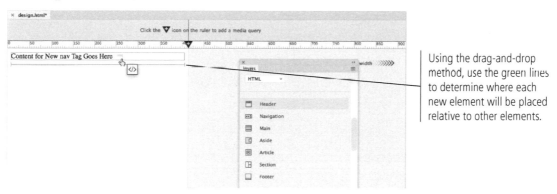

Using the drag-and-drop method, use the green lines to determine where each new element will be placed relative to other elements.

8. **In the Design pane, replace the placeholder text in the footer element with the following text:**

> **Site Design by Against The Clock, Inc.**

Remember, when the Live view is active, selecting text content is a three-step process:

1. First click to select the element.
2. Click again to select the element content.
3. Click and drag to highlight the text content you want to change or delete.

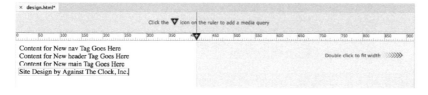

9. **In the CSS Designer panel, click the Add CSS Source button and choose Attach Existing CSS File in the menu.**

10. **In the resulting dialog box, click the browse button. Navigate to the file styles.css (in the site css folder) and click Open. Make sure the link option is selected, then click OK.**

11. **Click styles.css in the Related Files bar to show the CSS file in Code view. Review the defined selectors and property values.**

    Remember, clicking the styles.css file in the Related Files bar automatically changes to the Split view, and shows the selected file in the Code pane.

    Because we have already explained the process of creating CSS rules in great detail, we have provided you with a basic CSS file that defines rules for the body element and the four structural elements you just created. In a professional setting, you would have to define these rules on your own.

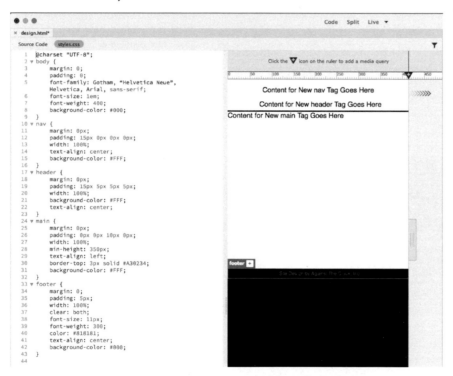

12. **Choose File>Save All, then continue to the next exercise.**

As you can see in the Design view, the current file structure is very basic. Despite its simplicity, however, this structure is perfectly suited to the site you are creating in this project — a basic site to present the client's information in a compact, easy to navigate user experience.

In this exercise you will add navigation links to the nav element, then define CSS to allow those links to all appear in the same line — taking up considerably less display space than a vertical list.

1. **With design.html open and the Live view active, select and delete the placeholder text from the nav element.**

2. **With the insertion point in the now-empty nav element, type:**

    Home [Return/Enter]

    Galleries {Return/Enter}

    Info

    When you press Return/Enter after the first word, that line is automatically tagged as a paragraph element. Each subsequent line also becomes a separate paragraph element.

    Do not press Return/Enter after the third word; this would result in a fourth empty paragraph element with a nonbreaking space character.

3. **Highlight the word "Home" in the Design pane. Using the Quick Properties Inspector, click the Hyperlink button and then define index.html as the link.**

    You can use the Quick Properties Inspector to define links at any time, even though the target pages don't yet exist.

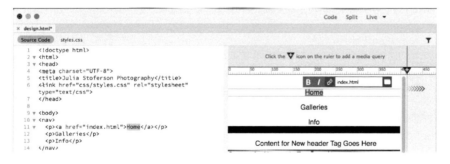

4. **Repeat this process to create additional links as follows:**

    "Galleries"   Link to galleries.html

    "Info"   Link to info.html

5. **Click styles.css in the Related Files bar to show that file in the Code pane.**

6. **Place the insertion point after the end of the existing code and define three new selectors:**

```css
nav p {
    margin: 0px;
    padding: 5px 10px 0px 10px;
    height: 20px;
    border-right: 1px solid #A30234;
}
nav p a {
    color: #A30234;
    text-decoration: none;
}
nav p a:hover {
    color: #2C9C8B;
}
```

Note:

Feel free to take advantage of the Code Hint menus that appear as you type.

In some cases, it is simply easier to type in the Code view to define CSS code — as you will do throughout the first part of this project. As you gain experience designing with CSS, you will develop your own preferences for accomplishing specific tasks.

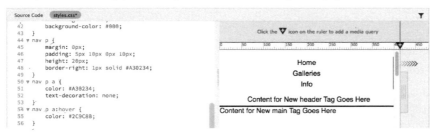

7. **Add a new property to the nav p a selector:**

text-transform: uppercase;

Note:

We have already explained the process for creating selectors in the CSS Designer panel, and we have already explained the meaning of these selectors in great detail.

By default, the case of letters appears as the letters are typed. You can use the **text-transform property** to change the appearance of letters in the selected element. Possible values include:

- **capitalize** transforms the first character of each word to uppercase.
- **uppercase** transforms all characters to uppercase.
- **lowercase** transforms all characters to lowercase.

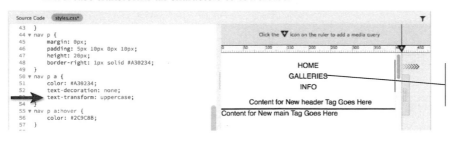

Text in the paragraph elements now appears in all uppercase.

8. **Add a new property to the nav p selector:**

   ```
   display: inline-block;
   ```

   The **display property** specifies the type of "box" that is used for an HTML element.
   The **inline-block** value allows elements to appear on the same line as preceding elements.

Each paragraph element moves into the same line.

9. **Create a new selector at the end of the code:**

   ```
   nav p:last-of-type {
       border-right: 0px;
   }
   ```

   CSS can be used to apply formatting to very specific elements, including certain instances of the same element within a specific container. In this case, you are defining formatting for only the last (**:last-of-type**) paragraph element (**p**) inside the nav element (**nav**).

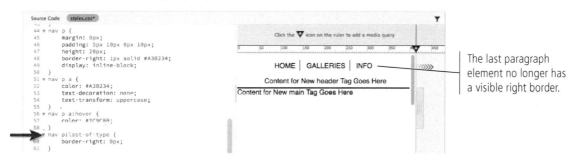

The last paragraph element no longer has a visible right border.

Using **p** as the base element in each example, other options for isolating specific instances include:

- **p:first-child** affects the p element that is the first child of its parent.
- **p:first-of-type** affects the p element that is the first paragraph of its parent.
- **p:last-child** affects the p element that is the last child of its parent.
- **p:nth-child(N)** affects the p element that is the nth child of its parent.
- **p:nth-last-child(N)** affects the p element that is the nth child of its parent, counting from the last child.
- **p:nth-last-of-type(N)** affects the p element that is the nth paragraph of its parent, counting from the last child.
- **p:nth-of-type(N)** affects the p element that is the nth paragraph of its parent.
- **p:only-of-type** affects the p element that is the only paragraph of its parent.
- **p:only-child** affects the p element that is the only child of its parent.

10. **Choose File>Save All, then continue to the next exercise.**

CONTROL IMAGE SIZE AND POSITION

Your client's site requires a number of images, which need to be placed in three separate ways:

- The logo will occupy the header of every page.

- A photo of your client taking a photo is the feature image in the main area of the home page.

- A series of photos, divided into two categories, need to be made accessible on the galleries page.

In this exercise, you will accomplish the first of these required tasks.

1. **With design.html open, make sure the Live view is active and show the page source code in the Code pane.**

   Leaving the Live view active allows you to immediately — and accurately — see the results of your code changes.

2. **In the Code pane, select and delete the placeholder text in the header element.**

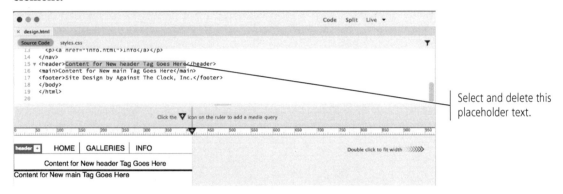

Select and delete this placeholder text.

3. **With the insertion point in the now-empty header element, define a new img element inside the header element using the following code:**

   ```
   <img src="images/jsp-logo.png" alt="Julia Stoferson Photography">
   ```

   When you first place an image, it is automatically placed at the file's original size, which is not appropriate for the small size of a mobile device. Fortunately, you can use CSS to force the image to fit into its containing element.

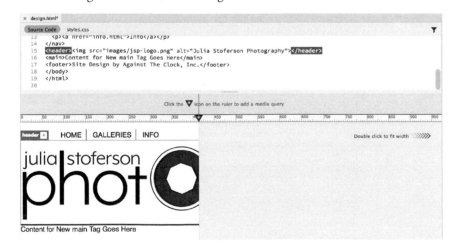

Note:

Again, feel free to take advantage of the Code Hint menus that appear as you type.

4. Click styles.css in the Related Files bar to show the CSS in the Code pane.

5. At the end of the existing CSS, create a new selector at the end of the code:

```
header img {
    width: 95%;
    height: auto;
}
```

By defining the width property with a value of 95%, the image in the header element will be 95% of its parent element's width. Since the header element has a width of 100% of its parent container (the body element), the logo is now 95% of the page width.

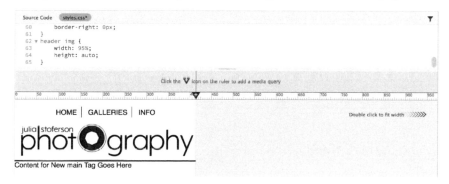

6. Click the handle on the right side of the display and drag until the display width is as wide as possible on your screen.

As you enlarge the display size, you can see the logo change size so that it still occupies 95% of the available display width. If you have a large enough monitor, you can see that the image quality eventually deteriorates when it enlarges too much beyond the image file's actual size.

Note:

The logo you are using in this exercise is 900 pixels wide. In a professional environment, you would have to determine an image's actual size on your own.

Click and drag this bar to enlarge the display width.

As the display and image enlarge, you might notice deterioration of image quality.

7. **In the Code pane, add another rule to the header img selector:**

    max-width: 900px;

    The **max-width property** prevents an image from enlarging beyond the defined size, which prevents the loss of quality you see when an image is enlarged too much beyond its actual physical size.

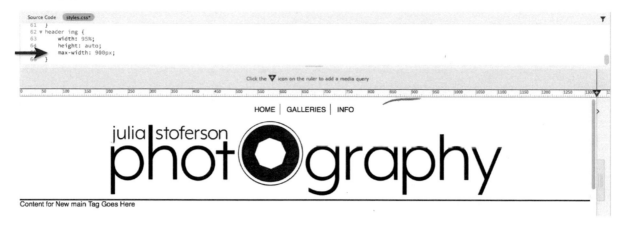

8. **Choose File>Save All, then continue to the next exercise.**

CREATE A SITE TEMPLATE

Design templates are a very useful tool for minimizing repetitive work, even in a site like this one that requires only three pages. In this exercise, you will create a site template from your basic file structure, then create the necessary HTML pages based on that template.

1. **With design.html open, turn off the Live view and close the Code view.**

    Remember, you can't work with templates when the Live view is active.

2. **Click in the Design view to make it active, then choose File>Save As Template.**

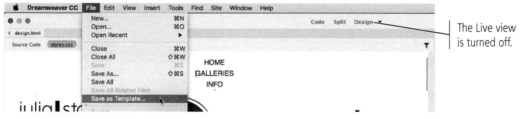

3. **Make sure Photography is selected in the Site menu, then click Save. When prompted to update links, click Yes.**

4. **In the Design view, highlight the placeholder content in the main element.**

5. **Click the Editable Region button in the Templates Insert panel.**

6. **In the resulting dialog box, type `PageContent` in the Name field, then click OK.**

Because you selected the placeholder text before defining the editable region, the new editable region is created around the selected text.

7. **Choose File>Save to save the template file, then close it.**

8. **In the Assets panel, click the button on the left of the panel to show only template files.**

If you don't see the template you just saved, click the Refresh button (↻) at the bottom of the panel.

9. **Control/right-click the existing template file and choose New from Template.**

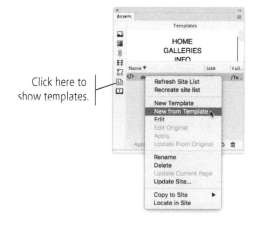

Click here to show templates.

10. Save the new file as **galleries.html** in the Photography site root folder.

11. Close galleries.html.

12. Repeat Steps 8–11 to create another new file named **info.html** from the design.dwt template file.

13. Repeat Steps 8–10 to create another new file named **index.html** from the design.dwt template file. Do not close the file.

14. With index.html open, show the Split view and turn on the Live view.

15. Use the Code pane to replace the placeholder text in the editable region with a new img element:

    `<img src="images/julia.jpg" alt="Julia Stoferson Photography">`

16. Use the Display Size menu to change the display to the iPhone 7 Plus size.

Because you used a compound selector to control the width of the image in the header element (in the previous exercise), the image you just placed is not affected by the width:95% property value. You have to define another width property to affect this image, which is placed in the main element.

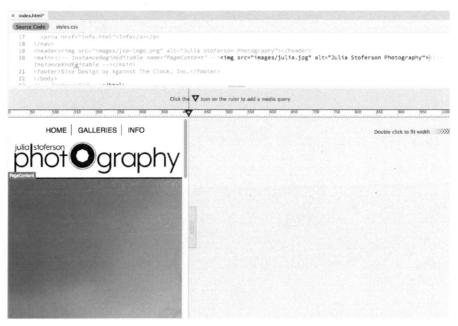

17. Show the styles.css file in the Code pane, then add a new selector to the end of the existing code:

```
main img {
    width: 100%;
    height: auto;
}
```

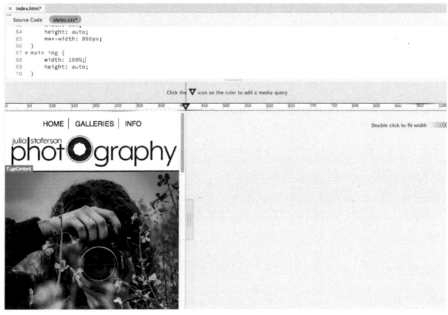

18. Choose File>Save All, then close index.html.

19. Continue to the next stage of the project.

Stage 2 Adding jQuery UI Elements

A **script** is a set of instructions that performs certain actions in response to an event —
generally something the user does, such as clicking an object. Although it was once
considered undesirable (or even unprofessional by some), JavaScript is now becoming
a *de facto* standard for adding interactivity in websites. JavaScript offers a number of
advantages to web developers, including (but certainly not limited to) the following:

Note:

*JavaScript is not the same
as the Java programming
language, despite the
fact that both share some
similar programming
structures.*

- It is supported by all current browsers on Macintosh, Windows, iOS, and
  Android operating systems.

- It does not require plug-ins to add interactivity to a web page. JavaScript
  scripts are interpreted and processed by the browser to produce the desired effect.

- It allows you to change a web page without reloading the actual HTML.

- It can be used to change or remove existing content, or even add new content to the page.

- It can be used to change the CSS that is associated with various page elements.

- JavaScript scripts can be embedded directly into HTML pages using <script> tags.

- If you want to execute the same scripts on multiple pages, you can create the scripts in an
  external JavaScript file (using the ".js" extension) and link that file to whatever HTML
  pages require the stored scripts.

JavaScript enables complex interactive interface objects, such as multi-level
navigation menus, tabbed panel sets, and so on. The code required to create these
common objects is fairly complex. However, because they are so common, the
necessary code already exists in many libraries — some of them free — that you can
download and use in your own sites.

Note:

*If you are pursuing a
career in web design
and development,
we highly encourage
you to continue your
education by learning as
much as you can about
JavaScript.*

Although JavaScript is not as confusing to learn as some kinds of scripting,
it is still a programming language that has its own syntax, vocabulary, logic, and
rules. Fortunately, Dreamweaver includes a number of tools for adding JavaScript
interactivity into an HTML page without manually writing a single line of code. In
this stage of the project, you will use those tools to change various page content based
on user interactivity, presenting multiple categories of information in a single HTML
page that loads only one time in the browser window.

 INSERT A JQUERY TABBED PANEL

jQuery is a JavaScript library that aims to make it easier to add JavaScript to a web
page. The library file stores a number of common tasks as methods, which can be
called by the script in your page; this means you don't have to rewrite the common
elements each time you want to implement the same common tasks.

Keep in mind that this is an extreme oversimplification of jQuery; basically, it's
little more than a definition. However, you don't really need to understand exactly how
it works to define the jQuery UI elements that are built into Dreamweaver.

1. Open **info.html** from your **WIP>Photography** folder and make the regular
   Design view active.

   It can be very difficult to work with the content of JavaScript elements when the Live
   view is active. You will build the basic structure in the regular Design view, then switch
   to the Live view to manage the appearance of the tabbed panel set.

2. **In the Design view, delete the placeholder text from the editable template region.**

3. **With the insertion point in the editable area, click the Tabs button in the jQuery UI Insert panel.**

The insertion point should be in the editable region.

As soon as you add a jQuery Tabs object, the Related Files bar shows a number of new linked files — three CSS files and two JavaScript library files are required for this object to work properly. All of the required JavaScript scripts are managed for you; you don't need to touch a single line of code for the object to function.

The default Tabs object contains three categories or headers. The first content area — the one associated with the "Tab 1" header — is visible in the Design pane.

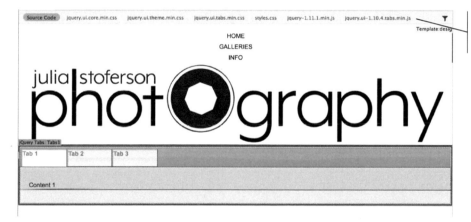

A number of files are required for the tabs to work properly.

4. **Choose File>Save. Read the information in the resulting message, then click OK.**

The CSS and JavaScript files required by the jQuery object must be included when you upload your site files to a web server. Dreamweaver automatically incorporates the necessary elements (including any images called by the JavaScript and CSS files) into your site folder when you save your HTML file.

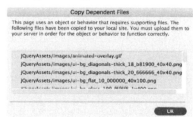

5. **In the Files panel, expand the jQueryAssets folder.**

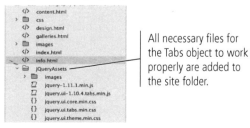

All necessary files for the Tabs object to work properly are added to the site folder.

6. **Click away from the Tabs object to deselect it.**

   After first creating the Tabs object, you have to deselect the newly created object before clicking the widget to select it and reveal its properties in the panel. This is a minor bug in the software, but one you should be aware of.

7. **Move the cursor back over the Tabs object.**

   When the cursor moves over a non-selected Tabs object, a blue widget appears at the top of the object. You can click the widget to select that object on the page.

8. **Click the blue jQuery Tabs widget.**

Click the widget to select the entire Tabs object.

Define object parameters in the Properties panel.

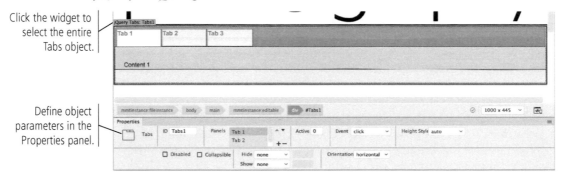

When the Tabs object is selected, you can use the Properties panel to define specific attributes of the Tabs object.

- **ID.** This is the ID attribute of the div that contains all elements of the Tabs object.

- **Panels.** This lists the categories or tabs in the object. You can use the Up and Down Arrow buttons to rearrange the panels; click the Plus (+) button to add a new panel; or click the Minus (–) button to remove the selected panel.

- **Active.** This option defines which section is visible by default when the Tabs object is first loaded. This number refers to a section's index value in the Panels list; the first item is 0 (zero), the second item is 1, the third item is 2, and so on.

- **Event.** This menu determines how a user can show a different tab section (click or mouseover).

- **Height Style.** This menu defines the height of the overall object (auto, fill, or content).

- **Disabled.** You can check this option to prevent a user from changing the visible section of the Tabs object.

- **Collapsible.** You can check this option to allow a user to collapse the active section without expanding a different section.

- **Hide** and **Show.** These menus apply animated effects when a user chooses a different tab. The Hide menu defines animation for the previously visible tab, and the Show menu defines animation for the newly visible tab. The attached fields defines the duration (in milliseconds) over which the animations occur.

- **Orientation.** This menu determine the basic structure of the Tabs object. Using the default horizontal orientation, tabs appear in a row at the top of the object. If you chose the vertical option, the tabs appear in a stack to the left of the content.

9. **Choose Content in the Height Style menu and leave all other options at their default values.**

10. **Save the file and continue to the next exercise.**

ADD TAB CONTENT

Content in an jQuery Tabs object is still HTML content; to add content to a Tabs object, you can simply type (or paste) in the relevant section. Because JavaScript shows and hides specific categories of content based on user interaction, only one content area appears at a time in the Design pane. To add content in a hidden content area, you first need to make that area visible in the document window.

1. **With info.html open in the regular Design view, select the "Tab 1" text in the first tab.**

2. **Type About to replace the default heading.**

   The text in a tab is still text, just like the text in any other element on the page. You can highlight it in the Design pane and type to change it.

   When the insertion point is flashing in a specific tab or tab section, the Properties panel shows options related to that text.

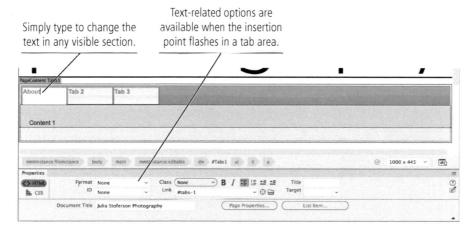

Simply type to change the text in any visible section.

Text-related options are available when the insertion point flashes in a tab area.

3. **Repeat Steps 1–2 to replace the text on other two tabs in the object:**

   "Tab 2" becomes Exhibits

   "Tab 3" becomes Contact

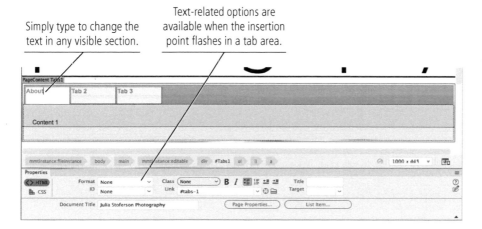

Simply type to change the text in any visible section.

Text-related options are available when the insertion point flashes in a tab area.

4. **Using the Files panel, open `content.html`.**

This file includes three sections of content; each should be pasted into the appropriate content area of the object.

5. **Select and copy the three paragraphs after the "About" heading.**

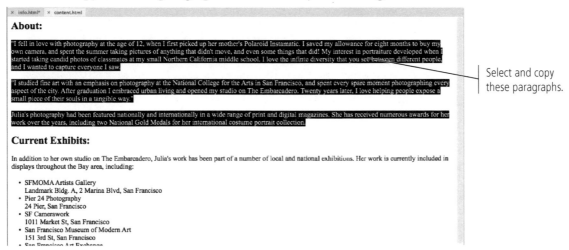

Select and copy these paragraphs.

6. **Make the info.html file active. Delete the default "Content 1" text in the visible content area, then paste the text you copied in Step 5.**

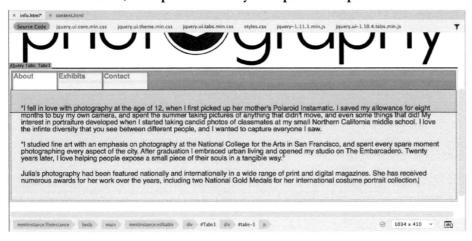

7. **Move your cursor over the Exhibits tab in the object.**

Moving the cursor over a tab in the selected Tabs object reveals an Eye icon; you can click that icon to show the content area for that tab.

Move the cursor over a tab to reveal the Eye icon.

Click the Eye icon to show the content for that tab.

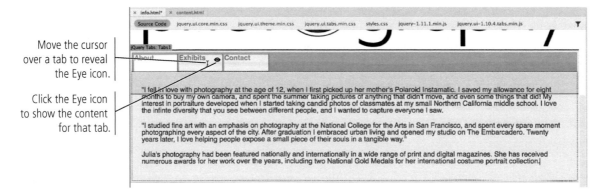

8. **Click the Eye icon to show the content area for the Exhibits tab.**

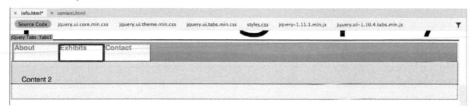

9. **Make the content.html file active, and copy the text after the second heading.**

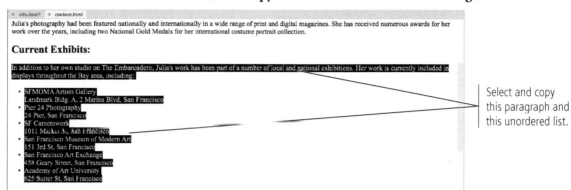

Select and copy this paragraph and this unordered list.

10. **Make the index.html file active, delete the "Content 2" placeholder text, then paste the copied text into the Content 2 area.**

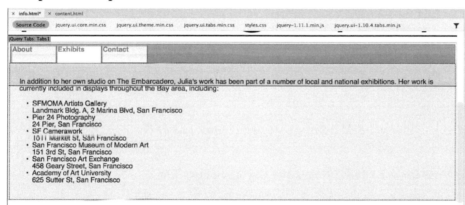

11. **Repeat Steps 7–10 to change the content in the Content 3 area (for the "Contact" tab).**

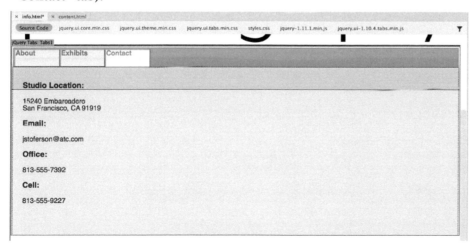

12. **Save all files, close content.html, and continue to the next exercise.**

CHANGE TAB CONTENT CSS

Many of the attributes related to a jQuery Tabs object do not function properly in the Design pane unless the Live view is active. The final step in this stage of the project is to review the tabs when all options are working, then make any changes that are necessary to make the file work within the context of the overall site.

1. **With info.html open, turn on the Live view.**

   You can now see formatting attributes that were not evident in the regular Design view. CSS that is automatically applied to the jQuery Tabs object defines the appearance of various elements of the object, such as the individual tabs, and the backgrounds behind the tabs and the content area. The built-in styles, however, do not affect the formatting of various elements within the content area. You have to define (or attach) CSS to control the appearance of those elements.

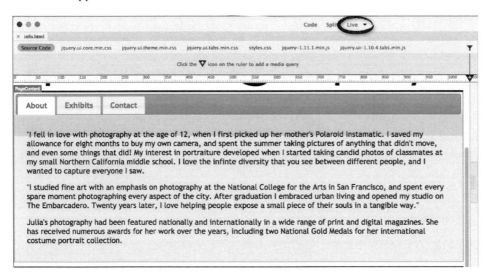

2. **In the CSS Designer panel, click the Add Source button and choose Attach Existing CSS File.**

3. **In the resulting dialog box, choose css/styles-tabs.css, then click OK.**

Note:

We provided this file with selectors to format paragraph elements, headings, unordered lists, and list items in the main element — where the tabbed panels are placed. (In a professional environment you would need to define these selectors on your own.)

It is important to realize that you can attach more than one CSS file to a specific HTML page. For very complex design jobs, this can be useful for more easily organizing and managing different aspects of the overall job.

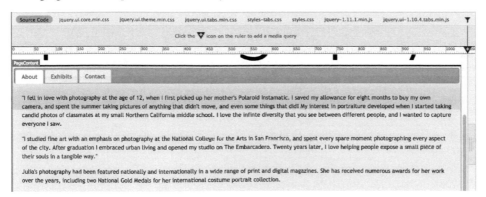

4. In the Live view, Command-Option-click (Macintosh) or Alt-click (Windows) the "About" tab to show the Code Navigator.

The Code Navigator lists all pieces of code related to the selected item. You can see that there are a number of CSS selectors — in several different files — that apply to the actual tabs in the Tabs object.

5. Move your cursor over the various selectors and review the defined properties.

Because the selector names that are defined in the predefined CSS files can be confusing, it's best to use the Code Navigator to find the property you want to modify.

Command-Option-click (Maintosh) or Alt-click (Windows) to open the Code Navigator.

Move your mouse over each selector to review the defined properties.

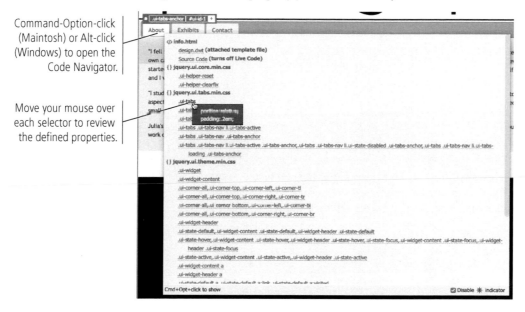

6. Click the .ui-state-default a,.ui-state-default a:link,.ui-state-default a:visited selector link in the Code Navigator.

Clicking a link in the Code Navigator automatically shows the related code in the Code pane, and selects the related selector in the CSS Designer panel.

For some reason, the CSS in the jquery.ui.theme.min.css is run together into a single line. Although the CSS does work properly without line breaks, it is almost impossible to distinguish the code you want to change. Fortunately, in this case, the CSS Designer panel makes it easy to accomplish the required tasks.

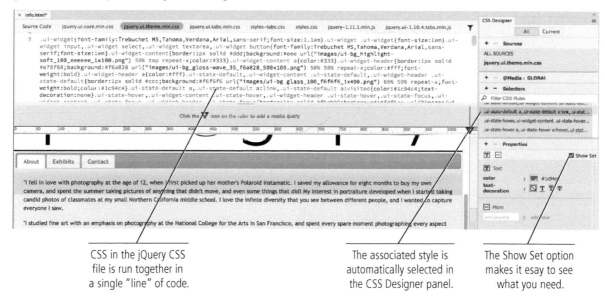

CSS in the jQuery CSS file is run together in a single "line" of code.

The associated style is automatically selected in the CSS Designer panel.

The Show Set option makes it easy to see what you need.

Grouping CSS Selectors

When two or more selectors have the same properties and values, they can be grouped to save time. For example, if you need three element selectors (h1, h2, and h3) with the same margin and padding values, you can write the code as:

```
h1 {
    margin: 0px;
}

h2 {
    margin: 0px;
}

h3 {
    margin: 0px;
}
```

Rather than defining three separate selectors, you can group them by typing all three selector names, separated by commas:

```
h1, h2, h3 {
    margin: 0px;
}
```

7. **In the CSS Designer panel, activate the Show Set option.**

8. **Change the color property of the active selector value to #A30234.**

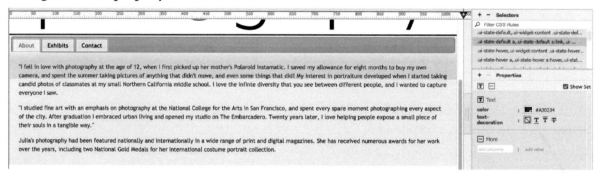

9. **Command-Option-click (Macintosh) or Alt-click (Windows) the first paragraph in the tab content area tab to show the Code Navigator.**

10. **Move the mouse cursor over the .ui-widget-content selector and review the settings.**

    This selector uses CSS shorthand to define a gray background color and a gradient background image at the top of each content area. You want the content areas to have a simple white background, so you are going to manually change this value.

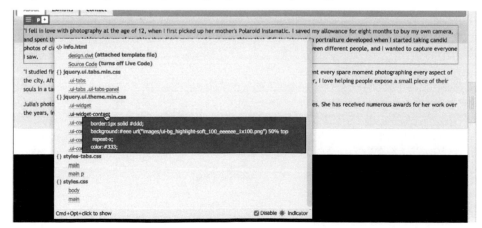

11. Click .ui-widget-content in the Code Navigator.

Due to a bug in the software, clicking a selector in the Code Navigator does not always automatically switch the CSS Designer panel to the appropriate selector. In this case, you have to manually click the selector in the panel to select it.

12. In the CSS Designer panel, click to select the .ui-widget-content selector.

13. In the Properties section of the panel, click the value field for the background property to highlight the existing value. Type #FFF to define white as the new value, replacing the entire previous value.

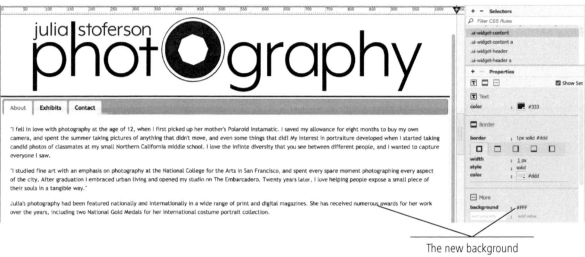

The new background property value removes the gray color and gradient.

14. With the Live view active, test the functionality of the tabs.

15. Use the Display Size menu to test the page in the iPhoto 7 Plus size.

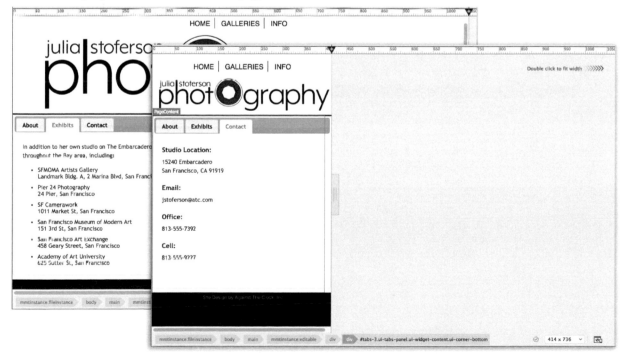

16. Choose File>Save All.

17. Close info.html, then continue to the next stage of the project.

Using Inspect Mode in Live View

In addition to using the Code Navigator, Dreamweaver's Inspect mode, which you can toggle on by choosing View>Inspect, makes it easy to find the page code and CSS styles that are associated with specific objects on the page.

When you move the mouse cursor over an object in the Design pane in Live view, different-colored highlights identify the defined padding, border, margin, and content areas of that object (the "box model").

The Code pane also dynamically changes to show code related to the highlighted object.

If the CSS Designer panel is visible, the panel also changes to show the rules and properties that are related to the object under the mouse cursor.

If you click an element in the Design pane, Dreamweaver automatically exits Inspect mode. Whatever code was highlighted remains selected and visible in the Code pane so you can make changes to the item you were highlighting when Inspect mode was still active.

An object's box model is highlighted when under the mouse cursor.

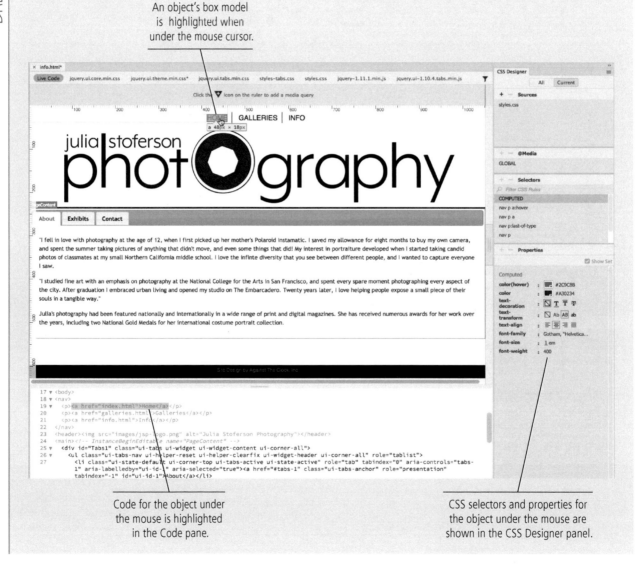

Code for the object under the mouse is highlighted in the Code pane.

CSS selectors and properties for the object under the mouse are shown in the CSS Designer panel.

Stage 3 Creating a JavaScript Photo Gallery

The final required task for this project is to create interactive photo galleries that can display your client's images within the compact layout that you are designing in this project. A JavaScript photo gallery is one of the most common ways to accomplish this goal.

Rather than reinventing the wheel, so to speak, you should know that a lot of JavaScript libraries for common tasks have already been created and are available through a basic internet search for little or no cost. (Please respect the licenses of these libraries; many are available free for personal use, but not for commercial use — in other words, anything you are charging someone money to create.)

In this project, you are going to use one of these libraries to build your photo galleries. **Lightbox**, created by Lokesh Dhakar, is a JavaScript library that displays images by filling the screen and dimming out the rest of the web page. The current version, Lightbox2, is 100% free to use in both commercial and non-commercial work, so long as you leave the developer's name, homepage link, and the license info intact in the provided files.

Note:

Full details about Lightbox2 are available at lokeshdhakar.com/ projects/lightbox2/

ATTACH EXTERNAL CSS AND SCRIPT FILES

In the previous stage of the project, you used tools built into Dreamweaver to add JavaScript interactivity. As you saw when you placed the Tabs object, Dreamweaver automatically created links to the external JavaScript and CSS files that are required to make the object function properly.

Because the Lightbox library is not part of Dreamweaver's built-in toolset, you have to manually link the page to the required external files.

1. **Open the file galleries.html from your WIP>Photography site and make the Live view active.**

2. **Click Source Code in the Related Files bar to show the page's HTML code in the Code pane.**

3. **In the Code pane, place the insertion point at the end of the closing </title> tag. Press Return/Enter to create a new line.**

4. **With the insertion point in the new line, click the Script button in the HTML Insert panel.**

   Rather than embedding JavaScript code directly in your HTML file, the <script> tag provides an easy way to manage JavaScript in a separate linked file.

The insertion point should be in this empty line.

5. **Navigate to the `lightbox-plus-jquery.min.js` file in the lightbox/js/ folder and click Open/OK.**

jQuery is required for Lightbox to function properly. The files included with the Lightbox package include a basic lightbox.js file and a lightbox-plus-jquery.min.js file.

Because the gallery page in this site does not already include a jQuery file, you are using the combined file that is provided in the Lightbox package. This file provides the script code that enables the Lightbox links you will define later.

6. **In the CSS Designer panel, click the Add CSS Source button and choose Attach Existing CSS File from the menu.**

7. **Click the Browse button in the resulting dialog box. Navigate to the `lightbox.css` file in the site's lightbox/css/ folder and click Open. With the Link option active, click OK.**

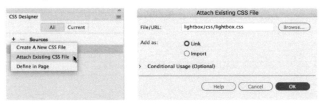

Note:

The lightbox/images folder includes a number of files that are defined in the lightbox.css file.

The lightbox-css file includes a number of selectors that define the appearance of various lightbox elements, including the mouseover behavior that shows "previous" and "next" buttons on either side of the lightbox image.

This line links the file to the lightbox JavaScript file.

This line links the file to the lightbox CSS file.

8. **Save the galleries.html file, then continue to the next exercise.**

CREATE THE LIGHTBOX IMG ELEMENTS

The Lightbox functionality requires an img element, which acts as a link to open a window that displays the full-size image. In this exercise, you will use the figure element to create two such images, each of which will open a separate Lightbox gallery.

1. With galleries.html open, use the Preview Size menu to change the Live view to the iPhone 7 Plus size.

   You are going to work primarily in the page code for this stage of the project; the Live view will provide a valuable preview of the code you define.

2. In the Code pane, delete the placeholder text from the editable template region.

3. With the insertion point immediately after the closing tag of the opening editable region marker code, press the Return/Enter key four times to add white space.

   White space in code is ignored by the browser when the page is rendered, but it is a valuable way to visually separate code elements so you can more easily distinguish different code elements.

Place the insertion point in the middle of the white space.

```
15 ▼ <body>
16 ▼ <nav>
17      <p><a href="index.html">Home</a></p>
18      <p><a href="galleries.html">Galleries</a></p>
19      <p><a href="info.html">Info</a></p>
20    </nav>
21    <header><img src="images/jsp-logo.png" alt="Julia Stoferson
         Photography"></header>
22    <main><!-- InstanceBeginEditable name="PageContent" -->
23
24
25
26        <!-- InstanceEndEditable --></main>
27    <footer>Site design by Against The Clock, Inc.</footer>
28    </body>
29    <!-- InstanceEnd --></html>
30
```

4. Place the insertion point in the middle line of white space, then type the basic code for a figure element:

```
<figure>
    <figcaption></figcaption>
</figure>
```

```
         Photography"></header>
22    <main><!-- InstanceBeginEditable name="PageContent" -->
23
24 ▼      <figure>
25            <figcaption></figcaption>
26        </figure>
27
28        <!-- InstanceEndEditable --></main>
29    <footer>Site design by Against The Clock, Inc.</footer>
30    </body>
31    <!-- InstanceEnd --></html>
32
```

   The HTML figure element includes a nested figcaption element to keep those two objects — the image and its caption — grouped together. You are going to create two separate image lightboxes, one for your clients "Portraits" collection and one for her "Dogs" collection. Including the figcaption element provides an easy way to attach a label that will identify each gallery in the layout.

5. Place the insertion point immediately after the opening <figure> tag and define an img element for the portrait1.jpg file:

```
<img src="images/portraits/portrait1.jpg" alt=" ">
```

6. **Place the insertion point between the opening and closing <figcaption> tags and type Portraits.**

Remember, in a previous exercise you defined CSS that causes img elements to occupy 100% of the available container width. Even though this image is 1000 x 1250 pixels, it is reduced to occupy only the available width of its immediate parent container.

7. **Click styles.css in the Related Files bar to show that file in the Code pane.**

8. **At the end of the styles.css file, define a new selector to control the appearance of the figure element:**

```
figure {
    margin: 5px;
    padding: 0px;
    width: 150px;
    display: inline-block;
}
```

9. **Create another new selector for the figcaption element:**

```
figcaption {
    font-weight: bold;
    text-align: center;
}
```

By limiting the size of the figure element to 150px wide, the nested img element is also reduced. Because the figcaption is also nested inside the figure element, the text-align property centers the caption within the defined width of the figure element.

10. Click **Source Code** in the Related Files bar to show that file in the Code pane.

11. In the Code pane, select and copy all code related to the figure element.

12. Create a line of white space after the existing figure element code, then paste another copy of the same code.

13. In the second copy of the figure element, make the following changes:

    Image source: **images/dogs/dog1.jpg**

    Caption text: **Dogs**

14. In the Code pane, select all code related to the two figure elements. Click the Div button in the HTML Insert panel.

The HTML Insert panel works in the Code pane as well as the Design pane.

The **div** element is a generic container-type element. Although it has largely been replaced by the specific HTML5 elements such as nav and section, it is still a useful tool for a variety of purposes that don't call for more specialized elements.

15. In the resulting dialog box, choose Wrap Around Selection in the Insert menu, then click OK.

In this case you are creating a container around the figure elements so that you can horizontally center the figure elements in the visible space without affecting other similar elements.

16. Show the styles.css file in the Code pane, then create a new class selector at the end of the existing CSS code:

```
.align-center {
    width: 100%;
    text-align: center;
}
```

17. Show the page source code in the Code pane. Place the insertion point inside the opening <div> tag and type to add the .align-center class:

```
class="align-center"
```

Remember, classes have to be manually applied to an element for the properties to apply. The two properties in the .align-center class produce the following results:

- The div extends the full width of its container (the main element)
- Content inside the div (the figure element) is centered horizontally inside the div's width.

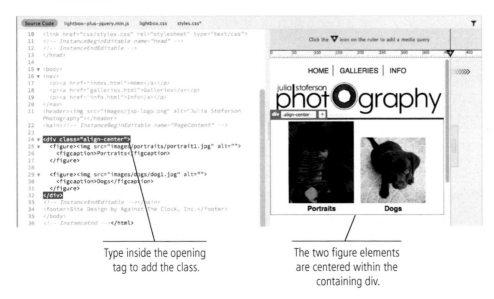

Type inside the opening tag to add the class.

The two figure elements are centered within the containing div.

18. Choose File>Save All, then continue to the next exercise.

DEFINE THE LIGHTBOX LINK OBJECTS

The final steps in this project are to list the images that should be included in each Lightbox, and then link the small images you just created to the interactive Lightbox functionality. Although this is a fairly simple process, it is entirely manual and can be tedious with a long list of images.

1. **With galleries.html open, place the insertion point in the source code at the end of the opening tag for the first figure element.**

2. **Press Return/Enter to move the `<img>` tag to the next line.**

3. **Place the insertion point immediately after the opening `<figure>` tag, then type:**
   `<a href="images/portraits/portrait1.jpg" data-lightbox="portraits">`

   This line converts the image into a link that will open a Lightbox named "portraits" that shows a larger version of the portrait1.jpg file.

   ```
   24 ▾ <div class="align-center">
   25 ▾   <figure><a href="images/portraits/portrait1.jpg" data-lightbox="portraits">
   26        <img src="images/portraits/portrait1.jpg" alt="">
   27        <figcaption>Portraits</figcaption>
   28      </figure>
   29
   30 ▾   <figure><img src="images/dogs/dog1.jpg" alt="">
   31        <figcaption>Dogs</figcaption>
   32      </figure>
   33    </div>
   ```

4. **Move the insertion point to the end of the `<img>` tag (outside the closing `>` character) and type `</`.**

   After typing the / character, Dreamweaver automatically closes the last open tag — in this case, the `<a>` tag that you just defined in Step 3.

   The contents of the `<a>` tag — in other words, content between the closing `>` character you typed in Step 3 and the closing `</a>` tag you add in this step — act as a link to open the Lightbox gallery.

   You must put the closing `</a>` tag <u>after</u> the `<img>` tag and not immediately after the closing `>` of the `<a>` tag.

   ```
   24 ▾ <div class="align-center">
   25 ▾   <figure><a href="images/portraits/portrait1.jpg" data-lightbox="portraits">
   26        <img src="images/portraits/portrait1.jpg" alt=""></a>
   27        <figcaption>Portraits</figcaption>
   28      </figure>
   29
   30 ▾   <figure><img src="images/dogs/dog1.jpg" alt="">
   31        <figcaption>Dogs</figcaption>
   32      </figure>
   33    </div>
   ```

5. **Choose View>Live View Options>Hide Live View Displays.**

   Although useful for development purposes, the Live view aids such as Element Displays can be distracting when testing JavaScript functionality.

6. **Click the "Portrait" image to test the Lightbox, then click the Lightbox Close button.**

   At this point you only see one image because you have not yet defined other images for the Lightbox.

| Click the image to open the Lightbox. | The lightbox shows a larger version of the image. | Lightbox code also defines Close button funcitonality. |

7. **In the Code pane, place the insertion point at the end of the first closing </figure> tag and press Return/Enter two times.**

8. **Create three new lines of code as follows:**

   ```
   <a href="images/portraits/portrait2.jpg" data-lightbox="portraits"></a>
   <a href="images/portraits/portrait3.jpg" data-lightbox="portraits"></a>
   <a href="images/portraits/portrait4.jpg" data-lightbox="portraits"></a>
   ```

   Each image must have the same data-lightbox attribute to appear in the same lightbox.

   ```
   23
   24 ▼ <div class="align-center">
   25 ▼     <figure><a href="images/portraits/portrait1.jpg" data-lightbox="portraits">
   26             <img src="images/portraits/portrait1.jpg" alt=""></a>
   27         <figcaption>Portraits</figcaption>
   28     </figure>
   29
   30         <a href="images/portraits/portrait2.jpg" data-lightbox="portraits"></a>
   31         <a href="images/portraits/portrait3.jpg" data-lightbox="portraits"></a>
   32         <a href="images/portraits/portrait4.jpg" data-lightbox="portraits"></a>
   33
   34 ▼     <figure><img src="images/dogs/dog1.jpg" alt="">
   35         <figcaption>Dogs</figcaption>
   36     </figure>
   37 </div>
   38 <!-- InstanceEndEditable --></main>
   39 <footer>Site design by Against The Clock, Inc.</footer>
   40 </body>
   41 <!-- InstanceEnd --></html>
   ```

Note:

Feel free to use the Code Hint menus to complete these lines of code, or simply type the full lines exactly as you see here.

9. In the Live view, test the Portraits image link.

10. Move your mouse cursor over the enlarged image and click the Next Image button on the right side of the image.

11. Review all four images in the Portraits Lightbox, then click the Close button in the bottom-right corner.

    Lightbox only shows navigation buttons that are relative to the active image. For example, the "Previous Image" button does not appear when you are looking at the first image because there is no image previous to the first.

Note:

If you want to include captions in Lightbox images, you can add the Title attribute to the code that defines the Lightbox images.

12. Repeat Steps 1–8 to define the existing dog image as a link to a second Lightbox. In this instance, use the images in the images/dogs folder and change the data-lightbox name to **dogs**.

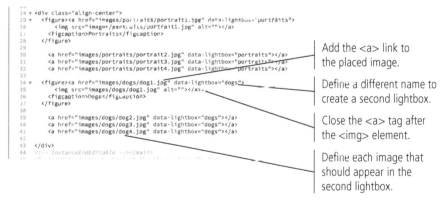

```
24 ▼ <div class="align-center">
25 ▼    <figure><a href="images/portraits/portrait1.jpg" data-lightbox="portraits">
26           <img src="images/portraits/portrait1.jpg" alt=""></a>
27        <figcaption>Portraits</figcaption>
28    </figure>
29
30        <a href="images/portraits/portrait2.jpg" data-lightbox="portraits"></a>
31        <a href="images/portraits/portrait3.jpg" data-lightbox="portraits"></a>
32        <a href="images/portraits/portrait4.jpg" data-lightbox="portraits"></a>
33
34 ▼    <figure><a href="images/dogs/dog1.jpg" data-lightbox="dogs">
35           <img src="images/dogs/dog1.jpg" alt=""></a>
36        <figcaption>Dogs</figcaption>
37    </figure>
38
39        <a href="images/dogs/dog2.jpg" data-lightbox="dogs"></a>
40        <a href="images/dogs/dog3.jpg" data-lightbox="dogs"></a>
41        <a href="images/dogs/dog4.jpg" data-lightbox="dogs"></a>
42
43    </div>
44    <!-- InstanceEndEditable --></main>
```

Add the <a> link to the placed image.

Define a different name to create a second lightbox.

Close the <a> tag after the <img> element.

Define each image that should appear in the second lightbox.

13. **Test the Dogs image link, and review all four images in the Dogs Lightbox.**

14. **Click the Close button in the bottom-right corner of the Lightbox.**

15. **Choose File>Save All, then close the galleries.html file.**

16. **Export a site definition named Photography.ste into your WIP>Photography folder, and then remove the site from Dreamweaver.**

Project Review

fill in the blank

1. The _____ panel can be used to create a new file from a Dreamweaver design template.

2. _____ is a JavaScript library that aims to make it easier to add JavaScript to a web page by storing a number of common tasks as methods.

3. JavaScript scripts can be embedded in an HTML page using the _____ tag.

4. The HTML _____ element includes a nested ___ element to keep an image and its caption grouped together.

5. A _____ element is a generic container-type element that is useful for purposes that don't call for more specialized HTML5 elements.

6. In _____, moving the cursor over a specific element reveals the box model of that element, the code related to the element (in the Code pane), and the CSS rules and properties that affect the element (in the CSS Designer panel).

7. Command-Option-click/Alt-click an element to open the _____, which shows all pieces of code related to the selected item.

8. The _____ can be used to prevent an element from exceeding a certain width.

9. The _____ value of the display property can be used to allow elements of the same type to appear on the same line as preceding elements.

10. The _____ selector can be used to select the first paragraph in a specific element.

short answer

1. Briefly explain how to create an inline navigation menu.

2. Briefly explain at least two advantages of using JavaScript.

2. Briefly explain how the Code Navigator helps to work with built-in jQuery UI elements.

Portfolio Builder Project

Use what you learned in this project to complete the following freeform exercise.
Carefully read the art director and client comments, then create your own design to meet the needs of the project.
Use the space below to sketch ideas; when finished, write a brief explanation of your reasoning behind your final design.

In order to increase marketing opportunities, your agency would like to create several more examples to showcase the ability to create a mobile-friendly site that works on multiple operating systems and browsers. Every designer in your agency has been asked to create a web page that showcases this type of design.

❏ Think of something you enjoy doing.

❏ Write clear text that explains the basic concept of your hobby. Consider including a basic explanation of the topic, historical information, links to external sites with related content, and even instructions on how your hobby works.

❏ Find or create graphics or images to illustrate your topic.

❏ Design a single web page using jQuery JavaScript to present your content.

Publishing for mobile devices is not only the future — it's the present. The photography site is an excellent portfolio piece to showcase our capabilities, but I would like our salespeople to be able to show off more than one example when they meet with current and potential clients.

To increase our agency's portfolio, I've asked every staff designer to create a single page that presents information in a compact, easy-to-navigate interface. I want this to be fun for you, and I want a range of different types of projects.

So, rather than give you a specific topic to work with, I want you to create a page about anything that interests you — your favorite sport, a personal hobby, how to train a pet iguana... whatever you feel passionate about.

_____

_____

_____

_____

_____

_____

_____

_____

_____

_____

_____

_____

_____

Designing sites that work equally well on a small smartphone screen and a full-size browser window is now a requirement for the professional web designer. In this project, you combined HTML, CSS, and JavaScript to present a lot of information in a compact, easy-to-navigate space that works in any display size.

JavaScript is quickly becoming a standard for interactivity in web design. It works on all current browsers, both for desktop and mobile devices, and allows considerable flexibility for manipulating the objects in an HTML page. This project incorporated Dreamweaver's built-in tools for adding jQuery user interface elements, as well as incorporating an external JavaScript library. If you plan to pursue a career in web design, we highly recommend you extend your education with more in-depth study of JavaScript and jQuery.

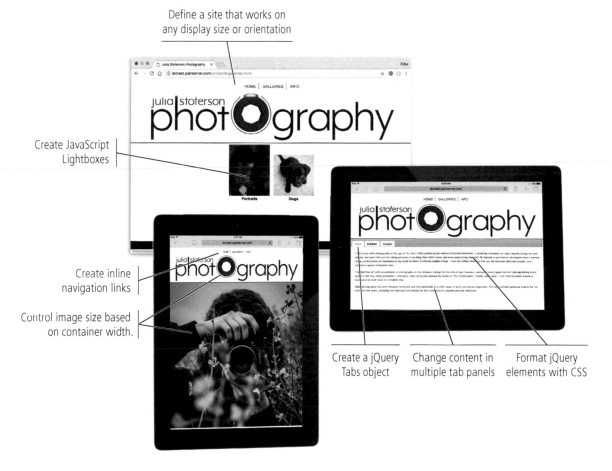

Define a site that works on any display size or orientation

Create JavaScript Lightboxes

Create inline navigation links

Control image size based on container width.

Create a jQuery Tabs object

Change content in multiple tab panels

Format jQuery elements with CSS

Bootstrap Responsive Page

You have been hired by the Chamber of Commerce to create a new web page for the city of Lancaster, California. You are going to create a single page that adapts to multiple display sizes so that the page looks good on both desktop and mobile devices.

This project incorporates the following skills:

- ❏ Creating a Bootstrap page
- ❏ Defining a responsive page grid
- ❏ Working with responsive page content
- ❏ Using CSS to control responsive page content
- ❏ Restricting element height and overflow
- ❏ Using the CSS Transitions panel

Project Meeting

client comments

In the past two years, millions of dollars have been spent to revitalize the downtown area. Dozens of new businesses have opened, including a number of specialty shops and restaurants.

Our area is visited by a large number of travelers, whether they are here for work or for one of the various national sports tournaments we host. We're also in the immediate path for people heading to the mountains from Los Angeles.

We want you to design a new web page that will help introduce The BLVD to the digital community.

art director comments

Designing responsive web pages can be complicated, but Dreamweaver makes it a bit easier than most other methods — and it's certainly better than designing multiple versions of the same page.

Your existing knowledge of CSS and HTML are going to be extremely important to working with responsive design. It can seem a bit confusing at first, but once you've created a couple of Bootstrap pages it becomes easier to understand.

After you finish the overall page layout, you should add some interactivity to the page. Again, Dreamweaver makes it fairly easy to create this interactivity directly in the page as long as you understand CSS.

project objectives

To complete this project, you will:

- ❏ Create a new Bootstrap page
- ❏ Define the Bootstrap page layout grid
- ❏ Insert responsive images
- ❏ Copy content into a Bootstrap page
- ❏ Use CSS to format page content
- ❏ Create new media queries
- ❏ Show and hide content in different layouts
- ❏ Restrict element height and overflow
- ❏ Use the CSS Transitions panel

Stage 1   Working with Bootstrap

Web designers have always had to deal with different display sizes when creating pages. For example, different users might have a 30″ desktop monitor or an 11″ laptop; a good web page should work effectively on both size displays, as well as anything in between. The explosive growth of digital tablets and handheld mobile devices (smartphones) further compounds the problem of designing for multiple display sizes, especially given the much smaller display sizes of these devices.

With HTML5 and CSS3, web designers now have the opportunity (and, many argue, the responsibility) to create pages that are optimized for viewing on whatever device a user chooses. Rather than creating multiple versions of a website for specific types of devices, we can use **responsive design** to create pages that automatically adapt to suit the device size that is used to display them.

Bootstrap is an HTML and CSS-based framework that allows much faster and easier web development, including responsive page design. Bootstrap CSS classes predefine the appearance of various elements, such as typography, images, and forms, as well as a variety of interactive components like navigation menus and image carousels. You can use Bootstrap to design a page that changes appearance, and even content, to present information in the best way possible given the screen size.

The tools built into Dreamweaver make it relatively easy to create responsive web pages using Bootstrap. However, you still need a solid foundational knowledge of CSS before you can efficiently and effectively take advantage of the available tools. You should understand how div tags work, and how to create the various types of CSS selectors to control the appearance of different page elements. You should also have a good working knowledge of basic Dreamweaver tasks, such as accessing the page code of various files (including the page source code and the code in related files).

Understanding the Bootstrap Page Grid

When you design using Bootstrap, the first thing you need to understand is the page grid that facilitates responsive page design. A Bootstrap page uses an underlying grid structure with 12 columns that extend the entire width of the page, regardless of the physical display size; the column widths adapt to whatever relative size is necessary based on the available space in the browser window. You then create row and column elements to contain the page content, and use predefined classes to determine the size of each column element on each size display.

Bootstrap recognizes four different screen sizes, as shown in the table below. The asterisk (*) in the listed classes is replaced by a number equal to the grid columns that element should span.

Display size	Bootstrap Designation	Display Width	Class for defining column span
Extra-small for phones	xs	< 768 pixels	.col-xs-*
Small for tablets	sm	768–991 pixels	.col-sm-*
Medium for desktops	md	992–1199 pixels	.col-md-*
Large for large desktops	lg	1200+ pixels	.col-lg-*

Note:

*Remember, the asterisk (*) is simply the number that defines how many grid columns the element should occupy. For example, an element using the **col-md-4** class will span 4 grid columns in the medium-display layout.*

When you create a new row with column elements, each column element spans all 12 columns of the underlying grid structure in the extra-small (xs) display size. If you define a different column span settings for the small display size, that width setting will persist throughout the medium and large sizes unless you define different settings for those displays as well.

The images to the right illustrate this concept. The grey vertical bars represent the underlying page grid; the green bars show the number of columns that will be spanned in each size layout using the classes as defined above each example.

You can change the number for each column element in a row, but the total of all column spans in the same row should be less than or equal to 12. If the total is larger than 12, some columns will appear in a second row in the display (although no coded row element is created).

Don't worry if this seems confusing at first. It will make more sense when you begin defining page elements in the next few exercises.

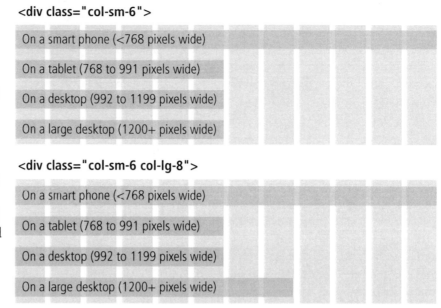

```
<div class="col-sm-6">
```

On a smart phone (<768 pixels wide)

On a tablet (768 to 991 pixels wide)

On a desktop (992 to 1199 pixels wide)

On a large desktop (1200+ pixels wide)

```
<div class="col-sm-6 col-lg-8">
```

On a smart phone (<768 pixels wide)

On a tablet (768 to 991 pixels wide)

On a desktop (992 to 1199 pixels wide)

On a large desktop (1200+ pixels wide)

Understanding Media Queries

Although we will explain media queries in greater detail later in this project, you also need to understand the basic concept now to better understand how responsive design works in general.

A **media query** is a way of defining different CSS code to apply in different situations — for example, defining different element sizes for different display sizes.

When a browser processes page code — including any linked CSS files — it follows a top-down approach. X applies unless and until it is specifically overridden by Y.

Say you have a CSS file that defines the h1 font-size property as 24px.

```
h1 {
    font-size: 24px;
}
```

If you want to change the font size of the h1 element for only medium displays to take advantage of the larger available screen space, you can add a media query using the following code:

```
@media (min-width: 992px) {
    h1 {
        font-size: 36px;
    }
}
```

If you wanted to change the font size again for large desktop displays, you could add another media query:

```
@media (min-width: 1200px) {
    h1 {
        font-size: 48px;
    }
}
```

The entire CSS file in this simple example would look like this:

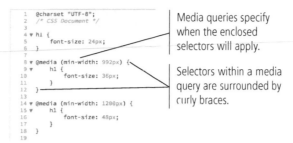

Media queries specify when the enclosed selectors will apply.

Selectors within a media query are surrounded by curly braces.

As the browser processes the code, it applies the first setting (font-size: 24px) to the h1 element by default. If a media query is triggered — if the display width is at least 992px — the browser applies the new defined property to the element (font-size: 36px).

One Final Note

The page you are going to create in this project should be considered a basic introduction to working with Bootstrap. You will create a page with two basic layouts — one for the extra-small and small layouts and one for the medium and large layouts. You will use a few basic Bootstrap components to implement the page design, and define a few simple media queries to control the appearance of page content in different layouts.

Keep in mind that there are many, many more options related to Bootstrap than what you will use to complete this project. Responsive design is quickly becoming the rule in professional web design, not the exception. We highly encourage you to continue your education in responsive design beyond what is covered in this project. Once you are comfortable with the skills and concepts that are explained here, create a new file using one of the built-in Bootstrap templates, then analyze the page structure, code, and attached CSS files. Experiment with some of the other components that are available in Dreamweaver's Insert panel.

 CREATE A NEW BOOTSTRAP PAGE

Dreamweaver directly integrates the ability to define a new Bootstrap page, either from scratch or using one of several built-in templates. Rather than dismantling an existing template to get what you need, you are going to start from the very beginning and create a new, blank Bootstrap page.

1. **Download BLVD_DW18_RF.zip from the Student Files web page.**

2. **Expand the ZIP archive in your WIP folder (Macintosh) or copy the archive contents into your WIP folder (Windows).**

   This results in a folder named **BLVD**, which contains the files you need for this project.

3. **In Dreamweaver, create a new site named BLVD, using your WIP>BLVD folder as the site root folder.**

4. **Choose File>New.**

5. **Select New Document in the left column an choose HTML in the Document Type list.**

6. **In the right side of the dialog box, click the Bootstrap tab.**

   When you create a new page in Dreamweaver, you can use the Bootstrap tab in the New Document dialog box to automatically integrate the required framework in your page.

7. **Choose Create New in the Bootstrap CSS section.**

   If you have a specific bootstrap.css file other than the default one — for example, you or someone else modified property settings to suit a specific need — you can use this option to attach it instead of using the settings in the Dreamweaver default file.

8. **Uncheck the Include a Pre-Built Layout option.**

   If this option is checked, Dreamweaver includes a number of placeholder elements in the new HTML page.

9. **Click the Customize button to show those options.**

   The default grid structure in Bootstrap uses 12 columns; The column gutters are the spaces between each column in the page grid, defaulting to 30px.

Note:

You can define different default values if you are sure of what you need for each different variation, but there is no real reason to do so.

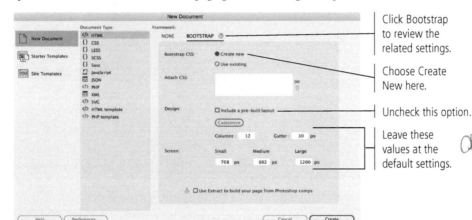

Click Bootstrap to review the related settings.

Choose Create New here.

Uncheck this option.

Leave these values at the default settings.

different values

10. **Click Create to create the new HTML page.**

11. **Choose File>Save. Save the new file as index.html in the BLVD site root folder.**

12. **Review the contents of the Files panel.**

    When you create a Bootstrap HTML page, Dreamweaver automatically copies several required files into your site root folder.

    The **bootstrap.css** contains all of the predefined classes for various responsive page elements. This file is locked by default, which means you can't accidentally change it. (You can unlock the file if you want to edit the file, but it's best to leave that file alone until you are more conversant with Bootstrap functionality.)

    The fonts folder contains a set of web font files that are used to create Bootstrap icons, such as a standard Home icon. The files in the js (JavaScript) folder help provide some of the responsive design functionality in older browsers that do not support HTML5.

no fonts folder

13. If the Code view is not visible, click the Split button in the Document toolbar to show the Code view.

14. Review the page code.

In Dreamweaver, a new Bootstrap page automatically includes the viewport tag in the page <head> code.

<meta name="viewport" content="width=device-width, initial-scale=1">

The **viewport** is the visible area of a web page on a specific device. Without the viewport tag, a web page will be universally shrunk to fit the available screen width on a particular device. Using the viewport tag, the page width is set to match the available screen width so that the actual page content is not reduced to fit in a smaller space.

- **width=device-width** sets the width of the page to match the screen-width of the device being used to view the page.

- **initial-scale=1.0** sets the initial zoom level when the page is first loaded by the browser. The "1.0" value means the page will display at 100% when it initially loads; a user can enlarge the zoom level using the pinch-and-zoom gesture.

> *Note:*
>
> *When you create a Bootstrap page in Dreamweaver, the new page automatically uses the HTML5 doctype.*

The viewport tag prevents page content from being reduced to fit smaller display sizes.

The page is linked to the bootstrap.css file.

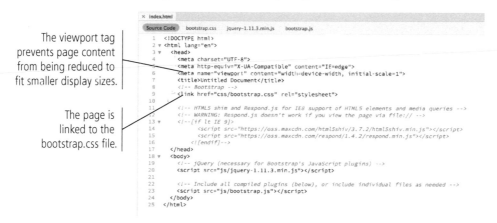

15. With the Live view active in the document window, review the Visual Media Queries Bar above the page.

Immediately below the Document toolbar, the Visual Media Queries Bar (VMQB) identifies the point(s) where another layout will be triggered based on size of the display being used to view a site. Each media query is represented by a colored block:

- Green bars are media queries that use only a max-width value.
- Blue bars are media queries that use both a min-width and a max-width value.
- Purple bars are media queries that use only a min-width value.

The values associated with each media query are displayed in the blocks on the VMQB. The arrows also provide a reminder of what defines each media query; min-width values show right-facing arrows and max-width values show left-facing arrows.

> *Note:*
>
> *You can toggle the VMQB on or off using the button in the Common toolbar (Window> Toolbars>Common).*

Green bars have only a max-width value.

Blue bars have both min-width and max-width value.

Purple bars have only a min-width value.

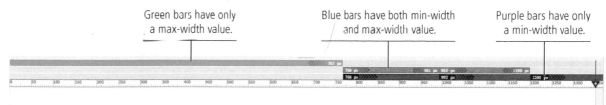

16. **Click the green bar on the left side of the VMQB.**

When you click a specific media query on the bar, the scrubber on the right side of the document window snaps to the breakpoint where that media query is triggered.

You can also drag the scrubber handle to manually resize the width of the display in the document window.

Click a bar to snap the display   Drag the scrubber bar handle to
view to the matching layout.   manually resize the display view.

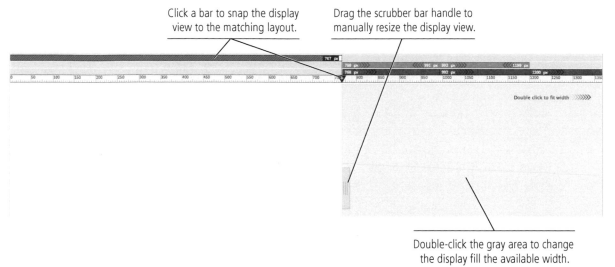

Double-click the gray area to change
the display fill the available width.

17. **Click the second purple bar (the one labeled 992px) to display the medium size layout in the document window.**

You might notice that there are both blue and purple bars for the small (min-width: 768px) and medium (min-width: 992px) size layouts. This is because the bootstrap.css file includes a number of separate media queries for each of these layout sizes. Some are based only on the min-width setting, while others have the min-width and max-width settings defined. Clicking either the blue or purple bar beginning with the appropriate min-width value will display the related layout in the document window.

Extra-small layout   Small layout   Medium layout   Large layout

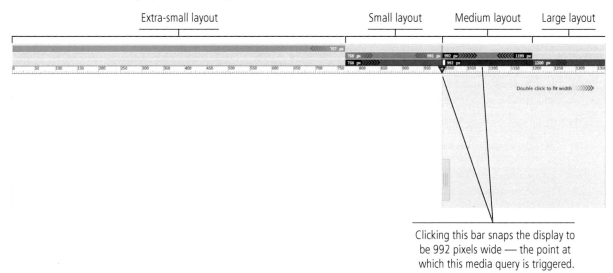

Clicking this bar snaps the display to
be 992 pixels wide — the point at
which this media query is triggered.

18. **Continue to the next exercise.**

More about the Visual Media Queries Bar

The Visual Media Queries Bar (VMQB) at the top of the Document window is not only informational, it is a useful tool for reviewing layouts based on existing media queries, creating new media queries, and even navigating to the code that is defined for a specific query.

If you Control/right-click a point on the VMQB, a contextual menu presents options to Go To Code or Delete Code; each submenu includes all media queries related to the width where you click.

- Choosing a specific query in the Go To Code submenu snaps the Code pane to show the selectors in the media query you choose.

- Choosing a media query in the Delete submenu presents a message that all selectors in the media query will also be deleted. Clicking OK finalizes the process.

EXAMINE BOOTSTRAP MEDIA QUERIES

Because a Bootstrap page defines four different layouts in one HTML page, the technology requires various selectors and media queries to control the appearance of element in various display sizes. In this exercise you will examine the selectors that make the basic work.

1. **With index.html open from the BLVD site, click the third purple bar (the one labeled 1200px) to display the large size layout in the document window.**

2. **Click in the document window to place the insertion point.**

   Clicking in an empty document automatically selects the body element.

3. **Click the Container button in the Bootstrap Components Insert panel to add that element to the page.**

   Using Bootstrap, all page content should be placed in a container element; there are two different container types to choose from:

   - A regular **container** element has fixed widths in the different layout sizes:

     - 1170px in the large size

     - 970px in the medium size

     - 750px in the small size

     - Full-width size in the extra-small display

     With the exception of the extra-small display, these widths are fixed regardless of the actual browser window or display size.

   - A **container-fluid** element has no defined width property; this type of element dynamically resizes with the browser window.

Note:

If you are using a laptop, you might need to iconize any open panels on the right side of your screen to review the large size layout.

Note:

You cannot put one container inside another container.

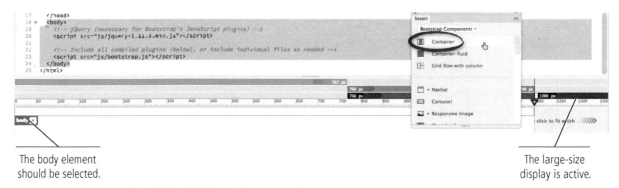

The body element should be selected.

The large-size display is active.

4. Review the code for the resulting element.

Bootstrap components are added as div elements; classes are automatically added to the new div elements to define the type of element. The bootstrap.css file, which is attached to the HTML file as soon as you create it, includes class definitions that define the objects' appearance and behavior.

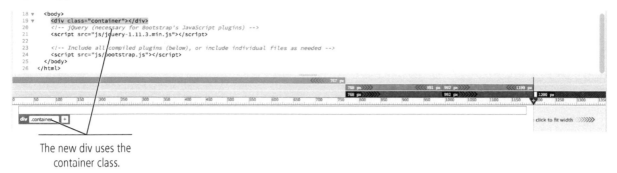

The new div uses the
container class.

5. Open the CSS Designer panel and activate the Current mode. In the lower section of the panel, make sure the Show Set option is checked.

6. If necessary, click the new container div element in the document window to select it.

7. In the CSS Designer panel, click to select the lowest .container selector.

Remember: When the Current mode is active, the panel shows only those selectors that affect the selected element.

As you can see, four .container classes apply to the div element that is selected in the document window. The media query associated with the highlighted selector appears bold in the @Media section of the panel.

CSS follows a top-down methodology. "Global" selectors apply to the element in all display sizes unless and until they are overridden by same-named selectors in specific media queries. The CSS Designer panel lists selectors in the reverse order that they appear in the actual CSS file.

In the image below, you can see that the last .container selector is active. In the @Media section of the panel, Global appears in bold. "Global" means that this selector does not exist within a specific media query; the defined properties apply regardless of which display size is active.

This selector defines automatic left and right margins, as well as 15px padding on the left and right sides of the element.

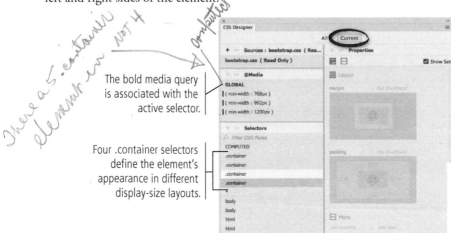

There a 5. container element Not 4
compiled

The bold media query
is associated with the
active selector.

Four .container selectors
define the element's
appearance in different
display-size layouts.

Note:

If you can make the CSS Designer panel wide enough, the Properties section moves into a second column in the panel. We use that mode in these examples to save space; feel free to use whatever interface arrangement works best for your workspace.

8. **Click the third .container class in the Selectors section of the panel, then review the properties that are defined for the active selector.**

In the @Media section of the panel, the (min-width: 768px) media query is bold to show that the active selector is defined within that media query.

This selector applies to the active element when the current display width is greater than 768px.

The only defined property for this selector sets the element width to 750 pixels. The line through the property name shows that this property is overridden by a later selector.

9. **Click the second .container class in the Selectors section of the panel, then review the properties that are defined for the active selector.**

In the @Media section of the panel, the (min-width: 992px) media query is bold to show that the active selector is defined within that media query. This selector applies to the active element when the current display width is greater than 992px.

The only defined property for this selector sets the element width to 970 pixels — this is the value that overrides the same value in the other .container selectors that appear earlier in the CSS file.

10. **Click the first .container class in the Selectors section of the panel, then review the properties that are defined for the active selector.**

In the @Media section of the panel, the (min-width: 1200px) media query is bold to show that the active selector is defined within that media query. The only defined property for this selector sets the element width to 1170 pixels; again, this is the value that overrides the same value in the other .container selectors that appear earlier in the CSS file.

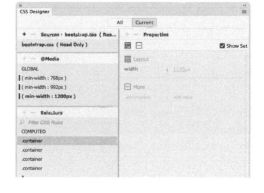

11. **Save the file and continue to the next exercise.**

DEFINE THE BOOTSTRAP PAGE LAYOUT GRID

As we explained at the beginning of this project, Bootstrap works based on an underlying page grid, which divides the page width into 12 equal columns. In this exercise you are going to define row and column elements to contain the page content; the size of the column elements will be based on the underlying page grid.

1. **With index.html open from the BLVD site, click the second purple bar (the one labeled 992px) to display the medium size layout in the document window.**

2. **With the container div selected in the document window, click the Grid Row with Column button in the Bootstrap Components Insert panel.**

3. **In the resulting dialog box, choose the Nest option and change the number of columns to 2.**

   The buttons on the left side of the dialog box determine where the new div will be placed — before, after, or nested inside — relative to the current selected element.

The div.container element is selected.

4. **Click OK to add the element to the page.**

5. **Review the results in the page code.**

   At its most basic, a responsive Bootstrap page is a series of row and columns that define the page layout. One new element with the row class has been added inside the container div that you created earlier. Because you defined two columns in the dialog box, two div elements with column classes have also been added inside the row element.

   In the document window, the new columns are visually identified by the dashed line in the middle of the row element. If you don't see the dashed line, open the Live View Options menu in the Document toolbar and make sure Hide Live View Displays is not checked.

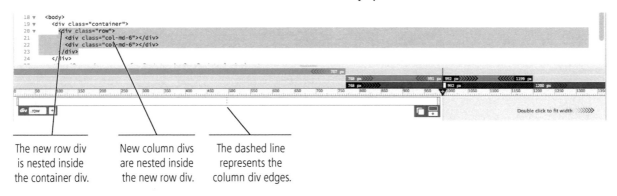

The new row div is nested inside the container div.

New column divs are nested inside the new row div.

The dashed line represents the column div edges.

   In Dreamweaver, what is visible in your document window determines exactly what is created when you add a new row with columns.

   - If the small size is active, column elements in the new row automatically adopt the .col-sm-* class.
   - If the medium size is active, column elements in the new row automatically adopt the .col-md-* class.
   - If the large size is active, columns in the new row automatically adopt the .col-lg-* class.

   In this case, the medium layout size is active in the document window; the resulting column elements have the .col-md-6 class applied.

   By default, new column elements are evenly divided across the 12 underlying page-grid columns. 12 divided by 2 equals 6, so each of the two resulting columns occupies 6 columns in the page grid.

Note:

If you add a number of columns that can't evenly divide into twelve, Dreamweaver rounds down to the nearest possible whole number. For example, say you add a row with five columns:

$$5 \times 3 = 15$$
$$5 \times 2 = 10$$

Because there aren't 15 columns in the grid, each new column element would occupy 2 grid columns.

6. **Click the max-width: 767px media query in the VMQB to show the extra-small size layout in the document window.**

When you change the display size in the document window, you can see the effect of how responsive design works. The two column elements in the row appear on top of each other; each column spans the entire document width.

Because the column element classes define a specific column width for only the medium display size, that setting does not apply to the extra-small (mobile) and small (tablet) display sizes.

Bootstrap follows a "mobile-first" approach, which means the design begins with the smallest display size. When you create a new row with multiple columns, each column defaults to extend across the entire underlying grid for the extra-small size page; that setting persists unless and until it is overridden for a different layout size. (You can define different column settings for the extra-small display, but the small size of many mobile devices means this is not usually recommended.)

Note:

The HTML page code is the same for all variations of the layout — which means the content in various divs will be the same regardless of which layout is active. The position and appearance of that content is controlled entirely through CSS classes.

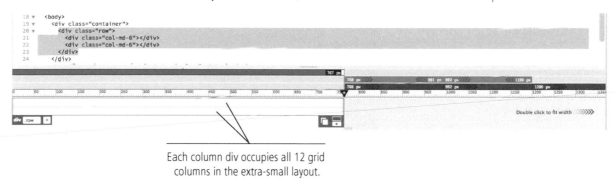

Each column div occupies all 12 grid columns in the extra-small layout.

7. **Click the min-width:1200px media query in the VMQB to show the large size layout in the document window.**

In the large display size, the column elements again adapt to only occupy six columns in the underlying page grid. Similar to the way CSS follows a top-down approach, Bootstrap follows a smallest-to-largest methodology; column settings apply unless and until they are overridden by a different setting in a larger display size.

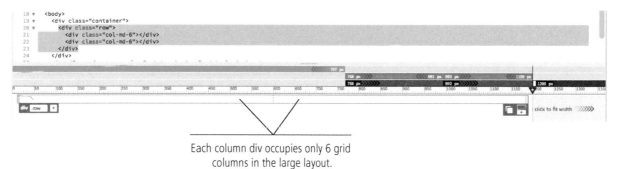

Each column div occupies only 6 grid columns in the large layout.

8. **Click the min-width: 992px media query in the VMQB to make the medium size layout active in the document window.**

9. **With the existing row div selected, click the Grid Row with Column button in the Bootstrap Components Insert panel.**

10. **In the resulting dialog box, choose the After option. With the No. of Columns field set to 3 (the default), click OK.**

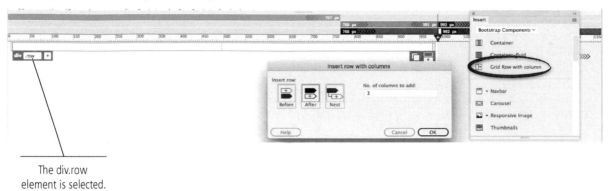

The div.row
element is selected.

Because you chose the After option, the new row div is added after the existing one. This row contains three column divs; the .col-md-4 class is applied to each because 12 page-grid columns divided by 3 column divs equals 4.

As with the column divs in the first row you created, these columns will extend the entire page width in the extra small and small layouts, but will only span one-third of the page width in the medium and large layouts.

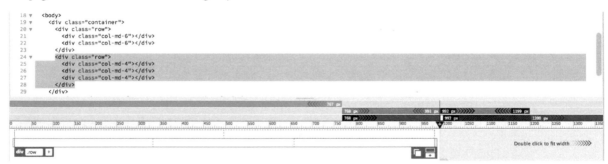

11. **With the second row div selected, click the Grid Row with Column button again. Choose the After option and change the No. of Columns field to 1. Click OK to create the third row in the grid.**

Because this row has only one column div, it uses the class .col-md-12. It will span the entire page width in all four layout sizes.

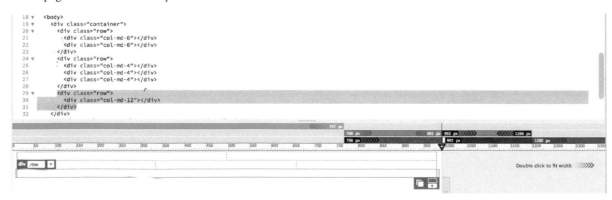

12. **With the medium size layout visible in the document window, click to select the left column of the first row.**

When the Live view is active, several on-screen controls are available to change the size and position of a column element, as well as add new columns to a row.

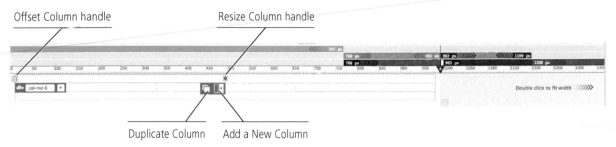

If you add a new column element to an existing row, it adopts the same class settings as existing columns. If, for example, you start two columns that use the .col-md-6 class, the new column element would also use the .col-md-6 class; 6 times 3 is greater than 12, so the third column in the row would be pushed into a new row (although no new row element is added).

13. **Click the Offset Column handle on the left side of the active column div and drag right until Element Display shows a second class of .col-md-offset-1.**

By default, columns appear at the left edge of their containing elements. The offset classes in Bootstrap are used to move a column div away from the left edge of its parent row. When you use the on-screen handle, Dreamweaver automatically adds the appropriate class to the column you are editing.

As you drag the handle, the left edge of the element snaps to each successive column in the underlying page grid. You can't offset a column by a specific physical measurement, only by a certain number of page grid columns.

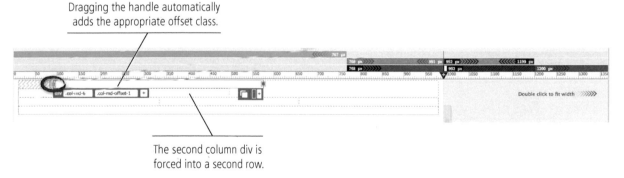

As you can see, the second column in the same row is pushed out of the grid row. (Again, no new row element is added). This is because the offset is added to the column widths, resulting in a number larger than 12 (the number of columns in the underlying page grid).

6	column 1 width
+ 6	column 2 width
+ 1	offset value of column 1
= 13	greater than 12

14. **Click the Resize Column handle on the right side of the active column element. Drag left until the Element Display shows the class .col-md-5.**

    As you drag the handle, the right side of the column element snaps to the underlying page-grid columns. Dreamweaver automatically adjusts the applied class to match the number you define by dragging.

    When you resize the first column element, the second element moves back into the same row because the overall width of both elements plus the offset of the first column is less than 12 — small enough to fit all elements into one row of the 12-column page grid.

Dragging the handle automatically adjusts the column-size class.

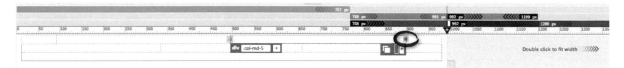

The second column div again fits in the first row.

Note:

You can't define an offset that results in a total great than 12 for a single element. For example, if a column spans 8 grid columns, you can't define an offset larger than 4 (8 + 4 = 12).

15. **Click to select the second column element in the first row.**

16. **Click and drag the Resize Column handle until the element spans five columns of the page grid.**

    The applied class automatically changes to .col-md-5, so the element spans 5 columns in the medium-size layout.

17. **Save the file and continue to the next exercise.**

 INSERT RESPONSIVE IMAGES

When you place a regular image into an HTML page, Dreamweaver automatically populates the width and height attributes of the **\<img>** tag based on the physical size of the placed image; when those attributes are defined, the image appears at a fixed size in the HTML page.

In a responsive web page, content should adapt to changing container sizes when elements adapt to different size displays. A responsive image, which does not have defined width and height attributes, is better suited to responsive page design.

Many of the built-in Bootstrap components — including responsive image placeholders — can be accessed directly in the Dreamweaver Insert panel without the need to write a single piece of code. In this exercise, you will add responsive images that adjust to fit the size of their containers.

1. **With index.html open, click to select the left column div in the first row.**

2. **In the Bootstrap Components Insert panel, click the arrow icon on the Responsive Image button. In the resulting menu, click the Default option.**

The button in the panel remembers the last-used option. If it already reads Responsive Image:Default, you can simply click the button to insert a new responsive image.

Bootstrap includes several options for changing the shape of a responsive image container. The default option simply places an image placeholder that will fill the width of the containing element. You can also choose a circle, rounded-corner rectangle, or a thumbnail (a container with a small amount of padding, a slightly rounded corner, and a light-gray border).

3. **Click the Nest option in the Position Assistant.**

When you place Bootstrap components, you have to decide where they will be placed relative to the active selection — before, after, wrapped around, or nested inside.

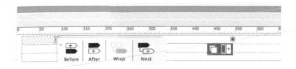

4. **With the resulting image placeholder selected in the document window, expand the images folder in the Files panel.**

5. **Using the Properties panel, click the Point to File button for the Src field and drag to the blvd-logo.png file.**

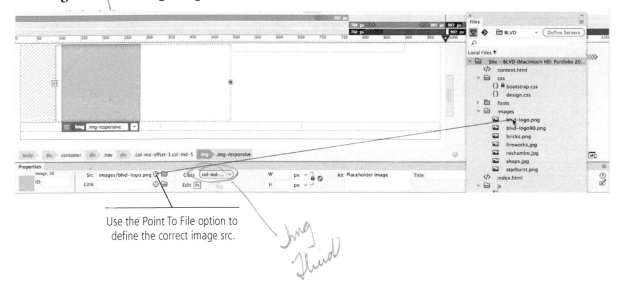

Use the Point To File option to define the correct image src.

6. **Change the Alt field text to The BLVD.**

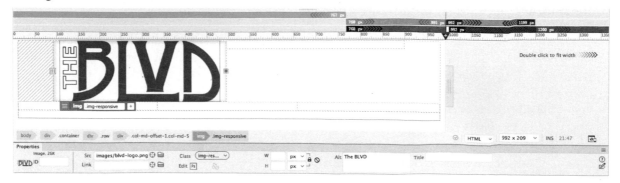

7. **Click the max-width: 767px media query in the VMQB to show the extra-small size layout in the document window.**

   Although you only placed the logo in the medium size layout, it appears in all variations. Remember, the responsive grid containers adjust the *appearance* of content and not the content itself. Anything you place in a div in one layout will appear in the same div in all variations. (More on this later when you use special "helper" classes to change the content that is visible in each layout.)

   Because this is a responsive image (using the predefined **.img-responsive** class), it adjusts to fill the width of the containing element. In the medium-size layout, you changed the containing column to only occupy 5 columns of the underlying page grid. In the small-size layout the same element spans all 12 columns, so the responsive image appears much larger.

8. **Click the min-width: 992px media query in the VMQB to show the medium size layout in the document window.**

9. **Save the file. Read the resulting message, then click OK.**

   Many Bootstrap components require specific files to function properly; when you save a file, Dreamweaver automatically warns you about those required files and copies them into your site folder as necessary.

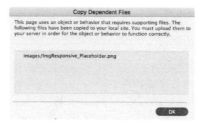

10. **Continue to the next exercise.**

COPY CONTENT INTO A BOOTSTRAP PAGE

We have provided the necessary content for this project in a regular HTML file. In this exercise, you are going to copy and paste the content into the appropriate page elements of the page. You can then make adjustments to various elements based on the actual content that appears in each element.

1: . With **index.html** open, open **content.html** from the site root folder.

> • This file includes the content that you need to place into the various divs in the page. Basic tags such as headings and paragraphs have already been applied.

2. Using the Code pane, select and copy the content on Lines 3–5 in the content.html file.

You can work in Code view or Split view to complete these steps.

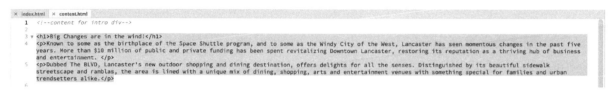

3. Make the index.html page active in the document window. In the Code pane, place the insertion point in the between the opening and closing div tags of the second column in the first row.

4. With the insertion point in place in the Code pane, paste the content you copied in Step 2.

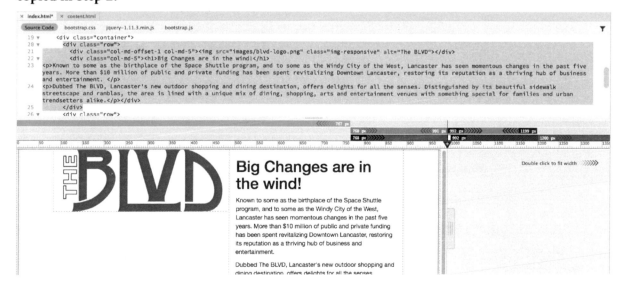

5. **Repeat Steps 2–4 to copy the various sections of content from the content.html file and paste them into the appropriate divs in the index.html file:**

Lines to Copy	Location to Paste
Lines 9–13	Second Row, First column
Lines 17–22	Second Row, Second column
Lines 26–32	Second Row, Third column
Line 36	Third Row, First (only) column

6. **Close the content.html file.**

After you paste all of the required content, you could delete the content.html file or move it into a cloaked folder to prevent it from being uploaded as part of the final site.

7. **In the Live view, click to select the image immediately below the "Shopping" h2 element.**

When you add a Bootstrap responsive image, the .img-responsive class is automatically added to the image you place. This class includes properties that force the image to fill 100% of the containing element (max-width: 100%).

The images that you pasted in the last few steps do not include the .img-responsive class, so it simply appears at 100% of its physical size. You need to add the appropriate class to the img element.

8. **With the image selected, click the Add Class/ID button in the Element Display.**

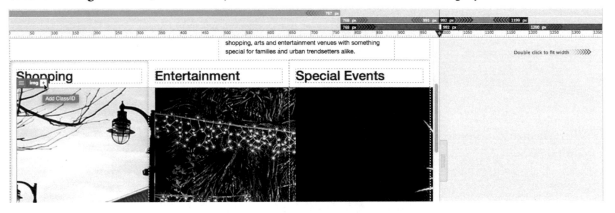

9. **In the resulting field, type .img-responsive, then press Return/Enter to add the new class to the selected element.**

With the .img-responsive class applied, the placed image is reduced to occupy only the width of the containing column element.

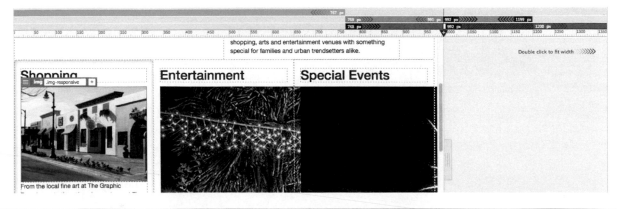

10. Repeat Steps 7–9 to add the .img-responsive class to the images under the Entertainment and Special Events h2 elements.

11. Using the VMQB, review all four layouts.

Once actual content is placed into the various divs, it becomes easier to see the effects of the different layout arrangements.

Extra-small layout (max-width:767px)

Small layout (min-width:768px)

Medium layout (min-width:992px)

Large layout (min-width:1200px)

12. Save the file and continue to the next exercise.

USE CSS TO FORMAT PAGE CONTENT

As you saw in the previous exercise, elements on the page use default formatting that is defined in the bootstrap.css file. You do not want to modify the bootstrap.css selectors; put simply, you should just leave this file alone.

Instead, you can attach another CSS file to store selectors for the appearance of various elements. This keeps layout-related selectors separate from design-related selectors, which will make it easier to find and modify exactly what you need if you (or someone else) want to make changes later.

Remember, the browser processes information in the order it is reached (in other words, first to last). When you attach a second CSS file to the page, it is added after the bootstrap.css file. Consider the following example, using a second CSS file named design.css. The page code looks like this:

```
<link href="css/bootstrap.css" rel="stylesheet">
<link href="css/design.css" rel="stylesheet">
```

In the bootstrap.css file:

```
h1, .h1 {
    font-size: 36px;
}
```

In the design.css file

```
h1, .h1 {
    font-size: 48px;
}
```

Note:

Bootstrap CSS defines the setting for the h1 element, as well as any element that uses an h1 class to identify an element as h1.

When the page is opened in a browser, the last-defined h1 property value — the one in the design.css file — will be used to define the element's appearance.

1. **With index.html open, click the min-width: 992px media query in the VMQB to make the medium size layout active in the document window.**

2. **Display the CSS Designer panel in All mode. Click the Add CSS Source button, and choose Attach Existing CSS File in the resulting menu.**

3. **Click the Browse button in the resulting dialog box. Navigate to the design.css file (in the site css folder) and click Open/OK.**

4. **Make sure the file will be added as a Link, then click OK.**

5. **In the CSS Designer panel, click to select design.css in the Sources section. Review the available selectors in the Selectors section of the panel.**

   In the Related Files bar, you can see that the new CSS file is now included as related to the index.html file. It is second in the list, which means any selector properties in this file will override the properties of same-named selectors in the first CSS file (bootstrap.css).

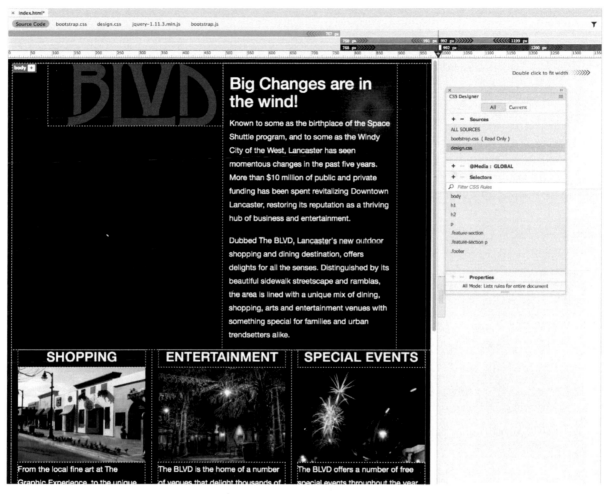

The file you just attached includes a number of selectors that define the appearance of your page's content. It also includes a .feature-section class, which defines the appearance of the Shopping, Entertainment, and Special Events content in the middle of the page.

The tag and selectors in the design.css file are automatically applied to the appropriate page elements. Class selectors only apply to elements where they are intentionally added, so you have to add the .feature-section class to the appropriate elements.

6. **Click to select the "Shopping" h2 element in the layout.**

   The Tag Selector at the bottom of the document window shows that this element is contained inside a div element. You need to add the .feature-section class to this div so the contained content is formatted properly.

Note:

It doesn't matter which size display is active at this point; we are using the medium-size layout simply for the sake of continuity,

7. **In the Tag Selector, click the div tag immediately before the h2 tag to select the entire div.**

   This div tag is the immediate parent of the "Shopping" content. You are applying the class to that div and not to the column div that makes up the page layout grid. The bootstrap.css file includes a number of settings for those elements that would make it very difficult to achieve exactly what you need. It is a better idea to use an extra containing div tag that does not impact the page layout grid.

8. **In the document window, use the Element Display to apply the .feature-section class to the selected element.**

   Remember, you have to type the preceding period in addition to the class name you want to define.

   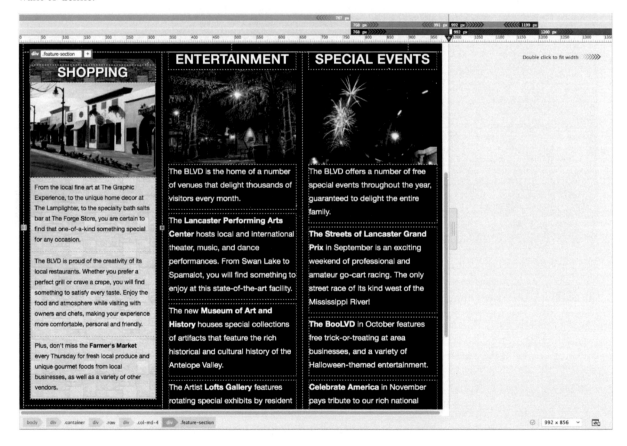

9. Repeat Steps 6-8 to apply the .feature-section class to the immediate parent divs of the Entertainment and Special Events content.

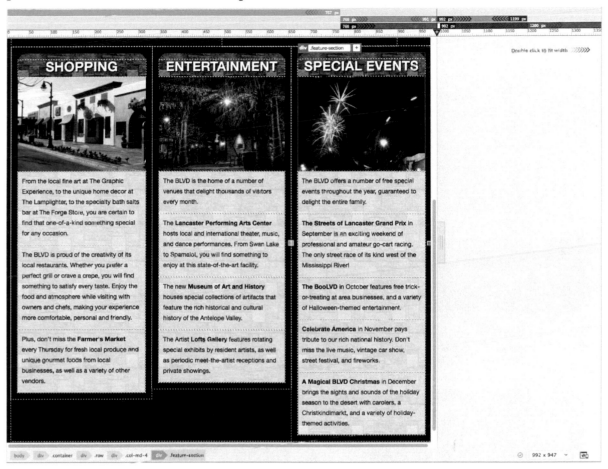

10. Save the file and continue to the next exercise.

CREATE NEW MEDIA QUERIES

You saw earlier that the bootstrap.css file used media queries to define different width settings for the column divs in different-size displays. In this exercise, you can use the same technique to define different appearances for content in various display sizes.

1. **With index.html open, use the VMQB to preview the four different layouts.**

   The point of using responsive design is to create files that adapt to the size of the media being used. By previewing the page at different sizes, you can see that some settings — specifically, font sizes — do not ideally suit all layout sizes.

Extra-small layout (max-width:767px)

Small layout (min-width:768px)

Medium layout (min-width:992px)

Large layout (min-width:1200px)

2. **Click design.css in the Related Files bar to show that file in the Code pane.**

   When you add media queries to a CSS file, you should remember that selectors apply until they are overridden by a later selector. You should then think about what you need to accomplish. For example, a media query uses the min-width statement to say:

   "The previous properties apply until the media width is X pixels or larger. Then use these properties."

   So, the first selectors in the file should define the options for the extra-small screen size and then define different selectors for each successive layout size.

3. Locate the h1 selector, and change the font-size property value to 20рх.

4. Locate the p selector, and change the font-size property value to 14рх.

5. Locate the .feature-section p selector, and change the font-size property value to 12рх.

These settings are more appropriate for the smaller display sizes. In the next few steps, you will define a media query to change the font-size properties for larger displays.

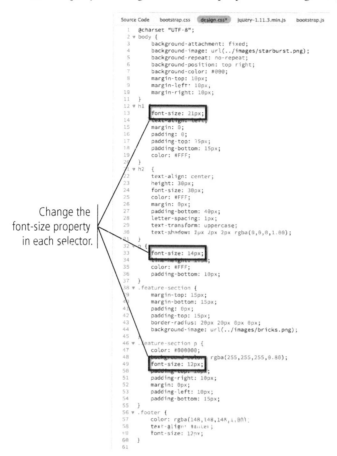

Change the
font-size property
in each selector.

Note:

As a rule of thumb, start small and work your way larger when you define different selectors for different media.

6. In the CSS Designer panel, select design.css in the Sources section, then click the Add Media Query button in the @Media section of the panel.

You can use this dialog box to define the conditions in which selectors in the query will apply. By selecting the design.css file first, the new media query will be added to that file.

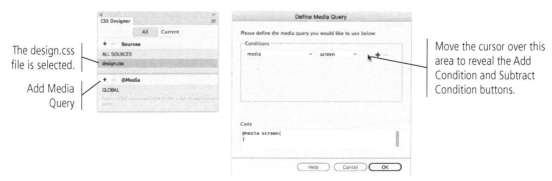

The design.css
file is selected.

Add Media
Query

Move the cursor over this
area to reveal the Add
Condition and Subtract
Condition buttons.

7. **With the first condition set to media:screen, move the mouse cursor to the right of that condition until the + and – buttons appear.**

8. **Click the + button to add a new condition to the query.**

9. **Open the first menu and choose min-width.**

   As you have already learned, media queries can be used to define different properties based on a specific set of conditions. Dreamweaver makes it very easy to add new media queries that define element appearance based on very specific conditions.

10. **Type 768 in the attached field, then press Tab to finalize the value.**

    The lower half of the dialog box shows the code that will be added to create the new media query.

11. **Click OK to create the media query.**

```
Source Code    bootstrap.css    design.css*    jquery-1.11.3.min.js    bootstrap.js
46 ▼ .feature-section p {
47        color: #000000;
48        background-color: rgba(255,255,255,0.80);
49        font-size: 12px;
50        padding-top: 10px;
51        padding-right: 10px;
52        margin: 0px;
53        padding-left: 10px;
54        padding-bottom: 15px;
55   }
56 ▼ .footer {
57        color: rgba(148,148,148,1.00);
58        text-align: center;
59        font-size: 12px;
60   }
61
62    @media screen and (min-width:768px){
63    }
64
```

The media query is added at the end of the design.css file.

12. In the Code pane, place the insertion point after the opening curly brace of the media query statement. Press Return/Enter, then create three new selectors:

```
h1 {
    font-size: 38px;
}
p {
    font-size: 18px;
}
.feature-section p {
    font-size: 15px;
}
```

This curly brace closes the media query; it was added for you when you defined the new media query.

```
Source Code    bootstrap.css    design.css*    jquery-1.11.3.min.js    bootstrap.js
61
62 ▼ @media screen and (min-width:768px){
63 ▼    h1 {
64             font-size: 38px;
65         }
66 ▼    p {
67             font-size: 18px;
68         }
69 ▼    .feature-section p {
70             font-size: 15px;
71         }
72     }
73
```

The original selectors defined a number of other properties for these selectors. You only want to change the font size based on the media size, so you do not need to include all of the properties that were included in the original selectors.

13. Use the VMQB to review all four layouts.

The smaller font-size properties only apply until the display size is larger than 767px.

Extra-small layout (max-width:767px)

Small layout (min-width:768px)

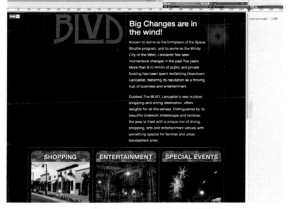

Medium layout (min-width:992px)

Large layout (min-width:1200px)

14. Choose File>Save All.

In this exercise you made changes to the CSS file, so choosing Save All ensures that any changes in all related files are saved.

15. Continue to the next exercise.

SHOW AND HIDE CONTENT IN DIFFERENT LAYOUTS

As we explained previously, the HTML page code is exactly the same for all variations of a responsive web page layout; the content in various divs will be the same regardless of which layout is being displayed. The position and appearance of that content is controlled entirely through CSS.

There is, however, a special CSS "helper" class in Bootstrap that allows you to hide different elements in different layouts. The HTML page code stays the same, but the applied CSS classes determine whether something is visible in a specific layout.

In this exercise, you will use this helper class to change the logo that is visible in different layouts.

1. With **index.html** open, make the medium-size layout active in the document window.

2. Click to select the logo image at the top of the page.

3. Click the Responsive Image:Default button in the Bootstrap Components Insert panel. Click the After button in the Position Assistant.

4. With the placeholder selected in the document window, use the Properties panel to change the image src to **blvd-logo90.png** (from the site images folder). Change the Alt field text to **The BLVD**.

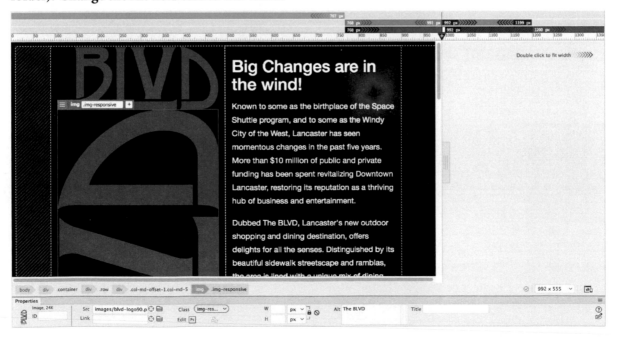

5. **Use the VMQB to show the extra-small size layout in the document window.**

6. **With the rotated logo selected in the document, click the Add Class/ID button in the Element Display. In the resulting field, type .hidden-xs.**

    You can apply the .hidden class to each size layout by appending the appropriate display-size abbreviation to the class:

    .hidden-xs   .hidden-sm   .hidden-md   .hidden-lg

7. **Press Return/Enter to finalize the new class.**

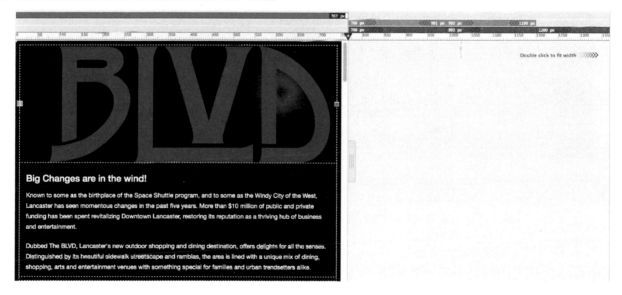

8. Use the VMQB to show the small size layout in the document window.

Keep in mind that the .hidden classes only hide an element in the specific layout that is defined in the class. In this example, you hid the vertical logo only in the extra-small layout. It is still visible in the other three layouts unless you add classes to hide it in those layouts.

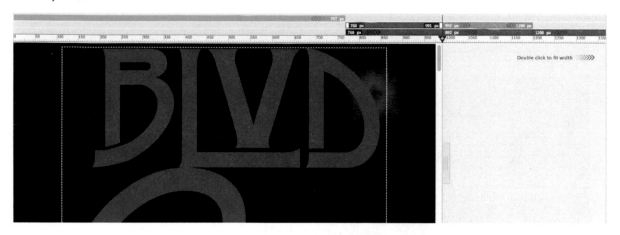

9. Repeat Steps 6–7 to add the `.hidden-sm` class to the vertical logo.

It is important to note that you are not changing the class you defined in Steps 6–7. You are adding a second class that controls the element's visibility in the small size layout.

More about Showing and Hiding Elements

The .visible classes are basically the inverse of the .hidden classes. If you apply the .visible-sm class to an element, that element will only be visible in the small size layout unless you add another class to make it visible in another size layout.

Using the .visible classes, you must also define how the element will be visible:

- **.visible-[size]-block**
  The element always starts on a new line and fills the width of the containing element.

- **.visible-[size]-inline**
  The element appears inline with other content, and occupies only as much space as necessary.

- **.visible-[size]-inline-block**
  The element appears inline with other content, but can have a specific defined height and width.

Class	Extra Small	Small	Medium	Large
.visible-xs-*	Visible	Hidden	Hidden	Hidden
.visible-sm-*	Hidden	Visible	Hidden	Hidden
.visible-md-*	Hidden	Hidden	Visible	Hidden
.visible-lg-*	Hidden	Hidden	Hidden	Visible
.hidden-xs	Hidden	Visible	Visible	Visible
.hidden-sm	Visible	Hidden	Visible	Visible
.hidden-md	Visible	Visible	Hidden	Visible
.hidden-lg	Visible	Visible	Visible	Hidden

* is the property that defines how the element will be visible.

10. **Use the VMQB to show the medium size layout in the document window.**

11. **Repeat Steps 6–7 to add the .hidden-md class to the <u>horizontal</u> logo.**

    In this case, you want the vertical logo to be visible so you are applying the .hidden-md class to the horizontal image.

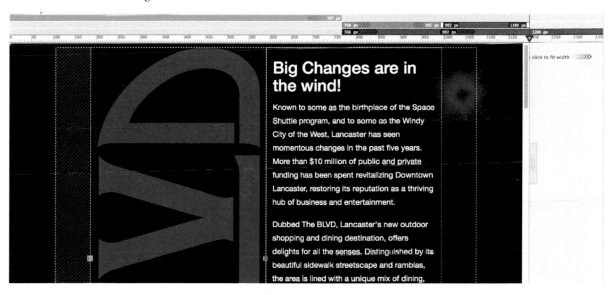

12. **Use the VMQB to show the large size layout in the document window.**

13. **Repeat Steps 6–7 to add the .hidden-lg class to the horizontal logo.**

14. **Click to select the vertical logo in the large layout, then use the Tag Selector to select its immediate parent (column) div.**

15. **Use the Resize Column handle to reduce the column div to span only 2 columns of the underlying page grid.**

    Dreamweaver makes it very easy for you to adapt different page elements as necessary; this type of change will not be uncommon when you begin working with actual client content instead of simply using placeholders to design different-size page layouts.

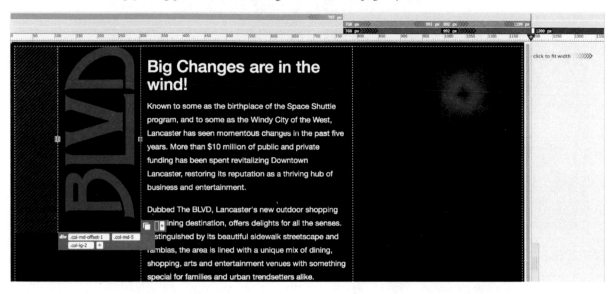

16. **Select the column div on the right side of the same row. Use the Resize Column handle to change the div to occupy 7 columns in the underlying page grid.**

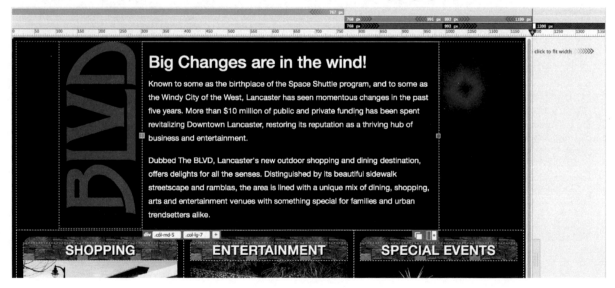

17. **Use the VMQB to show the medium size layout in the document window. Change the div with the logo to occupy 3 grid columns, and change the right div to occupy 7 grid columns.**

18. **Save the file and continue to the next stage of the project.**

Stage 2 Creating CSS3 Transitions

Before HTML5 and CSS3, animating something in a web page required an external file created in a separate application (such as Adobe Animate), or a script that would manage the change (such as the JavaScript that drives Spry objects like menu bars).

Features in HTML5 and CSS3 allow you to create animations directly in the HTML page without the need for Flash or JavaScript. This has several advantages. First, no plug-ins are required to support the animation because all of the changes (called transitions) are driven by CSS. Second, CSS3 transitions are fairly easy to create if you have a basic understanding of CSS selectors and properties.

Dreamweaver makes it very easy to define CSS3 transitions based on the selectors in a file. In this stage of the project, you will use two different methods to animate specific elements and properties.

RESTRICT ELEMENT HEIGHT AND OVERFLOW

CSS selectors give you extensive control over the elements on a page. In this exercise, you are going to force the three .feature-section elements to be a specific height in the extra-small layout, showing only the headings until a user taps the element. In the next exercise, you will add the transition that makes the overflow content visible.

1. **With index.html open, click the max-width:767px media query bar to snap the scrubber bar to that point.**

2. **Click the Plus Sign button on the ruler below the VMQB.**

   To create a new media query, click the Plus Sign button at the top of the scrubber bar. The current ruler position when you click this button determines the width that will be set in the new query.

Click the Plus Sign button to add a new media query at that point.

3. **In the resulting dialog box, choose design.css in the Select CSS Source menu and then click OK.**

Clicking the + button in Step 2 opens a dialog box; the current display view width is already filled in one of the fields.

You must also determine where to save the code for the new media query. The Select CSS Source menu includes all CSS files that are attached to the active page, as well options to define it in the HTML code of the active page (Define in Page) or Create a New CSS File to store the new media query.

4. **Show the `design.css` file in the Code pane, and locate the media query at the end of the existing code.**

You are adding the code in the next steps to the media query because you only want the change to apply to the extra-small (less than 768px) display size.

The design.css file is active in the Code pane.

This media query was added to the active file.

5. **Place the insertion point after the opening brace of the new media query. Press Return/Enter to start a new line, then type:**

```
.feature-section {
    max-height: 55px;
    overflow: hidden;
}
```

The **max-height** property allows an object to extend up to the defined height. This is different than the **height** property, which defines a specific, fixed height for the element.

However, by default, an element will occupy as much space as necessary to display all of its content. To hide the overflow content (called clipping the content), you also have to add the overflow property.

The **overflow** property determines what happens when an element contains more content than will fit into the defined space. Possible values for the overflow property include:

- **auto** adds scrollbars to the element only if some content is clipped.
- **hidden** clips the overflow content; only content that fits into the defined space will be visible.
- **inherit** applies the overflow value of the parent element.
- **scroll** adds scrollbars to the element even if there is no clipped content.
- **visible** causes all content to be visible, even if it appears outside the element boundaries.

6. Review the results of the new properties in the Live view.

It doesn't matter which size layout you are viewing; the height of the .container objects changes in all three versions.

7. Save all files, then continue to the next exercise.

 ## USE THE CSS TRANSITIONS PANEL

In this exercise, you will use the CSS Transitions panel to show the overflow content of the .container elements when a user's mouse hovers over them. Dreamweaver's CSS Transitions panel makes this process fairly easy; the required CSS code is created for you.

1. With index.html open, make the extra-small layout visible in the Live view.

2. Click to select the "Shopping" h2 element, then use the Tag Selector to select its immediate parent div element

You are going to add a transition to divs using the .feature-section class. If you don't select an element using that class before defining the transition, the class will be automatically added to whatever element is selected in the document window. This is simply a quirk of the software. To avoid applying an unwanted class to some random element, it's a good idea to select one of the targeted elements first.

3. Open the CSS Transitions panel (Window>CSS Transitions).

4. Click the Create New Transition button (the + icon) at the top of the panel.

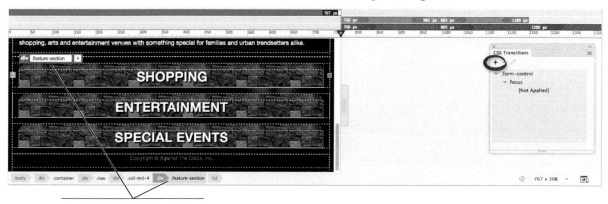

One of the .feature-section divs
is selected in the layout.

5. In the resulting dialog box, type `.feature-section` in the Target Rule field.

You could also open the attached menu and scroll to find the appropriate rule, but the list is very lengthy; every selector related to the active file (including those in all three linked CSS files) appears in this menu in alphabetical order.

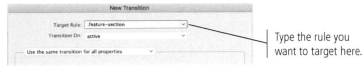

Type the rule you want to target here.

You know what you need to target, so typing is simply a faster solution.

6. In the Transition On menu, choose hover.

This menu determines what event will trigger the transition. In this case, the transition will occur when a user hovers the mouse over an element where the .container class has been applied.

7. Type `0.5` in the Duration field.

The duration is the time it takes for a transition to occur. Dreamweaver uses seconds (s) as the default time increment, but you can also choose milliseconds (ms) in the menu.

8. Type `0` in the Delay field.

The delay is a brief interval between the time the trigger event occurs and the time the transition begins.

9. In the Timing Function menu, choose Linear.

The timing function allows you to control the transition speed over the duration of the transition. In essence, you can make a transition speed up or slow down over time (called **easing**).

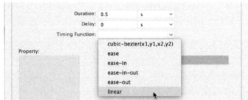

Easing in causes the transition to start slower and speed up over time. Easing out causes the transition to start faster and slow down over time.

10. On the left side of the dialog box, click the + button below the Property window, and choose max-height from the menu.

11. In the End Value field, type 999 and make sure px is selected in the secondary menu.

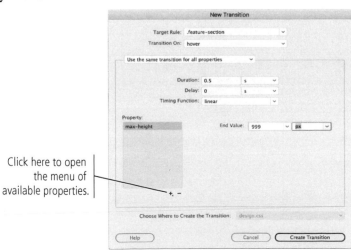

Click here to open the menu of available properties.

Note:

The menu at the bottom of the dialog box defaults to the file where the selected Target Rule is located.

12. **Click Create Transition to return to the document window.**

The CSS Transitions panel shows the new transition, as well as the instances where that transition occurs. There are three elements with the .feature-section class applied in this file, so the panel shows three instances of the defined transition.

13. **Show the design.css file in Code pane, and locate code for the .feature-section class in the second media query.**

Because this media query was active when you created the transition, the transition-related code was automatically added to the media query.

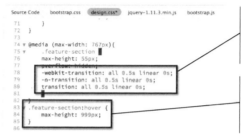

Transition properties (including necessary browser prefixes) are added to the .feature-section selector.

A new selector is added to define properties for .feature-section elements when the hover pseudo-class is triggered.

Code for the defined transition requires several versions for the various browsers. Remember, CSS3 is still in development and has not been universally adopted by all browsers. The transition property is not technically supported by any browser, so browser prefixes are required.

Each property line combines the various values into a single line (from left to right):

- The property that is affected by the transition. When this is "all," the same transition settings will apply to all properties that are being animated.
- The duration of the transition
- The timing function of the transition
- The delay of the transition

14. **Choose View>Live View Options>Hide Live View Displays.**

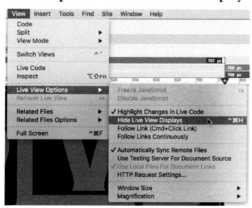

15. Move your mouse over any of the .feature-section elements to test the transition.

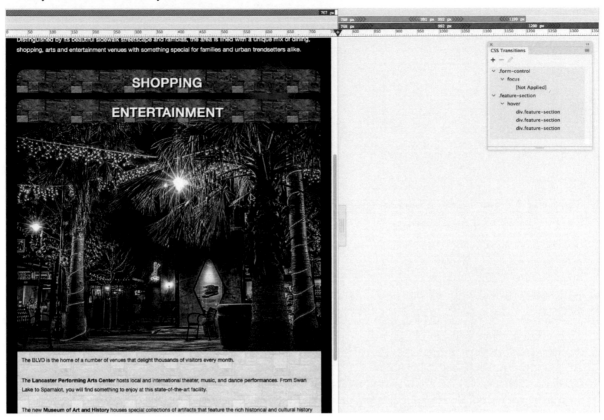

16. Display the Code pane for the index.html page.

As you might have guessed, the hover pseudo-class was designed for devices that use a mouse — in other words, desktop or laptop computers. Mobile devices, however, do not require a mouse; buttons and other interactive features on your site are enabled by touching the screen.

Using the Android OS, the hover pseudo-class is triggered by a touch/tap. This is not the case for iOS (iPhones and iPads), which does not trigger the hover behavior with a touch/tap. Fortunately, there is a very simple workaround to solve this issue.

17. Locate the first div that is identified with the .feature-section class.

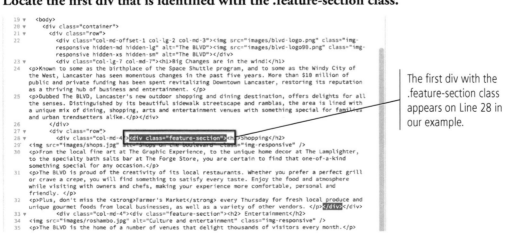

The first div with the .feature-section class appears on Line 28 in our example.

18. **Place the insertion point immediately after the opening div code and before the class definition.**

19. **Press the spacebar, then type `onclick=""`.**

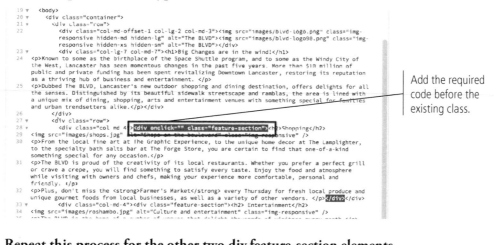

Add the required code before the existing class.

20. **Repeat this process for the other two div.feature-section elements.**

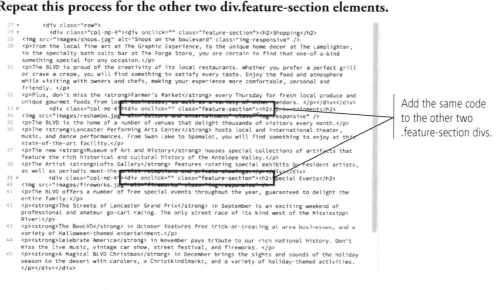

Add the same code to the other two .feature-section divs.

21. **Save all files and close them.**

22. **Export a site definition named `BLVD.ste` into your WIP>BLVD folder, and then remove the site from Dreamweaver.**

1. A Bootstrap page defaults to have _____ columns in the underlying page grid.

2. The _____ helper class can be used to hide an element in only the medium display size layout.

3. The _____ class would cause a column div in the small size layout to occupy 4 page-grid columns.

4. The _____ classes can be used to move an element away from the left edge of its containing element.

5. True or False: There is no difference between the behavior of .container and .container-fluid divs. _____

6. The _____ class creates an img element that adjusts to the maximum width available in the parent container.

7. True or false: You can change the HTML code for each div for each layout size in a responsive page layout. _____

8. A(n) _____ can be used to define different CSS properties based on the size of the display being used to view a page.

9. Animations in an HTML5 page are created by defining _____ properties for a specific CSS selector.

10. In a transition, _____ is the length of time it takes for the animation to be completed.

1. Briefly explain the concept of responsive design.

2. Briefly explain how columns relate to the underlying page grid in a Bootstrap page.

3. Briefly explain the process of creating a CSS3 transition.

Portfolio Builder Project

Use what you learned in this project to complete the following freeform exercise.
Carefully read the art director and client comments, then create your own design to meet the needs of the project.
Use the space below to sketch ideas; when finished, write a brief explanation of your reasoning behind your final design.

All professional web designers and developers need a portfolio to display their work to prospective clients. By completing the projects in this book, you have created a number of different examples that showcase your Dreamweaver skills.

The eight projects in this book were specifically designed to include a wide variety of skills and techniques, as well as different types of sites for different types of clients. Your portfolio should follow the same basic principle, offering a variety of samples of both creative and technical skills.

For this project, you are your own client. Using the following suggestions, gather your work and create your own portfolio.

❏ If possible, set up your own domain name to host your portfolio site. If you can't set up a personal domain name, use a free subdomain name from an established server company.

❏ Include links to sites you have created, whether the pages are kept in folders of your own domain or posted on other public servers.

❏ If you can't include links to certain sites, take screen shots and post those images on your site.

❏ For each sample site you include, add a brief description or explanation of your role in creating the site. (Did you design it? What techniques were used to build the site?)

❏ Be sure to include full contact information in a prominent location on your site.

project justification

_____

_____

_____

_____

_____

_____

_____

_____

_____

_____

_____

_____

_____

_____

As digital tablets and smartphones continue to gain market share, the way people browse the internet will continue to adapt to the capabilities of new technology. At least in part to meet the new needs of the mobile community, HTML5 and CSS3 are being developed to allow web designers more flexibility and functionality to create responsive web pages that work properly regardless of the medium being used to display the page.

It is important to realize that the evolution of mobile technology is faster than anything seen before in the communications industry. New devices are being introduced constantly, each with new capabilities and (in some cases) limitations. For the foreseeable future, we can continue to expect frequent and significant changes in both the actual devices and the tools we use to design for them.

This project introduced the concept of responsive design, focusing on the Bootstrap framework and the tools that Dreamweaver includes for building pages that adapt to different display sizes. Combined with a good understanding of HTML and CSS, the skills you learned in this project will be a strong foundation that will allow you to better manage the changing face of web design.

The second part of this project introduced CSS3 transitions, including the tools Dreamweaver provides for creating those transitions. Keep in mind that mobile devices do not have a pointing device; however, the hover behavior is triggered when a user taps those elements. We created these exercises to teach you the basic process for creating transitions in Dreamweaver, and we used the hover behavior because its familiarity can help to make it easier to relate what you are doing in this project to other projects. When you design responsive sites, you should carefully consider your options, and design to meet the needs of your audience.

Create a responsive layout that adapts to the size of the display

Define a media query to change properties based on the active display size

Define CSS3 transitions to change elements and properties based on user interaction

Index

Index

Index

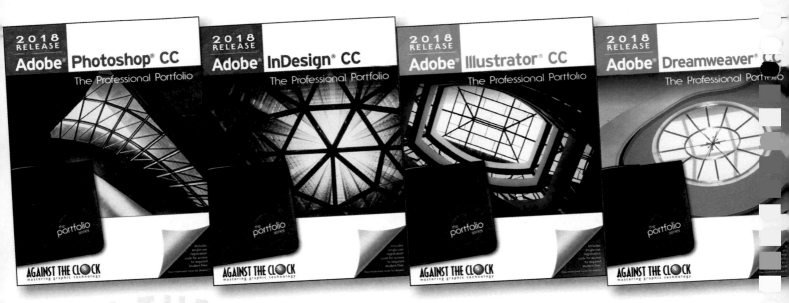